AF575457

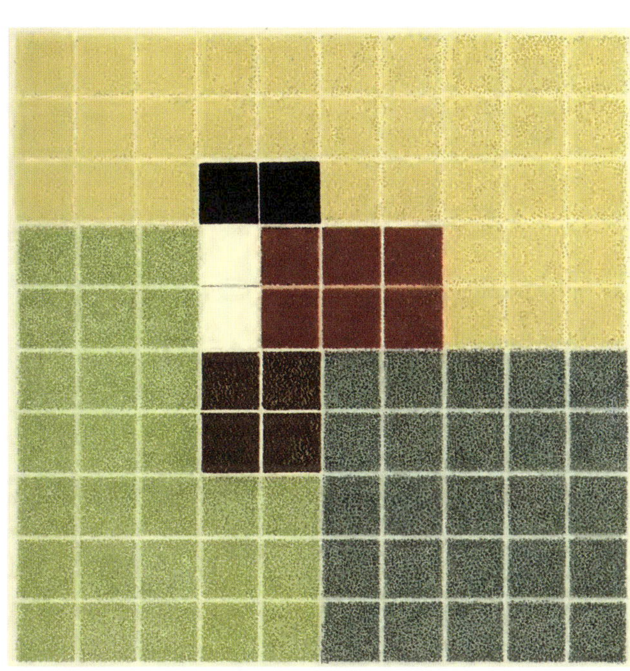

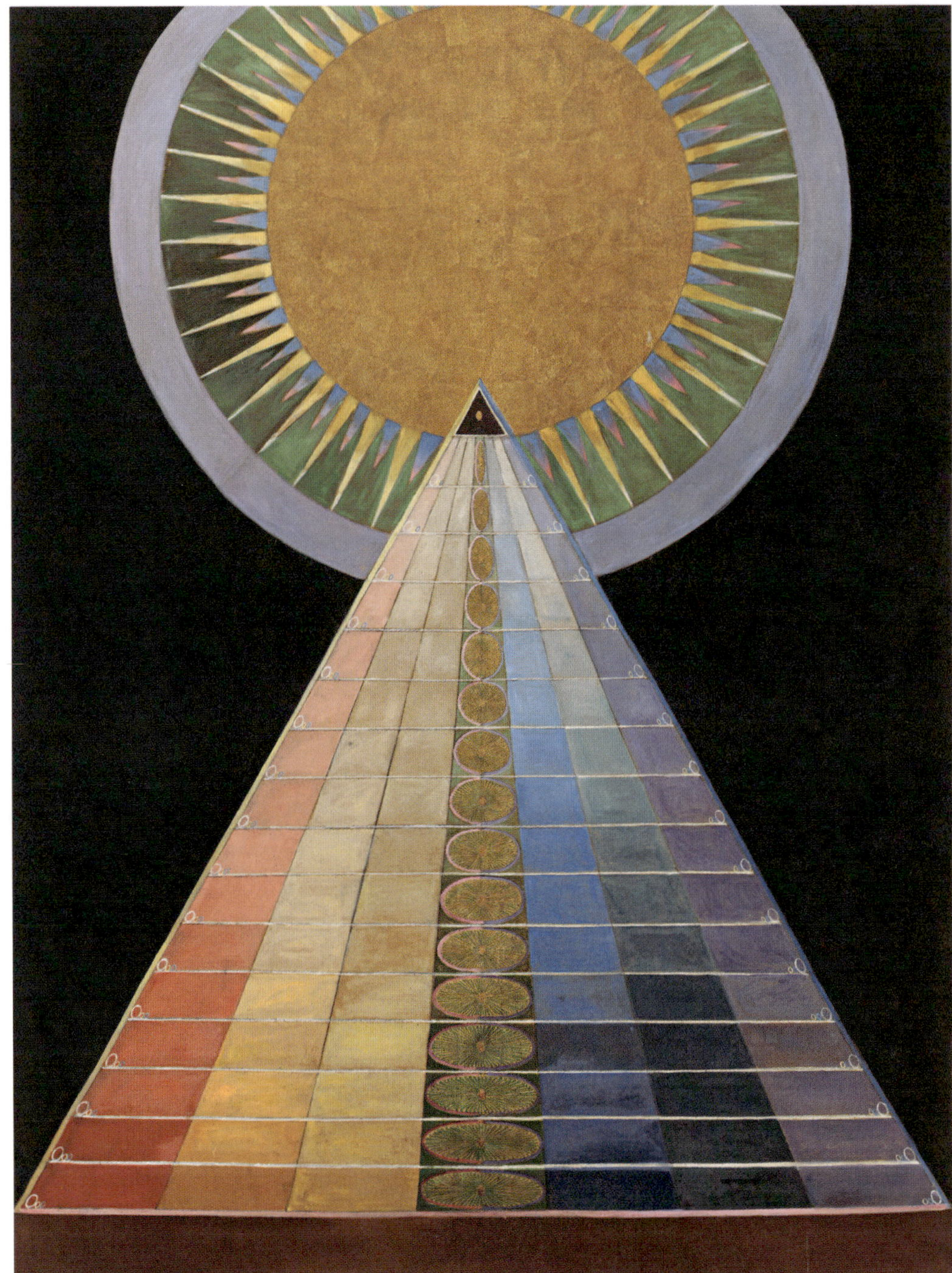

The Art of Colour

The History of Art in 39 Pigments

Kelly Grovier

YALE UNIVERSITY PRESS

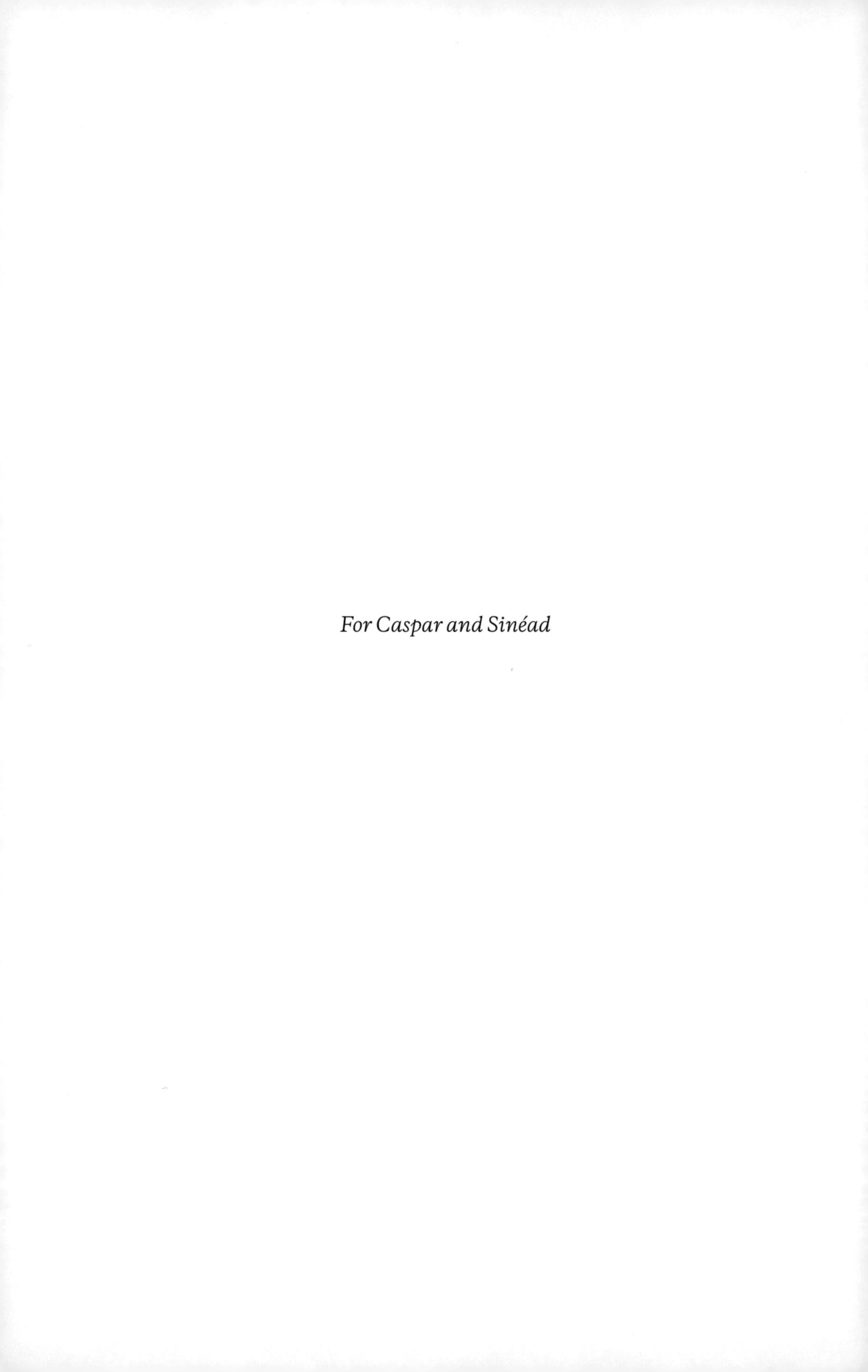

For Caspar and Sinéad

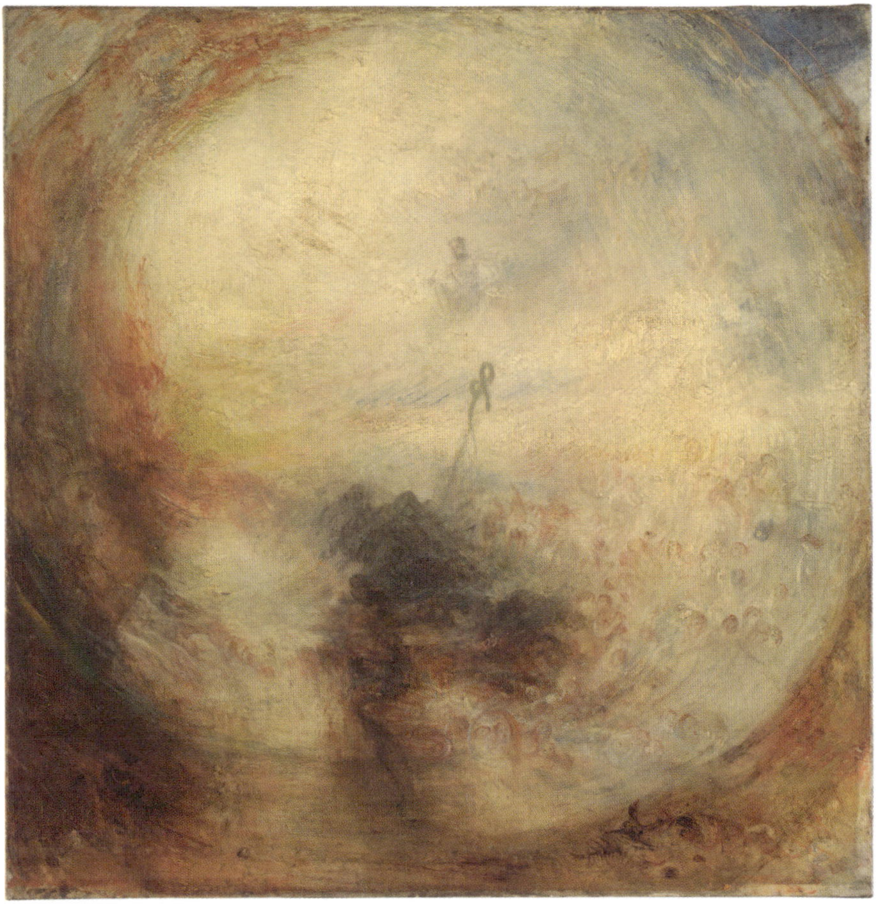

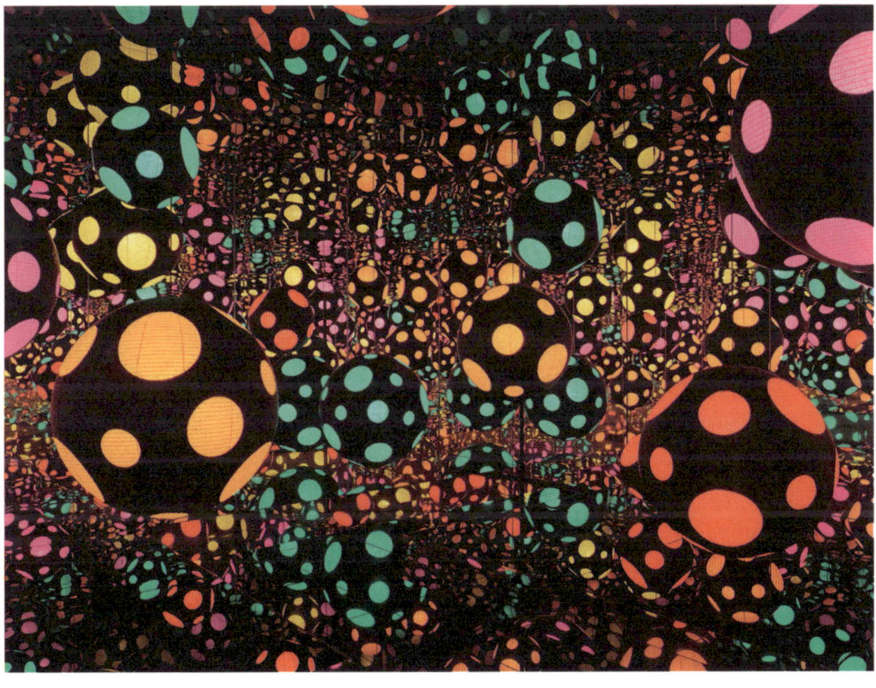

Contents

INTRODUCTION

Artymology

The kingdom of colours has within it multidimensional possibilities ... Each individual colour is a universe in itself.
Johannes Itten

'Colour', said the French Post-Impressionist Paul Cézanne, 'is the place where our brain and the universe meet.'[1] It is the very soul of art. Colour is what lures us into the mystery of Vincent van Gogh's *Starry Night* long before we begin to tangle with the restless geometry of its astral whorls. The undulating waves of cobalt blue and artificial ultramarine that crest and crash in the canvas's tempestuous sky and the almost subliminal hints of emerald green that halo the strange smudgy moon set an emotional stage that precedes conscious looking. Colour comes first. It's what the eyes feel.

We hardly need to know the pigments that Van Gogh used by their precise historical names, where or when they were discovered, or the complex processes necessary to make them palette-ready in order to register the pulsing power of *The Starry Night*. But what if we did? What if we knew that the artist's cobalt blue (a name derived from the German word *kobold*, meaning 'evil house spirit' or 'goblin'), whose swirls trouble the turbulent sky, shares a material bloodline with 14th-century porcelain glazed in the Ming dynasty? Or that the impastoed intensity of the sharp yellow moon was sculpted from clumps of dehydrated bovine urine secreted by cows force-fed a diet consisting solely of mango leaves? How would such revelations influence our reading of this indisputable masterpiece? How would it affect our relationship to the work – the way it moves us?

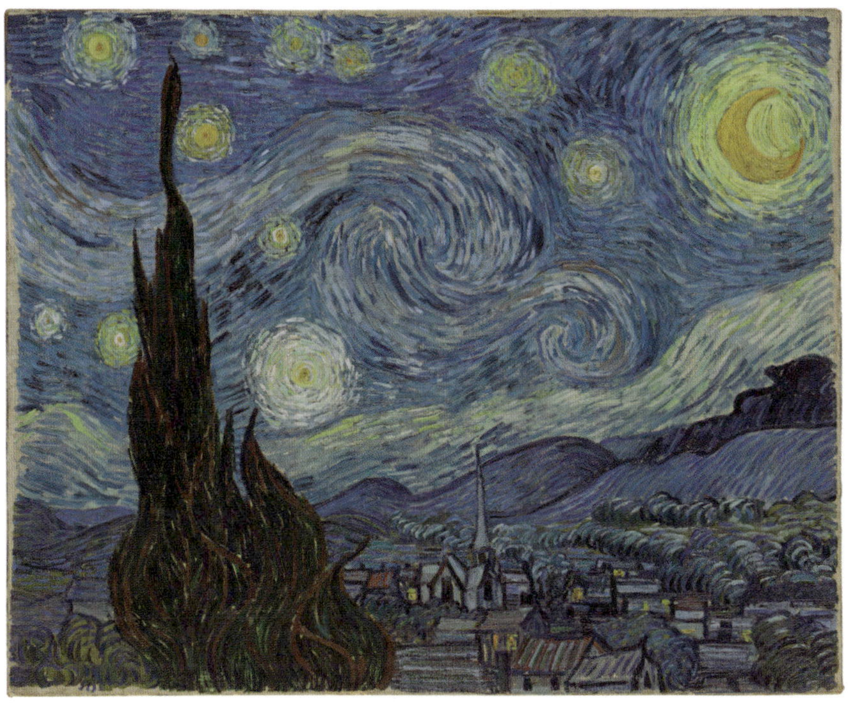

Vincent van Gogh, *The Starry Night*, 1889

This book begins with the simple premise that the biography of a pigment - its origins and adventures in cultural history - can unlock the spirit of a work of art in which it features. When it comes to appreciating a poem, say, or a novel, it is customary for scholars to consult the linguistic genesis of a given word, its birth and appearances in other literary works, in order to plumb a text's depths and access hidden meanings, or ones that may have faded over time. Whether or not the poet or novelist intended, or indeed was even aware of, a particular word's journey since its coinage is beside the point. Resonances are there, deliberately sewn or not. Words are absorbent, uncontainable, and pulsate significance irrespective of an author's will.

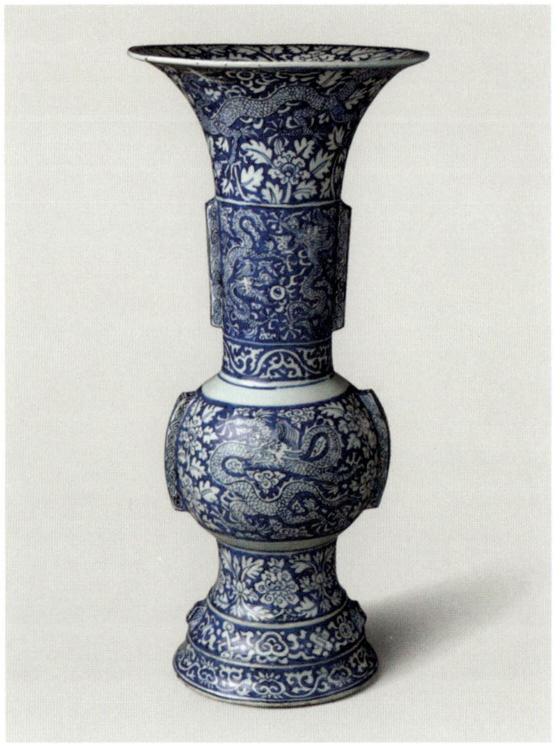

Temple vase with dragons amid flowers, China,
Ming dynasty, late 16th–early 17th centuries

Once a poem or novel is written, its DNA is the roots of language helixed into it, not its writer's.

So too with a work of art. Pigments are the syllables art speaks in. To understand what they are saying, it may be helpful to trace their discovery and track the gradual accrual of connotations over time. Where etymology involves establishing a word's genesis and evolution, perhaps we might call the approach pursued here, of mapping the emergence of a given pigment in order to appreciate more profoundly its significance in a given work, something analogous: *artymology*. So conceived, an *artymological* reading recognizes that paintings and sculptures, drawings and installations, are not merely ideas. They are things. The pigments that comprise them are not abstract concepts, but profoundly physical substances that possess the power simultaneously to command the surface of an artwork and to evaporate into nothing. 'Colour unmysterious', asserted the Victorian art critic John Ruskin, 'is wholly barbarous. Unless it loses itself and melts away, colour has no proper existence.'[2] Colour is at once everything and nothing at all. It may seem to cede its existence to the shapes of things – the objects and sitters to which interpretative priority is typically given. In truth, however, it controls the temperature of psychological space in which any reading occurs.

Artymology goes beyond a consideration of the conventional symbolism of colours – their myriad cultural associations in religion or science – to something grittier and more palpable. That's not to say it objectifies colour. Rather, it acknowledges that the pigments from which colours are coaxed are, inescapably, objects. And fascinating objects at that. Take, for instance, the pigments from which the tender triptych *The Virgin and Child with Saint Dominic and Saint Aurea, and Patriarchs and Prophets* by the medieval Italian painter Duccio di Buoninsegna is masterfully mosaicked into being. Commissioned by Niccolò degli Albertini da Prato (who became Cardinal Bishop of Ostia, near Rome, in 1303), the portable altarpiece has long been revered as a moving meditation on the exalted and exalting love between mother and son, one whose poignancy transcends its time. And so it is. But the work's transcendence is all the more astonishing when we reflect on the materiality of its making.

Although Mary's regal robe may appear to have been woven in an eternal elsewhere, in reality the resplendent garment was fashioned from the semi-precious metamorphic stone lapis lazuli, laboriously pulverized.[3] The dazzling pigment such arduous grinding creates is 'ultramarine', so christened for the

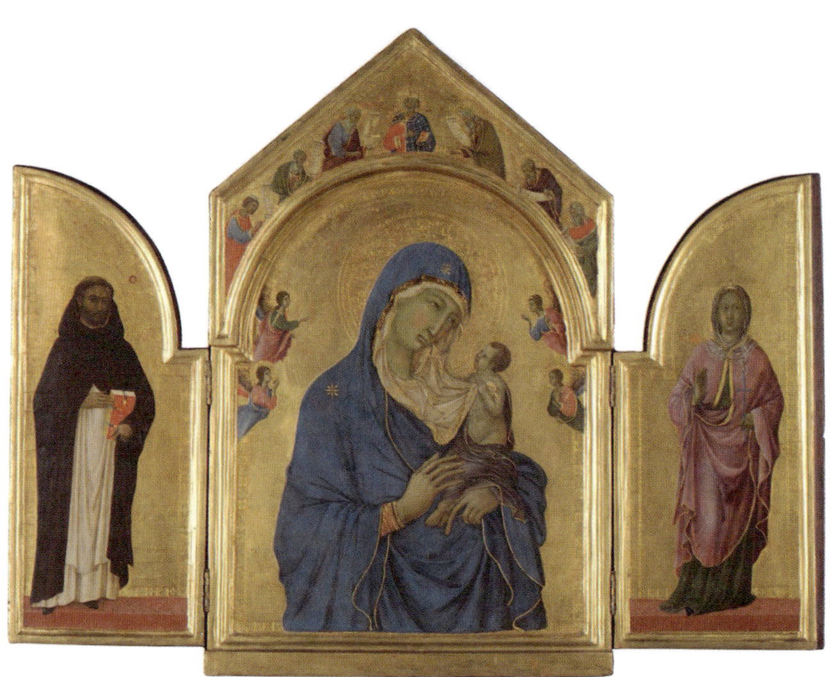

Duccio di Buoninsegna, *The Virgin and Child with Saint Dominic and Saint Aurea, and Patriarchs and Prophets*, c. 1312–15

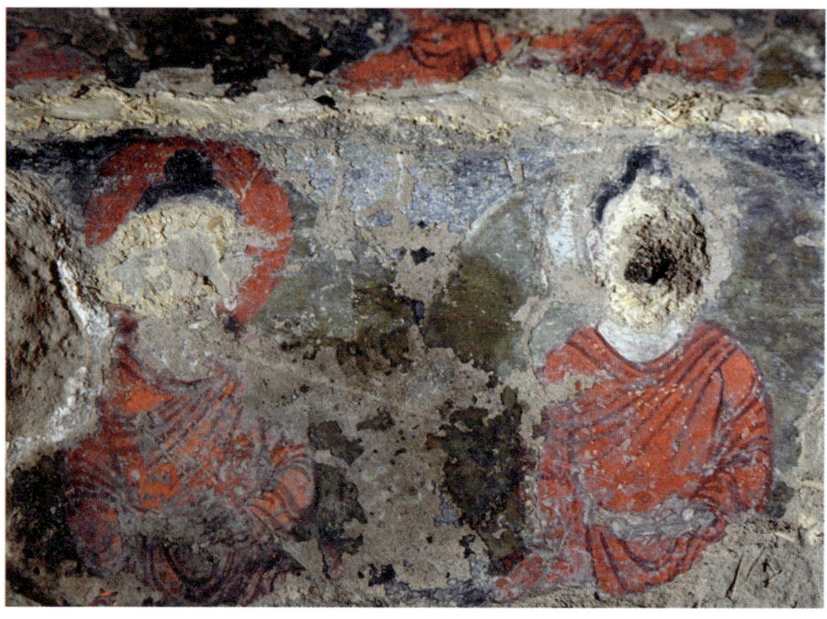

Buddha figures or bodhisattvas, Bamiyan caves, Afghanistan, *c.* 7th century CE

long journey it made back from 'beyond the sea' (the literal translation of the medieval Latin *ultramarinus*), where lapis lazuli was extracted from mines in Afghanistan. Seen in the context of that curious quarrying, without which the work we observe could not have come about, the love between Mary and Christ is suddenly displaced from the timeless, gold-hammered heaven in which it seems endlessly suspended to something darker, deeper and fustier - an uncanny interior space, a cave of the soul.

Duccio might have been surprised to learn that his reliance on lapis lazuli, which had become synonymous in early Christian symbolism with Mary and which dominates the triptych's central panel, ties his devotional work to 6th- and 7th-century Zoroastrian paintings found on the walls of cave temples in Bamiyan, Afghanistan - among the earliest known uses of the pigment[4] - as well as to works by 10th- and 11th-century Chinese, Indian and Anglo-Saxon artists. Although religiously exclusive in the devotional shapes they assume, these works have all been cut from the same geological cloth and, taken together, form a kind of fragmented and far-flung mosaic of spiritual searching.

Subtler, perhaps, but no less arresting is the eerie pallor of Mary's and Christ's complexions - a weird, wan amphibiousness that, when seen side by side with the underworld ultramarine of Mary's robe, creates the most affecting friction of colours. Over time, an underlayer of 'green earth' pigment, on to which healthier flesh tones were subsequently applied, has bled through. The result is a death-in-lifeness that magnifies the mysticism of the piece. Since antiquity, green earth has chiefly been derived from a pair of inorganic minerals found in abundance near Verona, giving rise to the common nickname 'Verona green'. Those minerals, glauconite and celadonite, are believed to have originated as marine clays formed from sea water near volcanic islands. The determination of these minerals to overwhelm the overlying whites and pinks that once occluded them intensifies the feeling that the intimate interplay between mother and child is not occurring in a removed and distant hereafter but is a natural force interwoven in the very fabric of the world we occupy - seismic in intensity and ancient as the seas. However unintended by the artist, the resilience of green earth, which overtakes the painting's flesh like a latent patina, reveals the irrepressible power of pigment. An artist's palette, after all, like the lyrical lexicon of a poet, possesses an uncanny agency unshackled to the will of the painter or sculptor who wields it. 'Colors', the Norwegian symbolist Edvard Munch sensitively observed, 'live a remarkable life of their own after they have been applied to the canvas.'[5]

For me, colour is more than merely an intriguing intellectual pursuit. Reconstructing the lost myths and forgotten scientific discoveries that have shaped the way artists have instinctively expressed themselves since time immemorial has changed who I am. My decades-long journey into the secret histories of colour has ground the very lens through which I perceive the world and comprehend the essence of human creativity. Colour, I have come to understand, is not simply the language in which painters and sculptors speak. It is a hidden knowledge - an essential truth.

It all started one early autumn day in September 2000. I had just taken my seat on a coach from Oxford to London, heading to the British Library, when my eye snagged on a headline in *The Times* newspaper: 'Florence skull yields portrait of Giotto'. Digging deeper, I was fascinated to learn how a team of palaeontologists and anthropologists had been able to determine that 'a deformed and misshapen' skeleton discovered years earlier beneath Florence Cathedral belonged to the late medieval Italian master who was responsible for what I have always felt to be among the most moving works in all of cultural history. Giotto's exquisite *Lamentation of Christ* for the Scrovegni Chapel in Padua, in which a choir of anguished

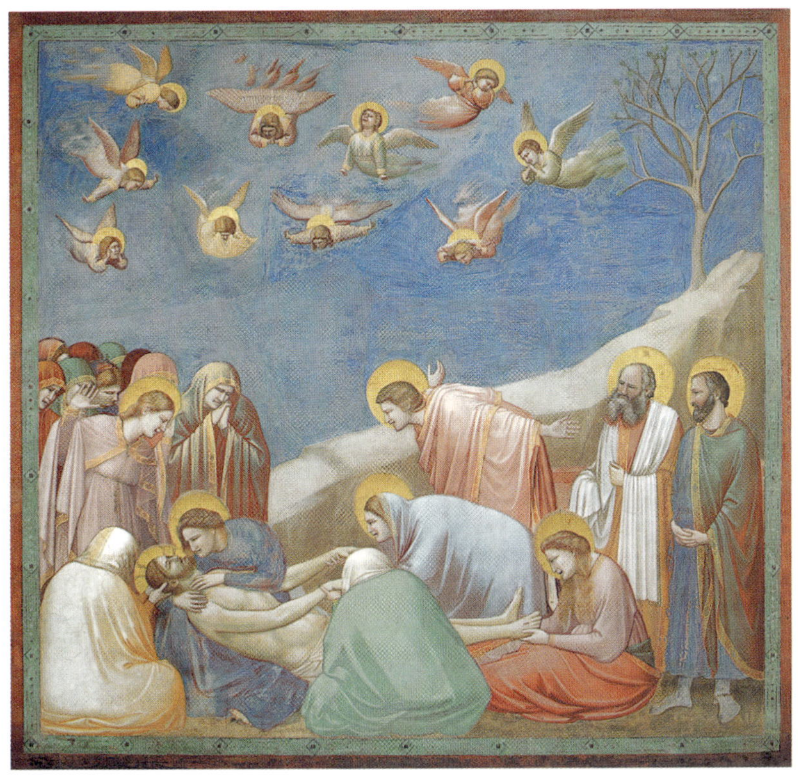

Giotto, *The Lamentation of Christ*, 1304–06

angels wail and whirl acrobatically above Christ's inert body, is more than a marvellous fresco. Its absorbing blue empyrean feels at once mystical and meteorological, inside and outside of time – the very atmosphere of the soul. Remarkably, according to the newspaper article, it wasn't DNA that had given away the identity of Giotto's remains, but art itself. Or, more to the point, colour.

'The bones', it was reported in *The Times*, were not only consistent with the tortured posture of a painter who had spent his life contorting his body in order to reach elevated frescoes,

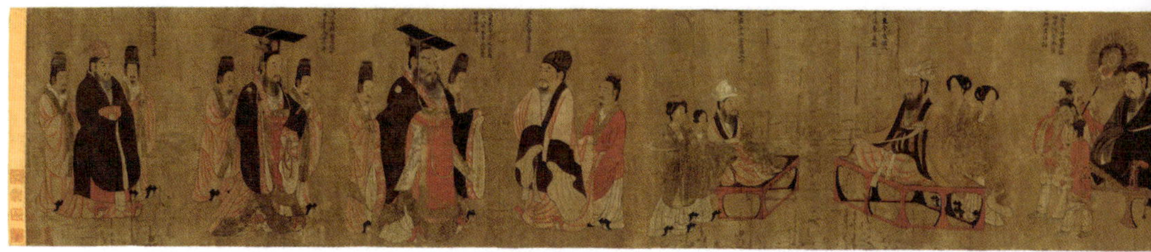

Attributed to Yan Liben, *The Thirteen Emperors*, China, Tang dynasty, late 7th century CE

as Giotto had; they also 'contained high levels of arsenic, lead, aluminium and manganese, and lead and copper – the main chemical elements in the colours used in Giotto's paintings'.[6] In the alchemy of death, Giotto, it seems, had become his own painting.

It struck me that, contrary to the way we conventionally conceive of colour when we discuss works of art – from the regal red symbolism that ignites the Tang-era painting *The Thirteen Emperors* to the decidedly deceitful yellows that artists have traditionally favoured when portraying Judas – pigments are more than purely intellectual concepts. They are made of grit and grime. They have weight and texture. They pulse through our veins and seep deep into our bones. They are capable of resurrection and tell secrets from the grave.

Inspired, I fumbled for a pen from my satchel and began scribbling in the margin of the rumpled newspaper a few lines that would become the basis of the first creative work I'd ever had accepted for publication: a poem entitled 'Giotto', which became a kind of contract with myself to learn more about the elusive subject of colour. Even as I was jotting about Giotto, describing the 'pigment metals ... traced in the blood, sticking to his bones like plaster',[7] I was conscious that my words were little more than a shaky start – the beginning of a journey, not its

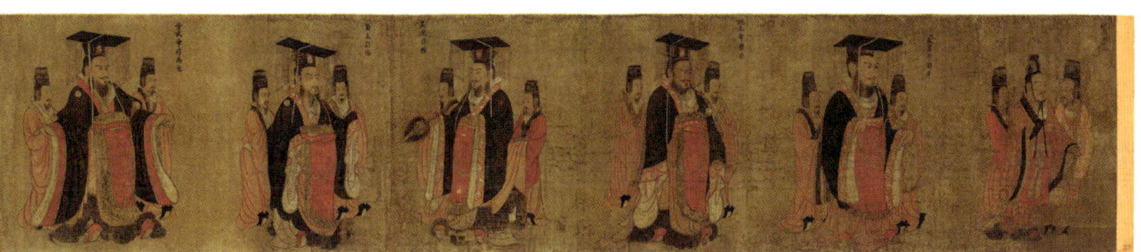

end. Somehow, atoms of elements forged billions of years ago in the furnace of distant stars, propelled by stellar explosions, had made their way to the tip of Giotto's brush. From there they were deployed by the artist to share a timeless existence not only with the sombre seraphs and fractured physique of Christ in the artist's fresco, but also, in time, with Giotto's own bent and buried bones. Colour was simultaneously an indestructible substance and a haunting ghost - a material spirit that could transcend time, collapse space, and blur the border between life and art. I had to know more.

Thus began my obsession with the lost legends of pigments, whose silent syllables articulate a different history of art from the one we are accustomed to reading. My preoccupation with tracing the provenance of the elements that comprise artists' pigments was fed fortuitously by a pair of extraordinary studies on the subject. A groundbreaking book by the science writer Philip Ball, *Bright Earth: The Invention of Colour*, which magisterially sets out the chronology and complex processes of colour concoction from antiquity to modern times, appeared the year after I stumbled across the story about Giotto's remains. A year after that, Victoria Finlay's captivating chronicle, *Colour: Travels Through the Paintbox*, took readers on a guided global expedition in search of the indigenous homes of a vast array of painterly hues. Where Ball sits us before percolating cauldrons in the past to witness the first forging of new pigments, Finlay places in our palm a cochineal beetle that she has just plucked from the flower of a prickly pear cactus in a colonial town in Chile – daring us to clench our fists and release the crimson blood from which a coveted red has been made since the 2nd century CE.

Hooked, I soon found myself consuming every book on the history of artists' materials, antiquated and new, that I could find – from the 14th-century Italian painter Cennino Cennini's seminal manual on pigment preparation, *Il libro dell'arte* (The Book of Art), to the contemporary art historian John Gage's authoritative studies *Colour and Culture: Practice and Meaning from Antiquity to Abstraction* (1993) and *Colour and Meaning: Art, Science and Symbolism* (1999); and from the 19th-century English chemist George Field's influential *Chromatography; or, A Treatise on Colours and Pigments, and of Their Powers in Painting* (1835) to the cultural historian Kassia St Clair's elegant compendium of chromatic portraits, *The Secret Lives of Colour* (2016), and countless others besides.

These studies began to kindle in me a fascination with an aspect of the sprawling subject that I had not found explicitly addressed: how the life of a pigment – its origins and adventures – shapes our experience of the masterpieces in which it figures. How, in other words, do a painting's colours colour us? How is it that a work's pigments can sink so deeply into the very fabric of who we are that they help us recognize ourselves in moments of self-excavation? It became increasingly clear to me that colour was more than an evocative aspect of artistic representation. It's what connects us with works on a more profound level than we consciously realize. If 'the painter', as Marcia Hall astutely asserts in her eloquent study *The Power of Color: Five Centuries of European Painting*, 'performs complex balancing acts in composing with color',[8] are we merely passive spectators in the mesmerizing spin of palettes? Or are we called upon actively to participate in the performance by recognizing the resonances and appreciating the materiality of the metaphors that painters compose with pigments? I wanted to learn not only *about* colour but also *from* it. 'Always with color', as the Renaissance scholar David Kastan observes in his wide-ranging meditation on the subject, *On Color*, 'there is something more than meets the eye.'[9]

I began to believe that a deeper consciousness of colour had the potential to complicate and enrich every aspect of our experience of art. Consider metaphor, that most basic dimension of art we look towards to transport us elsewhere. Colour has the capacity to make metaphor literal by imposing an empirical 'otherwhereness' – one that is absorbed into the tapestry of a work. Take the pair of poised peacocks in Tintoretto's dynamic *Origin of the Milky Way* (*c.* 1575), a canvas that imagines the mythic moment when the infant Hercules, sucking too hard on the breast of the goddess Juno, is shoved aside and a spray across the firmament from Juno's chest forms the Milky Way. Hidden from us are the hundred all-seeing eyes that Juno, according to myth, has taken from the poly-pupilled giant Argus Panoptes and imprinted on the folded wings of the peacocks. Nevertheless, the principal pigment that Tintoretto has used to describe the birds' dreamy blue plumage, azurite, ensures that we can still have magnified vision and can gaze all the way to a far-off elsewhere. Derived from the stone *Lapis armenius* (or 'stone of Armenia', a name that reflects where it was mined in Tintoretto's time), the azurite that glistens from the peacocks' feathers drags a distant land into the fabric of a painting that is, after all, all about the elasticity of immeasurable space. A peacock's tongue may not be able to carry a transportative tune, and its wings may not have the aviationary strength to propel it with ease across continents. But because of the power of pigment, the motionless migration of Tintoretto's majestic peacocks can whisk us to the remotest of realms.

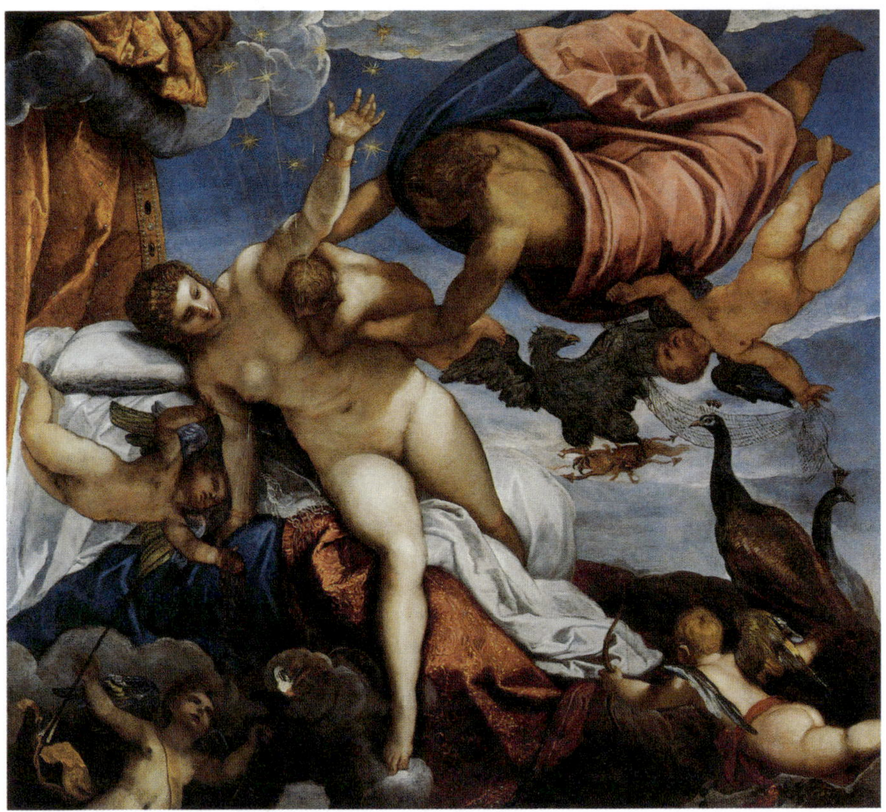

Jacopo Tintoretto, *The Origin of the Milky Way*, c. 1575

In the pages that follow, an artymological eye is turned to thirty-nine of the most significant pigments (and two metals) that have shaped the story of art. (It is important to note that the word 'pigment', which is related to the Latin stem of *pingere*, meaning 'to tint', 'to colour', 'to portray', is employed in the book's subtitle in the broadest possible sense and, admittedly, with a slight sleight of hand. The term's ambit has been stretched to accommodate not merely distilled, extracted, or powderized minerals suspended in a medium such as oil, as is traditional, but any substance, natural or synthetic, used by artists to impart colour, including soluble dyes.) The book is organized into ten chapters, each devoted to a single colour and to the principal materials from which that colour has been derived by image-makers since Stone Age humans first began creating pictures more than 45,000 years ago. The book also presents, inserted between these chapters, a series of nine 'Colourful Minds' spreads. Each of these two-page features draws the reader's attention to a key moment in the evolution of colour theory, from the publication in 1704 of Isaac Newton's groundbreaking treatise *Opticks; or, A Treatise of the Reflexions, Refractions, Inflexions and Colours of Light* to Swiss painter and theorist Johannes Itten's influential *The Art of Color*, which appeared in 1961. These features, which also call attention to the extraordinary contribution of female thinkers to the story of colour theory, are intended to serve as palette-cleansers between the pigment-heavy chapters that come before and after. The 'Colourful Minds' features are distinct from, yet run parallel to, the book's primary argument, thus establishing a 'light-motif', as it were, of ever-evolving theoretical insights that have helped fashion the way artists have perceived colour.

Whether muscled into brilliance by long-forgotten prehistoric artists seizing on bones and branches near to hand, concocted serendipitously by medieval alchemists in their pursuit of the Philosopher's Stone, or synthesized with scientific precision by modern-day chemists, the pigments explored in this book have left indelible marks on cultural consciousness. Like the ores and minerals from which many derive, these pigments have tended to settle beneath the surface strata of our conscious seeing as if deliberately deferring to the mere illusion of the objects and sitters they deceptively depict. My aim is to reassert the elemental primacy of pigments in our relationship with works of art, to pull them back into the light, and to acknowledge the formative role they play in shaping our appreciation and our awe.

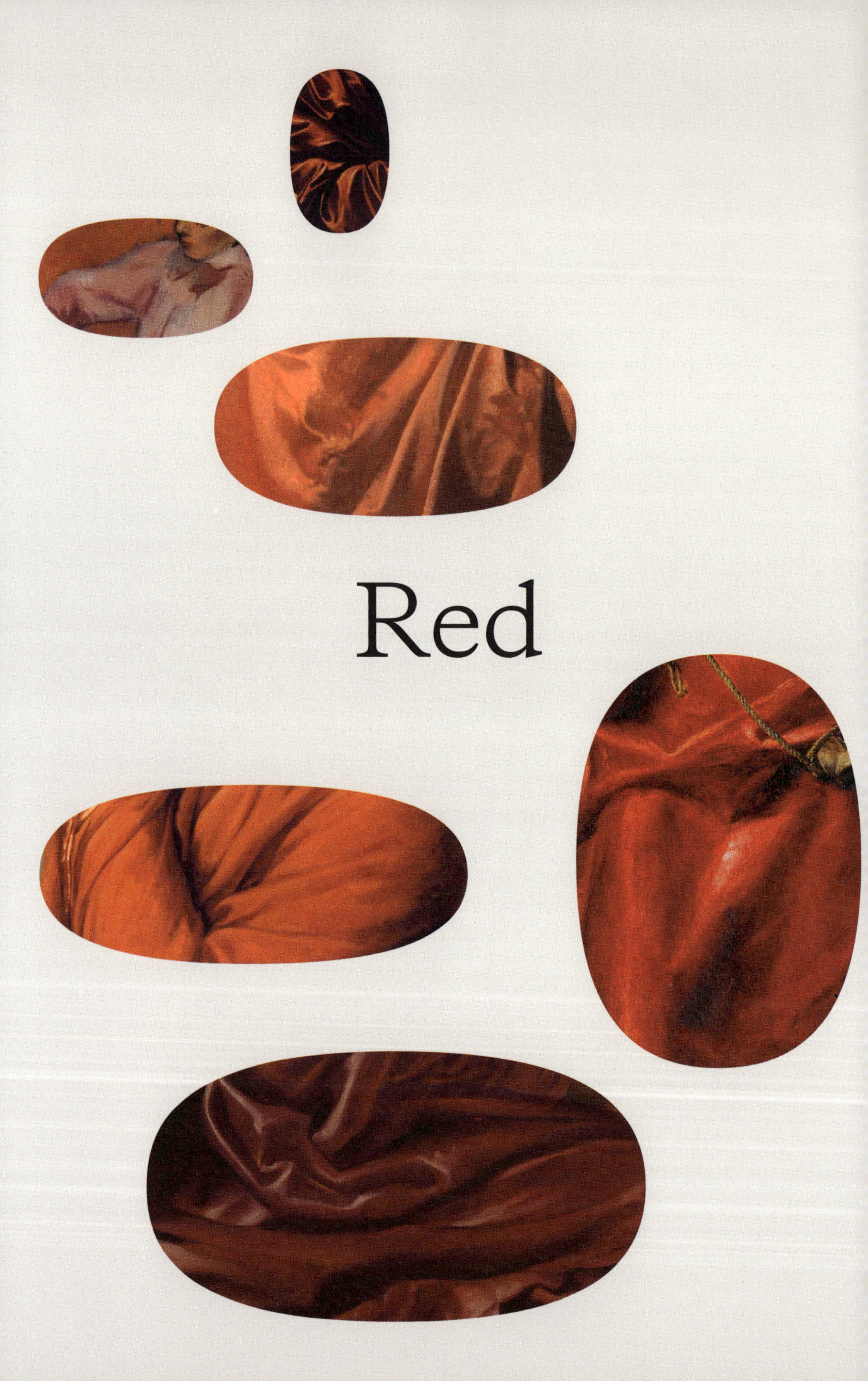

Red

'Look, Papa, oxen!' With those three words, shouted in excitement in 1879 by the daughter of an amateur Spanish archaeologist, the story of art was rewritten. What eight-year-old Maria was marvelling at as she stood with her father, Don Marcelino Sanz de Sautuola, in a cave in northern Spain was a pulsing pageant of Palaeolithic bison painted above them on the stone ceiling of the sprawling, multi-chambered complex.[1] So resonant and pristinely preserved was the ruddy red that vibrated from the beasts' bodies, it is little wonder that Sautuola, after sharing with the world the extraordinary discovery, would find himself accused of perpetrating an elaborate forgery by scholars who refused to accept that primitive hands were capable of such enduring grandeur.

Subsequent scientific analysis of the Altamira Cave paintings, which remain to this day among the most compelling examples of prehistoric art ever uncovered in Europe, has confirmed the authenticity of the Stone Age wonders and estimated the date of their creation to around 13,000 BCE – making them three times older than either Stonehenge or the pyramids of Giza.[2] The principal materials used by the primaeval painters have also been identified. The striking black outlines that define the bisons' bodies are down to a deft handling of charcoal, as is the alluring illusion of smoky depth in which they seem to shudder – an aesthetic innovation historians had long attributed to artists of much later eras.[3]

Red Ochre

But what really makes the muscular creatures sizzle and soar in their static stampede is a russet resplendence to their fur that the Stone Age artists magicked from natural clay earth rich in unhydrated iron oxide – or what is commonly called red ochre. The mineral responsible for the depth of colour in this prehistoric pigment is hematite.[4] That name, an ancient one, is

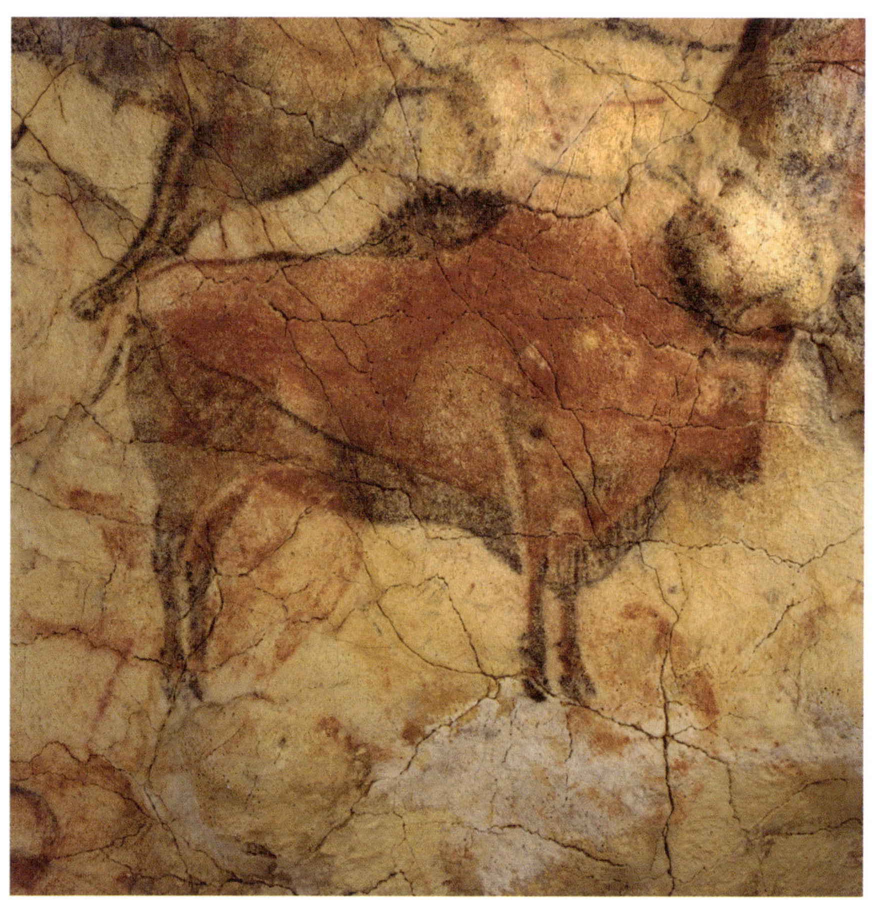

Altamira Bison, Cave of Altamira, Spain, *c.* 13,000 BCE

Red Ochre

derived from the Greek phrase '*aematitis lithos*' (or 'blood stone'), a term attached to the rust-red ore by the classical polymath Theophrastus in the 4th century BCE. Among the oldest (if not indeed the earliest) of sources from which humankind derived pigments for creating images, hematite is the lifeblood of art. It has been found in almost every prehistoric work and continues to be used to this day.

Over time, the mineral came to be valued not only for its use as an aesthetic tool but also for the wide range of medicinal properties it was purported to possess. Four centuries after Theophrastus coined the ore's name, the Roman naturalist and philosopher Pliny the Elder would attest to its ability to aid in recovery of everything from 'burns' to 'haemorrhoidal discharges'. 'It is marvellously useful', Pliny insists,

> *as an application for bloodshot eyes, and, taken internally, it acts as a check upon female discharges. To patients vomiting blood, it is administered in combination with pomegranate-juice. It is very efficacious also for affections of the bladder; and it is taken with wine for the cure of wounds inflicted by serpents.*[5]

While very much a substance of this world, hematite was increasingly perceived as possessing an almost supernatural ability to return one's troubled flesh to health. By the medieval era, the mineral's reputation as a miracle cure had accelerated. In his lyrical *Liber lapidum* (Book of Stones), the 11th-century French poet and bishop of Rennes, Marbodius, devoted an entry to the healing power of hematite, which he describes as 'a stone created to help humankind'.[6] The influential lapidary, which would go on to be translated into French, Provençal, Italian, Irish and Danish by the early Renaissance, advised that hematite, when 'mixed with egg white, and smeared on swollen eyelids, it heals them, and dim vision too, by banishing the blurriness'.

Whether Caravaggio knew of Marbodius's Book of Stones when he created his double portrait of Martha and Mary Magdalene (*c.* 1598), which captures the intimate moment when the former converts the latter from a life of the flesh to a life of the spirit – 'banishing', as it were, her 'dim vision' – the rumpled red right sleeve of Mary's robe, which crests and crumples at the very centre of Caravaggio's canvas, has been woven from hematite-rich red ochre. The fabric's delicate drama – the sheen of its crisp summits and the shadowy depths of its valleys – is as absorbing as the penetrating dialogue between Martha and Mary. Caravaggio has been careful to intersow his picture with dutifully literate and conventionally Christian symbols that make clear the spiritual transformation that is taking place before our eyes: the orange blossom, an oft-rehearsed symbol of purity, that Mary holds to her chest; the ivory comb and convex mirror, emblems of 'worldly vanities renounced', as the art historian Andrew Graham-Dixon has observed.[7] But the red-ochre sleeve shimmering at the dead centre of the painting setwws a deeper mood and materially connects the painting, whether intentionally or not, with a longer tradition of human healing.

Red is never what it seems. It signals something deeper. 'Red', the British Indian sculptor Anish Kapoor has said, 'is the colour of the interior of our bodies ... in a way it's inside out.'[8] From the colour's first occurrence in image-making tens of thousands of years ago to its saturation of such absorbing works as Artemisia Gentileschi's jolly *Virgin and Child with Rosary* (1651) and Élisabeth Louise Vigée Le Brun's scarlet-soaked portrait of Countess Varvara Nikolayevna Golovina (*c.* 1797–1800), red has throbbed, thrumming proof of art's vitality. Over time, red ochre would be joined by a host of other materials from which

OPPOSITE TOP Michelangelo Merisi da Caravaggio, *Martha and Mary Magdalene, c.* 1598

OPPOSITE BOTTOM Artemisia Gentileschi, *Virgin and Child with Rosary*, 1651

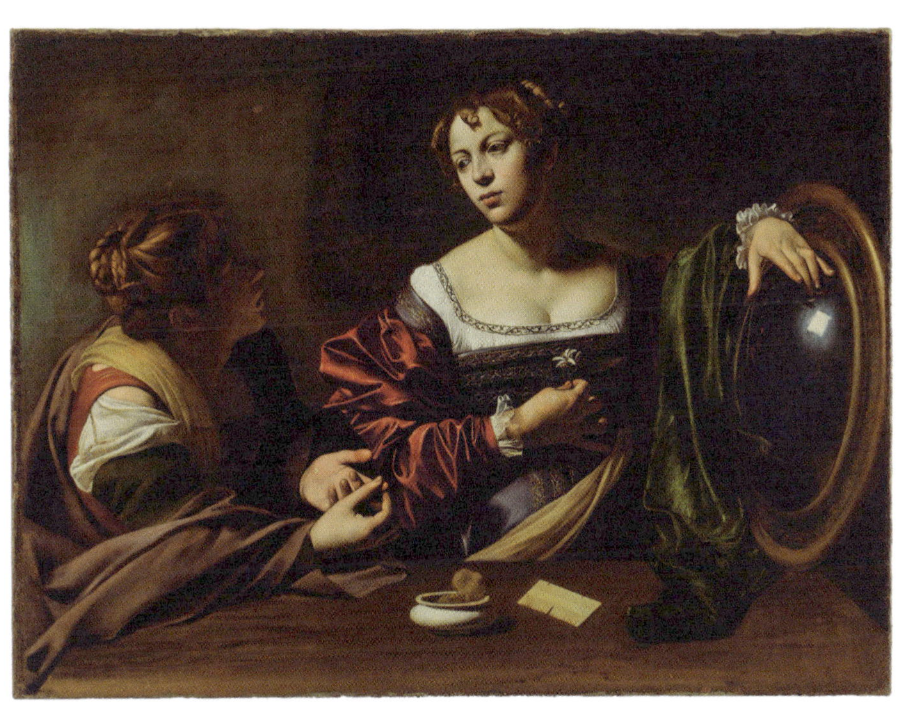

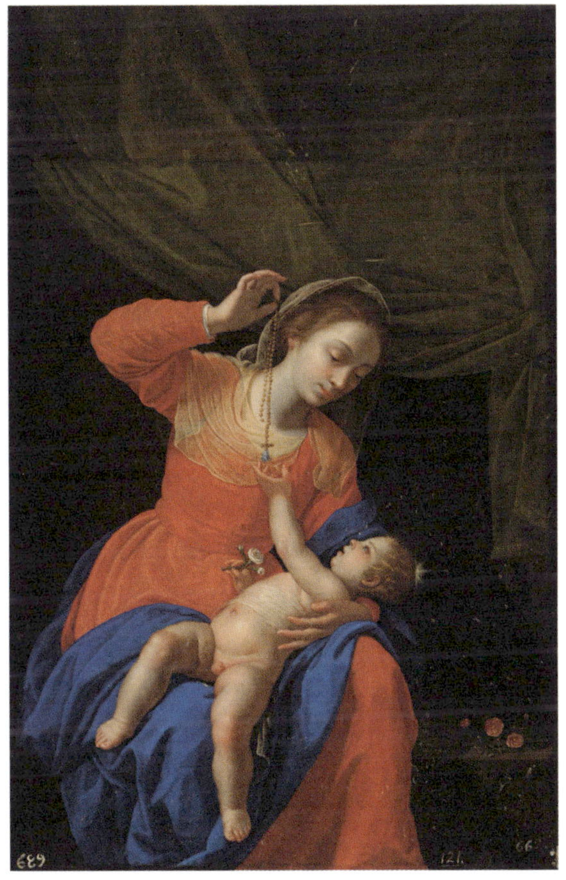

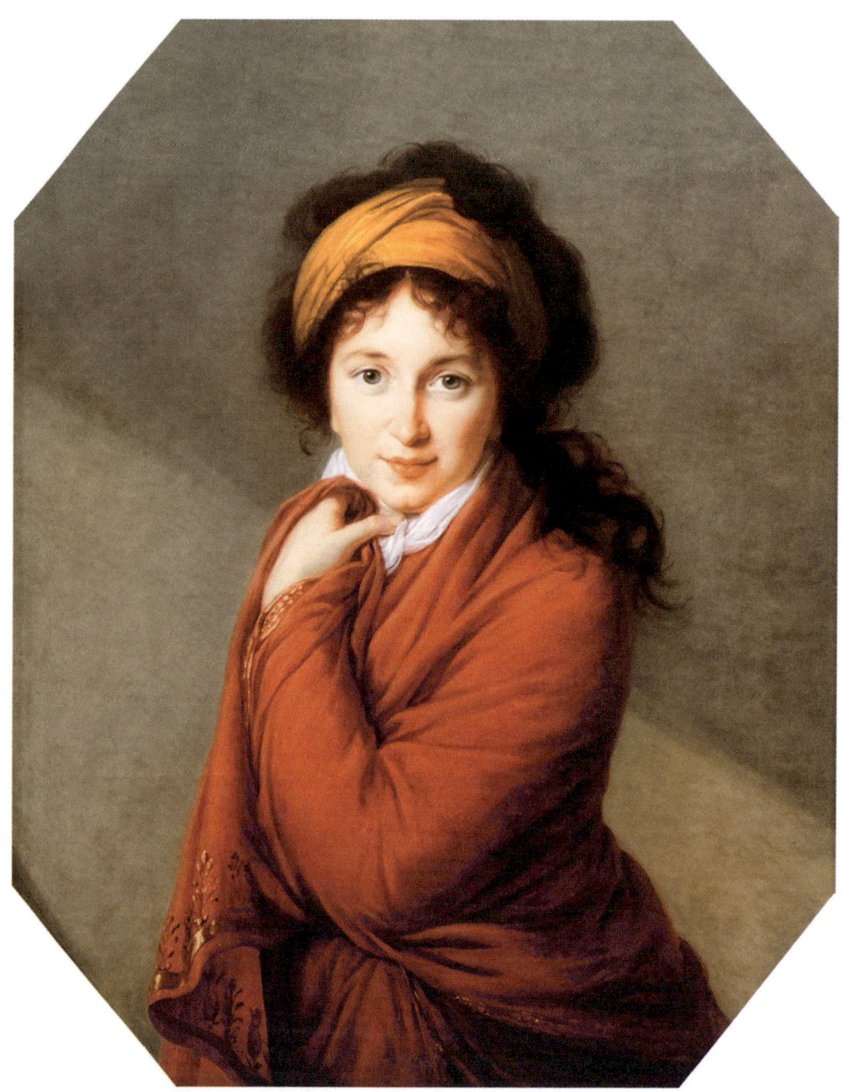

Élisabeth Louise Vigée Le Brun, *Portrait of Countess Golovina*, *c.* 1797–1800

rosy pigments could be pounded, pestled and powderized into service. Here we take a closer look at some of the most important and intriguing.

Carmine

How better to portray the conquering of supernatural power than to harness supernatural colour? That is what the Flemish master Peter Paul Rubens believed he was doing when he turned the rumpled dress of Delilah – the Philistine woman who famously coaxed her lover, Samson, into divulging the source of his great strength – into a surging ocean of carmine. Ancient in origin, carmine is a red colourant that has been used as a pigment and dye for at least the last 10,000 years.

For centuries, a teensy, seed-like burl from which carmine was extracted – first by crushing, then by boiling the pulverized remains – was understood to be a mysterious entity that magically transformed from a gritty little grain into a miniscule animal. This persistent misconception gave rise to the saying 'dyed in the grain'.[9] As microscopes improved, understanding of the nature of kermes – the name for this curious creature, which was gathered from pistachio and sumac trees in southern Europe – evolved. By the middle of the 18th century, it was widely believed that kermes was actually a tiny fruit inside of which spontaneously hatched a small insect whose infinitesimal wings vibrated with an otherworldly red that must be harvested at precisely the right moment before it fluttered off. '[T]hose berries,' wrote the English writer Godfrey Smith, compiler of the guidebook *The Laboratory, or School of Arts* (1756), 'when ripe, contain an insect of crimson red, which, if not timely gathered, will disengage itself from the shell and fly away.'[10]

This was a red with urgency and a mind of its own – a red that bides its time, waiting patiently to reveal its true intensity.

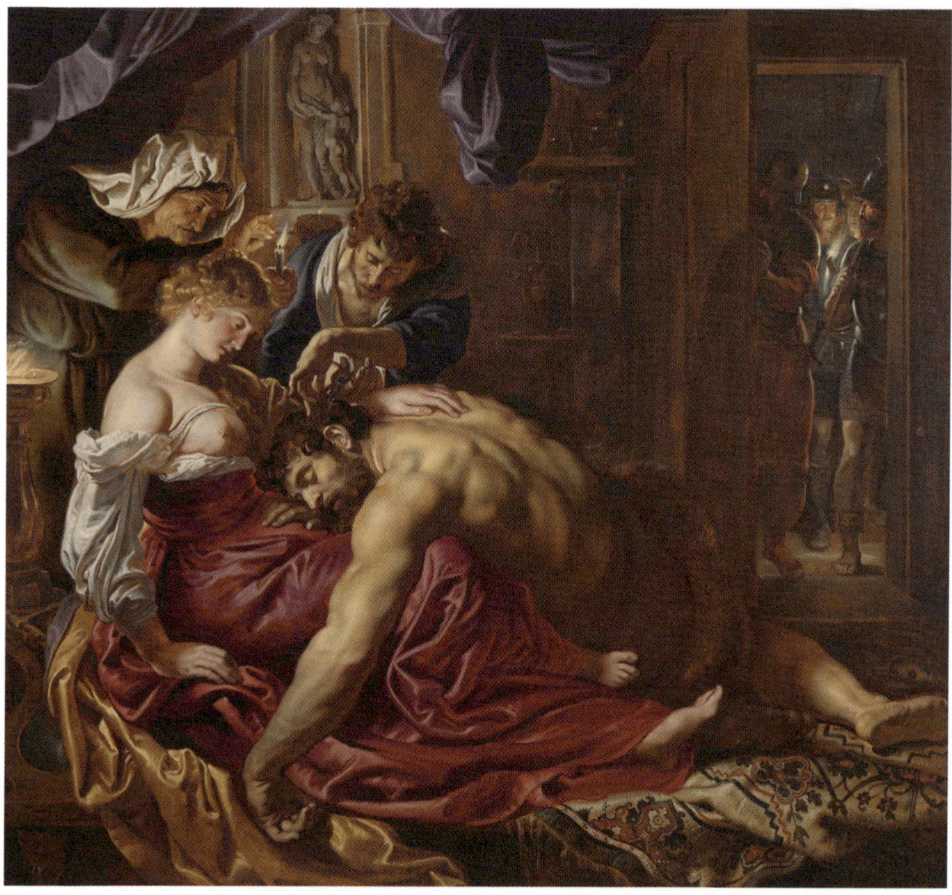

Peter Paul Rubens, *Samson and Delilah*, c. 1609–10

By drenching Delilah in a crimson derived from countless pestled kermes (a single ounce of the pigment required the crushing of 2,400 insects), Rubens echoes in colour the complexities of her character – at least as far as his age understood the strange nature of the pigment's origin. In the early 1700s, a century after Rubens had made his painting, the Dutch Golden Age microscopist Antony van Leeuwenhoek succeeded in ascertaining that there was no berry or grain in which a kermes hibernated, but only the insect's own crunchy chassis – a revelation that had slipped the attention of Godfrey Smith. In time, the colonial discovery of another scale insect on cacti in South America from which a similar dye and pigment could be extracted weakened the demand for kermes-derived carmine. Although the New World carmine, culled from cochineal, may have had further to travel, it could be harvested more frequently than kermes and was considered stronger.

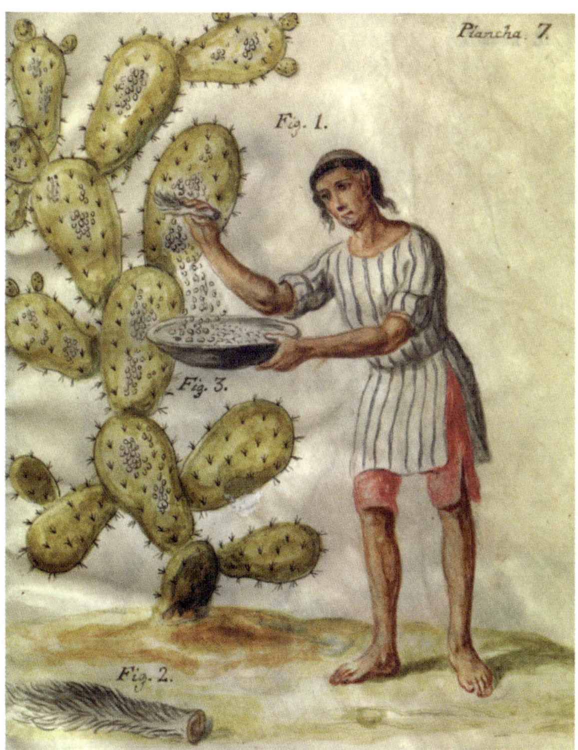

Cochineal collection, illustration from José Antonio de Alzate y Ramírez, *Memoria sobre la naturaleza, cultivo, y beneficio de la grana ...*, 1777

Rose Madder

Some colours dazzle the eye. Others sink deep into our bones. Rose madder, a luminous red hue derived from the root of the herbaceous perennial plant *Rubia tinctorum*, is one of these.[11] In 1736, an English surgeon by the name of John Belchier could hardly believe his eyes when his friend, a cotton printer, served him a joint of pork with a resplendent crimson bone jutting from the meat. When Belchier asked how his host had managed to produce such an arresting effect, without 'the least Alteration in Colour or in Taste' to the flesh,[12] he learned that his friend's livestock had been fed a diet of bran boiled in the same copper pot that the printer had used to print his calicoes bright red.

Keen to see if he could repeat the trick himself, the surgeon began experimenting on a clutch of hens back home. In fact, Belchier was retracing steps made two centuries earlier by the French astronomer and physician Antoine Mizauld, who may have been the first to record the effect on an animal's bones of consuming residue from the dye. 'I fed them with a Paste made of Wheatmeal and Powder of Madder-roots', Belchier would later attest in a scholarly treatise published in the *Philosophical Transactions of the Royal Society*, 'and gave them an Infusion of the same Root to drink, which I was in hopes they would have no Dislike to.' Although Belchier was wrong about the agreeableness of his concoction ('at the end of some Days, they could not relish the Mixture, of which they eat very little,' he observed, 'and wasted away visibly'), he was right about the effect of the madder root on the birds' bones.

'By looking at the Bones on the Under-Side of the Wing,' Belchier noted, 'which have no other Covering than thin Skin', he was amazed to see how the osseous architecture beneath the translucent membrane was soon 'tinged of a fine Rose-colour'.[13] The tireless surgeon went on to test the phenomenon by spiking the diet of pigeons and turkeys, the bones of which also turned 'a lively Rose'. When Belchier extended his experimentation to plants, however, lacing the soil in which they grew 'with a good Quantity of Madder', he 'found nothing, either in the Leaves, Stalks or Flowers'. It seems that alizarin, the organic compound responsible for the red colouring in madder, requires calcium to reveal its magic.[14] Over the course of the ensuing decades and centuries, Belchier's research would lead to significant advances in our understanding of anatomy and bone growth.

Belchier's long-forgotten experimentation is instructive of the penetrating power of this particular type of red in art history. Since antiquity, alizarin has been isolated from madder root to create both a dyestuff for textiles as well as a painter's pigment. Frequently used to convey the lush luminance of a subject's clothing, the hue is capable of accentuating hidden intensities. Painters sensitive to its piercing potency have reached for it to signify deeper mysteries pulsing beneath the surface fiction of their brushstrokes.

Rose madder proved an irresistible colour for Christ's flowing robe, which vibrates lustrously at the centre of one of the most transfixing works by the Spanish Renaissance master El Greco, *The Disrobing of Christ* (1577–79). Embattled on all sides by hecklers jostling to strip him of his clothes and dignity as he is marched to crucifixion, Christ gazes serenely towards heaven. But his eyes are a misdirection, a head fake. For now, our focus is and must be on his body, moments away from unmerciful punishment. No other pigment than bone-staining rose madder, from which El Greco has almost exclusively sculpted the rippling red robe that shrouds Christ's physique (save for a few flecks of lead white), can convey the vivid lividity of his imminent sacrifice.[15]

A century later, the Dutch Baroque painter Johannes Vermeer would use rose madder to complicate his *Girl with the Wine Glass* (1658–59), as the sheen of his subject's silk tabard dress echoes the lucency of Christ's robe in El Greco's painting.

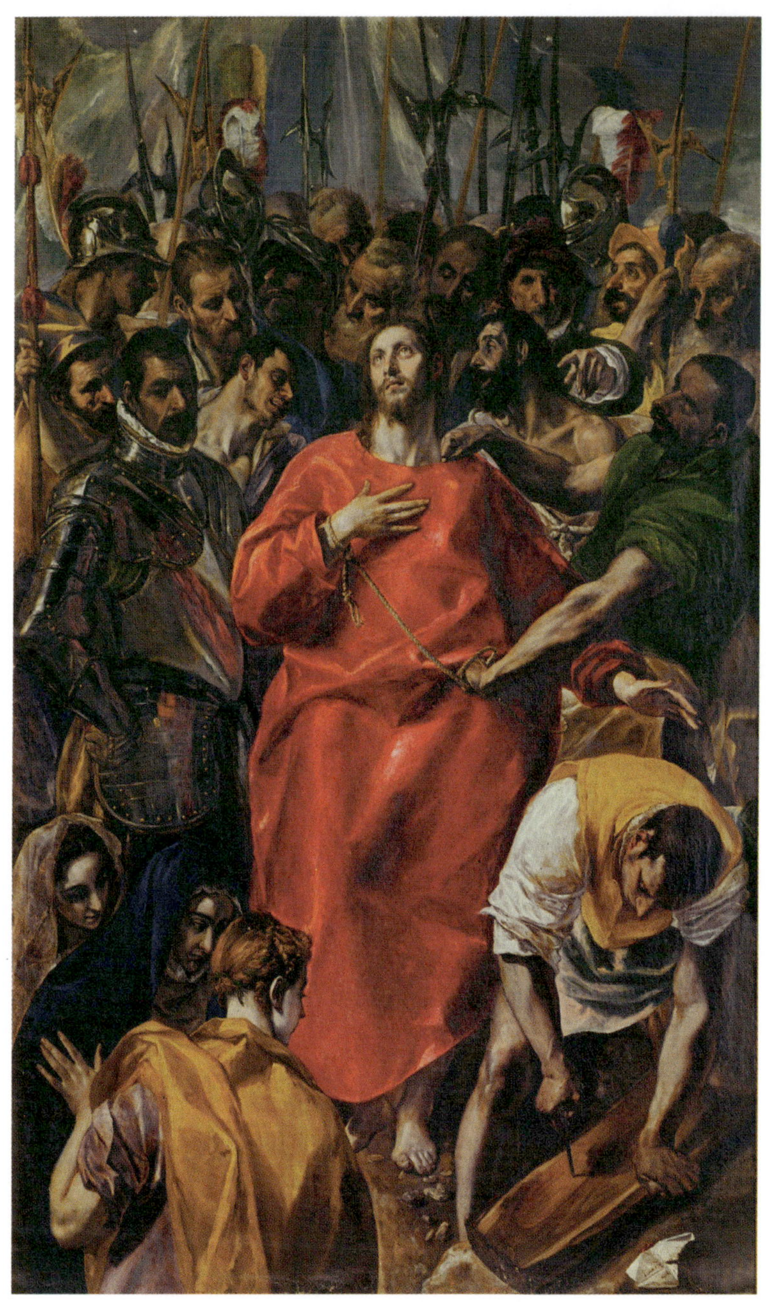

El Greco, *The Disrobing of Christ*, 1577–79

Rose Madder

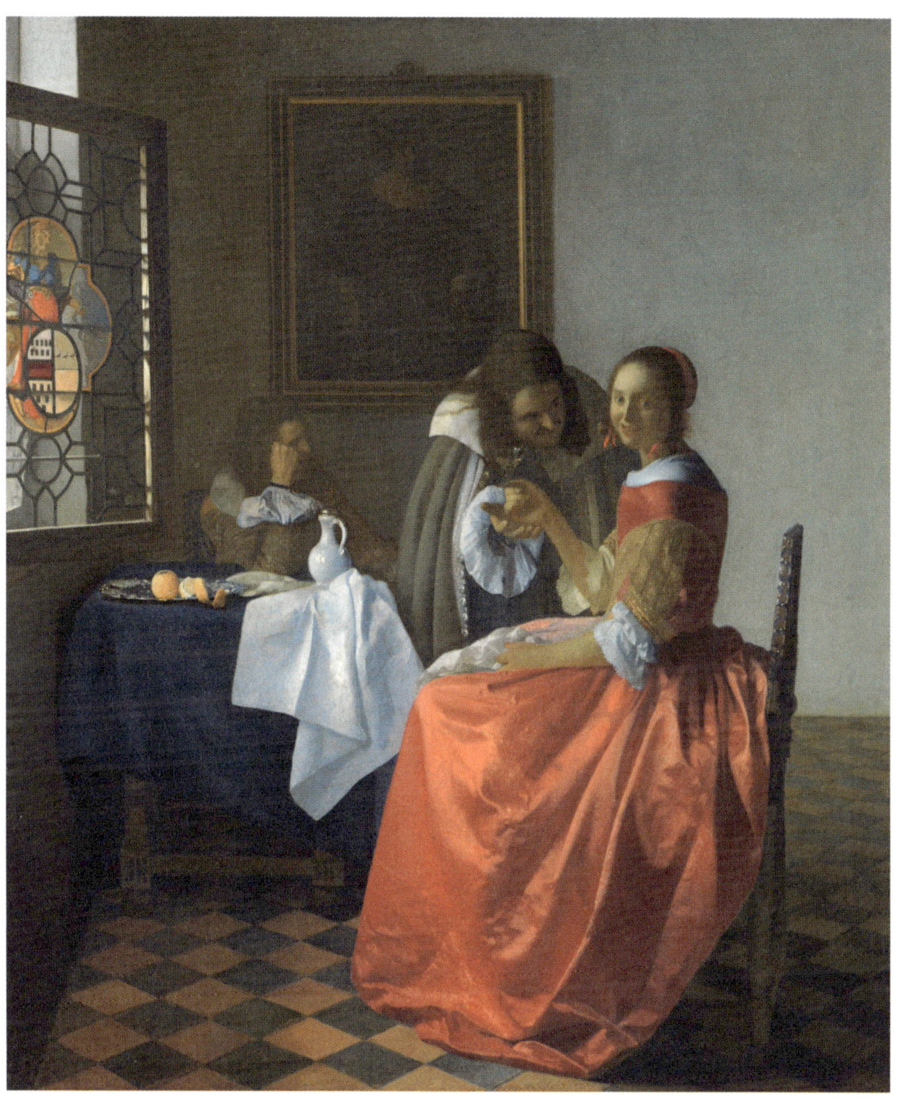

Johannes Vermeer, *The Girl with the Wine Glass*, 1658–59

Rose Madder

The vulnerable body of the young woman, whom we see plied with alcohol by a visiting suitor as a chaperon nods off in the corner of the painting, is once again brought subliminally to the surface of the painting by Vermeer's choice of rose madder to cover an underlayer of vermilion - a pigment with smouldering secrets of its own.[16]

Vermilion

Vermilion is a colour forged in fire. It ignites everything it touches, imbuing it with inner incandescence - an interior knowledge of its own fiery fleetingness. 'Vermillion is a red with a feeling of sharpness, like glowing steel.'[17] That's how the pioneering Russian artist and theorist Wassily Kandinsky described the fierce refulgence of the bright-red pigment in his soulful treatise on the essence of image-making, *Concerning the Spiritual in Art* (1911). Originally created by crushing into a highly toxic powder - cinnabar, a sparkling red mineral that embodies the scarlet effulgence of its volcanic origin - 'vermilion has the charm of flame,' Kandinsky observed, 'which has always attracted human beings.'[18]

Surviving fragments of inscribed ox scapula and turtle plastron used as props in pyromantic ceremonies in the 2nd millennium BCE by members of the Shang dynasty in China (whose use of vermilion is among the earliest recorded) corroborate Kandinsky's description of the pigment's spirit and appeal. Vermilion was used to paint symbols carved by diviners into these crude vessels as petitions to their deities for good fortune. The carefully scraped scapula or printed plastron was then subjected to fire until it shattered from the intense heat. The cryptic shards of bright vermilion text that resulted from the curious kilning of bone and shell required expert spiritual interpretation, like a scorched deck of Tarot cards.

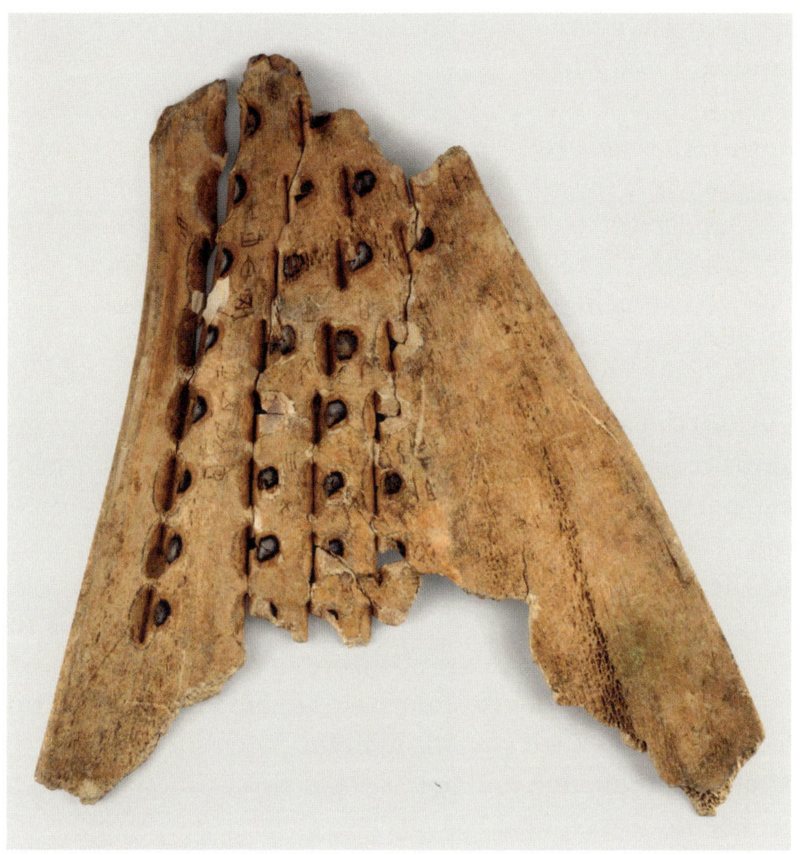

Oracle bone, China, 16th–10th centuries BCE

Romans couldn't get enough of the pigment either. Despite its rarity, its jaw-dropping expense and the dangers that its toxicity posed, they were drawn like moths to its lethal flicker. Not only did they doll up their statues with the poisonous powderized fire, they laced their cosmetics with it too, transforming their lips and cheeks into ill-fated flames.[19] According to Pliny the Elder, access to the mines in north-west Spain from which the cinnabar was extracted and imported for conversion into vermilion was strenuously restricted. 'Nothing is more carefully guarded', Pliny wrote.

> *It is forbidden to break up or refine the cinnabar on the spot. They send it to Rome in its natural condition, under seal, to the extent of some ten thousand pounds a year. The sales price is fixed by law to keep it from becoming impossibly expensive, and the price fixed is seventy sesterces a pound.*[20]

By the Middle Ages, a process of concocting vermilion synthetically from a secret recipe of sulphur and mercury had been perfected by alchemists who were convinced that the conjuring of such scintillation from the drabness of base elements put them a short stride away from the miracle of magicking gold itself. Cennino Cennini, the gifted Florentine artist, teacher and, as we have seen, author of the influential pedagogic tome *Il libro dell'arte,* took pains to help his students and readers navigate their way through the potential pitfalls of the pigment's production and use. 'I am leaving out the system for this,' Cennini explained,

> *because it would be too tedious to set forth in my discussion all the methods and receipts. Because, if you want to take the trouble, you will find plenty of receipts for it, and especially by asking of the friars. But I advise you rather to get some of that which you find at the druggists' for your money, so as not to lose time in the many variations of procedure. And I will teach you how to buy it, and to recognize the good vermilion. Always buy vermilion unbroken, and not pounded or ground. The reason? Because it is generally adulterated, either with red lead or with pounded brick.*[21]

Among the many recipes for vermilion that Cennini had in mind was an especially evocative formula recorded by the 12th-century compiler of the seminal manual to medieval arts, *De diversis artibus* (On Various Arts). 'Take sulphur', the author, known as Theophilus, wrote, 'and add it to two equal parts mercury, weighed out on scales.'

> *When you have mixed them carefully, put them in a glass jar. Cover it all over with clay, block up the mouth so that no fumes can escape, and put it near the fire to dry. Then bury it in blazing coals and as soon as it begins to get hot, you will hear a crashing inside, as the mercury unites with the blazing sulphur. When the noise stops, immediately remove the jar, open it, and take out the pigment.*[22]

Embodying the spirit of transformation from one substance to another, vermilion has been enlisted by artists keen to capture objects or figures in the throes of metamorphosis. Titian's altarpiece panel painting, *The Assumption of the Virgin,* which the Venetian Renaissance master created for the Basilica di Santa Maria Gloriosa dei Frari between 1516 and 1518, is exemplary of that desire. Portraying the Virgin Mary as she is mystically assumed into heaven at, or instead of, her physical death (the point remains a subject of dogmatic debate), the altarpiece establishes a continuity between the earthly realm that she is departing and the eternity to which she ascends by cloaking the chief figures in the spectacle - a pair of apostles at the bottom, Mary in mid-flight and God waiting to receive her - in varying shades of vermilion. By cutting them all from the same chromatic cloth, Titian is making as much a theological point as an aesthetic one. We, all of us, mortal and divine alike, are in an eternal state of fiery flux.

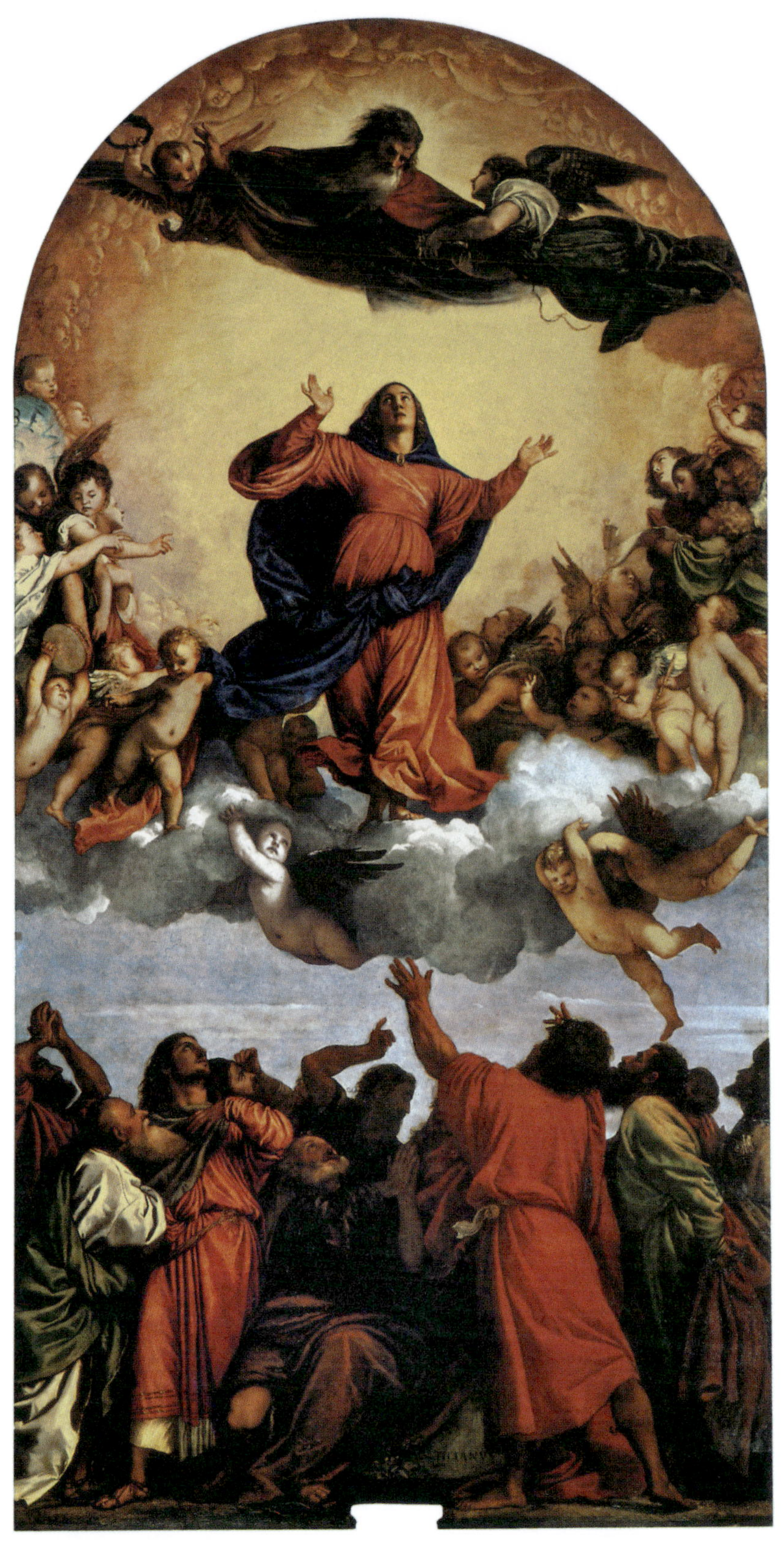

Titian, *The Assumption of the Virgin*, 1516–18

Red Lead

Speaking of flux, vermilion was often rather confusingly known by artists and writers by another name - one that, in fact, properly designates an entirely different shade of red: minium. Also called 'red lead', minium is characterized by a warmth that flickers towards orange and is best known for its use by medieval manuscript writers who relied on its embering radiance to illuminate their texts. Elaborate historiated initials, as well as many of the other readerly cues that punctuate these early texts, including paragraph marks (or pilcrows) and rubrics, were also set out in minium by specialists who came to be known as 'miniators'. Over time, any type of small-scale creation would come to be known by a derivative of this curious job title: miniature.

Like the synthetic form of vermilion, minium could be cooked up by anyone prepared to follow a few prescribed steps. '[T]ake a pot that has never been used', instructs the *Mappae clavicula*, a medieval handbook for creating craft materials such as dyes and glass, 'and put sheets of lead in it. Fill the pot with very strong vinegar, cover and seal it. Put the pot in a warm place and leave it for a month.'[23] Patience paid off. 'Next,' the Latin text goes on to say, 'take the pot, uncover it, shake out the deposits around the sheets of lead into a ceramic pot, and then place [it] on the fire. Stir the pigment constantly, and when you see it turn white as snow use as much of it as you like; this pigment is called basic lead white, or ceruse.' But it was the final step in the ritual that would produce the greatest surprise: 'Then take whatever is left on the fire, and stir it constantly until it becomes red ... remove it from the heat and allow it to cool.'

For centuries, artists were content to stop there. Coaxed as it was from snow white and hovering between simmering red and roasted orange, minium typified the very essence of transformation, and was used to inflect with fire everything from Diane's dress in Titian's *Death of Actaeon* (*c.* 1559–75) to the bedside table in Van Gogh's *Bedroom in Arles* (1888). In 1772, however,

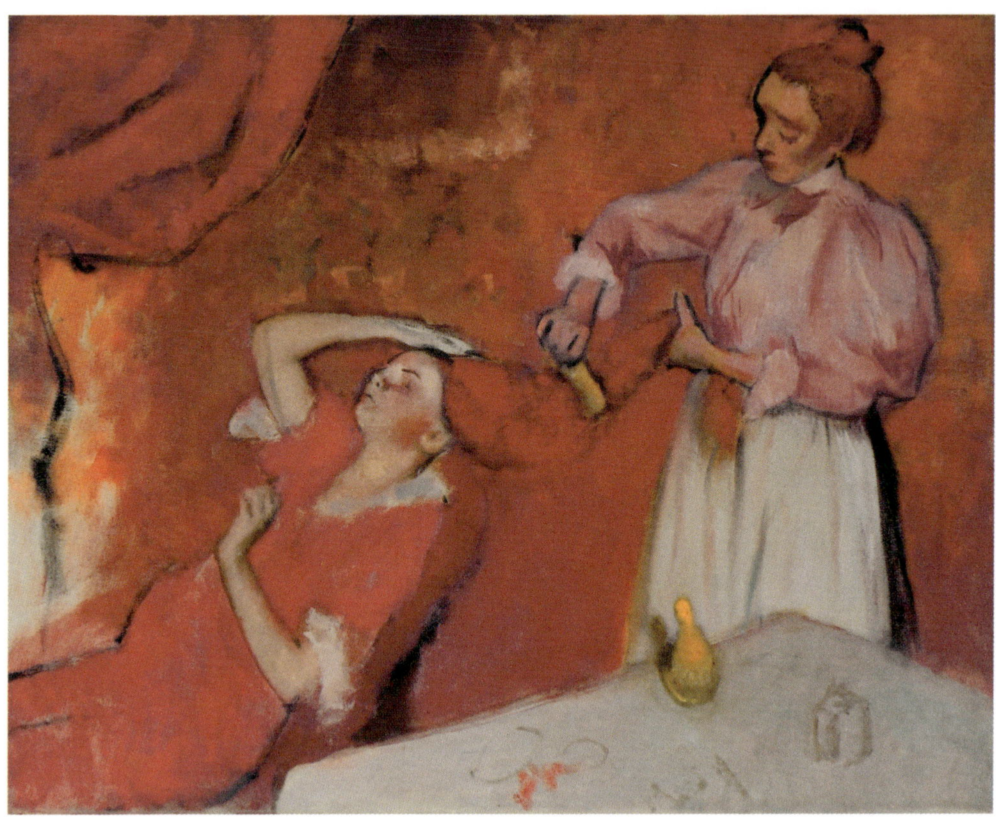

Edgar Degas, *Combing the Hair ('La Coiffure')*, c. 1896

the English natural philosopher and pioneering chemist Joseph Priestley went further and changed the course of science by pushing the pigment to its limit by heating it until his beaker rattled above the candle and emitted a 'crackling noise'. Doing so, Priestley observed, produced a gas (or an 'air', as he called it) that was so pure that, when it was pumped into a chamber filled with mice, the creatures were suddenly energized and stayed alert twice as long as they had when breathing ordinary air. Sucking it in himself, Priestley attested to the air's invigorating power. He called the gas that minium respired 'Dephlogisticated Air', mistakenly believing that it had been cleansed of a mythical impurity 'phlogiston'.[24] Today, we call it oxygen.

Perhaps no painting in the history of art demonstrates a greater sensitivity to the inspiriting potential of minium than Edgar Degas's sweetly sinister *Combing the Hair* (*c.* 1896).[25] A percolating assortment of several declensions of red – from the vermilion that dominates the dress of the girl whose scalp is roughly ripped back to the red ochre that saturates the rumpled curtain in the upper left of the canvas, which threatens to sweep down at any moment – the crush of crimsons in Degas's work is almost suffocating. Save, that is, for the murky mizzle of minium that engulfs the servant in a radiant cloud. Its strange warmth sustains our stare, keeps it curiously oxygenated amid the asphyxiation, as it crystallizes the inscrutable servant into eternal mystery.

Isaac Newton's *Opticks*

(1704)

The English mathematician, physicist and astronomer Isaac Newton began investigating the essence of colour as a student at Cambridge University in the 1660s, while quarantined to avoid the plague that was then sweeping England. Newton challenged the classical notions of colour, attributed to the ancient Greek philosopher Aristotle, that had stood for 2,000 years: that there were only two primary colours - blue and yellow - and that all the colours we see are associated with the four elements - earth, air, water and fire. Although the Romantic poet John Keats would later accuse Newton (albeit light-heartedly) of 'unweaving the rainbow' and demystifying its beauty, his insights changed forever how artists perceive colour.

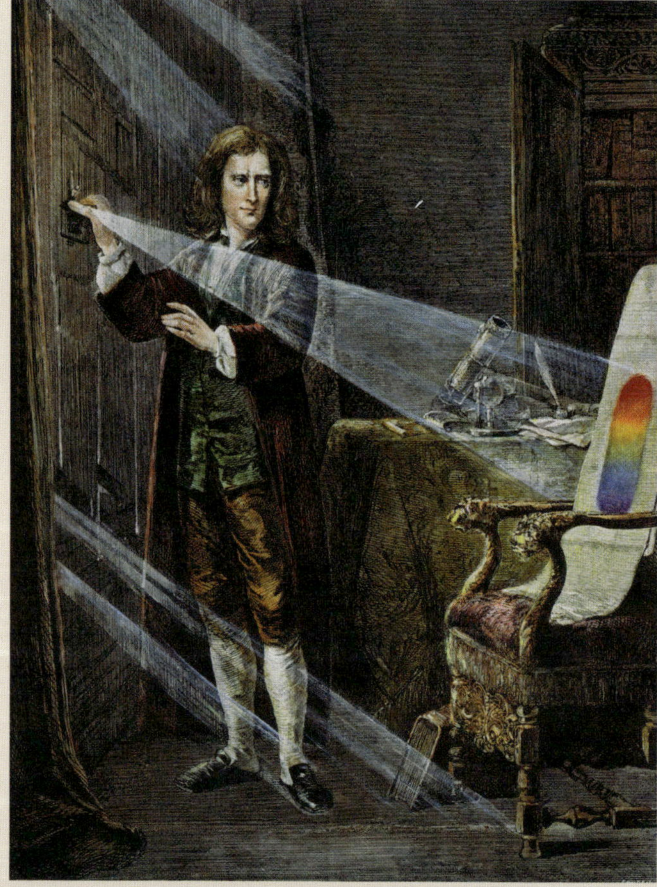

In 1666, Newton analysed the behaviour of beams of light as they passed through a hole drilled in the shutters of his student rooms at Cambridge University. Using glass prisms positioned at various angles first to split the white light into a spectrum of colours and then to reweave it, Newton proved that colour is intrinsic to light.

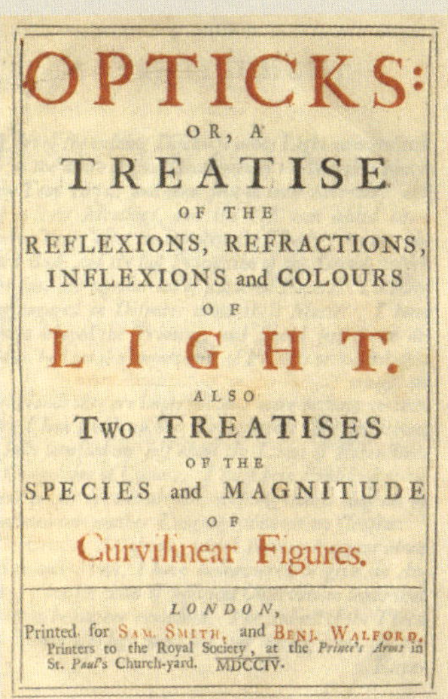

OPTICKS:
OR, A
TREATISE
OF THE
REFLEXIONS, REFRACTIONS,
INFLEXIONS and COLOURS
OF
LIGHT.
ALSO
Two TREATISES
OF THE
SPECIES and MAGNITUDE
OF
Curvilinear Figures.

LONDON,
Printed for SAM. SMITH, and BENJ. WALFORD,
Printers to the Royal Society, at the Prince's Arms in
St. Paul's Church-yard. MDCCIV.

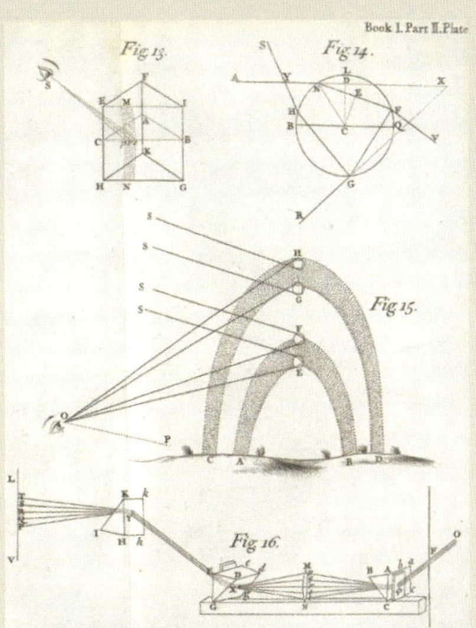

Published in 1704, Newton's pioneering study *Opticks* (title page seen here) chronicled the results of his nearly forty years observing the nature of light and our perception of colour.

Newton's dispassionate analysis of atmospheric optics was perceived by the Romantic writer John Keats as reductive, resulting in the clinical dissection of a rainbow's beauty.

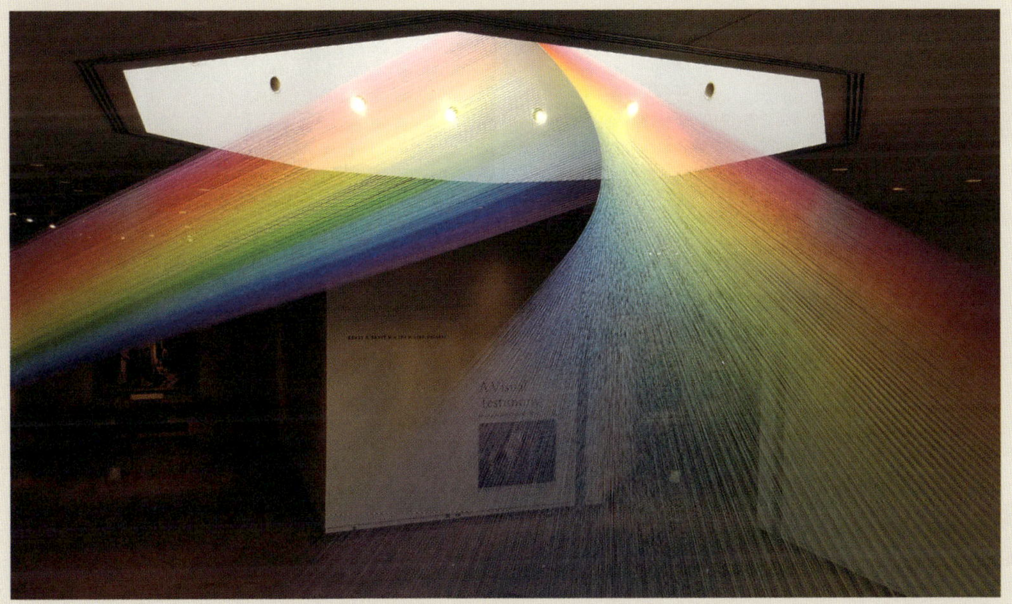

Newton's observations took that most seemingly impalpable of things, colourful light, and transformed it into something tangible: scientific equations. In our own age, Mexican-born contemporary artist Gabriel Dawe is similarly concerned with the nebulous nexus where light and materiality blur. Using miles of fine polyester sewing thread that he delicately stretches and arcs into diaphanous veils for his series of mesmerizing installations *Plexus*, Dawe miraculously weaves a colourfully static mist.

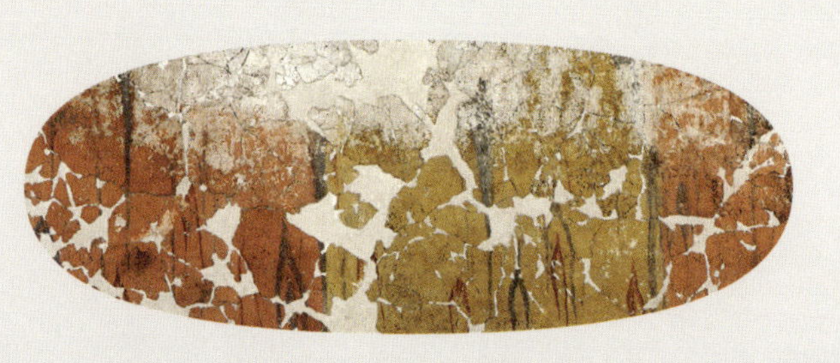

Orange

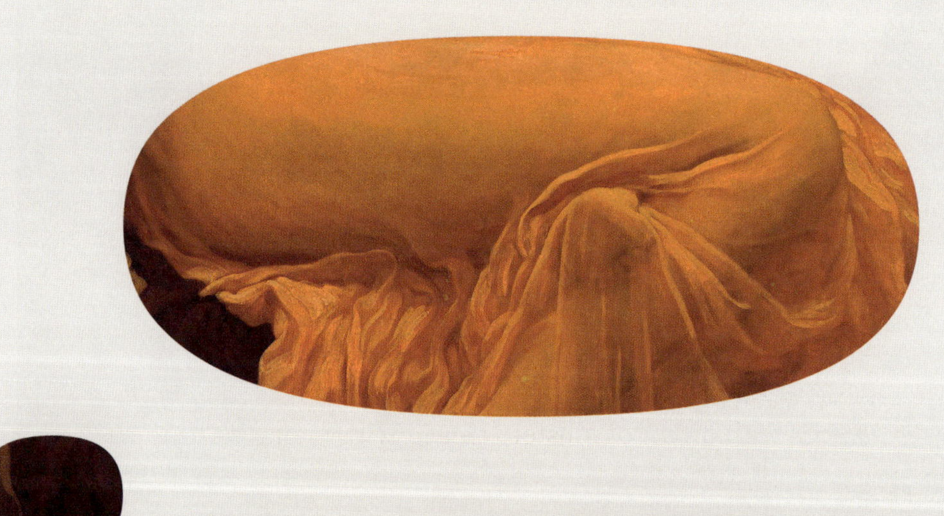

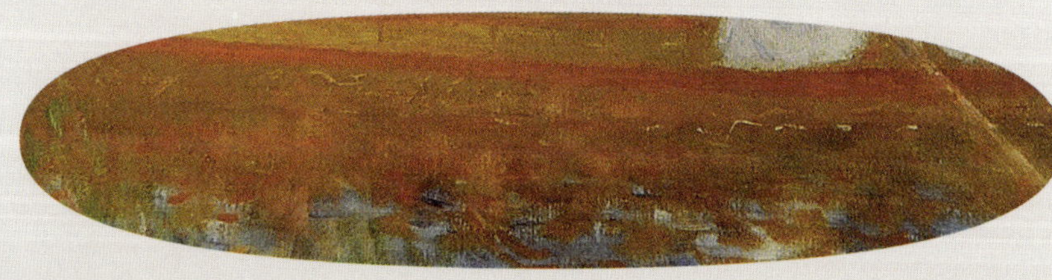

Rarely lost for words, the 14th-century English poet Geoffrey Chaucer was happy to fashion from French and Latin the language he needed if it didn't already exist. According to the *Oxford English Dictionary*, countless words we use today, from 'blab' to 'blaspheme', 'trickle' to 'twitter', make their first known appearance in Chaucer's writings. His *Nun's Priest's Tale* alone is credited with giving us such indispensable vocabulary as 'cottage' and 'digestive', 'tiptoe' and 'poop'. But when it came simply to describing the cinnamony fur of a fox – a colour for which the English language had not yet got around to crafting a word – even Chaucer (who coined 'cinnamon') was at a loss. When the proud rooster Chauntecleer, the hero of the *Nun's Priest's Tale*, dreams of an approaching fox, we're rather drably told the creature's 'colour was be-twixe yelw & reed'. Until the citrus fruit itself finally rolled its way from China (where it had been growing for more than four millennia) to Britain two centuries after Chaucer, the English were content with lazily sticking the word for yellow (*ġeolu*) on to the word for red (*rēad*). For centuries, the ungainly *geoluread* was apparently good enough. In time, a corruption of 'naraga' – the Sanskrit word for the zesty fruit – would be squeezed into a fresh English word 'orange', a word that would soon double for the colour.

Orpiment

Whether they knew quite what to call it or not, artists have never been in any doubt about the visual power of orange. Since antiquity, whenever painters were determined to invest their work with an air of mystery tinged with menace – as if the work possessed a dangerous, secret knowledge – they reached for orpiment, among the earliest substances from which the colour orange could be wrought without concocting it artificially from a mixture of primary reds and yellows. A sparkling arsenic sulphide mineral whose name is derived from the Latin *auripigmentum* (meaning 'gold pigment'), orpiment is found either near volcanic cracks and fissures or when realgar (a deeper-coloured arsenic sulphide) begins to decay. For centuries, the mineral's deceptive resemblance to gold defined its reputation and made it the obsession of alchemists and of those who craved what alchemists were struggling to create.

Pliny the Elder devotes a short chapter in his sprawling compendium of knowledge, *Naturalis Historia*, to 'procuring gold; by making it from orpiment'. He teases the reader with an anecdote recalling Caligula's abortive efforts to distil from the sulphite's raw state a worthwhile proportion of precious metal. 'It is just the colour of gold, but brittle, like mirror-stone', Pliny writes. 'The substance', he says,

> *greatly excited the hopes of the Emperor Caius, a prince who was most greedy for gold. He accordingly had a large quantity of it melted, and really did obtain some excellent gold; but then the proportion was so extremely small, that he found himself a loser thereby. Such was the result of an experiment prompted solely by avarice: and this too, although the price of the orpiment itself was no more than four denarii per pound. Since his time, the experiment has never been repeated.*[1]

Orpiment's obstinate refusal to divulge the secrets of making gold seems only to have added to its allure. As did its extreme toxicity. Convinced that any substance this dazzling – despite the presence of highly poisonous arsenic in its composition – must possess within itself some hidden healing properties, naturalists from ancient China to medieval Europe experimented with orpiment as a miracle cure. 'The Javanese and the Chinese do not regard it as a poison,' observed the 17th-century

German botanist Georg Eberhard Rumphius in his quirky conspectus *The Ambonese Curiosity Cabinet*, 'but will also administer it without fear to a body, but in small quantities, wherein they are not careful enough in my opinion. After all, it was observed in the year 1660, in Batavia [the Netherlands], that it was given to a woman who became mad from it, and crawled up the walls like a cat, the quantity having probably been too large.'[2]

That menacing mixture of glitz and peril - of something that possesses simultaneously the secrets of health and fortune and of madness and death - seems instinctively to have heightened the appeal of orpiment also as an artist's tool. In his *Il libro dell'arte*, Cennino Cennini, the Renaissance authority on the art of colour, takes pains to point out both the wonders that can be 'coaxed' from orpiment as well as the risks involved in communing with it. 'This color is, to start with, the most refractory color to work up that there is in our profession,' Cennini notes, echoing Pliny's characterization of the mineral as a kind of refractory 'mirror-stone'.

> *And so, when you want to work it up, put the amount you want on to your stone; and, with the one which you hold in your hand, proceed to coax it, little by little, so as to squeeze it from one stone to the other, mixing in a little of the glass of a broken goblet, because the powder of the glass attracts the orpiment to the roughness of the stone. When you have got it powdered, put some clear water on it, and work it up as much as you can; for if you were to work it for ten years, it would constantly become more perfect. Be careful of soiling your mouth with it, lest you suffer personal injury.*[3]

At once dazzling and dangerous, orpiment inflects works with inscrutable lustre. Although shabby from the elapse of

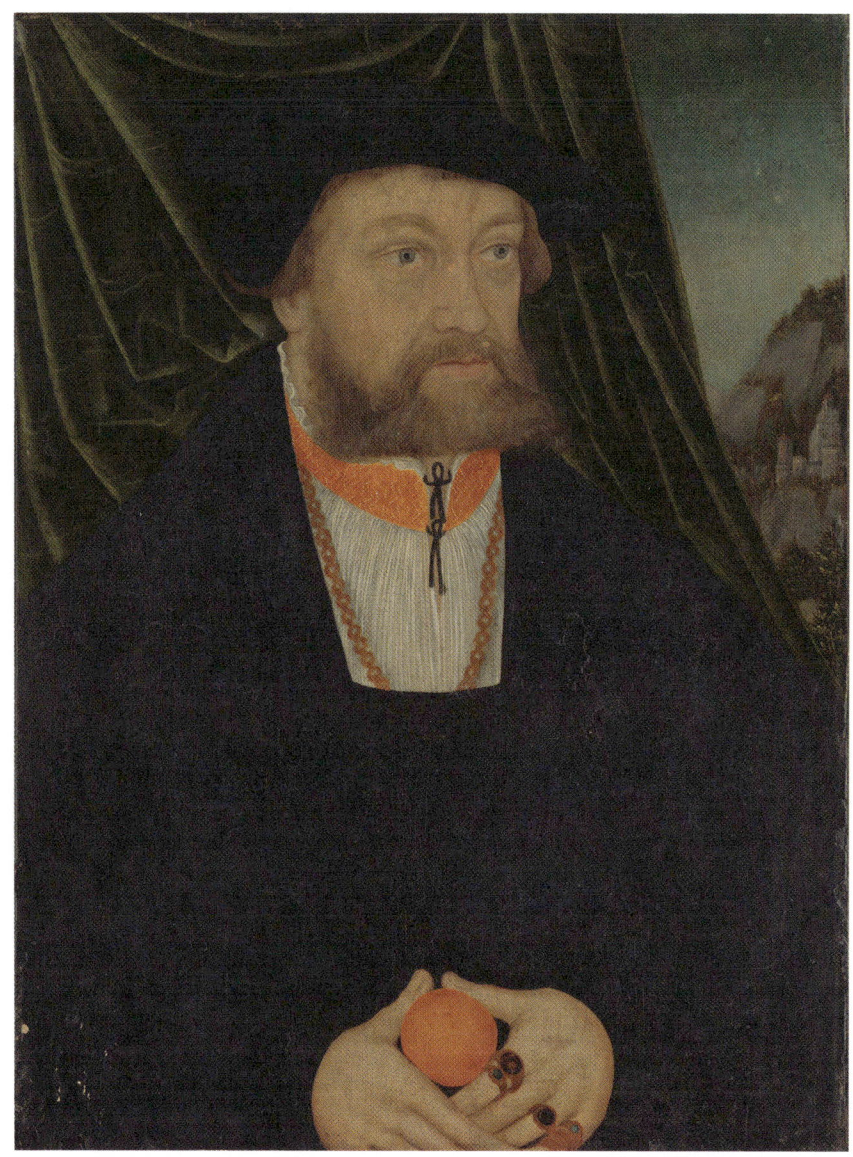

Circle of Lucas Cranach the Elder, *Portrait of a Man*, 1537

Orpiment

centuries and scrubbing by restorers, a 16th-century portrait of a middle-aged man holding an orange (a painting that may come from the workshop of the German Renaissance master Lucas Cranach the Elder) is characteristic of the power of this enigmatic pigment. Caught in half profile, with sealed, unreadable lips, the anonymous subject stares into empty space, lost in contemplation of life's irresolvable mysteries. Neither sanguine nor sorrowful, delighted nor depressed, he seems to sit outside human emotion. His scholarly cap suggests that he is well accustomed to such a posture of aloof reflection - a dispassionate observer of the world he inhabits.

The careful choreography of the sitter's fingers, which clasp the citrus fruit in a self-conscious manner that calls to mind the sign language of an occult society, invests the portrait with intrigue. The fruit's tangy, incongruous glisten (concocted from orpiment) in a painting otherwise dominated by the drabness of the sitter's cloak and the heavy velvet folds of the curtain behind him echoes the bright embroidery of his clementine collar (which also bears traces of the pigment). The coordination intensifies the suspicion that the orange he holds is not an incidental prop, but a key to the portrait's meaning - a tangy talisman that transports the sitter to a realm of pure thought.

Saffron

In 1546, a pair of unprincipled pepperers, Hans Kölbele of Nuremberg, Germany, and Lienhart Frey, from Thalmässing, were burned alive. Their crime? Selling the exceedingly pricey spice saffron surreptitiously diluted with the shrivelled florets of much cheaper plants, such as calendula and safflower. Kölbele and Frey were not just set alight for their offence; their bodies were malodorously smoked at the stake along with the 'adulterated' wares that the pair had peddled to unsuspecting customers.[4] Two months later, an accomplice, Elss Pfragnerin, was apprehended and, for his part in the scheme, buried alive.

Such prosecutions and punishments had become customary since the establishment in 1441 in Nuremberg of a so-called *Safranscau* (or 'saffron inspection') aimed at curbing the counterfeit practice of 'falsifying' what was (and remains to this day) the world's most expensive spice. Treasured since antiquity for its alleged medicinal properties and for its ability to yield a crisp, otherworldly orange hue when used as a pigment or dye, saffron has managed perennially to command an exceedingly high price (the value in 2020 stood at $10,000 per kilogram[5]), chiefly because of the intensive labour required to harvest it.

To produce a single gram of saffron, stigmas from more than 150 *Crocus sativus* flowers (each containing 'three tubular, filiform orange-red stigmas ... about an inch in length'[6]) must be delicately tweezed by hand. The coveted crocus flower blooms briefly in the autumn, and the window of time one has to shuck the crimson stigmas from the centre of the plant's violet petals is vexingly small – 'a few days only', Pliny the Elder lamented. In 1444, Jobst Findeker found out the hard way just how serious the *Safranscau* was in its determination to deter fraudsters who might cut corners and spike their inventories with additives to pad their profits. With a parcel of the spice he had debased hung around his neck, Findeker too was set on fire.[7]

Questions of purity have always been bound up with saffron, perhaps most famously in its use as a dyestuff for colouring Buddhist robes a vibrant yellow-orange that denotes the renunciation of the material world – a tradition that dates back millennia. From 10th-century BCE Persia, where threads of the spice were woven into funeral shrouds and ritually offered to deities, to ancient Greece, where legendary leaders Cyrus the Great and Alexander the Great treated their war wounds with it, saffron has also been cherished for its purported restorative powers. The cure-all of cure-alls, saffron has been prescribed to

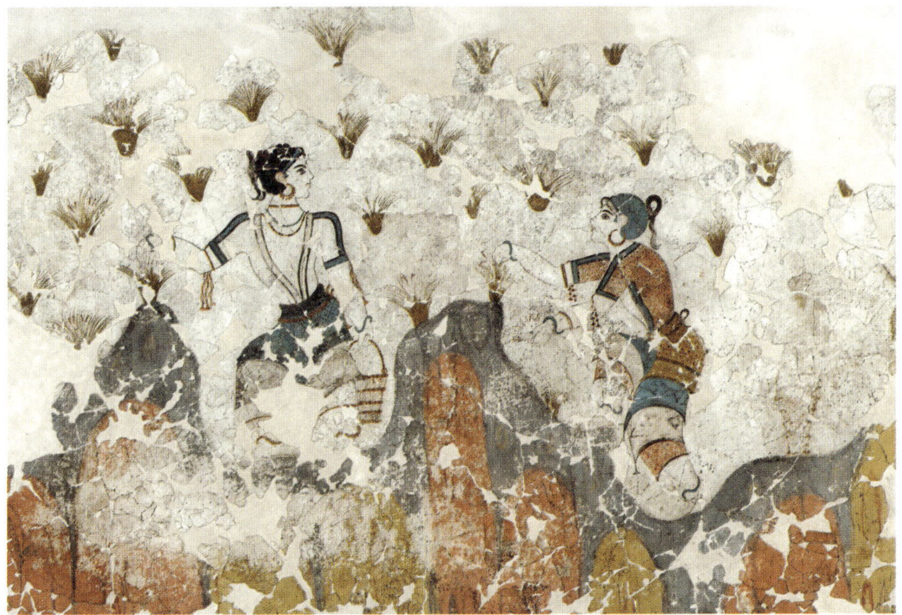

The 'Saffron Gatherers' fresco (detail) from the upper storey of Xeste 3 at Akrotiri, Thera (Santorini), Greece, 16th century BCE

treat everything from diseases of the eye to asthma, menstrual problems to depression. Believing it could cleanse both the soul and the body, Cleopatra is reputed to have perfumed her bath water with liberal lashings of the spice, especially before rendezvous with men.[8]

Saffron's reputation as a wonder drug hardly diminished over time. 'The moderate use of it', according to John Gerard in his famous 16th-century illustrated botanical handbook *Herball; or, Generall Historie of Plantes* (1597), 'is good for the head, and maketh the senses more quick and lively, shaketh off heavy and drowsy sleep, and maketh a man merry.' So miraculous was the spice, it even leant itself to being the perfect metaphor for illustrating the purifying power of Christ. 'As the saffron-bag

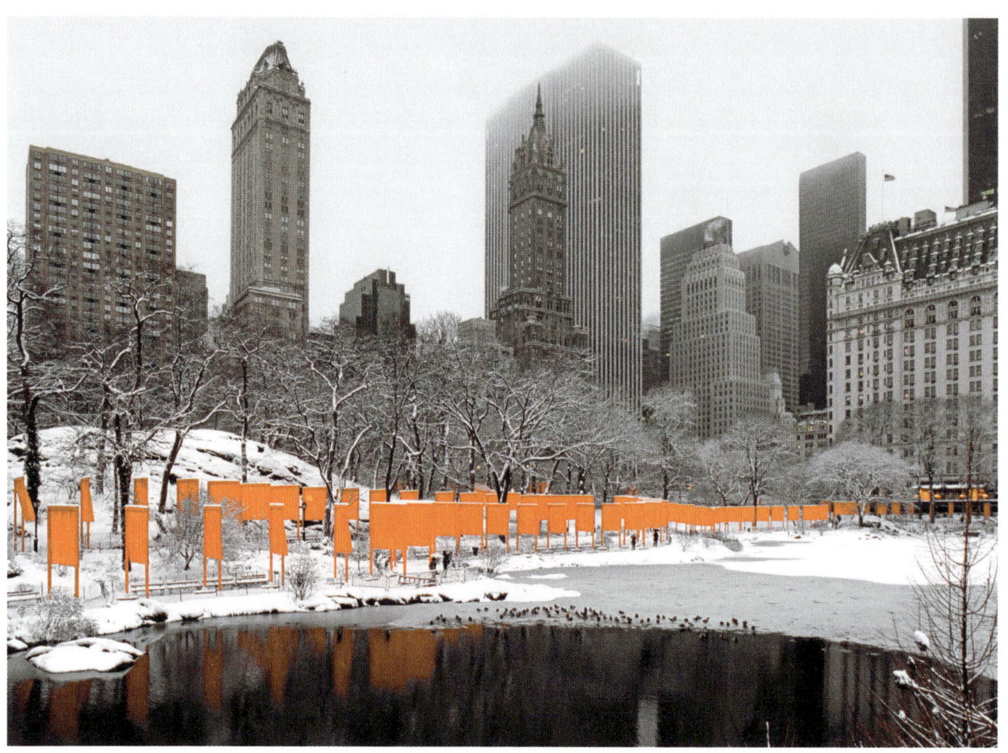

Christo and Jeanne-Claude, *The Gates, Central Park, New York City*, 1979–2005

that hath been full of saffron, or hath had saffron in it,' the English preacher Hugh Latimer proclaimed in a sermon in 1548 (seven years before he, himself, would be burned at the stake for denying transubstantiation), 'doth ever after savour and smell of the sweet saffron that it contained; so our blessed lady, which conceived and bare Christ in her womb, did ever after resemble the manners and virtues of that precious babe that she bare.'[9]

As a potent pigment and dyestuff, saffron has been in use since the Upper Palaeolithic period. Traces of *Crocus sativus* have been found on the paintings of prehistoric beasts discovered in caves in Iraq dating back fifty thousand years.[10] In medieval Europe, the spice became a key ingredient in conjuring gold on the vellum pages of illuminated manuscripts. To produce the lustrous effect, 'take pure tin finely scraped,' Theophilus explains in his influential creative companion *De diversis artibus*, 'melt it and wash it and apply it with glue upon letters or other places you wish to ornament with gold. When you have polished it with a tooth, take saffron, with which silk is coloured, moistening it with clear of egg without water, and when it has stood a night, on the following day cover with a pencil the places which you wish to gild ...'[11]

That the mystique of saffron has survived undiluted into our own age is powerfully illustrated by one of the most ambitious installations undertaken by the celebrated contemporary art duo Christo and Jeanne-Claude. In January 2005, the artists occupied a snow-covered Central Park in New York City by erecting 7,503 enormous, 4.9-metre-high (16 feet) door frames from which were draped as many large, flowing swathes of fabric, each dyed an arresting saffron. *The Gates*, which took some 26 years to plan and stretched 37 km (23 miles) through the pathways of the park, transformed the shared municipal space into a mesmerizing maze of mystical thresholds.

Chrome Orange

The prohibitive premium that pure saffron commanded meant that, however desirable its refulgence, any practical usefulness the spice held for artists as a workaday pigment was severely limited. Most painters were simply priced out. That all began to change on 26 July 1761, when the German mineralogist Johann Gottlob Lehmann, hard at work analysing mineral deposits in a gold mine in Russia's sloping, forested Ural mountains, stumbled across a curious, four-sided crystal the likes of which he had never seen before. Misidentifying the chemical nature of the mineral, which glistened the same gorgeous deep orange as saffron, Lehmann christened the extremely rare substance Siberian Red Lead, after the region in which the Berezovsky gold deposit, where he discovered it, is located. In due course, the mineral would be properly desynonymized from red lead and given a distinct name of its own: 'crocoite', after the Greek word for 'saffron', whose colour it so closely resembled.

It would be another generation after Lehmann's discovery, however, before any real headway could be made in transforming the scarce mineral crocoite into a practical artistic tool. In 1797 a French pharmacist, Louis Nicolas Vauquelin, began experimenting with the unusual crystal, first pestling it into a fine powder before boiling it 'in a saturated solution of carbonate potash'. Vauquelin's calibrated fiddling paid off. After an 'effervescence of considerable duration' finally settled and a period of 'spontaneous evaporation' passed, he eventually found himself face to face with an isolated element of 'crystals of a beautiful orange red' that no one had ever produced before.[12] In honour of the sheer brilliance of the colour that he had whittled down from Lehmann's mineral, the new element was christened 'chromium', after the Greek word for colour, 'chroma'.[13]

Not long after Vauquelin's isolation of the element chromium, abundant deposits of a related crystalline mineral, chromite, were discovered in Paris and near Baltimore, Maryland. Despite its dull, dingy and unpromising complexion, chromite was also found to be composed of usable chromium – a fortuitous revelation that was quickly capitalized upon to produce a much more affordable saffron-coloured pigment. The turn of events would have a profound impact on the history of image-making.

It wasn't long before a luminous 'chrome orange', as the commercial pigment was called, which had long seemed off-limits to painters without the deepest of pockets, began to ignite canvases. Impressionist Pierre-Auguste Renoir's *The Skiff (La Yole)* (1875), which charmingly portrays a pair of young women enjoying a gentle jaunt in a rowing boat on a sunlit river Seine in summer, is indicative of the impulse. It has been acknowledged by historians that the striking contrast of the bold brushy blues of the water and the vibrancy of the orange skiff in the painting is handled with an astute awareness of the theory of colour contrasts that the French chemist Michel Eugène Chevreul proposed in 1837, which argued that the

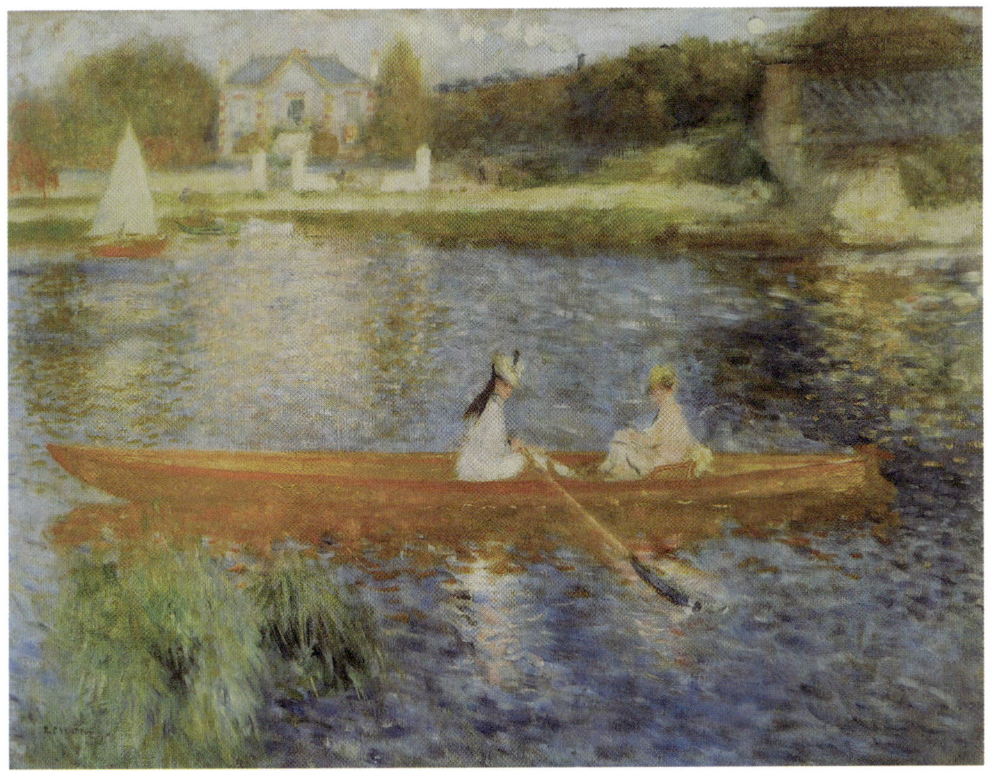

Pierre-Auguste Renoir, *The Skiff (La Yole)*, 1875

complementary colours – blue and orange – are intensified when placed side by side.[14] But the ready availability of the alluring orange may have tempted Renoir also to contest aspects of Chevreul's influential theories. 'Orange is a colour', Chevreul contends in a section of *The Principles of Harmony and Contrast of Colours, and Their Applications to the Arts* on wall-hangings, 'that can never be much employed, because it fatigues the eye too much by its great intensity.' Throwing caution to the summer wind, Renoir saturates the skiff in a celebration of orange shades he manages to muster from a variety of yellows, all held in unchecked check by a diaphanous frame of scintillating saffron-esque chrome orange that structures the vessel, forever ferrying the pair to an unknown and unknowable elsewhere.[15]

Perhaps the most well-known instance of chrome orange's sudden seepage into cultural consciousness would arrive twenty years after Renoir's lyrical canoe in the form of British artist Sir Frederic Leighton's preposterously famous lambent portrait of a dozing nymph, *Flaming June* (1895). Where Renoir's sprightly skiff absorbs into its wistful skin an awareness of the colour's age-old association with purity, Leighton's slumbering young woman – whose depiction melts Michelangelo's sombrous marble allegory *Night* into a meditation on arresting colour – is uneasy in her repose. Like the deep, subterranean mines from which the pigment that articulates her physique is sourced, the subject in *Flaming June* sinks below the line of the horizon, as if suggesting her interment or return to a hidden grave. 'The sleeper in *Flaming June* is at once serene and ominous,' the art historian Keren Rosa Hammerschlag has observed. 'To her left, orange drapery becomes brown, which then becomes dark purple and blue, as though her form is in the process of melting from the flaming June heat.' In a reverse chain of reactions, *Flaming June* silently retraces the steps that Vauquelin followed to create the very pigment that describes its subject, as if returning her to a state that is irreducibly raw and undiscovered.[16]

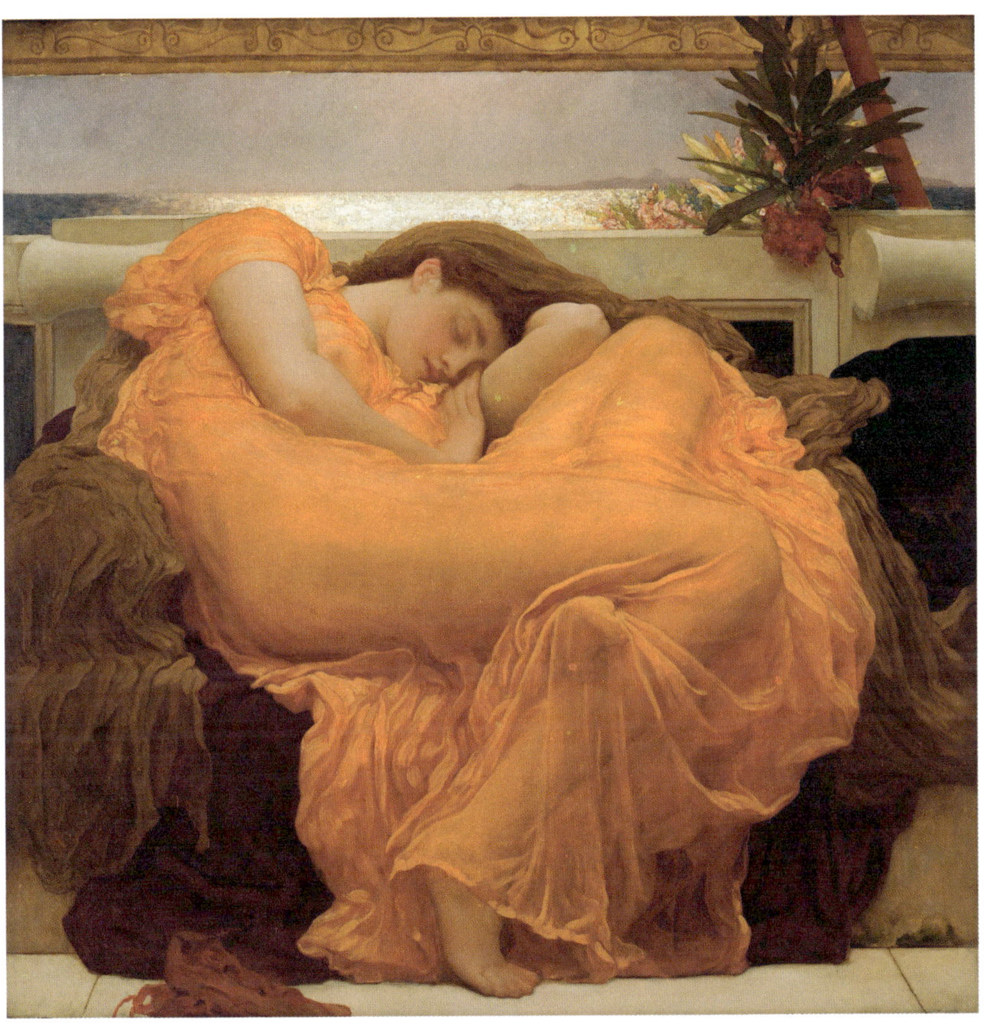

Frederic Leighton, *Flaming June*, 1895

Cadmium Orange

In 1818, a striking notice appeared in the 29th volume of the distinguished, learned German journal *Annalen der Physik*: 'Discovery of Two New Metals in Germany'. The publication's editor, the physicist Ludwig Wilhelm Gilbert, chronicled the respective circumstances by which the pair of unrelated discoveries had come about. One was attributed to the findings of a physician, Dr Lorenz Chrysanth von Vest, who was examining nickel and cobalt-pyrite deposits found in the woody mountains near his university in Graz, Austria, when he noticed a substance embedded in the pyrite that didn't resemble anything he had ever seen before.

Von Vest liked the name 'Sirium' for the new element he'd discovered, believing that 'Vestium' – as proposed by Gilbert in honour of the fourth largest object in the asteroid belt located in 1807 – was too close to his own name and would appear self-regarding. To be fair, only a few years earlier, in 1809, Von Vest's friend, the botanist Carl Ludwig Willdenow, had named a new genus of flowering plant, *Vestia*, after him. The quandary over the best name for the mineral ('Junonium' was also a strong contender) proved embarrassingly premature after a tag team of astute contemporaries, including Sir Humphry Davy and Michael Faraday, double-checked Von Vest's work and concluded the substance he had isolated wasn't new at all, but merely impure nickel.

The other 'new' metal unveiled by Gilbert in his article in *Annalen der Physik* proved considerably sturdier to the tests of time and would leave an indelible mark on the history of image-making. Its story began in 1817 when J. C. H. Roloff, an inspector of pharmaceutical products in Magdeburg, Germany, noticed that a popular zinc-oxide ointment (the predecessor of modern-day calamine creams) was curdling in colour from brilliant white to a rather concerning yellow. Fearing the creams had been contaminated with arsenic, Roloff immediately sent samples off for expert analysis and also alerted the supplier of the remedies, Carl Samuel Hermann, of his concerns.

Impatient for results, Roloff kept squinting through his microscope and became increasingly convinced that what was tainting the tinted zinc oxide wasn't a poison, but a new element that had never before been observed. At the same time, the chemists that Roloff had consulted, as well as another pair of eyes – those belonging to Professor Friedrich Stromeyer in Berlin, to whom Hermann had sent a sample – had all reached the same conclusion and would all subsequently vie for the glory of having found a new, rare metal: 'Cadmium', so called after the Greek word for 'calamine'.

It wasn't long before the new element was being poked and prodded to unlock its potential. When cadmium was heated in hydrogen sulphide gas, it was soon discovered, a powdery compound was created called cadmium sulphide. Further tinkering with the proportions of sulphur and selenium yielded the most extraordinarily intense pigments, which ranged in shade from deepest red to zingiest yellow. An outrageous orange, somewhere in between, was especially transfixing. Unlike its predecessors wrung from realgar, orpiment, saffron and crocoite, cadmium orange harmonizes itself to a different kind of chromatic music and seems almost to carry notes of its chemical contrivance. There is nothing in the outward complexion of pure cadmium's dull-grey shimmer that suggests the promise of brilliant colours lurking inside. This isn't a shade one simply plucks from the centre of a flower, or whose dazzling volcanic crystals are stumbled across by a hot spring.

Cadmium orange is a hue whose ferocity of lustre feels cooked-up – the by-product of incorrigible scientific efforts to break the visible world down or to galvanize a latent luminosity from something ostensibly lithic and dead. In that respect, it seems somehow fitting that cadmium should have come to life at almost the very same moment that Mary Shelley gave

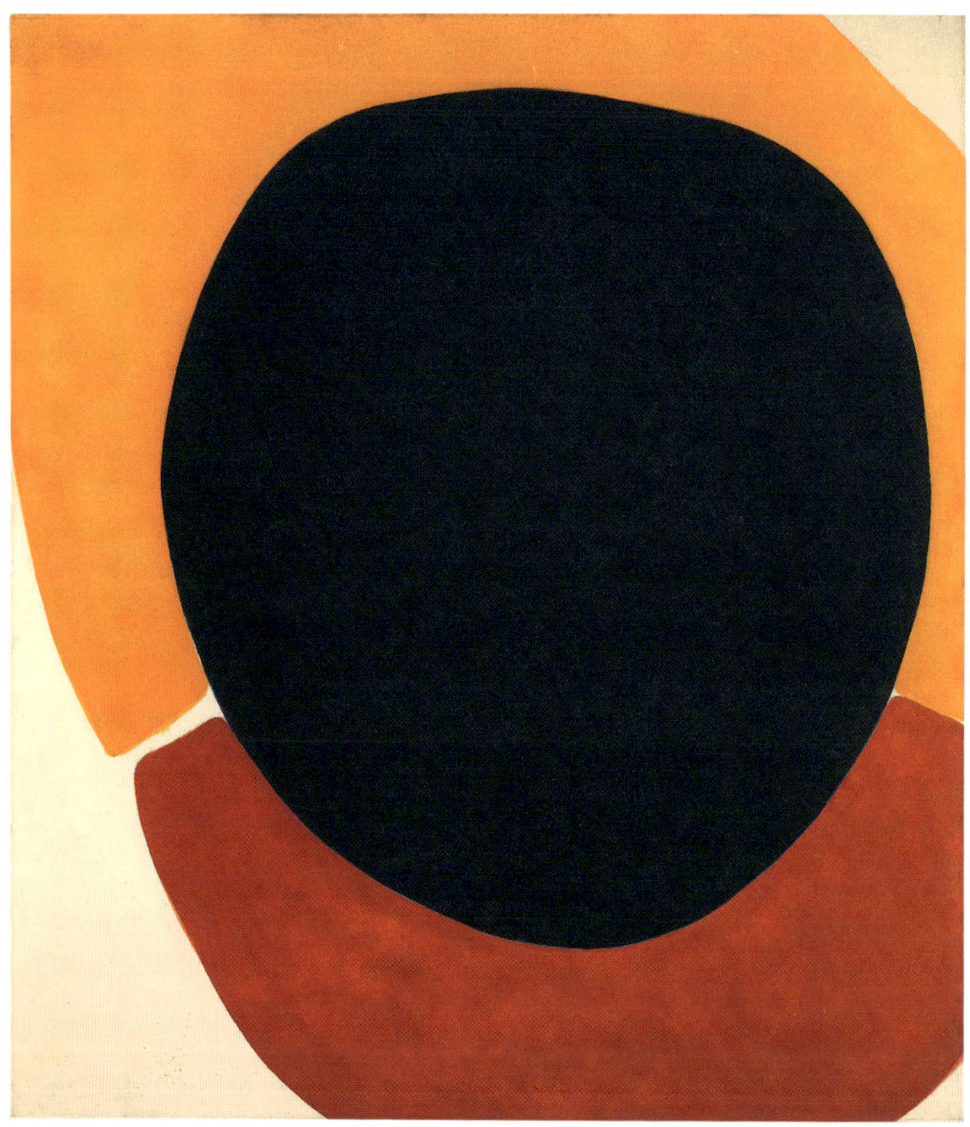

Jules Olitski, *Cadmium Orange of Dr. Frankenstein*, 1962

birth to that most famous allegory of unrestrained science and invigorated inertia, *Frankenstein* (1818). Implying some poetic compatibility between those two cultural shapes, Russian contemporary artist Jules Olitski's colour-field painting *Cadmium Orange of Dr. Frankenstein* (1962) is among the most captivating paintings to employ the pigment.

The work was created the same year that the world endured the anxieties of the Cuban Missile Crisis, which threatened to unleash nuclear weaponry across the globe. The canvas is dominated by the ambiguous swell of a dark sphere. Does the ominous orb represent the annihilating potential of a split atom or the toxic aura of a fizzled-out world? Who can say. All that's clear is that the shapeless shape is emerging from a cadmium-orange case that has hitherto contained it, as if to suggest that the colour itself is an unexplored realm – that further levels of reality spin inside it, still waiting to be discovered.

Tobias Mayer's *The Affinity of Colour Commentary*

(1775)

When he was not mapping the moon and calibrating its movements in lunar tables, the 18th-century German astronomer and cartographer Tobias Mayer devoted himself to deepening our understanding of colour. In 1758, Mayer devised an ingenious, triangular-shaped diagram comprised of twenty-eight shaded hexagons that illustrate the gradations of the three primary colours (examples of which he placed in the diagram's three corners using daubs of cinnabar, gamboge and azurite). Hardwired to conceive things in multiple dimensions, Mayer proceeded to explode his diagram into a pyramid of stacked, three-dimensional layers, in order to demonstrate subtler variations in a shade's brightness. The result was a schematic – published posthumously by Georg Christoph Lichtenberg in 1775 – that anticipated modern-day computer models that plot colour in three-dimensional space.

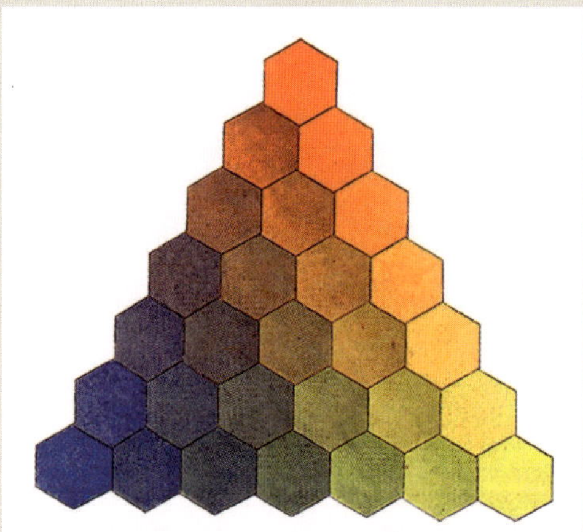

To help readers visualize Mayer's schema for conceiving shades of colour, the physicist Georg Christian Lichtenberg created the elegant diagram above. The primary colours – red, blue and yellow – occupy the triangle's three corners and are fashioned from the pigments cinnabar, azurite and gamboge, respectively. Gradations created when these primary colours are combined with each other to varying degrees can be seen in the diagram's hexagons.

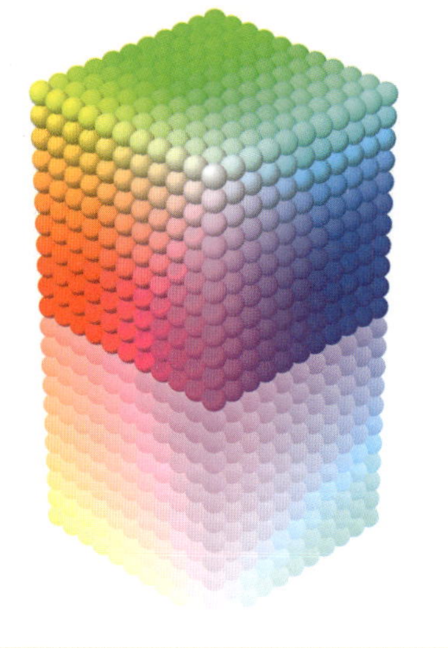

Mayer's ingenious design anticipated 3D colour modelling. Mapping Mayer's concept to a cube, so-called RGB colour models show red increasing along the x-axis, green increasing along the z-axis, and blue increasing along the y-axis.

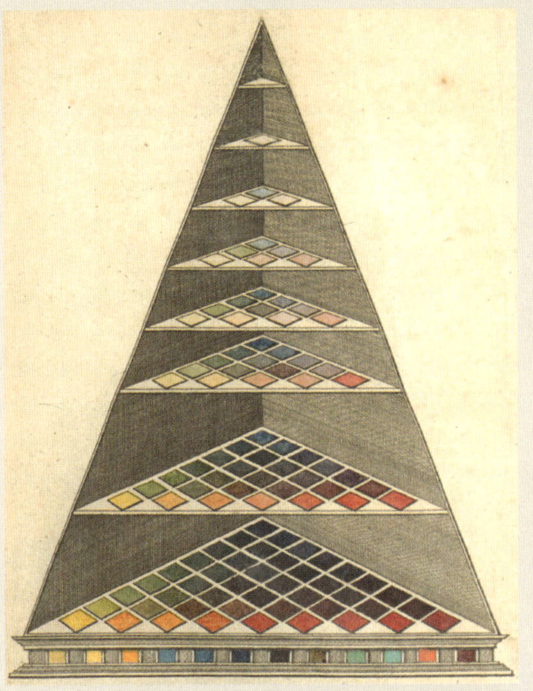

Like Lichtenberg, the German astronomer Johann Heinrich Lambert was inspired by Mayer's deceptively simple diagram for understanding the progression of hues between primary colours. In order to help textile merchants keep track of their inventory of dyes, Lambert endeavoured to expand Mayer's concept into three dimensions. Lambert's pyramidal model is comprised of seven 'floors' and demonstrates the gradual ascendance of hues from darker ones (at the bottom) to lighter ones (at the top).

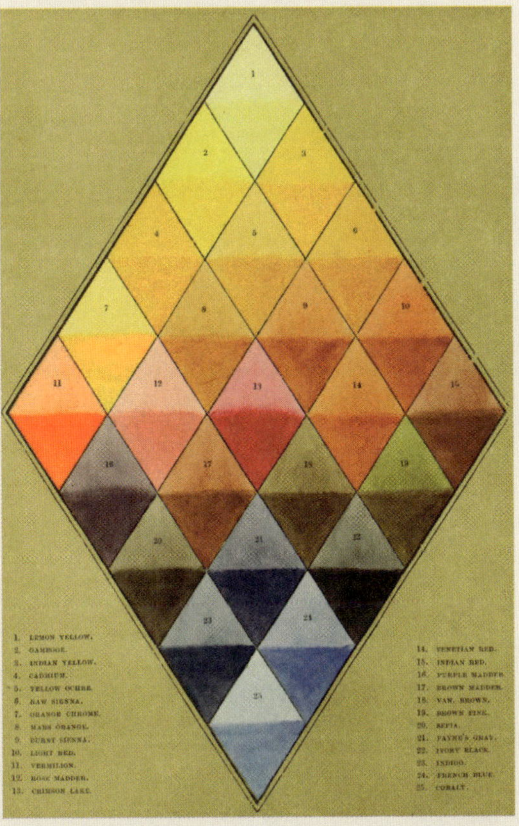

A century after the posthumous publication of Mayer's treatise in 1775, the impact of his ideas on artistic practice was still being measured. Echoing the vibrant geometry of his schema, a table entitled 'Harmonious Arrangement of Twenty-Five of the Most Useful Pigments' enriched British artist and writer George Barnard's practical guide *The Theory and Practice of Landscape Painting in Water-Colours*. The diamond-shaped diagram organizes the gradation of painterly pigments into a luminous lozenge, with lemon yellow at the top and cobalt blue at the bottom, and a band of varying shades of red (vermilion, rose madder, etc.) running along the shape's equator.

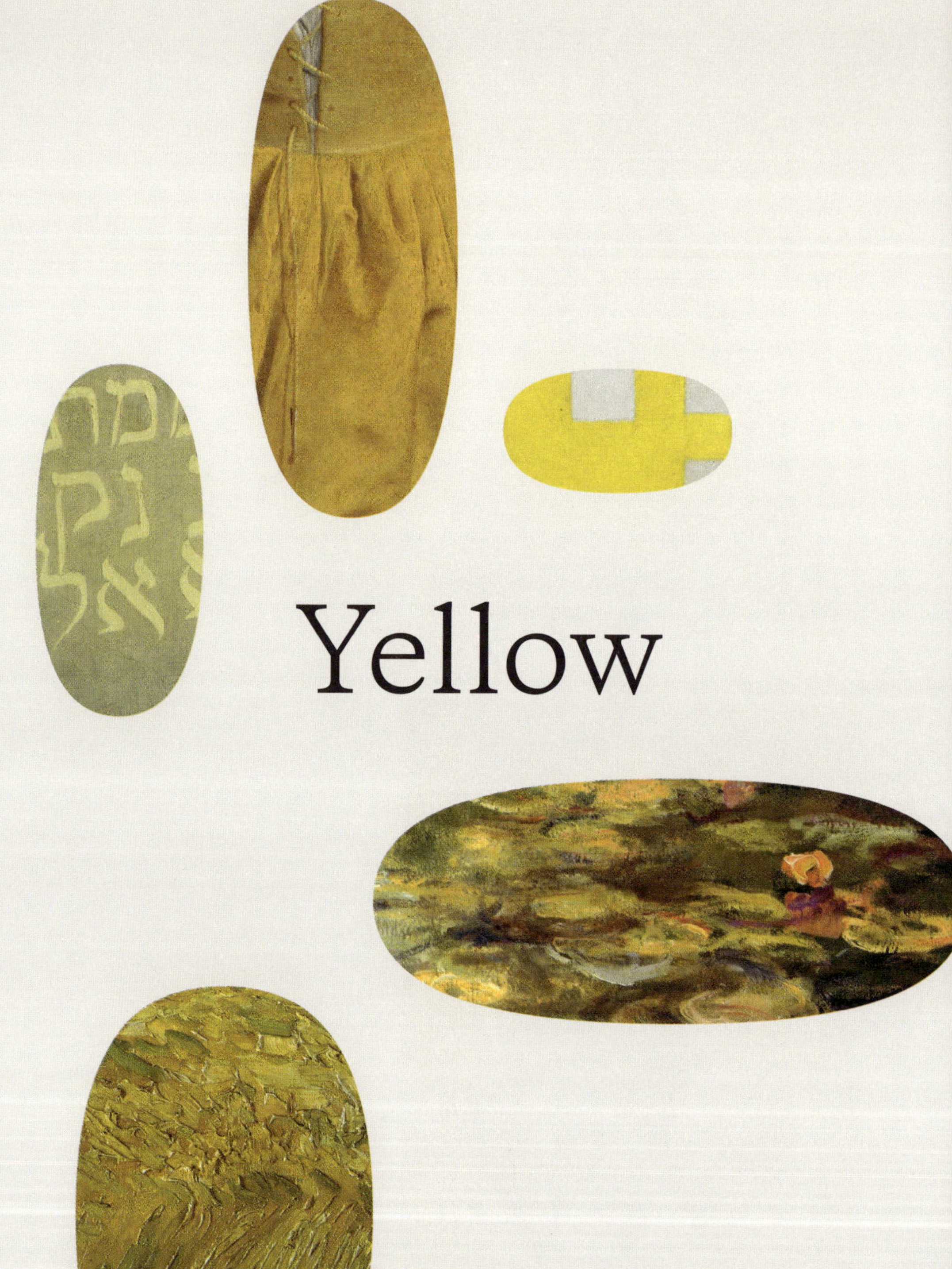

Yellow

Yellow is impossible to pin down. Emblematic of power and prestige in the East, the colour has hung off the shoulders of Chinese royalty since the mytho-historical reign in the 3rd millennium BCE of the Yellow Emperor, a cosmic ruler credited with creating the Chinese state. At the same time, yellow is the shade of shameful cowardice in the West, where it has drooped off depictions of a dastardly Judas since the Middle Ages. Yellow is as redolent of riches and gold's reflective shimmer as it is with sickness, the failing of the flesh, and the inner turmoils that bring up bile. Yellow is at once the colour of aspiration and dilapidation. 'There is nothing in the world that is not mysterious,' the Argentine essayist Jorge Luis Borges once reflected, 'but the mystery is more evident in certain things than in others: in the sea, in the eyes of the elders, in the color yellow, and in music.'[1] Tom Stoppard, the British playwright, has found the colour similarly enigmatic, setting it apart from the rest of the colours with which we experience experience. 'The colours red, blue and green are real', he writes in *Rosencrantz & Guildenstern Are Dead*, but 'the colour yellow is a mystical experience shared by everybody.'[2]

Yellow Ochre

In September 2003, a team of archaeologists examining fragments of fabric found half a century earlier in a buried tomb in Gordion, the capital city of ancient Phygia, described the results of their forensic analysis as 'unusually exciting'.[3] X-rays of the textile's weave revealed traces of an iron-oxide mineral called 'goethite'. First identified in 1806 by the German mineralogist Johann Georg Lenz, who named his discovery after the literary polymath Johann Wolfgang von Goethe – a pioneering theorist of colour (see page 104) – goethite is the primary component of a yellow iron ore known as 'limonite', which, in turn, is responsible for giving us one of the very earliest pigments known to cultural history: yellow ochre.

The scientists who confirmed traces of the mineral were excited because the fabric on which the pigment was found - likely a robe that had been dyed a dazzling gold - was not just any old funeral shroud. It was one that adorned the ceremonially entombed body of Gordias, the father of the legendary King Midas (famous in Greek mythology for his ability to turn everything that he touched to gold). No source for the famous myth of tactile transformation of threads from base substance into gold has ever been found. The discovery of garments associated with Midas that had, themselves, undergone some semblance of alchemy was therefore especially intriguing.

Gordias's lamé-like robe was hardly the first instance of yellow ochre's use as either a dyestuff or an artistic pigment. Some 17,000 years ago, goethite-rich limonite was responsible for exalting a horse painted on the walls of the Lascaux caves. It was later used by ancient Egyptian artists to adorn the tomb of Nakht, the scribe and astronomer of the Egyptian deity Amun. There, the pigment transformed the bodies of women into refined and eternal figures from another world. Since antiquity, the pigment has been in continuous use. With an opulence that punches above the modest price of its weight, it can be found enriching everything from the flowing dress of one of the angels floating beside Christ, catching the blood dripping from his hands, in Raphael's *The Crucified Christ with the Virgin Mary, Saints and Angels* (*The Mond Crucifixion*; c. 1502–03) to Christ's resplendent flesh in Tintoretto's *Christ Washing the Feet of the Disciples* (c. 1575–80) to the yellow slipper worn by the subject of Degas's *After the Bath, Woman Drying Herself* (c. 1890–95).

OPPOSITE Raphael, *The Mond Crucifixion*, c. 1502–03

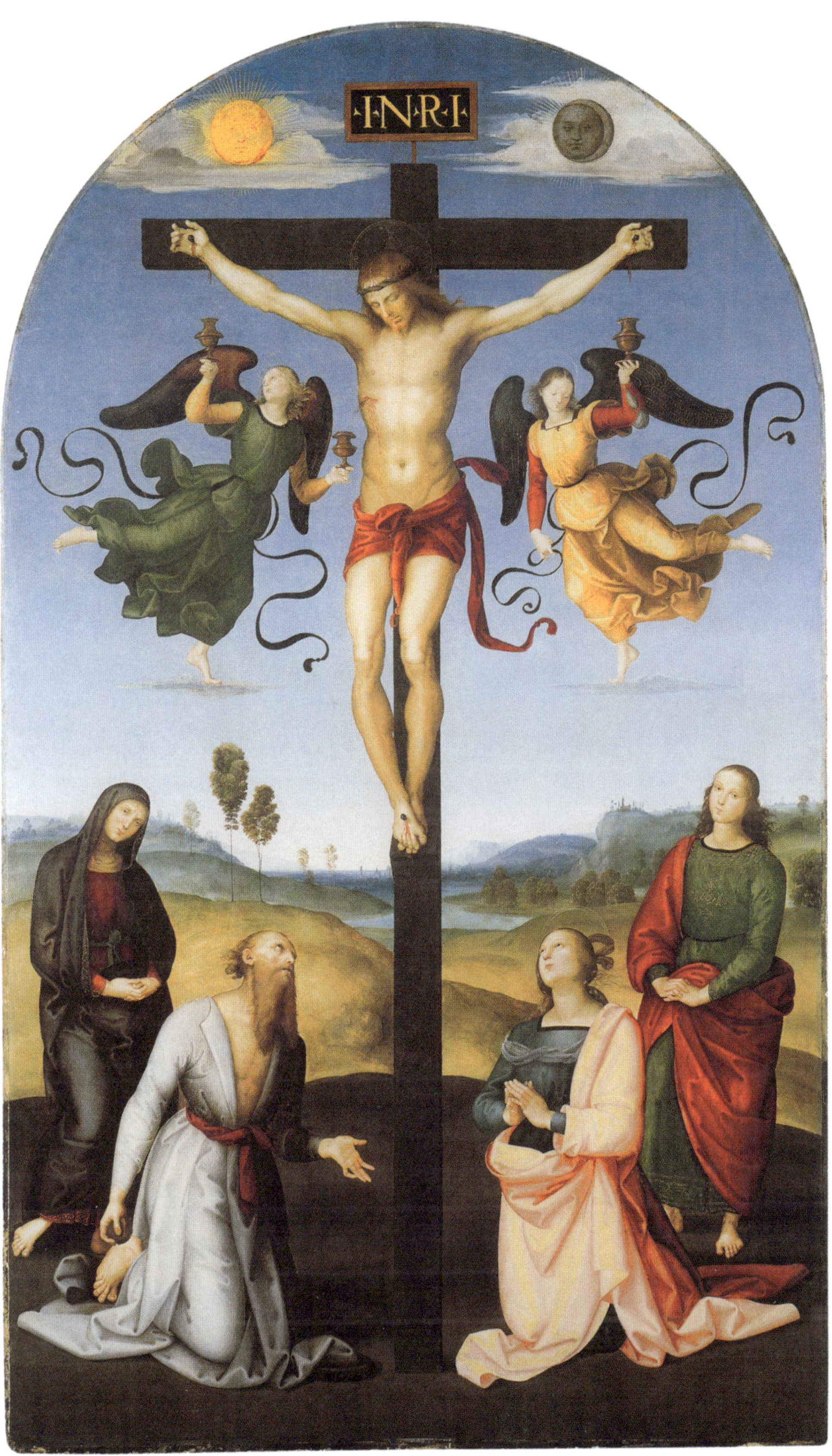
·I·N·R·I·

Lead-tin Yellow

Had it not been for the curiosity in 1940 of a researcher at the Doerner Institute in Munich, devoted to the study of artists' materials and colour technology, the mysterious identity of one of the most significant pigments used in Western art between the 13th and 18th centuries might have remained unsolved to this day.[4] Surprised by how often analysis of yellow samples from German paintings from the 15th and 16th centuries contained appreciable proportions of tin in addition to lead, Richard Jacobi tried his hand at reverse-engineering such a pigment himself.

Jacobi soon discovered that, depending on how high he heated his homespun mixture of three parts lead monoxide and one part tin dioxide, a diverse range of yellows could be concocted – from a murky mustard to a light zesty chiffon.[5] And just like that, Jacobi had cracked the code of a curiously ubiquitous, yet utterly elusive formula for *Blei-Zinn-Gelb* (or lead-tin yellow) that had avoided detection for centuries by masquerading under a variety of aliases in different regions without anyone ever cottoning on that they all derived from the same secret Old Master recipe.

That the method for preparing lead-tin yellow as a distinct, stand-alone pigment (of two principal types, with or without the addition of glistening quartz) managed to evade detection until the 20th century is astonishing given how prevalent we now know its use was. From generation to generation, the technique of magicking shades of yellow from powdered lead heated with tin had been passed down from medieval frescoists to 18th-century landscape painters like a secret knowledge. Expunge it from the history of image-making, and everything from the creamy wad of discarded fabric that cushions the foreground of Titian's *Bacchus and Ariadne* (1520–23) to the delicate dialogue between the sun-ignited curtain in the upper left-hand corner of Vermeer's *Woman Holding a Balance* (c. 1664) and the gentle swell of her belly would vanish. Thought to be

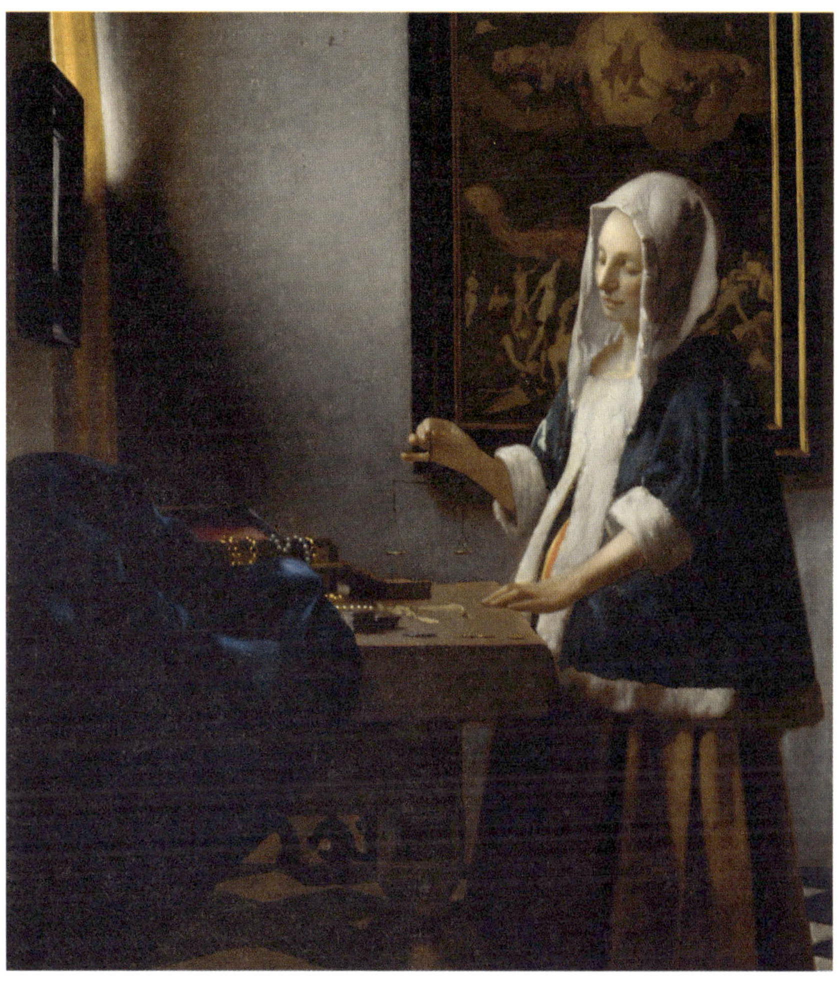

Johannes Vermeer, *Woman Holding a Balance*, c. 1664

a portrait of Vermeer's wife, as if caught poignantly weighing their family's future, the latter canvas is profoundly personal; and Vermeer's reliance on lead-tin yellow to articulate the miracle of life's ignition is testimony to the power he placed in that particular pigment.

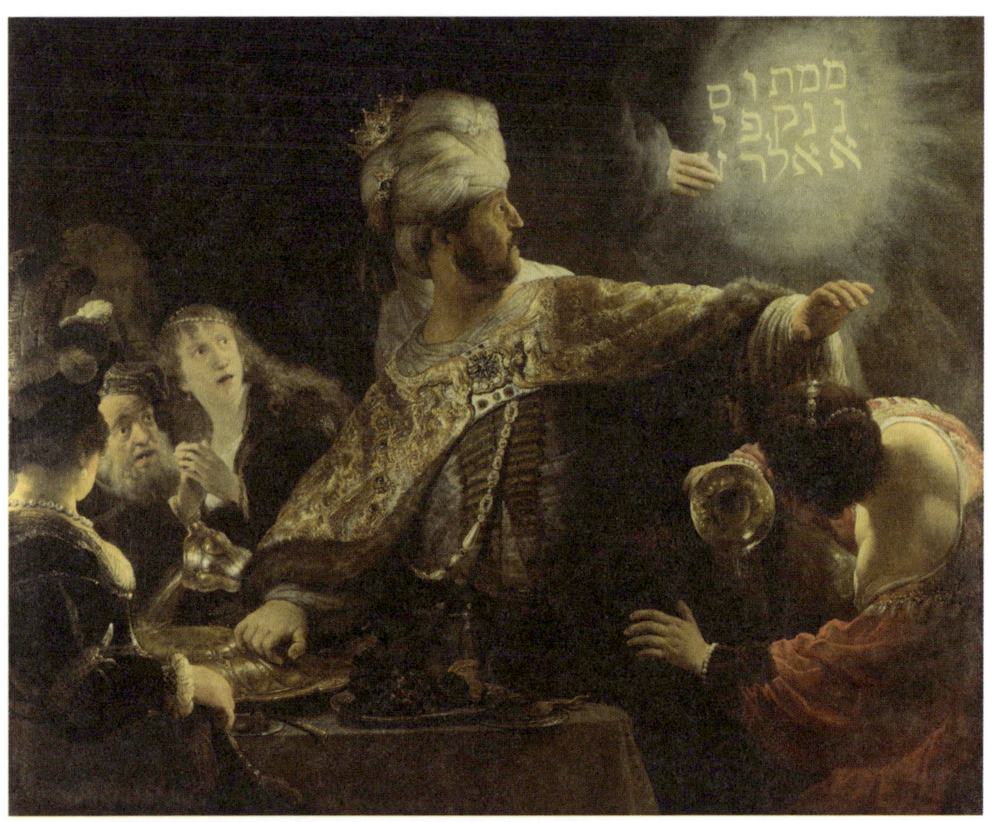

Rembrandt, *Belshazzar's Feast*, c. 1636–38

In Rembrandt's *Belshazzar's Feast* (*c*. 1636–38), the dazzling brocade cloak of the son of the Babylonian king Nebuchadnezzar, who has stolen from the Temple in Jerusalem the golden goblets he now uses to host a drunken knees-up, is intricately woven from whispers of lead-tin yellow. So too are the cryptic words that suddenly appear on the wall behind him, inscribed by the hand of God, portending the downfall of Nebuchadnezzar's kingdom. Two centuries after Rembrandt created his masterpiece, ignited by the magic of lead-tin yellow, the pigment – like the Babylonian reign whose demise it foretells - would also disappear. To this day, no one knows why the use of lead-tin yellow would cease so suddenly and so completely. From the middle of the 18th century, not a single trace of the pigment's employment has been found.[6]

Naples Yellow

In 1904, Paul Cézanne sat sniffily scrutinizing the palette of Émile Bernard, his friend and fellow Post-Impressionist. Preoccupied with the essence and importance of colour (he once asserted 'there is nothing but colors and in them the light'[7]), Cézanne was mortified by how limited Bernard's range was. 'You paint only with that?' Cézanne queried. 'Yes indeed,' Bernard proudly replied. 'Where is your peach black,' Cézanne demanded, 'your sienna, your cobalt blue, your burnt crimson lake ...?' Above all, the stupefied Cézanne wanted to know why there was no Naples Yellow.[8]

That Cézanne was dumbfounded by the absence of Naples Yellow from his friend's inventory almost certainly says more about the artist's insatiable appetite for colour than it does about the true breadth of Bernard's materials. By the beginning of the 20th century, the heyday of Naples Yellow had come and gone. But, for the space of nearly a century - from the mysterious demise of lead-tin yellow around 1750 to the middle of the 19th century - Naples Yellow (also known as 'antimony yellow') had eclipsed lead-tin yellow. Among the oldest synthetic pigments ever concocted, the compound of lead antimonate has been in use since the days of the pharaohs. A recipe for the colour passed down orally from generation to generation was memorialized in the early 17th century by the Italian miniaturist Valerio Mariani da Pesaro. 'You can also make this yellow of a fuller colour and more beautiful',

Pesaro says, taking care to explain how patience is among the chief ingredients:

> *by taking 6 ounces of burnt lead and 4 ounces of antimony and one ounce of Alexandrine Tutty and 1 ounce of salt, and this all mixed together you grind it finely and put it on plates ... if it will come out too much cooked and if there is a fire and it is melted, then you will grind it finely again putting the material back on new plates, you will put it on a lower fire and if necessary, one will repeat it several times and this way it will turn out beautifully.*[9]

Without realizing it, Pesaro and those who followed his recipe found themselves fabricating a synthetic version of a naturally occurring mineral, bindheimite, which, despite its stunning appearance, like ossified sunshine, seems rarely to have been mined to produce the pigment in its own right. Over time, Naples Yellow revealed its pitfalls as a pigment and developed a reputation for being unreliable, 'assum[ing] a greenish tint', according to one 19th-century handbook for young painters, and 'attack[ing] certain other colors'.[10] A simmering pugnacity and propensity to kick against the tempo and temperament of adjoining colours on a canvas complicate the ambiance of works into which Naples Yellow is injected. The mellifluous notes floating from the fingers of the musician in Orazio Gentileschi's *Lute Player* (c. 1612–20) are accompanied by a quiet cacophony of colour in the clash of the strident gold sheen of her rumpled dress (crafted in large measure from Naples Yellow) against the scarlet velvet covering of the musician's stool and the olive-green throw that shrouds the table at which she is sitting.

Although the painting may at first seem an innocent celebration of musical harmonies, the scatter of competing instruments before the musician, each silently clamouring

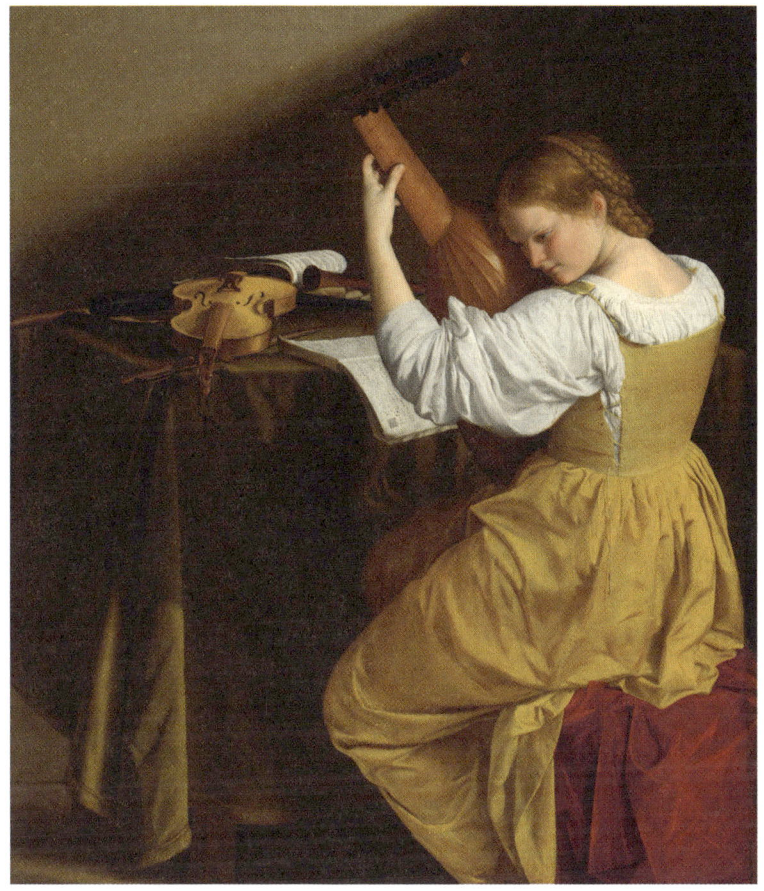

Orazio Gentileschi, *The Lute Player*, c. 1612–20

for her attention, and the aggressive slant of shadow cast on the wall above her, setting a psychologically dramatic stage, suggest that this is really a work of intense internal tensions, whose temperature is determined chiefly by the modulations of yellow that command our focus. Three and a half centuries later, Naples Yellow will serve as the plank our eyes are made to walk into the exploded centre of David Hockney's *A Bigger*

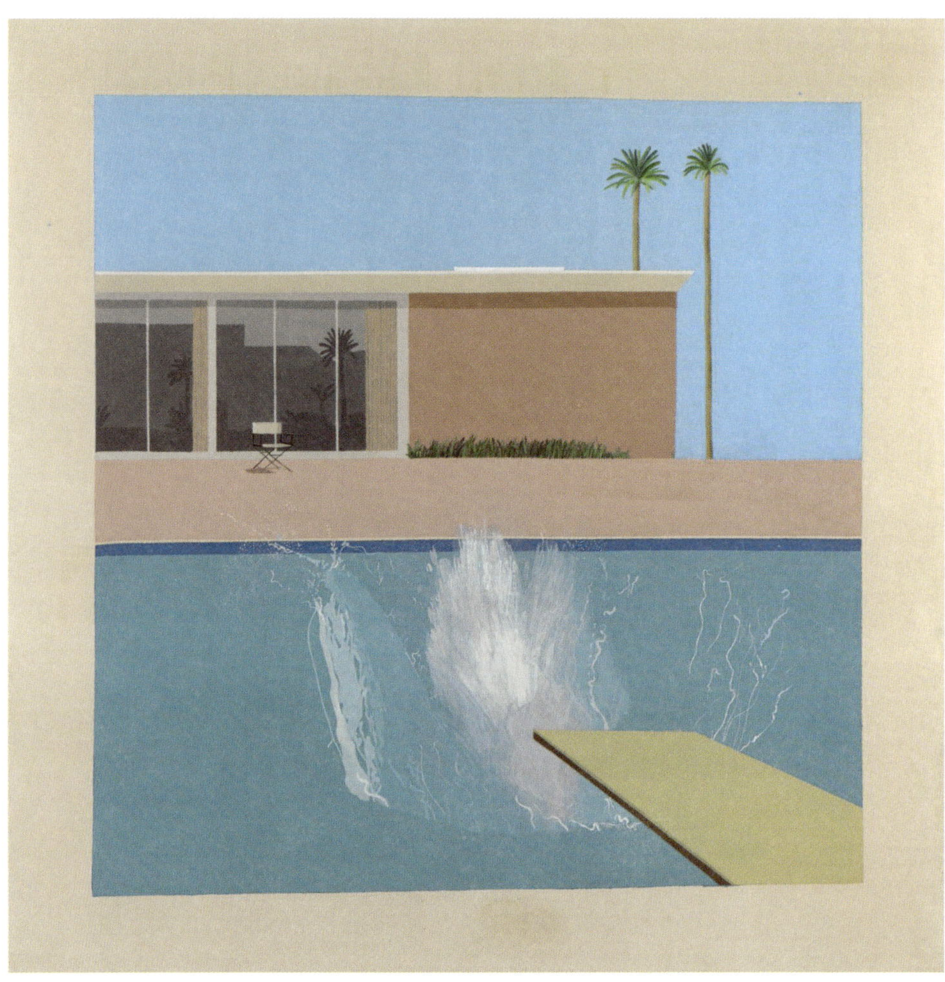

David Hockney, *A Bigger Splash*, 1967

Splash (1967). Although the pigment had long fallen out of favour with artists, here, the jarring juxtaposition of the suspended splay of swimming-pool water and the incommensurate calm of the yellow diving board - which our minds know must still be vibrating - establish an affecting artificiality that rhymes with the flawless finish of the minimalist house and the unblemished blue of the Formica sky. Fashioned from a yellow from another era, the diving board emphasizes an out-of-syncness to the painting that is only heightened by the utter evaporation of the diver who created the 'bigger splash', but who - like Naples Yellow itself - seems to have jumped out, dried off, and flip-flopped away centuries ago.

Indian Yellow

'I myself saw mango leaves lying before the cows, the collection of urine, and the manufacture of *piuri*. So the real source of this kind of *piuri* is now beyond any doubt whatever.' This recollection, taken from a letter that ranks among the strangest and most unsettling documents in the history of art, appeared in the *Journal of the Society of Arts* in November 1883. The substance to which Trailokya Nath Mukharji, a Bengali civil servant in the British Indian Department of Revenue and Agriculture, is referring - 'piuri' - is one of many names by which an intense marigold pigment (also called Indian yellow) was known in the 19th century.

Mukharji set about tracking down the pigment's source after receiving a letter that Sir Joseph Hooker, director of Kew Gardens, sent in January 1883 to the India Office. Hooker was keen to know the true origin of Indian yellow, which had been making its way into artists' paint boxes in Europe for more than a century in the form of chalky green-gold orbs whose ammonic pong smacked of stale animal secretions. Determined to get to the bottom of the pungent pigment, Mukharji trekked to Monghyr, where he uncovered a disconcerting custom for manufacturing the colour. Mukharji attests to having witnessed with his own eyes 'a sect of gwalas (milkmen)' producing *piuri* by feeding their cows 'solely with mango leaves and water, which increased the bile pigment, and imparts to the urine a bright yellow colour'. 'The cows treated with mango leaves', Mukharji proceeds to report,

> *are made to pass urine three or four times a day by having the urinary organ slightly rubbed with the hand, and they are so habituated to this process that they have become incapable of passing water of their own accord. The urine is collected during the whole day in small earthen pots, and in the evening put over a fire in an earthen vessel. The heat causes the yellow principle to precipitate, separating it from the watery portion. It is then strained with a small piece of cloth; the sediment is made into a ball, and dried first on charcoal fire and then in the sun, when it is ready for the market.*[11]

Although Mukharji was unable to confirm that the cows subjected to this inhumane treatment died prematurely, he reports that they 'looked very unhealthy'. So unsettling is the alleged practice for producing Indian yellow, it is hardly surprising that some recent historians and critics, reflecting on Mukharji's account through a contemporary cultural lens, have questioned his veracity. When the British writer Victoria Finlay attempted to locate any surviving vestiges of the insalubrious industry that Mukharji had described by travelling to Monghyr herself in 2002, she came up empty. 'I will always wonder', Finlay concluded, 'whether this story is simply an example of someone gently, and literally, taking the piss.'[12]

A scientific analysis of a historic sample of Indian yellow published in the journal *Dyes and Pigments* in January 2019, however, found that the pigment indeed 'presented hippuric acid, a ruminant metabolite found in urine', thus establishing for the first time a 'substantial link between animal urine and the pigment Indian yellow'.[13]

In June 1889, six years after Mukharji had made his way to Monghyr, Vincent van Gogh smeared a dab of Indian yellow on his palette and, with his brush, whisked into edgy effulgence a crisp, clenching crescent moon in the corner his iconic canvas *The Starry Night* (see page 9). Knowing what we know of the artist's own tortured psyche at the time (he had only just checked himself into the Saint-Paul-de-Mausole mental asylum at Saint-Rémy-de-Provence near Arles a month earlier, in May 1889), this semicircle of sharp impastoed piss, squeezed from tormented creatures, seems a fitting emblem with which to cauterize the turbulent cosmos of his troubled soul.

Chrome Yellow

A few weeks after completing *The Starry Night*, Van Gogh returned to the psycho-atmospherics of his soulscape in his stirring *Wheat Field with Cypresses* (1889). Only here, the yellow that he reaches for to capture the restless rustle of golden stalks is chrome yellow, a close cousin of the chrome orange that we saw earlier igniting Sir Frederic Leighton's *Flaming June*, created a few years later. Although the celestial orb and the field of grain are broadly cast in the same colour genus of yellow, the difference in emotional resonance between the tremor of *The Starry Night*'s moon and the sunny swish of wheat is striking.

Constructed from a pigment coaxed from recently discovered caches of chromite, the wheat crop of the later work feels far less fraught – as if the artist were deliberately trying to

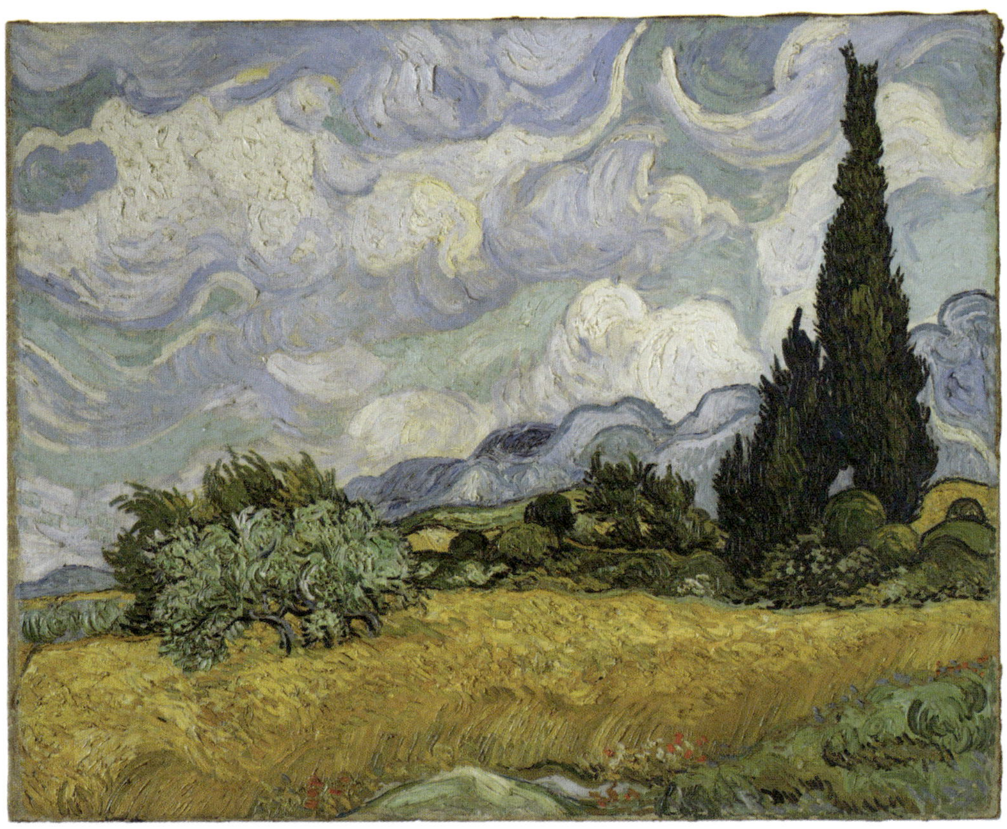

Vincent van Gogh, *Wheat Field with Cypresses*, 1889

lay a foundation of sturdier emotional ore on which to mount a recovery. The seeds of Van Gogh's chrome-yellow field will find themselves carried on a current of imagination into the consciousness of countless significant paintings over the course of the next several decades, accenting everything from the chiffon shirt in Henri Matisse's portrait of fellow Fauvist André Derain (1905) to the mustardy trapezium at the centre of Russian Supremacist Kazimir Malevich's geometrically beguiling *Painterly Realism of a Football Player* (1915).

Cadmium Yellow

In the preceding chapter, devoted to the story of the colour orange, we explored the chance discovery in the first half of the 19th century - from a pot of discoloured calamine cream in a German pharmacy - of cadmium pigments, whose introduction coincided with the gradual rise of Indian yellow. Neither cadmium orange nor its sibling, cadmium yellow (produced by varying the proportions of sulphur and selenium heated with the freshly found cadmium), would gain traction on the artist's palette until the second decade of the 20th century, when industrial demand for their use and improved manufacturing techniques for producing cadmium sulphide after 1917 made the pigments affordable options for painters.[14]

Commercial commodification, however, is hardly the first thing that springs to mind when contemplating the transcendent shimmers of diaphanous lemon light that shudder from the surface of Claude Monet's glorious *Water Lilies* (1919). Seemingly at furthest remove from the concerns of industrial efficiency, the lily pads that Monet masterfully sculpts from deftly dabbed dollops of cadmium yellow are paradoxically weightless in their gravity and become an evaporative substance that defies its own heft. The result is something almost mystically at odds with the mechanical realities of its making that conjures an 'infinitude', as the French art critic René Gimpel described Monet's painting on a visit to the artist's studio in 1919, in which 'water and sky have neither beginning nor end'. Although the particular cadence of colour that cadmium yellow was capable of producing may have only recently been made available to Monet, his work summons the spirit of a moment that precedes time. 'We seem to be present', Gimpel lyrically observes, 'at one of the first hours in the birth of the world. It is mysterious, poetic, delightfully unreal.'[15]

Although the smudgy music and evaporative vibrations of Monet's *Water Lilies* may not immediately call to mind the angular geometry and pristine perpendicularities of the pioneering abstractionist Piet Mondrian's late masterpiece *Broadway Boogie Woogie* (1942–43), the works' mutual reliance on cadmium yellow ensures that their energy is powered by the same source. For decades, Mondrian had committed himself to helping humanity recalibrate its soul by creating minimalist canvases of measured lines and fields of pure primary colours that he believed were aligned with the invisible principles that underpin our existence.

Soon after his arrival in New York City in 1940, escaping the war-weary Europe of his birth and upbringing, Mondrian sensed a compatibility between his spiritual project and the raw rhythms of boogie-woogie music that thrummed through the city's nightclubs. *Broadway Boogie Woogie* encapsulates the artist's determination to merge these impulses on to a single surface. At first glance, the canvas pulses with a vibrant vibe that resists the fleeting ephemeralities of this world and seems a perfect melding of mind and music. And yet the yellow bands that surge through the work like liquid electricity, funnelled into the flow of the painting from the recently industrialized cadmium yellow, make certain that the painting remains materially tethered to the faceless factory grind of the here and now.

Arylide Yellow

By relying on cadmium yellow for the ripe rhythms of their resplendence, Monet's and Mondrian's masterworks share another surprising element at odds with their soulful spirits: extreme toxicity. Noxious to the nose and poisonous to the touch when produced, cadmium colour proved less than desirable. An accelerating awareness of the dangers to health involved in the making and use of the pigments led to their eventual replacement by less lethal options. They were largely eclipsed

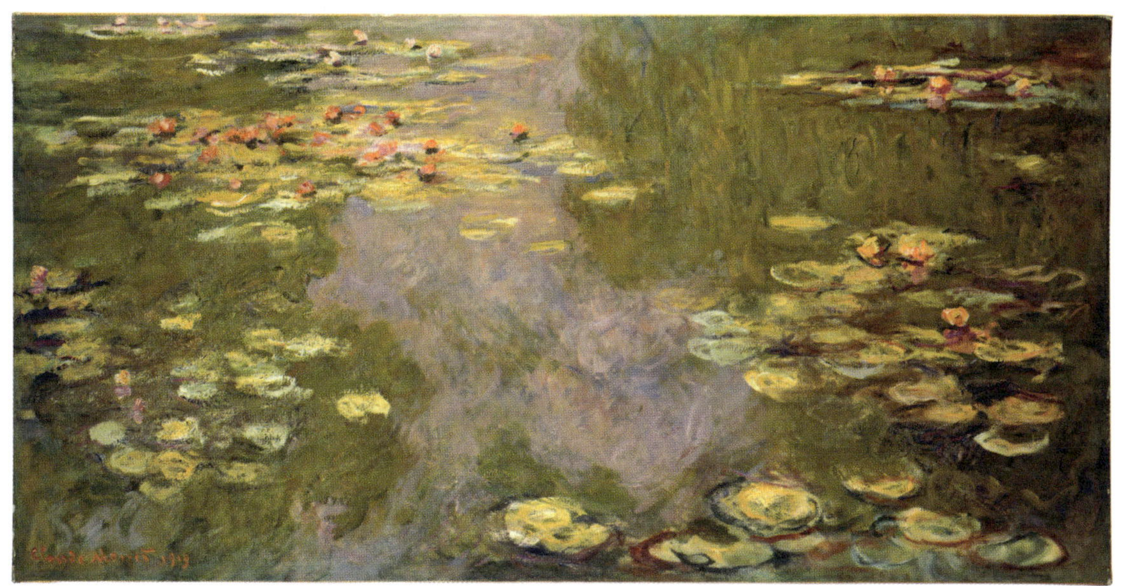

Claude Monet, *Water Lilies*, 1919

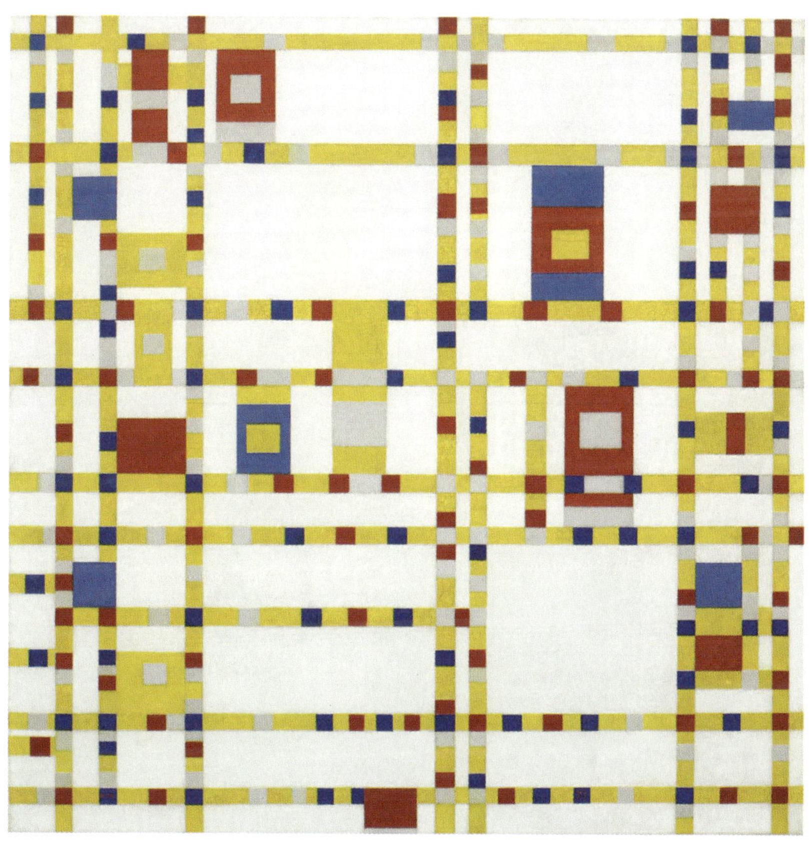

Piet Mondrian, *Broadway Boogie Woogie*, 1942–43

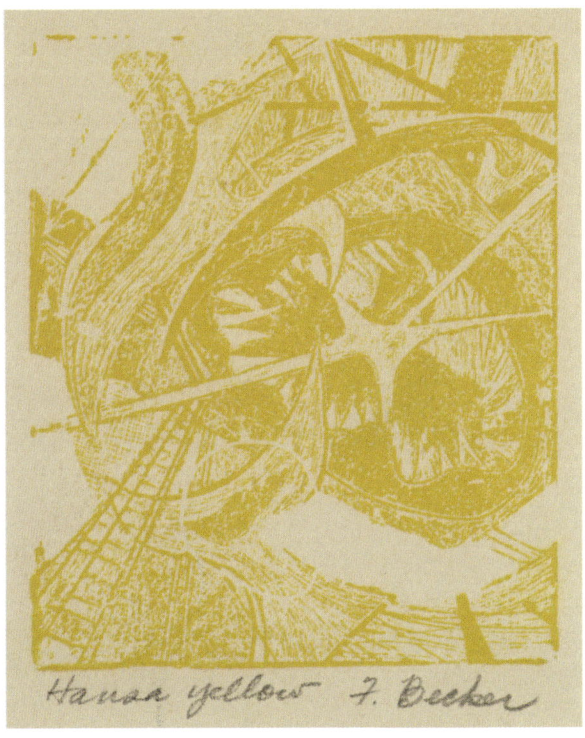

Fred Becker, *Hansa Yellow*, 1947

after a pioneering German chemist discovered how to take two nitrogen atoms and double bind them into an organic pigment. 'To all whom it may concern,' begins the patent filed with the US patent office in 1910 by the enterprising scientist, 'be it known that I, HERMANN WAGNER, Ph. D., chemist, a citizen of the Empire of Germany ... have invented certain new and useful Improvements in New Mon'oazo Dyestuffs and Processes of Making Same, of which the following is a specification.' 'The new dyestuffs', Wagner went on to explain, 'are distinguished by a remarkably pure yellow tint and at the same time by excellent fastness to light and good insolubility in oil, alcohol and Water.' It would be another decade however before Wagner's breakthrough would yield commercial pigments that were widely available.

Once on the shelves of art shops, arylide yellow, reassuringly free of health warnings, began to leave its mark. To lend the newfangled pigment an air of tradition, it was promoted by merchants under the name 'Hansa yellow', calling to mind the medieval trade network the Hanseatic League. This was an inexpensive yellow, so sturdy and stable in its resonance that it needn't be rationed or savoured in smidges as some earlier yellows had been. Indeed, so weighty was its verve, the American sculptor Alexander Calder used it by the square foot as a hefty sounding board against which a twisting torso-scaled amorphous physique (dangling from a jutting rod) gently swivels in his part-mobile, part-painting wall sculpture, *Form Against Yellow* (1936). Calder's lyrical red cut-out of a fluid figure moves with the motion of a swimmer casting shadows in a sea of sun. This was a yellow that writ itself large as a force that could drown the world in its manufactured sprightliness. The ambiguity of 'against' in the title of Calder's work, which implies both a thing's physical and psychological position, suggests something latently suspect about the surge of this particular colour. The sense of warning suggested by Calder's work - of a yellow cautioning against yellow - is amplified by the edgy geometry of American printmaker Fred Becker's 1947 engraving *Hansa Yellow*. Part of a series of four images entitled *Hooks and Eyes*, the eerie intaglio print relies for its effect on the lure of Piranesian vectors and foreshortened lattices to impel our gaze into the unflinching abyss of a fang-encircled pupil snarling at us from the centre. In Becker's vision, yellow doesn't beckon. It devours.

Mary Gartside's *Essay on Light and Shade, on Colours, and on Composition in General* (1805)

It is remarkable enough that Mary Gartside's book of 1805, *An Essay on Light and Shade, on Colours, and on Composition in General*, is the first treatise on chromatic theory ever published by a woman. Of particular significance, however, is the sequence of audacious abstract illustrations that Gartside, an amateur painting instructor, included in her pioneering work. Intended to demonstrate the harmonies of colour and the gradations of brightness, the eight so-called blots she created for the book anticipated by more than a century works by Wassily Kandinsky, Kazimir Malevich and Piet Mondrian, artists who are widely credited with the invention of non-figurative art. Gartside's expressive explosions of diaphanous colour adhere neither to the physical form of flowers nor to the feeling of light being reflected off their surface, yet somehow suggest both. Her pioneering ideas looked forward to many modalities of modern art, including Impressionism, Abstract Expressionism and the flowerscapes of Georgia O'Keeffe.

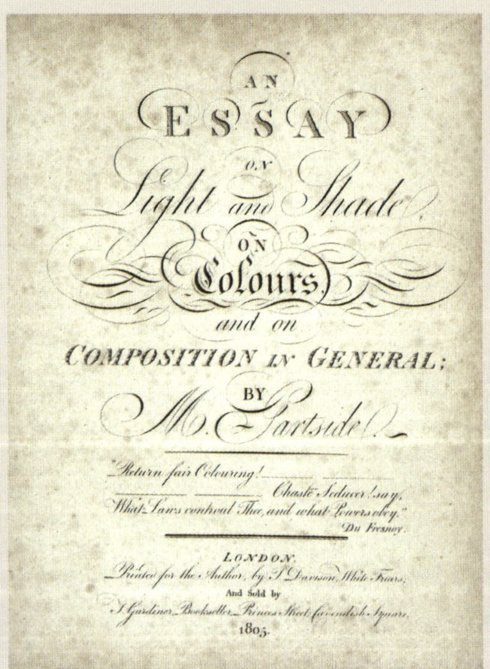
AN
ESSAY
ON
Light and Shade
ON
Colours,
and on
COMPOSITION IN GENERAL;
BY
M. Gartside.

"Return fair Colouring! ——
—— Chaste Seducer! say,
What Laws controul Thee, and what Powers obey."
Du Fresnoy.

LONDON,
Printed for the Author, by T. Davison, White Friars;
And Sold by
J. Gardiner, Bookseller, Princes Street, Cavendish Square.
1805.

Modestly introduced by its author as little more than a guidebook for 'the ladies I have been called upon to instruct in painting', Mary Gartside's unprecedented book *An Essay on Light and Shade, on Colours, and on Composition in General* (title page seen here) is the first treatise on colour theory ever published by a woman. Gartside's study predates by half a decade Johann Wolfgang von Goethe's celebrated treatise *Theory of Colours* (1810) and anticipates Goethe's own effort to recalibrate Newton's conception of the spectrum of colours that comprise white light and to inflect it with a painterly urgency it arguably lacks.

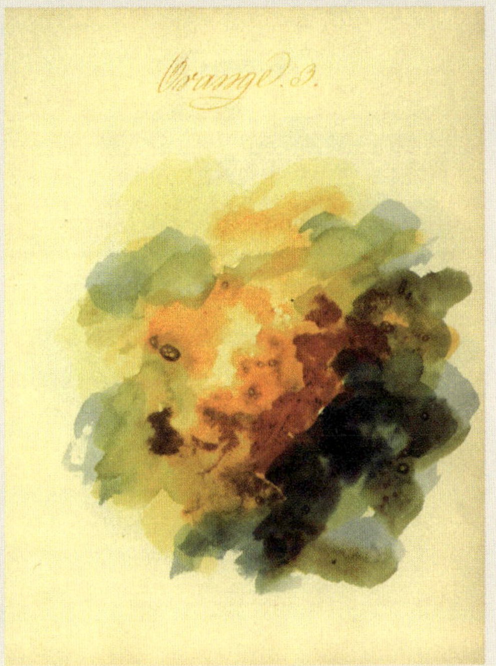

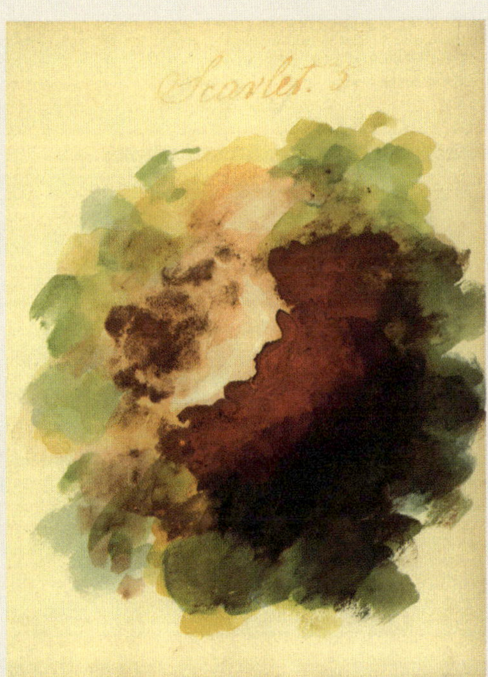

Appended to Gartside's study is a remarkable series of eight abstract watercolour 'blots' unlike any work produced previously by a writer or artist of any gender. While appearing to anticipate the amplified floralscapes that the American artist Georgia O'Keeffe began producing in the 1920s, Gartside's blots are untethered to any settled shape. While they may conjure the essence of exploding petals, they do not meticulously describe them. Neither wholly literal nor fanciful, Gartside's blots pave the way for experiments in non-figurative painting that will occupy the imagination of artists a century later. Titled, in turn, 'White', 'Yellow', 'Orange', 'Green', 'Scarlet', 'Blue', 'Violet' and 'Crimson', these evanescent experiments (three of which are shown here) are intended to illustrate each hue at fluctuating degrees of intensity. Where Tobias Mayer before her and Goethe afterwards relied on rigid geometric shapes to embody their theoretical concepts, Gartside employs a more organic and impressionistic visual device. By doing so, she emphasizes the core aim of her endeavour: to distinguish form from the luminous energies of pure colour.

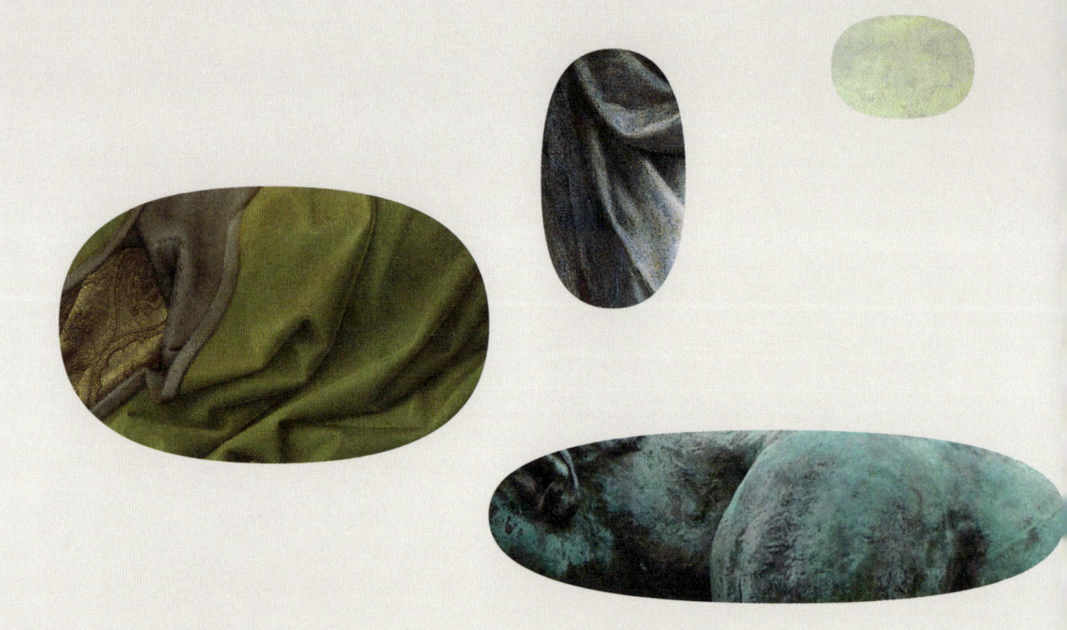

Green

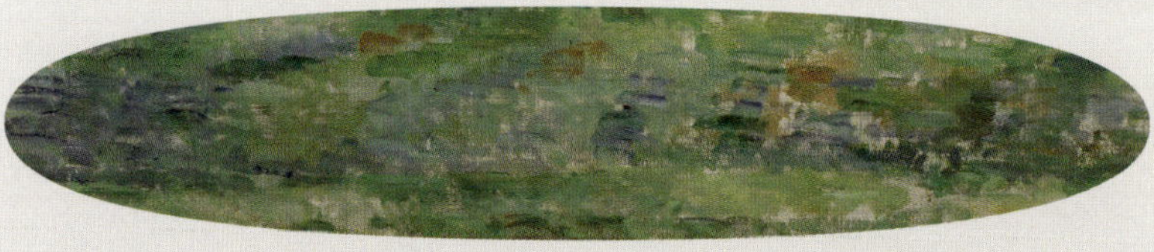

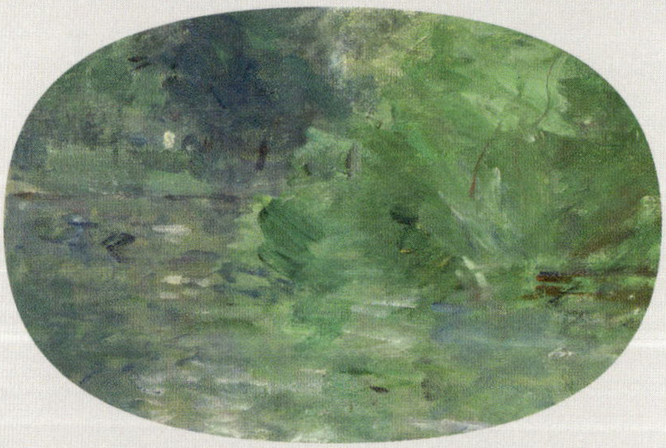

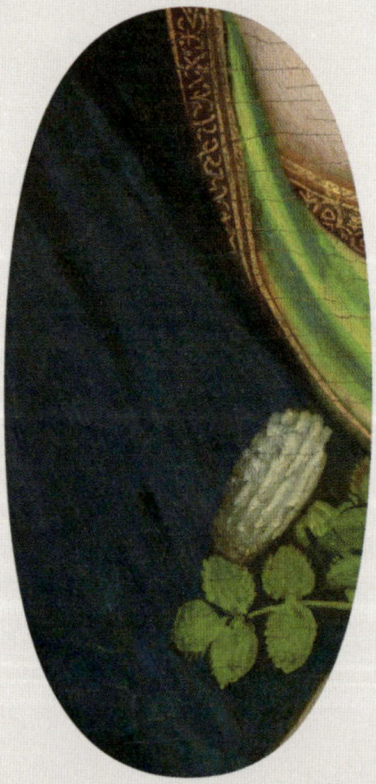

Green may be among the most conspicuous characteristics of the external landscape – the boast of buds and leaves and grasses – but it is also a colour that finds its way inside us and gets under our skin. Its needles needle our subconscious. 'Green, oh how I want you green', begins Spanish poet Federico García Lorca's intense 'Sleepwalking Ballad', whose somnolent lines seem to ebb and flow on the shore of consciousness:

Green wind. Green limbs.
The boat on the sea
and the horse on the mountain.
With the shadow around her waist
she dreams on her balustrade,
green skin, her hair green,
with eyes of shivering silver.
Green, oh how I want you green.[1]

In Lorca's hands, green is at once tantalizingly tactile and utterly beyond our grasp. 'Nobody knows what's going on', Lorca himself confessed of his beautifully befuddling ode to green, 'not even I, for poetic mystery is also a mystery to the poet who communicates it, but who very often is unaware of it.'[2] A colour that is ambiguously emblematic both of nature's regeneration and of flesh's gangrenous degeneration, only green can command such mesmerizing mystery.

Verdigris

Nothing can evaporate an object into weightless thought, or a meditation on the elapse of time, like a ghostly patina oxidizing on its skin. Strip the Statue of Liberty of the alluring layer of blue-green copper carbonate that has gradually formed on its surface since its dedication in 1883, and its poignancy would

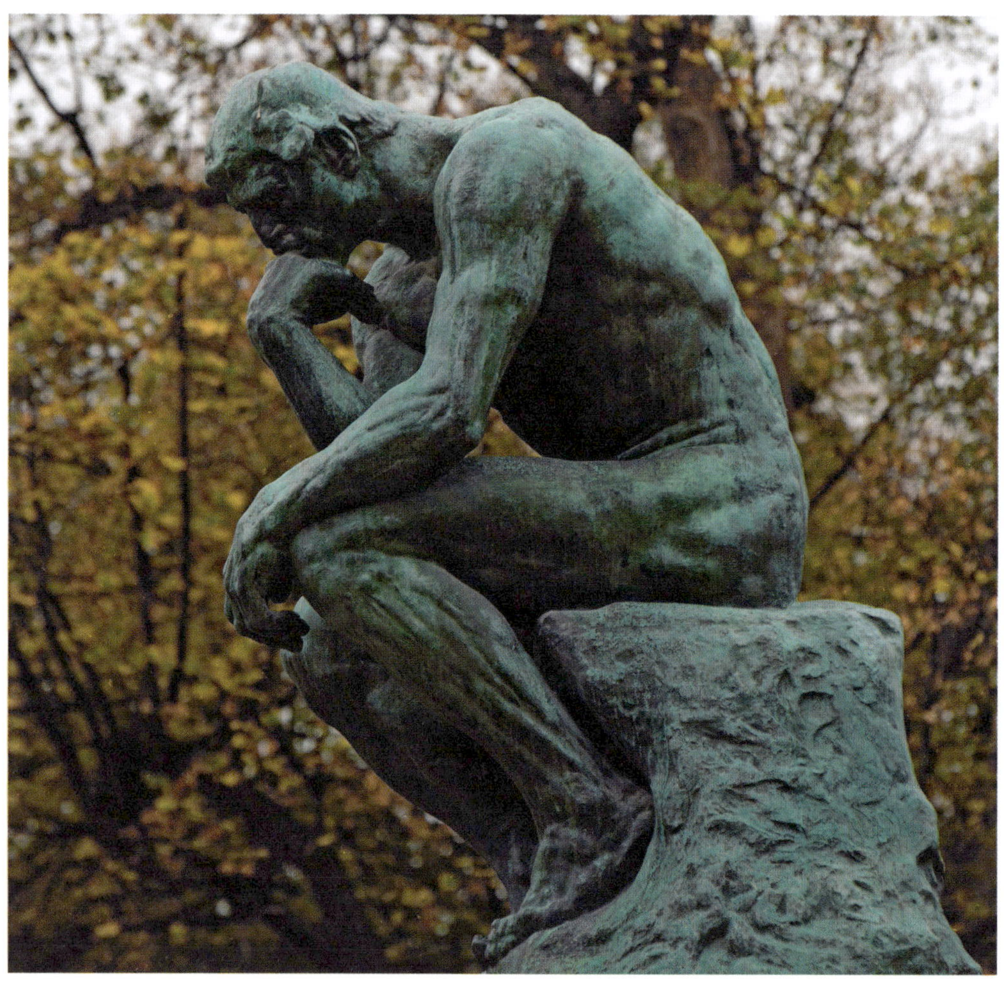

Auguste Rodin, *The Thinker*, 1903

be severely diminished. The enticing tarnish gives the levitating work its stationary swagger - its soul-cred. The lines that the American poet Emma Lazarus ventriloquized the statue to say - 'Give me your tired, your poor, / Your huddled masses yearning to breathe free / The wretched refuse of your teeming shore. / Send these, the homeless, tempest-tost to me' - can only credibly issue from the sealed lips of a toughened spirit as world-weathered as those she embraces. She herself is the scarred spirit she welcomes.

Impatient for that poetic crust to form on his own bronze works, the 19th-century French sculptor Auguste Rodin instructed his studio assistants to take matters into their own hands, take aim, and urinate on his freshly cast bronze creations, aware that the natural acids could accelerate the chemical reaction.[3] The eerie algae-coloured coating that builds naturally on the surface of untreated copper when exposed to the elements (or weed on) for years and decades was the source, when scraped loose into a powder from the metal on which it gathers like an alien frost, of one of the earliest green pigments used by artists: verdigris.

Although attractive in its own right, verdigris (a word formed in Old French in the 12th century, meaning 'green of Greece') doesn't always play nice with other pigments it is placed beside, and has the tendency to tarnish anything it touches. Since antiquity, a tried-and-tested hack for accelerating verdigris's production was well known to artists, who, following a recipe proposed by Theophrastus, placed copper plates or bowls 'over lees of wine'; 'the rust which it acquires by this means', he explains, 'is taken off for use'.[4] Three centuries later, Pliny will expand on his Greek predecessor's instructions and assert that leaving these vessels to steep inside sealed earthenware jars filled with vinegar for nine days works best. In addition to producing a serviceable pigment, Pliny says a salve can also be concocted from the ripe residue - an ointment that 'eats away the callosity of fistulas and of sores round the anus' and, not least, 'removes leprosy'.[5]

By the start of the Renaissance in Italy, verdigris had developed a reputation as a pigment that can dazzle and disappoint in equal measure. 'Take care never to get it near any white lead,' Cennini warns, 'for they are mortal enemies in every respect. Work it up with vinegar, which it retains in accordance with its nature. And if you wish to make a most perfect green for grass ... it is beautiful to the eye, but it does not last.'[6] Over time, verdigris had the tiresome tendency to sully into something dull and dim. The leaves and grass of countless Old Master paintings – from Botticellis to Bronzinos – curdled from lucent lushness into dreary drabness.[7]

Handled properly, verdigris can retain its amphibian sheen and transform a subject into something sublime, salvaged as if from an inner depth – a shipwreck of the soul. Like the patina from which it derives – a protective corrosion that preserves the underlying object from further damage or deterioration – verdigris is a paradoxical pigment that seems almost to displace the essence of things to the watery elsewhere from which it has been recovered or removed. Van Eyck, who clads the enigmatic bride in *The Arnolfini Portrait* (1434) in acres of the colour, knew precisely what he was doing. The shimmer survives. So did Rogier van der Weyden, who, a few years after Van Eyck's famous painting, would encrust his portrait of Mary Magdalene reading (a detail from his altarpiece *Virgin and Child with Saints*) in the same pigment, tempering its intensity with an admixture of lead-tin yellow. The result is a durably delicate figure who feels at once fragile and timeless, protected yet vulnerable – quietly cocooning in its own spiritual second skin. Nor has verdigris lost any of its mystique in modern times. In her entrancing tangle of verdant shades, *portrait of a mare at night* (2019), the Swiss-born abstract artist Liliane Tomasko unweaves the carefully threaded chrysalides in which her famous forebears cloaked their subjects

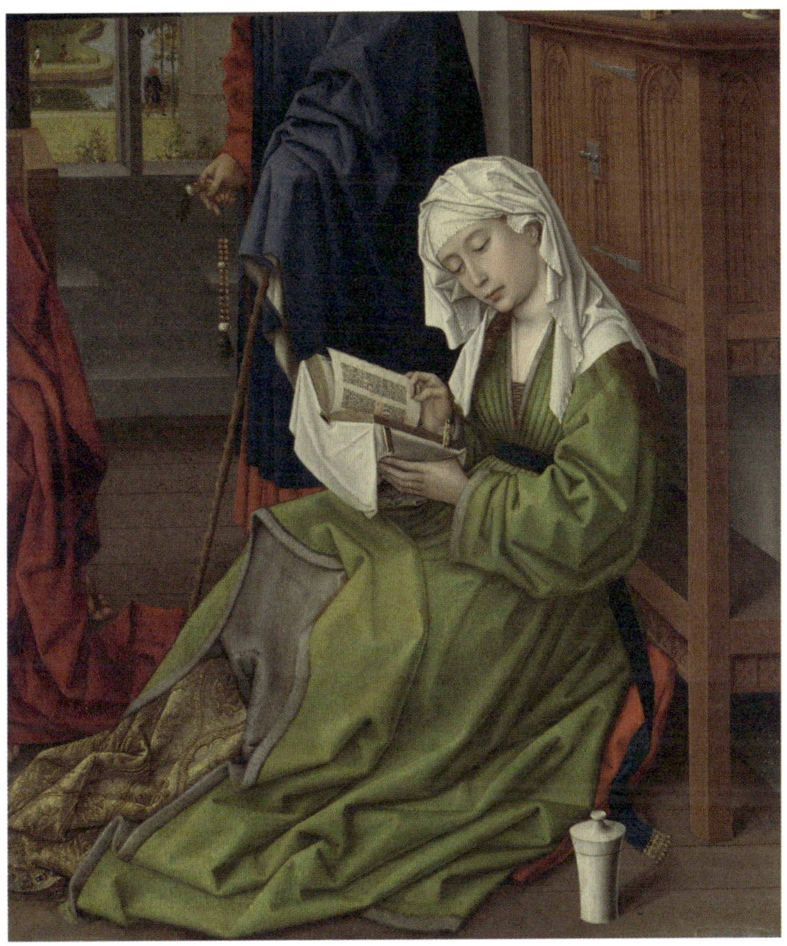

Rogier van der Weyden, *The Magdalen Reading*, fragment from the altarpiece *Virgin and Child with Saints*, before 1438

to reveal the raw energies of verdigris vibrating silently beneath the silk. Fascinated by the forces – invisible and uninterrogatable – that govern the dominion of our sleep, Tomasko's work seeks to disentangle the material world of wakeful perception from the immaterial threads we cling to when unconscious (a project she

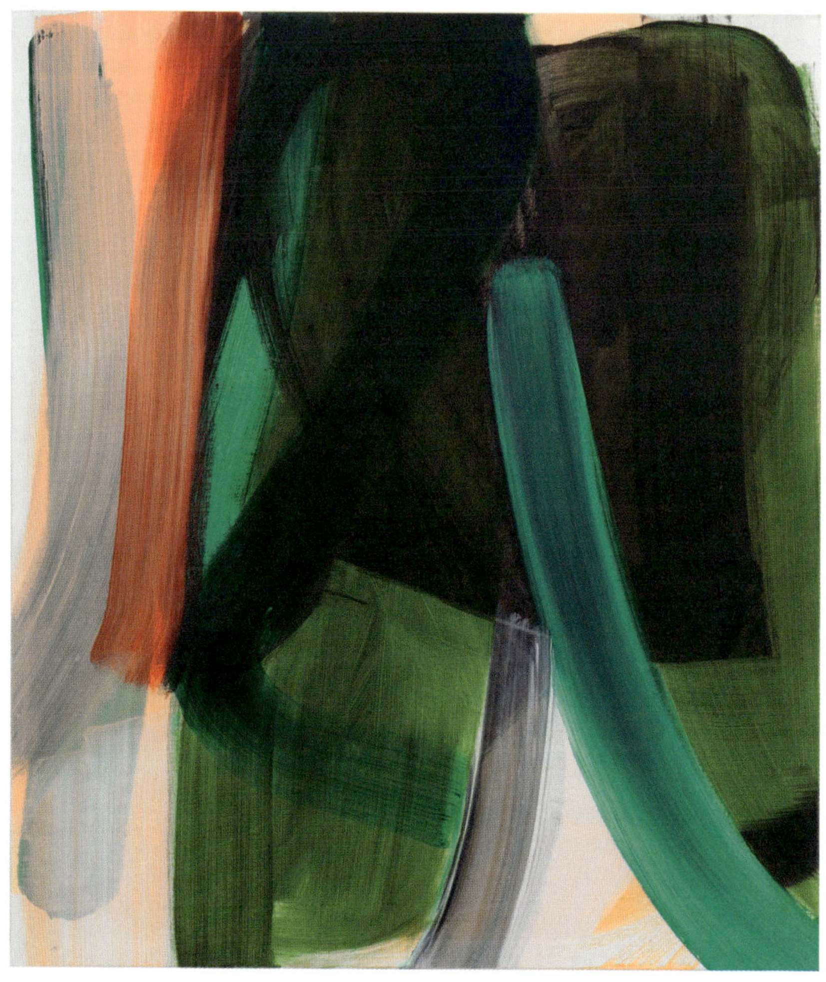

Liliane Tomasko, *portrait of a mare at night*, 2019

hints at in the unpicking of the morphemes that comprise 'portrait of a nightmare' into the fragmented formula of her teasing title). No hue more intuitively evokes the intractable alchemies of imagination more vividly than verdigris, a thrumming thrust of which throbs at the heart of her painting.

Malachite

In use since prehistoric times, verdigris would eventually be joined as a source for generating green pigment by the brittle copper carbonate malachite – a mineral that forms fragile fibrous stalactite masses, like prickly verdant porcupines, in deep underground fractures. In ancient Egypt, this particular incarnation of lustrous green was associated with the soul's rebirth in an eternal realm free from suffering. Such paradise was designated 'The Field of Malachite'.[8] In contrast to other minerals we've looked at, such as orpiment, to release the malachite's magic there is a point of diminishing return to its levigation, or milling with water. Cennini warns us that 'if you were to grind it too much, it would come out a dingy and ashy color.' Instead, he insists the colour must be coaxed by a subtler ritual of delicate sousing. 'When you have got it worked up,' he writes,

> *put it into the dish; put some clear water over the color, and stir the water up well with the color. Then let it stand for the space of one hour, or two or three; and pour off the water; and the green will be more beautiful. And wash it this way two or three times, and it will be still more beautiful.*[9]

A century before Cennini, the Parisian scholastic Bartholomaeus Anglicus compiled an encyclopedic compendium entitled *De proprietatibus rerum* (On the Properties of Things), in which he devotes an entry to malachite and the cultural connotations it had accrued since antiquity. Describing the mineral as 'more lurid green than the emerald', Bartholomaeus attributes to the 1st-century Greek physician Dioscorides the belief that malachite 'saves children from harmful evils and mishaps; and whoever bears it on his left side, no wicked thing shall grieve him'.[10]

•

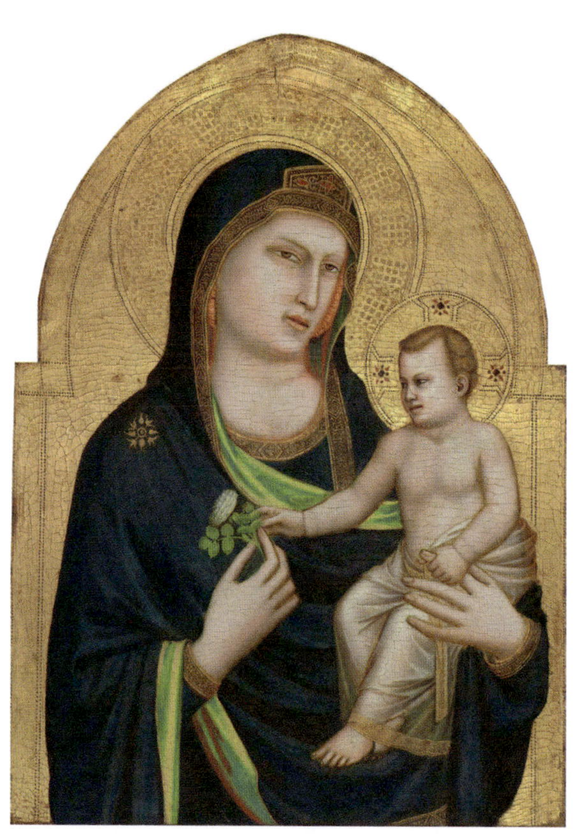

Giotto, *Madonna and Child*, c. 1310/1315

Whether Raphael was conscious of the many traditions surrounding the mineral, a reverberation of malachite's mystique ineluctably intensifies his *Sistine Madonna*, a dramatically staged painting that Vasari described as 'a truly rare and extraordinary work'.[11] Commissioned in 1512 by Pope Julius for the church of San Sisto, Piacenza, the painting imagines a vaulted Mary, tip-toeing on a pedestal of clouds while holding an inscrutable, saucer-eyed infant Christ. The plush green curtains that appear to have been just pulled wide to reveal the mother and child, hovering in heaven, have been magicked from malachite. The mineral's ability to herald the hereafter has resonated since the early 14th century, when Giotto inflected with malachite the elegant gown that engulfs the Virgin in his *Madonna and Child*.

Amplifying its intensity in Raphael's painting, the pigment is picked up by the sash worn by Saint Barbara, the patron saint of mining, who levitates on Mary's left, as if deliberately invoking the legend Bartholomaeus ascribes to Dioscorides of malachite's protective power when it comes to the safety of children. Once spotted, malachite grinds the spiritual lens through which the work frames its own sublimity.

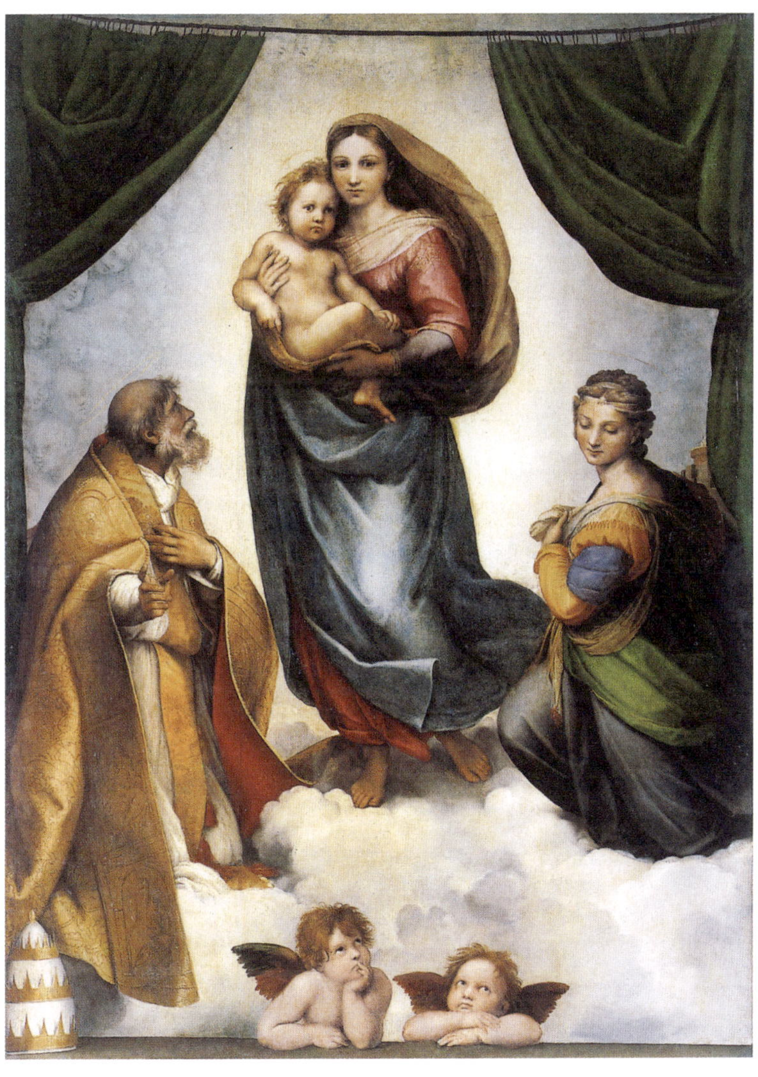

Raphael, *The Sistine Madonna*, 1512–13

Emerald Green

'My wallpaper and I', Oscar Wilde quipped shortly before he died in a Paris hotel in 1900, 'are fighting a duel to the death. One or the other of us has to go.'[12] If legend is to be believed, three quarters of a century earlier, on a remote volcanic island in the South Atlantic Ocean, Napoleon Bonaparte found himself on the losing end of a similar quarrel. Literally. Analysis of a lock of the French military leader's hair suggests that he may have died as a result of toxic exposure to arsenic, which was a key component of the wallpaper that adorned the fusty room in which Napoleon died in exile on St Helena in 1821.

According to one theory of what finally did him in, a conspiracy of mould (which can grow quickly on the walls in St Helena) and damp air that suspended arsenic fumes and fungal spores may have helped deliver the toxin to the dejected figure's defeated body. The source of the poison in this hypothesis would have been the copper arsenite that laced the green fleurs-de-lis pattern of the wallpaper – one of the countless products to benefit from a relatively new type of pigment discovered by the German-Swedish pharmaceutical chemist Carl Wilhelm Scheele in 1775. Conscious of the potential health hazards involved in using the pigment, Scheele kept his anxieties to himself as his invention caught fire with the public. It would be a century before a connection was made between the popularity of so-called Scheele's green and the mounting death toll of those who spent time around it, including countless children whose parents found the hue sufficiently soothing for a nursery.

In 1814, a close cousin of Scheele's green was discovered coincidentally in two different European labs – once in the Bavarian city of Schweinfurt (where the pharmacist Friedrich Wilhelm Ruß and the industrialist Wilhelm Sattler were tinkering with concoctions of verdigris, vinegar, white arsenic and sodium carbonate), and again in Vienna by the Austrian entrepreneur Ignaz von Mitis.[13] More dazzling to the eye and

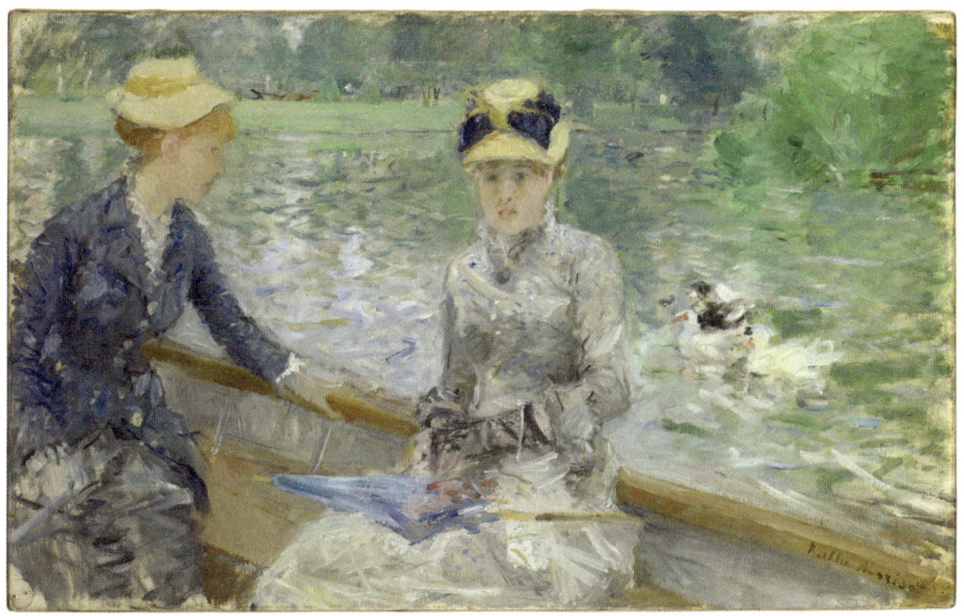

Berthe Morisot, *Summer's Day*, c. 1879

friendlier to the painter's canvas than Scheele's green, *vert de Schweinfurt*, as the resulting pigment came to be known locally – or 'Paris green', 'Vienna green' and 'emerald green' elsewhere – soon took off with artists, who were as in the dark about the dangers of inhaling the pigment's harmful fumes as Napoleon himself.

The French painter Berthe Morisot was among those drawn to this particular iteration of green, which George Field described as 'lighter, more vivid, and more opaque' than Scheele's green. 'Its vivid hue', he wrote in *Chromatography*, 'is almost beyond the scale of other bright pigments, and immediately attracts the eye to any part of a painting in which it may be employed ... yielding spring tints of extreme brilliancy and beauty'.[14] Where Field recommended the colour be 'discreetly used', and imagined 'a touch on a gaily painted boat or barge' as its ideal deployment, Morisot, in her painting *Summer's Day* (*c.* 1879), refrains from using the colour to articulate the boat that carries the pair of young women leisurely drifting on dappled water. Instead, she boldly wallpapers the highly gestural horizon of green trees with expressive slashes of the pernicious pigment. The result unsettles the summer scene with an uneasy verdancy that seems uncomfortable in its own skin – a green that feverishly tosses and turns.

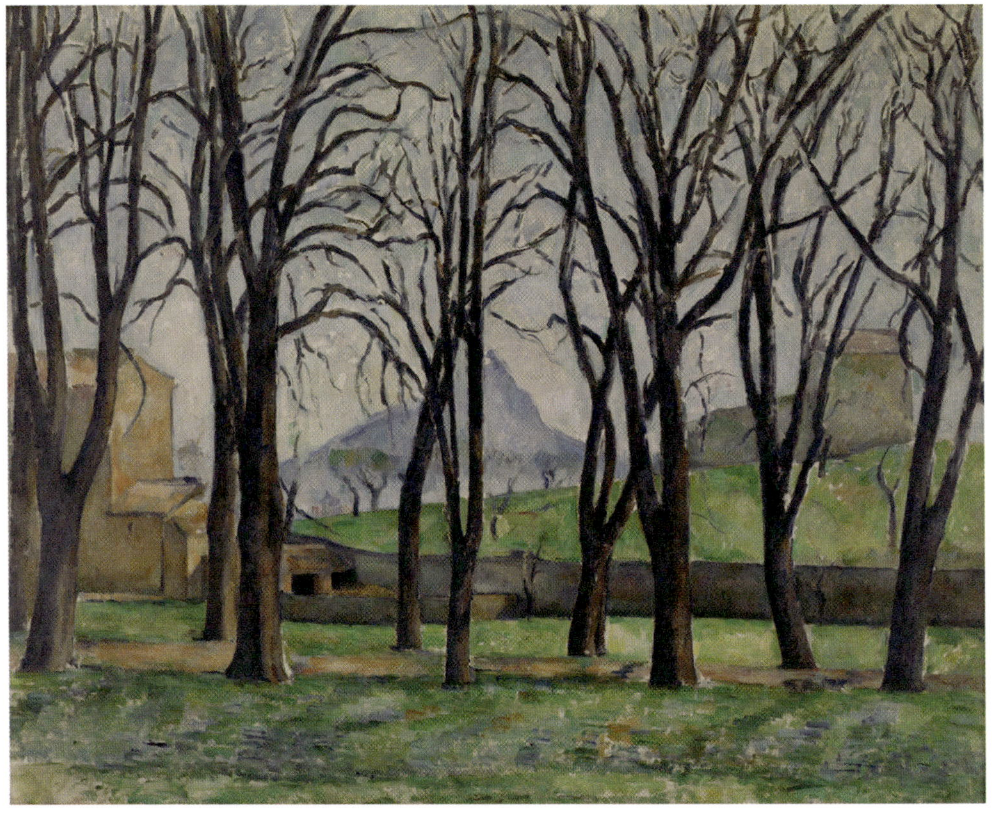

Paul Cézanne, *Chestnut Trees at Jas de Bouffan*, *c.* 1885–86

Half a decade later, Cézanne will make comprehensive use of emerald green in nearly every aspect of his wintery *Chestnut Trees at Jas de Bouffan* (c. 1885–86), a work he undertook the year his father, with whom he'd had an emotionally intense relationship, died. Here, Cézanne allows the colour to accent not only the lighter and darker patches of grass and the shifting light on the tan house to the left, but also the stone wall that cuts across the canvas, the skeletal trunks of leafless trees and the sepulchral sky they shatter. The only shape he resists tainting with the toxic pigment is the grey-blue thrum of Mount Victoire, beckoning in the distance – a shimmering totem he increasingly came to associate with the eternal pulse of indomitable nature. Make what you will of that.

Viridian

In the rich slants of trunk-shade that soulfully striate the foreground of Cézanne's painting, traces of still another type of green pigment can be found, one whose French name – *vert emeraude* – makes for easy confusion with emerald green. Better known outside France as viridian, this glistening green with a delicately diaphanous dimension – ideally suited to the Impressionists' desire to alchemize the solidity of things into delicate declensions of light – squeezed itself on to artists' palettes at the end of the 1850s. It was then that the French chemist C. E. Guignet stumbled across a way to hydrate (or put water molecules) into the crystal lattice of chromium that Vauquelin had discovered sixty-five years earlier (see page 56). Guignet was not, in fact, the first to create hydrated chromium oxide, but was commercially savvy in expeditiously licensing his method to manufacturers. Twenty years earlier, a pioneering Paris-based colourist, Pannetier, was the first to unlock the secret formula for viridian, but kept it close to his chest.[15]

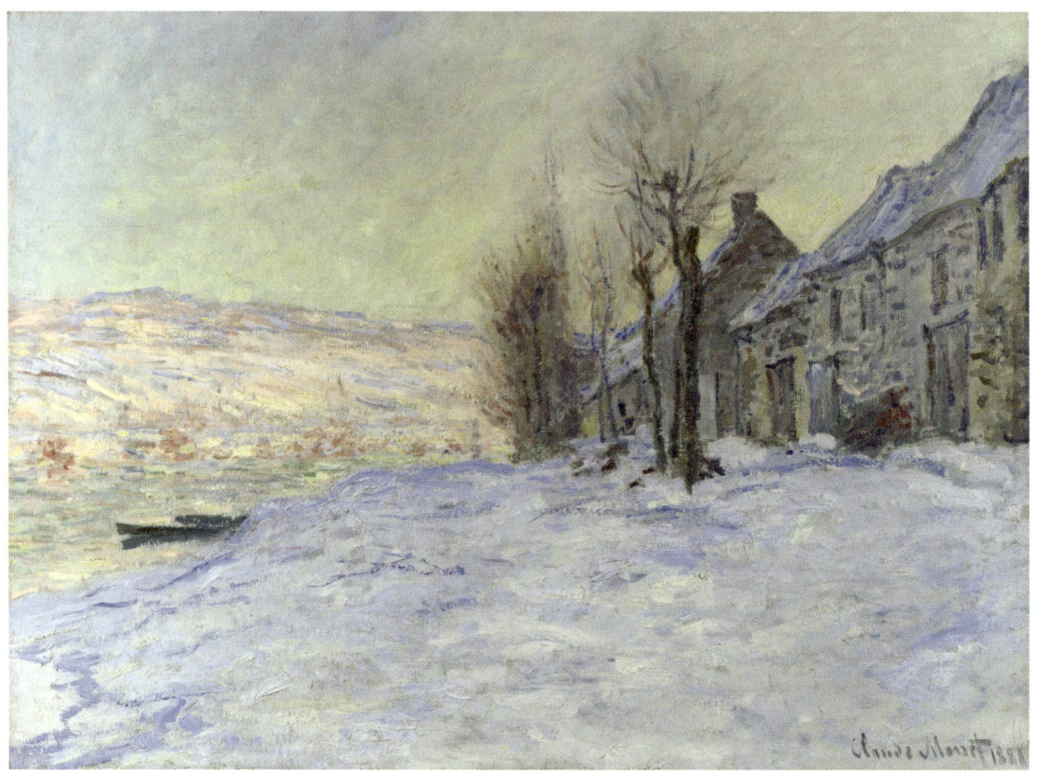

Claude Monet, *Lavacourt under Snow*, c. 1878–81

What distinguishes viridian is an inherent paradox in its temperament. On the one hand, as implied by its very name (derived from the Latin stem *viridis* meaning 'blooming, vigorous'), the pigment offers itself as bold, palpable and robust, 'being not unlike the richest velvet', as George Field describes it. On the other hand, there is an almost mystical translucency to the colour that complicates its tangibility. 'Pure and clear as the emerald,' Field goes on to say, viridian 'may be called the Prussian Blue of Greens, of such richness, depth, and transparency is it.'[16] That paradox, which accommodates at once a precious physicality we can touch and hold (or can hold us) and the transport of an airy metaphysicality that can carry us elsewhere, almost subliminally invigorates the stark, wintery splendour of Claude Monet's *Lavacourt under Snow* (c. 1878–81).

The canvas depicts a small clutch of houses along a curve of the river Seine near Vétheuil, a commune to the north-west of Paris where Monet had moved in the spring of 1878 during a period of intense financial struggle. At first glance, it's easy to equate the accumulation of snow as a metaphor for the piling-up of trouble and unsold paintings. But it's the subtle glint, echoing across the track of seemingly impassable snow, of delicate vertical slivers of viridian that describe the windows of the stone house on the right and which construct the slender skiff on the bank of the river opposite that generates the poignancy of the painting. Viridian is both the palpable portal out of the quotidian concerns of this world and the vehicle that can convey our spirits elsewhere. Taken together, the vertical and horizontal viridian axes Monet has carefully calibrated in his canvas are the lines of longitude and latitude along which its static journey moves.

COLOURFUL MINDS

Goethe's *Theory of Colours* (1810)

In the eyes of the German poet and thinker Johann Wolfgang von Goethe, Isaac Newton's colour theories did not so much deepen our understanding of colour as cloud it, obscuring it with scientific obtuseness. To appreciate colour, Goethe believed, one would be better advised to consult a philosopher, not a physicist. Our experience of colour, he maintained, was at once 'allegorical, symbolic [and] mystic'. Insisting that every colour we perceive 'spontaneously and of necessity ... produce[s] another', complementary one, Goethe constructed a complex colour wheel 'arranged in a general way according to the natural order ... for the colours diametrically opposed to each other in this diagram are those which reciprocally evoke each other in the eye. Thus, yellow demands violet; orange [demands] blue; purple [demands] green; and vice versa: thus ... all intermediate gradations reciprocally evoke each other; the simpler colour demanding the compound, and vice versa.' To each of the three primary colours (red, yellow and blue) and the three secondary colours (orange, green and purple), Goethe attached a particular quality, ranging from 'beautiful' to 'common'. The attribution of character traits to colours would have a significant impact on a wide range of artists, from J. M. W. Turner to Joseph Albers, Wassily Kandinsky to Paul Klee.

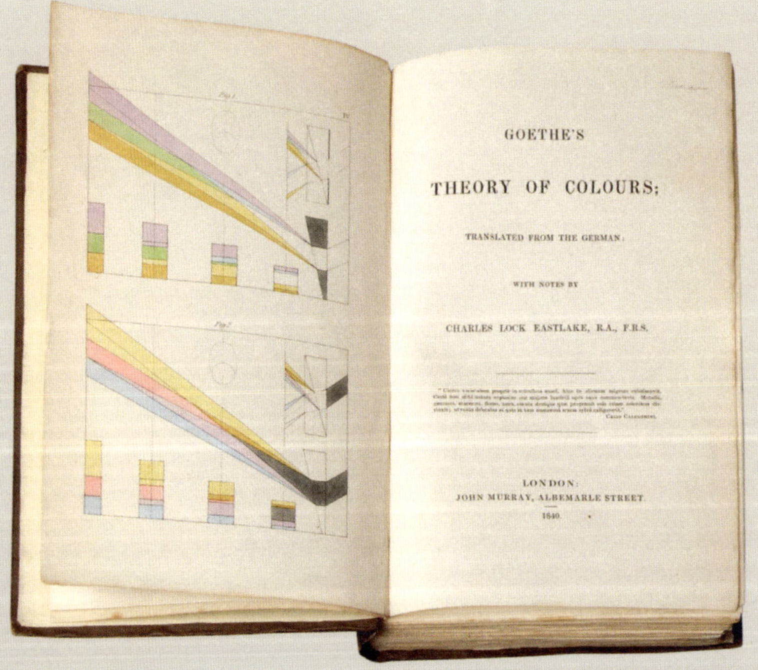

GOETHE'S

THEORY OF COLOURS;

TRANSLATED FROM THE GERMAN:

WITH NOTES BY

CHARLES LOCK EASTLAKE, R.A., F.R.S.

LONDON:
JOHN MURRAY, ALBEMARLE STREET.
1840.

Insisting that Newton's theories of colour were clinically removed from the realm of actual experience, Goethe's *Theory of Colours* (1810) resolves to restore the context of lived reality and 'to prove by numberless cases that colour is produced by light as well as by what stands against it'.

Goethe's famous colour wheel encapsulates his assertions about the relationship between colour and human emotion. Synchronizing hue and mood in its suspended spin, the diagram aligns yellow with feelings of 'bright serenity', yellow-red with 'extreme excitement', blue with 'a stimulating negation', shades of violets with 'unquiet feelings', red with 'grace and attractiveness', and green with the mind's 'repose'.

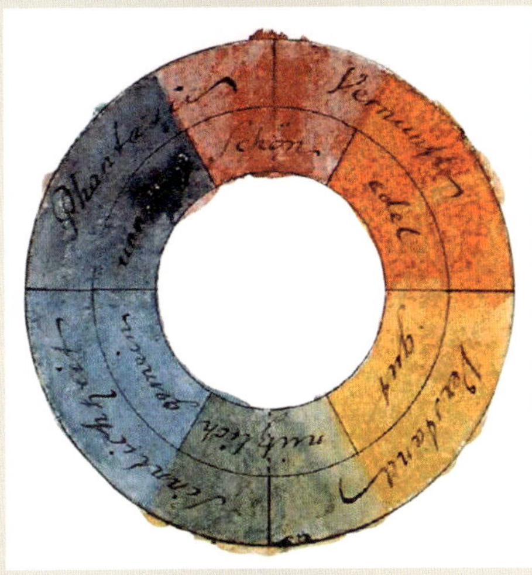

Goethe's theories exerted a great influence on the imagination of thinkers and artists alike, including the philosophers Arthur Schopenhauer and Ludwig Wittgenstein and the painters J. M. W. Turner and Hilma af Klint (see page 2). In what sense, precisely, Turner's 1843 canvas *Light and Colour (Goethe's Theory) – The Morning after the Deluge – Moses writing the Book of Genesis* can be read as a comment on Goethe remains the source of some debate.

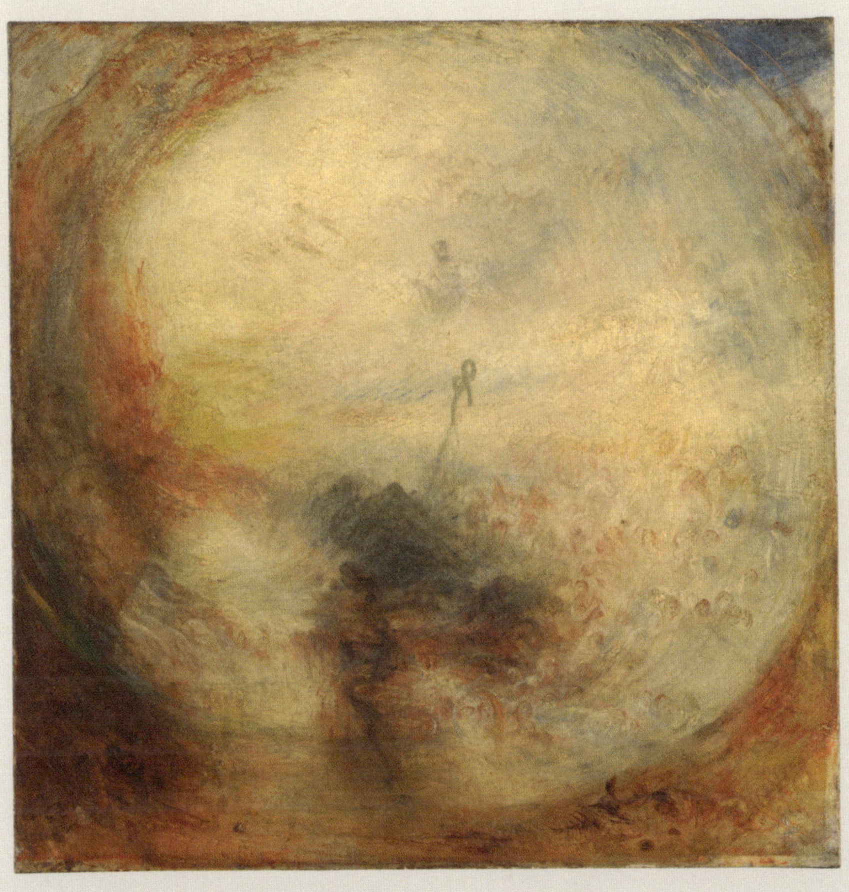

Blue

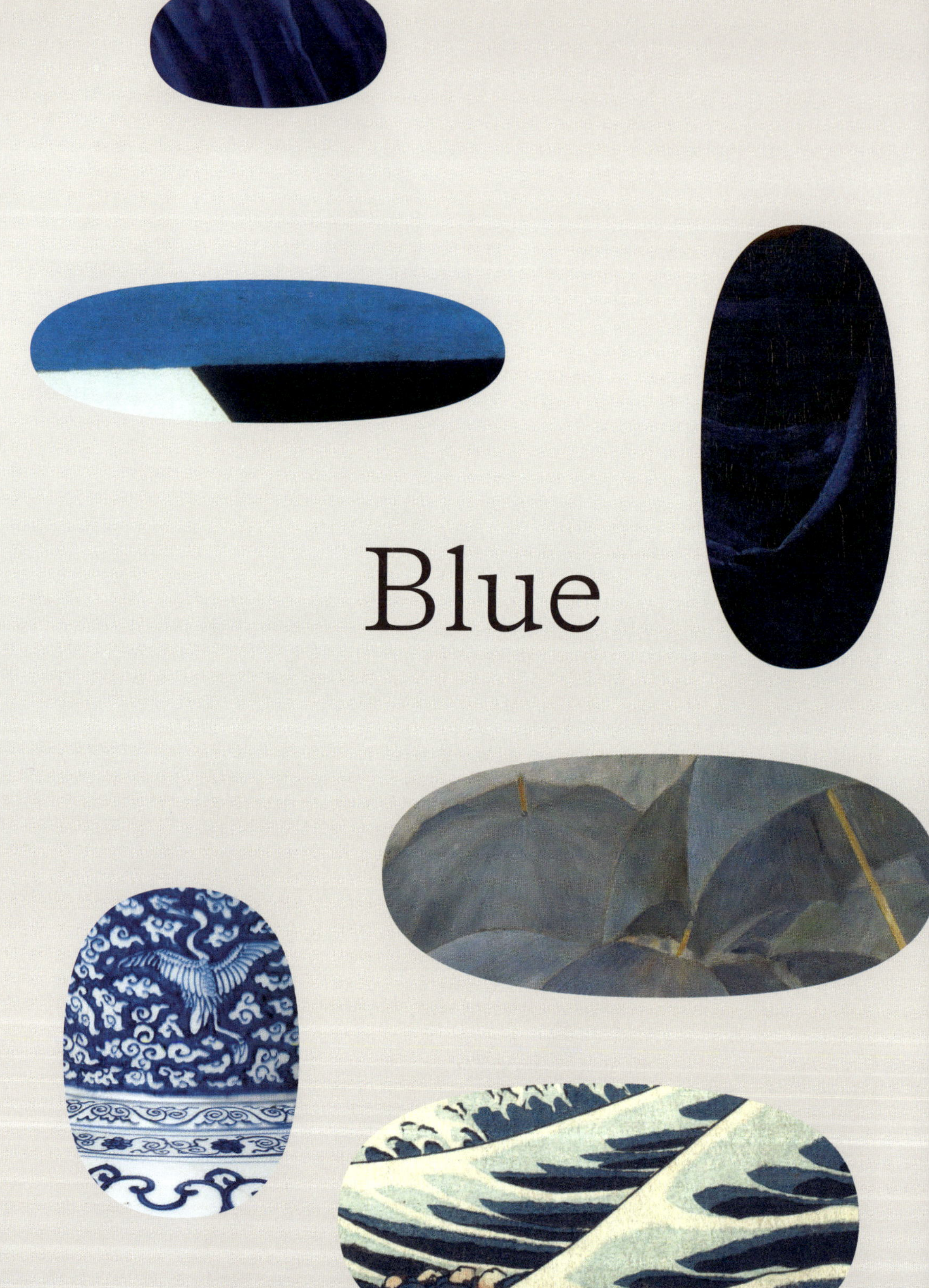

Blue eludes. It 'has no dimensions,' the 20th-century French artist Yves Klein insisted,

> *it is beyond dimensions. At first there is nothing, then there is profound nothing, after that a blue profundity. Other colors bring associations to concrete, material and tangible ideas, while blue recalls at most the sky and the sea, but also Western spirituality and Eastern mysticism, the symbol of eternity and ... what is most abstract in tangible and visible nature.*[1]

As we will discover, Klein was not content merely to sing the blues; from the late 1950s until his death in 1962, aged just thirty-four, he immersed himself in the task of inventing an immersive new shade - one that seemed to absorb into itself countless contradictory cultural connotations that the colour has accrued since antiquity. While the ancient Greeks didn't bother with coining a word for it (believing blue a variation of green), Egyptians synthesized a special ethereal shade they called *irtyu* with which they devotedly decorated the tombs of their honoured dead. At once evasive and evocative - by far the rarest of the primary colours to occur in nature, yet the prevailing colour of the planet when seen from space - blue both abounds and beguiles; it is neither here nor there.

Azurite

No one knows for sure who first connected the colour blue with sadness. Some attribute the emotional link to the English medieval poet Geoffrey Chaucer, who describes downcast lovers parting company in his poem 'The Complaint of Mars' as being weighed down with 'teres blewe' and a 'wondyd herte'.

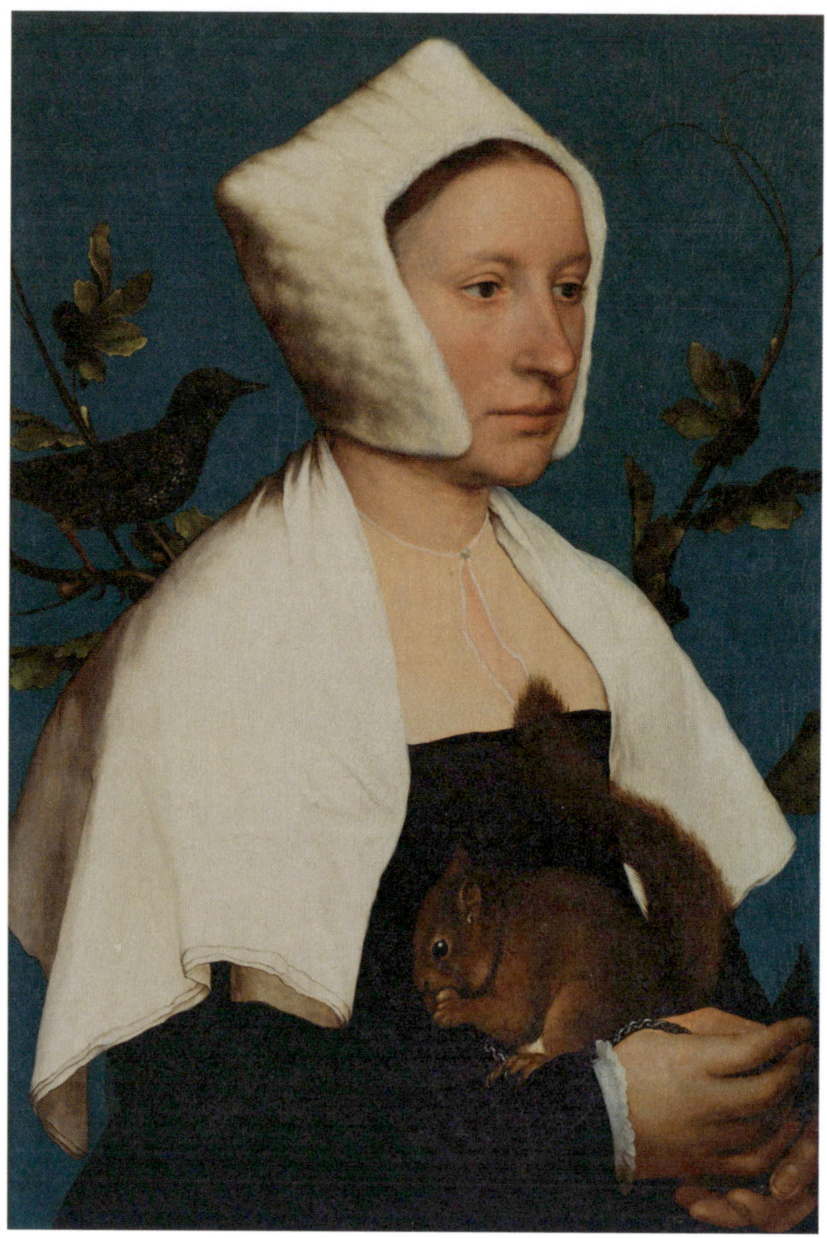

Hans Holbein the Younger, *A Lady with a Squirrel and a Starling*, c. 1526–28

It is likely, however, that the association goes back further still. In his encyclopedic treatise on depression, the 17th-century English writer Robert Burton alludes to a curious remedy for despondency gleaned from the ancient teachings of the eminent Greek physician Alexander of Talles. According to Burton's famous *Anatomy of Melancholy* (first published in 1621), the deep-blue copper mineral azurite – known in antiquity, as we have seen, as *Lapis armenius* – was 'much magnified by Alexander', who believed 'all melancholy passions might be cured by it'.[2] The presumed action of the antidote, which requires that the mineral be 'well washed, that the water be no more coloured, fifty times some say', is almost homeopathic in its reliance on the intensifying effect of dilution: a washed away blue that washes away blueness.

In due course, deposits of the copper carbonate azurite would be discovered throughout Europe (in France, Hungary, Germany and Spain), a development that helped establish its use in Western art until the beginning of the 18th century. That the pigment itself, whose preparation required patient purification of the pulverized mineral by milling it with water, continued to carry with it the propensity to plumb the depths of a subject's psyche enriches our response to Hans Holbein's enigmatic *A Lady with a Squirrel and a Starling* (*c.* 1526–28). The genius of Holbein's oil-on-oak painting – thought to be a portrait of Anne Lovell, wife of a personal attendant of Henry VIII – lies in its juxtaposition of material and immaterial textures.

Our eye marvels at the mastery of fabric – the delicate rumples in Lovell's linen shawl, the diaphanous sheen of her chemise, and the softness of the Russian ermine-pelt cap. A fabulous finesse with feathers in the artist's handling of the starling (its presence, it is said, is likely a pun on 'Harling', a parish in Norfolk, where the sitter lived), together with the buoyant bristle of the squirrel's tail (an animal that figures in the Lovell coat of arms), alert us to the fact that the portrait goes beyond the contours of literal likeness. Captured in the prime of her life and in the very year she gave birth to a son, Thomas, there is nevertheless a sombreness to the portrait - an air of melancholy that the azurite background only accentuates.

Holbein would not have recognized the word 'azurite' as the name for the pigment he used to conjure the solemn theatre of the mind in which he metaphysically locates his sitter. It would be another three centuries after he completed *A Lady with a Squirrel and a Starling* that a French mineralogist, François Sulpice Beudant, would coin the term. Holbein would likely have known the pigment by either 'mountain blue', chessylite (after the mines in Chessy, Rhône, eastern France, where a rich deposit had been discovered) or, more likely still, 'citramarine', meaning 'on the near side of the sea' - a designation intended to distinguish azurite from a far more precious and mysterious pigment that came from 'beyond the sea': ultramarine.

Ultramarine

Ultramarine is a miracle of a colour. That the intense blue pigment, which transforms countless medieval and Renaissance works into mesmerizing marvels, was ever concocted at all is among the great wonders of art history. Like its sibling azurite, ultramarine is derived from a naturally occurring substance - the semi-precious stone lapis lazuli, which, for centuries, hailed exclusively from a system of remote mines in the mountain range of Badakhshan, Afghanistan. Unlike azurite, however, isolating the usable pigment component (a blue phosphate mineral called lazurite) from the myriad unwanted ingredients that clog lapis lazuli (including calcite, sodalite, pyrite, augite, diopside, enstatite, mica, hauynite, hornblende, nosean and löllingite) proved an intractable task for the ancient Greeks and ancient

Egyptians alike. It wasn't until the 6th century that the artists who constructed frescoes around the heads of colossal sculptures of Buddha in Bamiyan, Afghanistan (some 500 km/310 miles to the south-west of Badakhshan), managed to unlock the painterly potential of ultramarine. Unfortunately, those groundbreaking relics, which had survived for centuries, were lost in 2001 when the Taliban leader Mullah Mohammed Omar declared that the Buddhas were idols and ordered them destroyed.

Sourcing the raw stone from its hiding places in Sar-i-Sang (Valley of Stones) was itself no mean feat. 'Under the spot to be quarried', the 19th-century Scottish naval officer and explorer John Wood, who witnessed the age-old technique first-hand, chronicled in his travelogue *Narrative of a Journey to the Source of the River Oxus*, 'a fire is kindled, and its flame, fed by dry furze, is made to flicker over the surface. When the rock has become sufficiently soft, or to use the workman's expression, nurim, it is beaten with hammers and flake after flake knocked off until the stone in which they are in search is discovered. Deep grooves are then picked round the lapis lazuli, into which crowbars are inserted, and the stone and part of its matrix are detached.'[3] Other accounts of the arduous process describe the use of ice water, splashed against the smouldering stone, to stun it into shattering. There is little doubting that ultramarine was truly the product of shock and awe.

But acquiring chunks of the absorbing stone, whose rich blue hue turns the specks of pyrite into a firmament of stars, was only half the battle. Separating the constellations of fool's gold and other unwelcome debris (which, if left in and ground up with the lazurite, results in a sombrely subfuscous grey) from the dazzle of deep space surrounding it requires astonishing patience. Cennino Cennini, who was utterly seduced by ultramarine and described it as 'a color illustrious, beautiful, and most perfect, beyond all other colors; one could not say anything about it, or do anything with it, that its quality would not still surpass', believed its excellence justified that he 'discuss it at length ... to show you in detail how it is made'. 'To begin with,' Cennini says, 'get some lapis lazuli' and 'pound it in a bronze mortar, covered up, so that it may not go off in dust', then put it on a slab 'and work it up without water'. After that, sift it through a sieve 'and pound it over again', 'bear[ing] in mind that the more finely you work it up, the finer the blue will come out.' The next step requires melting together a handful of additional ingredients, including 'six ounces of pine rosin from the druggists, three ounces of gum mastic, and three ounces of new wax, for each pound of lapis lazuli'. This concoction is then strained 'into a glazed washbasin' and mixed together with 'a pound of the lapis lazuli powder' to form a 'plastic'.[4]

It is crucial, Cennini insists, that you 'always keep your hands well greased' with linseed oil as you work this freshly forged 'plastic' over a little 'for at least three days and three nights'. Only now are you ready 'to extract the blue from it'. This requires first making 'two sticks out of a stout rod, neither too thick nor too thin; and let them each be a foot long; and have them well rounded at the top and bottom, and nicely smoothed'. Once you've created these sticks, use them, one in each hand, to 'turn over and squeeze and knead this plastic', to which you have added a bowlful of 'lye, fairly warm'. Working the lye-soaked plastic with the sticks 'this way and that, just as you work over bread dough with your hand', you will eventually 'see that the lye is saturated with blue'. At this point, draw the lye off into a glazed 'porringer' – or small bowl with a handle – 'and put as much lye again onto the plastic, and press it out again'. 'When the lye is quite blue, put it into another glazed porringer. And go on doing this for several days in the same way, until the plastic will no longer color the lye; and then throw it away, for it is no longer any good.'

Now you're getting somewhere. Once you have filled as many porringers as possible, Cennini instructs that you 'arrange all these porringers in front of you on a table' in the order that you have squeezed the blue lye from the plastic, remembering to use 'your hand [to] stir up in each one the lye with the blue which, on account of the heaviness of this blue, will have gone to the bottom'. By so arranging the generations of extractions, he says, you will 'learn the yields of the blue', 'bearing in mind that the first yields are the best, just as the first porringer is better than the second', and so on. 'Every day' from here, Cennini says, you must 'drain off the lye from the porringers, until the blues are dry. When they are perfectly dry, do them up in leather, or in bladders, or in purses, according to the divisions which you have.'

The sweat and stamina necessary to extract ultramarine was worth it, both aesthetically and financially. Until an artificial version was finally fabricated in the 19th century, ultramarine, squeezed like blood from stone, fetched a higher price than any other pigment and was, pound for pound, pricier even than gold. It's tempting, of course, simply to acknowledge, as many historians have, that the exorbitant price placed on ultramarine added to its lustre and made it the obvious choice to extol the most exalted subject in art history - the Virgin Mary. It is true that, all tallied, the acreage of intense blue devoted to Mary's robes in countless portrayals of her since the Middle Ages - from Gerard David's *Virgin and Child with Saints and Donor* (*c.* 1510) to Sassoferato's *The Virgin in Prayer* (1640-50) - doubtless makes her the dearest subject in the history of art. But expense alone does not account for what infuses the unreal radiance of ultramarine with heightened cultural potency. The colour's intensity seems almost to shudder with a knowledge of its own wrenching evulsion - the gruelling ordeal of its punishing production. Ultramarine, like Mary herself, who must witness the torture and murder of her own son, has been through the wringer and come out the other side more majestic. The two are radiant not in spite of what they've undergone, but because of it.

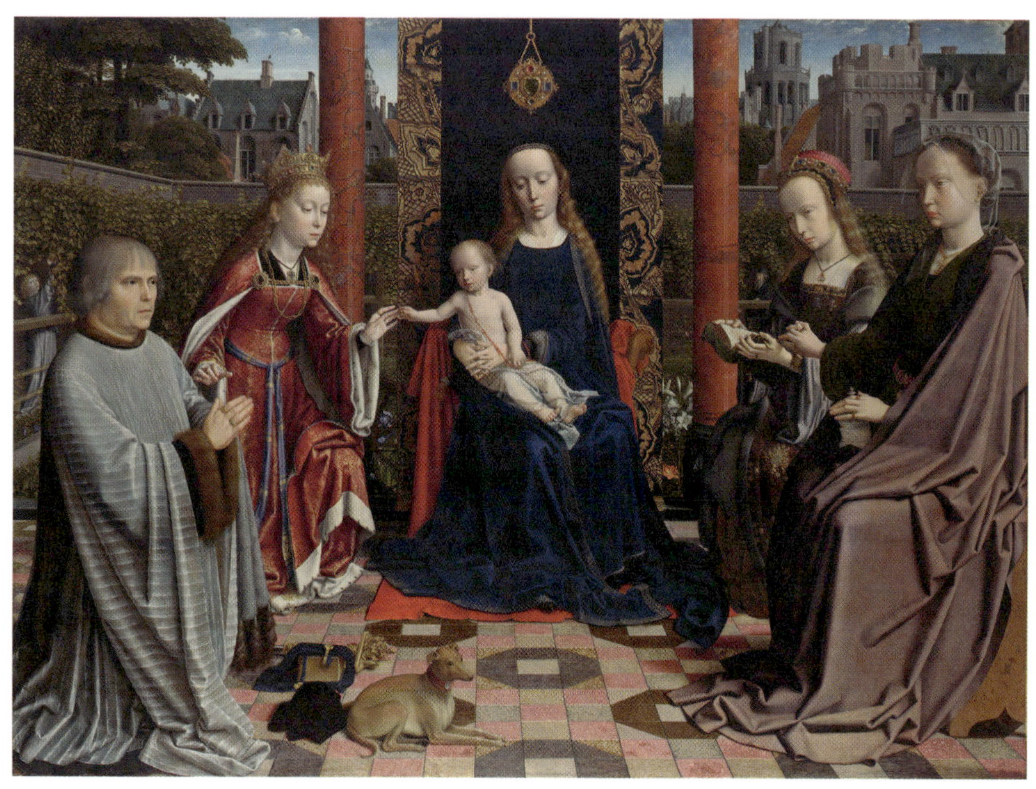

Gerard David, *The Virgin and Child with Saints and Donor*, probably 1510

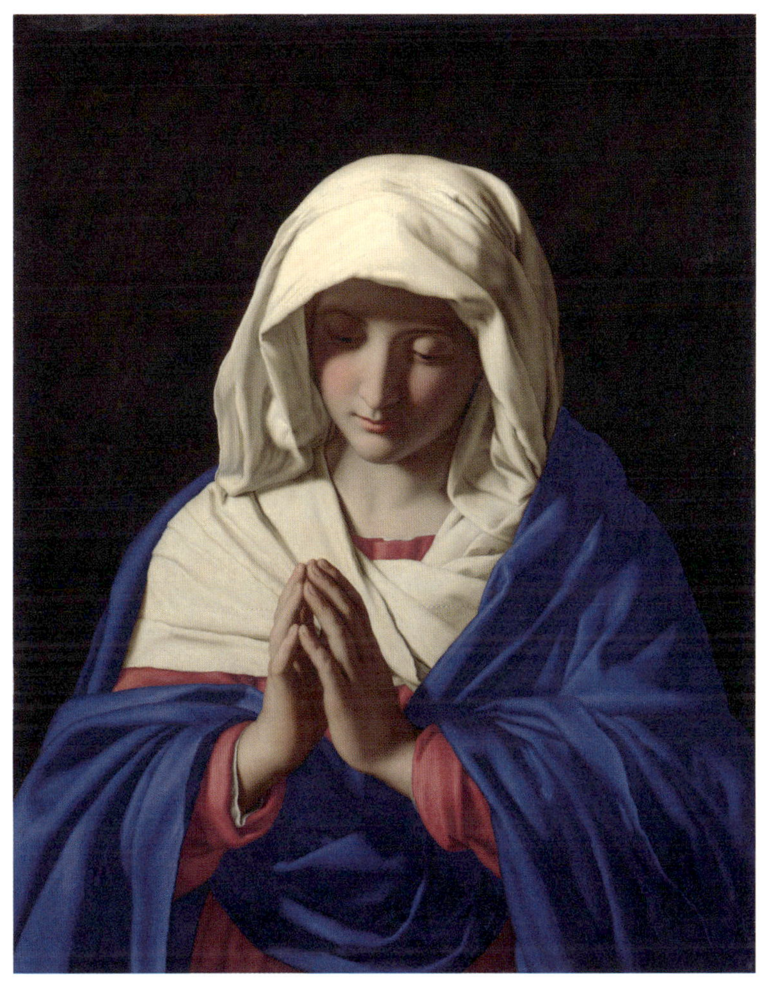

Sassoferrato, *The Virgin in Prayer*, 1640–50

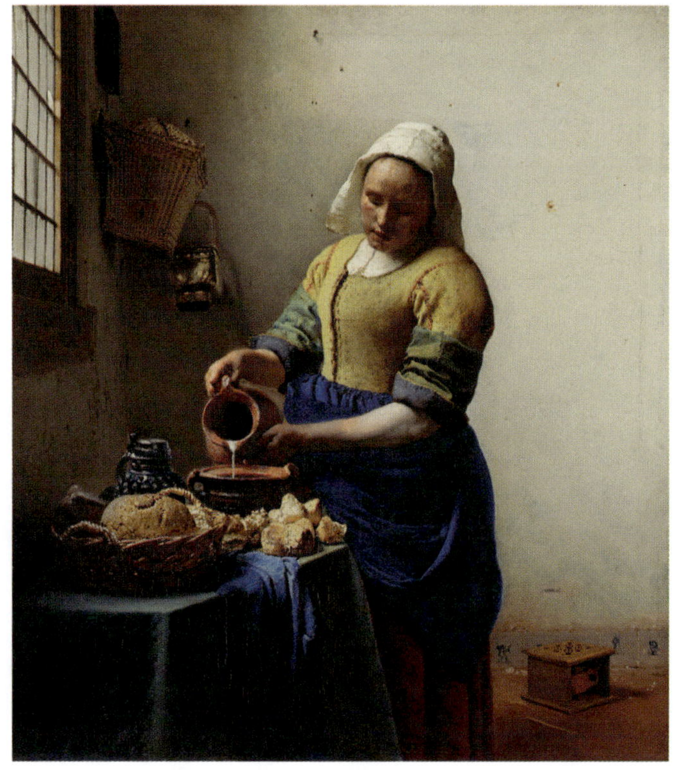

Johannes Vermeer, *The Milkmaid*, c. 1660

The manner of its making crushes ultramarine into meaning. An essence purified by tribulation, it glints richly with an inner nobility hewn by fortitude. That's what makes it the perfect pigment to capture the unpretentious grace not only of the subject of Vermeer's *Milkmaid* (c. 1660) – whose intense blue apron has been both painted with pure ultramarine in the first instance and then, to underline the point, glazed with it – but also of the pensive dwarf who affectingly looks our way in Diego Velázquez's *Las Meninas* (1656), her billowy crinoline dress drenched in the stuff. Beneath its sheen of superficial splendour, ultramarine carries with it the weight of its own patient purgation, inflecting everything it touches with a hint of the mineral's inner mettle. The frozen instants of Vermeer's and Velázquez's works, painted only a few years apart, are hardly enough to distil full profiles of their respective subjects. Yet there is an alluring humility to these portraits, a poignancy, that ultramarine - and ultramarine alone - can coax to the surface.

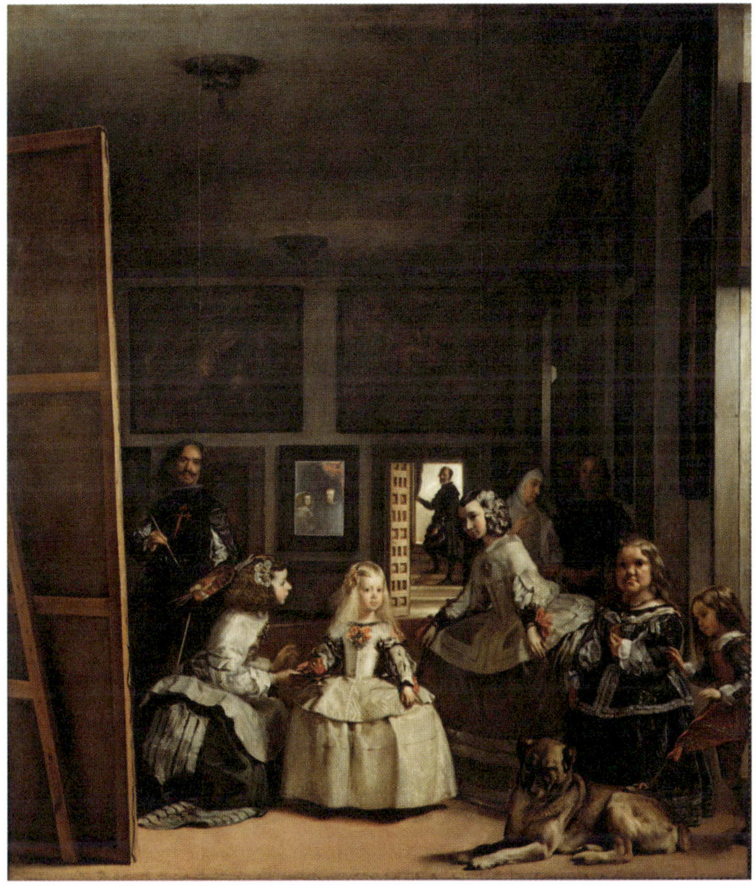

Diego Velázquez, *Las Meninas*, 1656

Cobalt Blue

Speaking of coaxing, there is another blue hue whose identity is entangled with the myth of conjured spirits: cobalt blue. Not harnessed for use on the painter's palette until the 19th century, when the French chemist Louis Jacques Thénard synthesized cobalt salts with alumina to create an affordable, stable and suitably robust blue pigment in 1802, cobalt blue is so-named for its connection with a menacing medieval myth. Meaning literally 'gremlin' or 'goblin', German *kobold*, so the legend goes, is the name of a malicious spirit that bedevilled miners trespassing into the secret corridors of the earth. When prospectors found themselves sick and dying after handling the rich blue smaltite ore in silver mines, they attached the superstitious name to the offending substance. Eventually, an 18th-century Swedish mineralogist, Georg Brandt, would reveal that an entirely new metal, one that is bound up with crude smaltite (the first metal discovered since antiquity), was in fact the real source of the trouble, as it invariably brought with it the highly pernicious metalloid arsenic.[5] Although there was nothing supernatural about its toxicity, the ominous nickname, 'cobalt', stuck.

Chinese ceramicists were obsessed with the colour and made exquisite use of it, most notably in their celebrated 'blue and white' pottery created between the 14th and 18th centuries. Meanwhile, back in Germany, an obscure 17th-century female alchemist and author of the occult tome *On the Key to the Cabinet of the Secret Treasure Room of Nature* unlocked one of cobalt's most extraordinary qualities – an ability to shine momentarily into resplendence and then vanish completely. Known to history only by her initials, 'D. J. W.', the enterprising adept isolated a cobalt compound that was curiously chameleon under certain conditions. 'When the cobalt was prepared and turned into a solution with which to write,' reports the historian and sociologist Kristie Macrakis, who chronicles

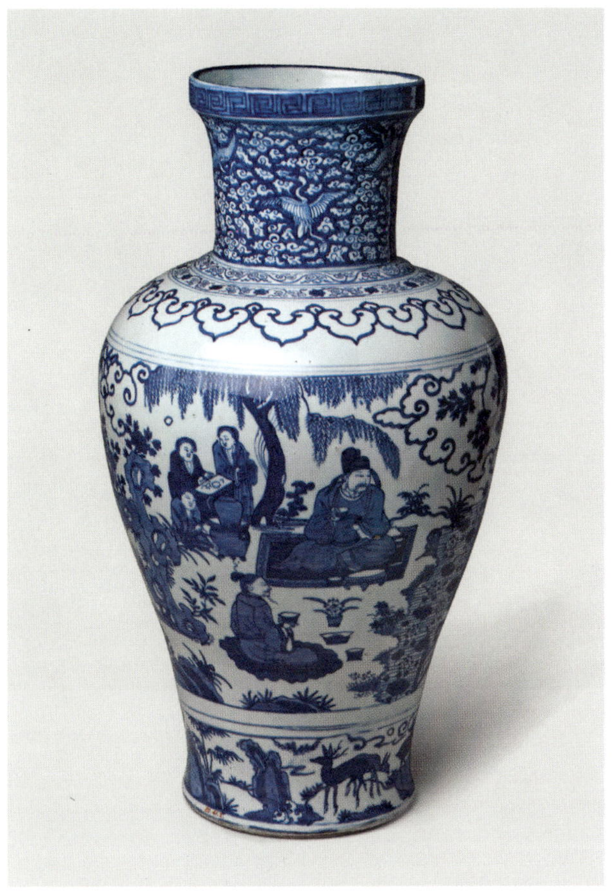

Vase with poet Zhou Dunyi, China, Ming dynasty, 1587

D. J. W.'s breakthrough in her study *Prisoners, Lovers, and Spies: The Story of Invisible Ink from Herodotus to Al-Qaeda*, 'it was clear, but it produced a fabulous blue-green color when heated.' Most astonishing of all, Macrakis notes, 'the writing disappeared when cooled.'[6]

The ensuing decades would witness a spirited continental tussle between French and German scientists keen to explain

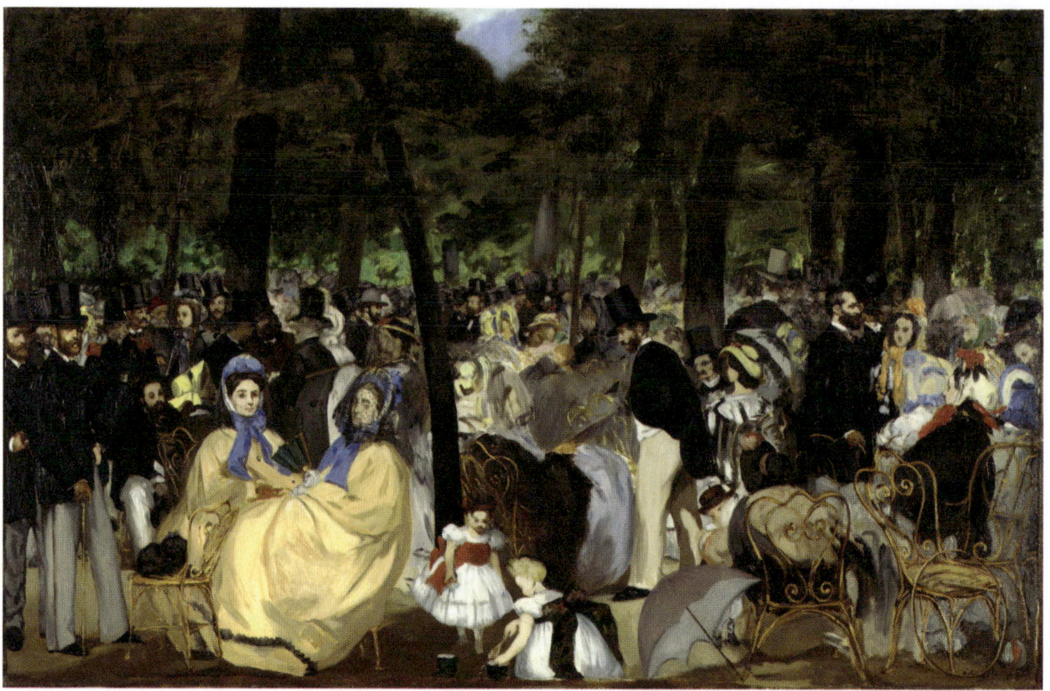

Édouard Manet, *Music in the Tuileries Gardens*, 1862

(and to take credit for explaining) the precise chemical processes responsible for cobalt's magical power to dazzle then disappear. Much to the chagrin of German scientists who believed that they had cracked cobalt's code first, it was a Frenchman, Jean Hellot, who gave the secretive substance the name by which it would widely be known: 'Hellot's Sympathetic Ink'. Among the most fascinating applications of the fleeting blue hue, aside from its use as a tool by spies composing clandestine missives, was its role in the creation of breathtaking fire screens that began to appear in Paris in the middle of the 18th century. At first glance, and prior to a flame being kindled behind them, these fashionable partitions would seem to depict nothing more than an austere winter scene of leafless trees, articulated by a spare armature of Indian-ink lines denoting nude branches. 'The artist then painted a solution of cobalt chloride on the screen,' Macrakis explains. 'The cobalt was invisible initially, but as soon as the heat from the fire reached the screen, the barren winter landscape magically turned into a verdant landscape. When the heat was removed, the landscape became barren winter again.'

In these evanescent visions, cobalt amounted to nothing less than the secret ingredient of life's ephemeral plenitude. In Édouard Manet's groundbreaking *Music in the Tuileries Gardens* (1862), often cited as 'the first modern painting' for its sketchy style and elusive subject, cobalt's transformative potential is put to ingenious use. The work, a hustle of rustling textures as a crowd of Parisian intellectuals and their families gathers in the shade of chestnut trees for a concert near the Louvre, is admired for its informal celebration of informality – the seemingly unstaged shuffle of fabrics, shadows and flesh suspended in a flash by canvas and brush. An especially intriguing episode in the painting's meditation on the fleetingness of time is the poignant mirroring of two ladies identically clad in fashionably billowy, cream-coloured gowns in the foreground of the work – twins but for the gap of years between them. The pair, who sit to the left of the work's centre (near to the artist's own stick-wielding self-portrait at the edge of the canvas), are perfect reflections of each other, the same self separated by generations. Manet's decision to enwreathe their countenances with bonnets sculpted from cobalt blue, a bracing hue that snags our eye more sharply than nearly any other pigment in the work, only accentuates the suggestion that the two visages are time-elapsed portraits of a single person at different moments in the span of life's flame. The result is a work that seems to shudder before our very eyes, like a fire-screen that flickers in a hot breath between the winter and spring of existence.

Cerulean

At the same moment that Manet was creating his early masterpiece, the English colourman George Rowney began marketing a scintillating spin on cobalt blue inspired by the work of a Swiss chemist, Albrecht Höpfner, who had begun experimenting almost a century earlier with adding tin oxides to the pigment. Christened by Rowney 'coeruleum', meaning 'sky-coloured' (a name that would eventually smooth into 'cerulean'), the chromatic cousin of cobalt would strike a chord with imaginations as seemingly far flung in vision and verve as Paul Signac's and Pablo Picasso's - an emotionally sonorous chord that continues to resonate to this day. For the stacked horizons of his ongoing series of abstract soulscapes, *Landline* - brushy bands that blur the borders between the flow of air and water, thought and breath - the Irish-American artist Sean Scully hears in the pulse of cerulean blue an affecting echo of the colour of a tricycle that he rode as a small child around the streets of London, where his family moved when he was a toddler after a homeless start on the streets of Dublin in the 1940s. 'I remember I had a bicycle. And I'll never forget it. It was cerulean blue,' Scully once told me. 'Cerulean blue is that lovely pale blue. I will never forget the colour of that little bicycle, a three-wheeler. I used to ride all around the Old Kent Road on my own, and make up these fantasies about where I was going.'[7]

Listening to the mute jangle of Scully's blue-strung 'Landlines', fluid instruments that harmonize the physical and psychological, we too are transported to a boundless realm that ripples outside of place and time. In *Landline Blue See* (2016), painted six decades later when Scully was seventy-one, the full spectrum of blues is on display. At its equator, a band of cerulean divides the painting's consciousness into the interdependent hemispheres of hereness and thereness, body and mind, innocence and maturity, and serves as a pivotal rung in the ladder of the soul. The tricycle of Scully's childhood, which seems to

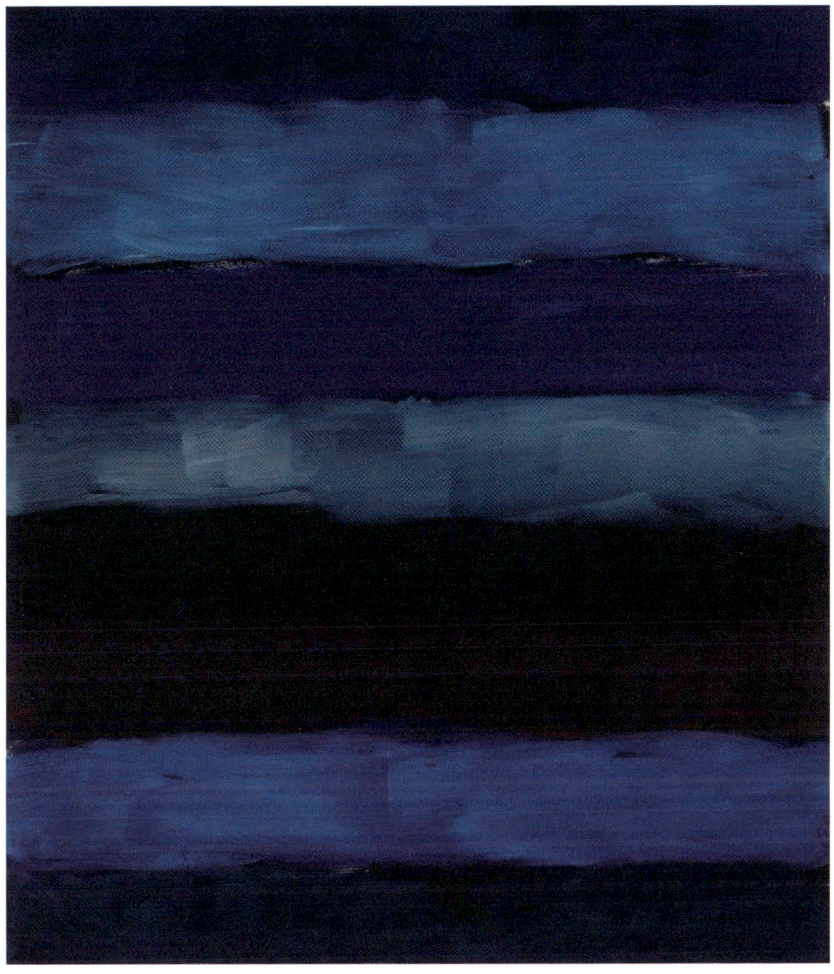

Sean Scully, *Landline Blue See*, 2016

symbolize the freedom of self-propelled conveyance through the world and which he has compared with the 'Rosebud' sleigh in Orson Welles's *Citizen Kane* – an intractable talisman of intense memory – still spins in his mature work, still provides the pedalled traction of perceiving and recording what it means to be alive.

Prussian Blue

According to legend, one of the more curious chapters in the life of the colour blue was written in Berlin in the early years of the 18th century.[8] It was then, some time around 1706, that the shadowy German occultist Johann Konrad Dippel was busy in his lab endeavouring to concoct a universal elixir for all human ailments – a diversion that occupied the imaginations of many alchemists stymied in their search for the elusive Philosopher's Stone. A congenitally colourful figure, Dippel was born in Castle Frankenstein in 1673. His tendency to meander the shadier margins of respectable intellectual enquiry, including efforts to transfer souls with a funnel from one cadaver to another, has led some literary scholars to suspect he may be the inspiration for Mary Shelley's famous fictional scientist.

On this particular occasion, it was Dippel's failure that proved an unexpected boon, both to himself and to culture. Resigned to the fact that his elixir recipe was still in need of serious tinkering, he went to discard the claggy concoction of potash (or wood ash soaked in water), to which he'd added a healthy ladle of bovine blood, when the dye maker with whom he shared his workshop, Johann Jacob Diesbach, suddenly stopped him. Diesbach, as it happens, was up against the clock trying to fill an order for cochineal red (see page 31) when he realized that he was fresh out of potash – a key ingredient in producing the pigment. Recycling Dippel's leftovers, Diesbach was apparently unconcerned by the interjection of a little animal blood in a brew that already contained the pulverized bodies of countless scarlet insects and was intended to be red anyway. Who would need to know about the secret additive?

Rather than intensifying the resulting dye, however, the adulterated potash appeared, at first, to yield a very weak pink solution that Diesbach knew would be unacceptable to his client. With no option but to try and make the makeshift mixture work, Diesbach resolved to reduce the concoction and concentrate the colour. For a moment, the effort seemed to pay off. The hue began to deepen in the vat. He kept stirring and was surprised to see the emulsion suddenly turn purple ... and then blue![9] Not just any blue, either, but a stunning hue that surpassed the vigour of azurite and appeared to rival the resplendence of ultramarine.

Dippel, who was better versed in the whys and wherefores of chemical reactions than Diesbach, concluded that the contamination of the dye with blood was responsible for producing what we now know today as potassium ferrocyanide – the first purely synthetic pigment ever produced. The pair recognized immediately the commercial potential for their chance discovery and did their best to keep its fluky formula under wraps as they began ramping up production of the new pigment. The art world would soon be awash in what would become known as Prussian Blue, after the region of its accidental conception.

A year after their fortuitous collaboration, Dippel was on the run, fleeing the arms of the law that were hoping to nab him for one or other of his dubious initiatives, leaving Diesbach behind to capitalize on the lucrative recipe. Dippel eventually set up shop in the Netherlands, where he established a rival operation to Diesbach's enterprise in Berlin. For well over a decade the two succeeded in controlling the market for Prussian Blue, until a German apothecary by the name of Caspar Neumann managed to reverse-engineer the pigment's code in 1723. Neumann soon shared the elaborate formula (which required '4 ounces of well-dried and finely powdered ox blood') with the English naturalist John Woodward, who, in turn, published it in the *Philosophical Transactions of the Royal Society* in 1724, effectively ending Dippel and Diesbach's monopoly.

The bewitching backstory to Prussian Blue's inadvertent invention – how it emerged murkily from the mist of a conjurer's cauldron – added to the colour's allure and inflected its lustre. 'Nothing is perhaps more peculiar than the process by which one obtains Prussian blue,' Jean Hellot would observe decades later, 'and it must be owned that, if chance had not taken a hand, a profound theory would be necessary to invent it.'[10] Stable, less toxic and (perhaps most significantly of all) more affordable than its predecessors, Prussian Blue was quickly adopted by artists. In Italy, Giovanni Antonio Canal was among the first to embrace the pigment. His *Stonemason's Yard* (*c.* 1725), in which Canaletto (as he was commonly called) captures the muscular music of an impromptu construction site from which a refurbishment of the church of San Vidal was being conducted, is, at first glance, a poetic tribute to the tussle of tough textures, as dawn light scrapes against a cacophony of wood huts and shattered stone. The imagined mingle of a cock crowing and a child crying intensifies the hectic atmosphere. But Canaletto has sealed his curious kettle of shadows and sounds with an incongruously ethereal lid: an evaporative sky magicked from the semi-translucence of a Prussian Blue, tinging his vision with an inchoate mysticism - an unexpected alchemy that, like the pigment itself, transcends the sum of its visceral parts.

A century later, the Japanese *ukiyo-e* artist and printmaker Katsushika Hokusai will reach for Prussian Blue as the colour best suited for striating the static surge of his famous *Great Wave* (the first image in his series of woodblock prints *Thirty-six Views of Mount Fuji, c. 1830–32*), infusing the inscrutable work with a literal layer of material mystery. The sublimity of the image relies for its effect on the endlessly suspended peril of the three crews who remain for eternity just beyond the clutch of the rabid foam's rapacious fingers. By sculpting

OPPOSITE TOP Canaletto, *The Stonemason's Yard*, *c.* 1725

OPPOSITE BOTTOM Katsushika Hokusai, *Under the Wave off Kanagawa*, also known as *The Great Wave*, from the series *Thirty-six Views of Mount Fuji*, *c.* 1830–32

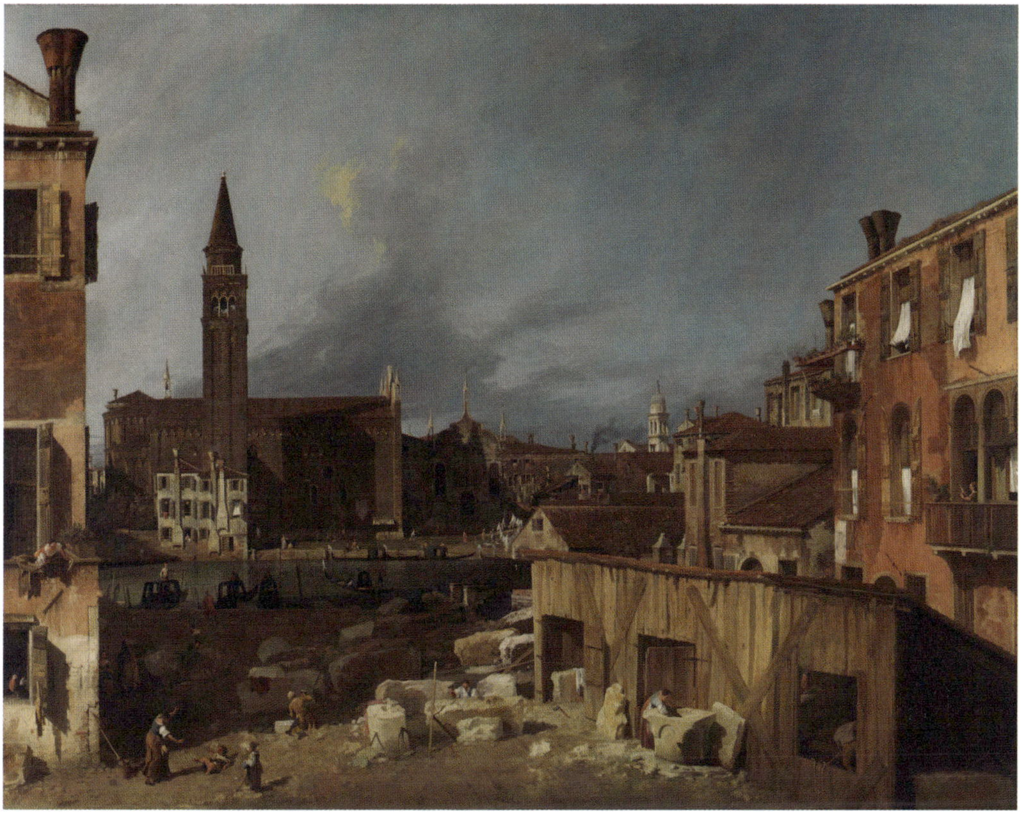

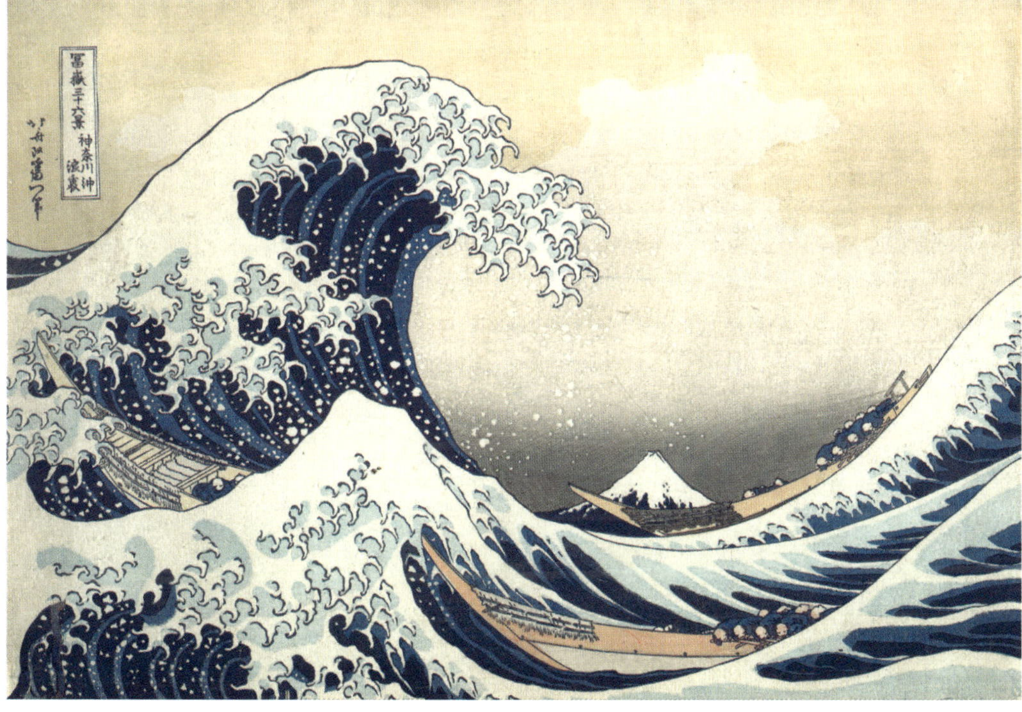
冨嶽三十六景
神奈川沖
浪裏

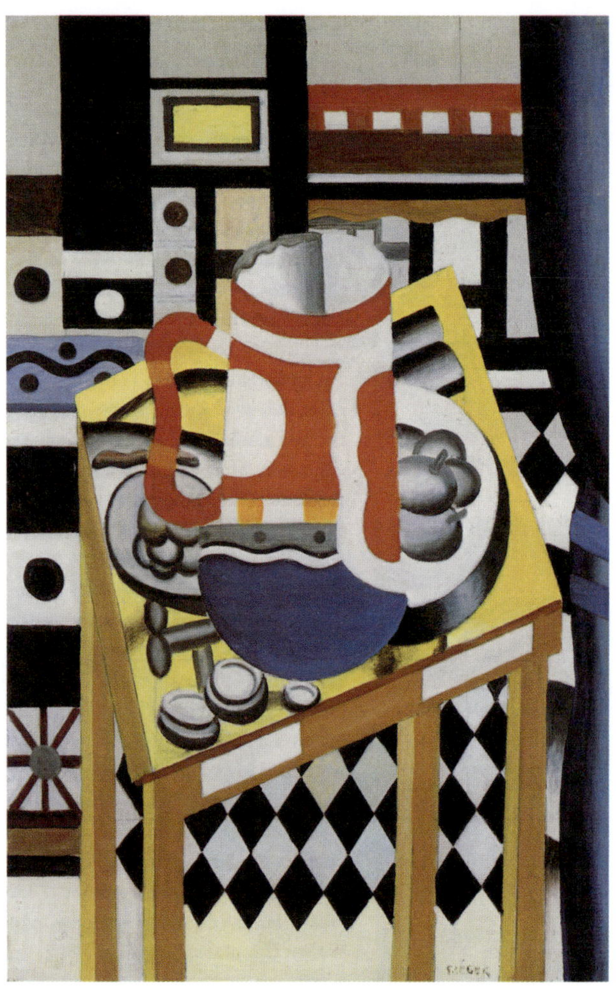

Fernand Léger, *Still Life with a Beer Mug*, 1921–22

the colossal crest of his bloodthirsty wave, which is thicker than water, from a pigment whose ferocity depends on the admixture of actual blood, Hokusai laces his scene with a haematic hermeticism. The esoteric genesis of Prussian Blue establishes an unexpected bloodline that links works as disparate in meaning as Canaletto's absorbing *Stonemason's Yard*, Hokusai's thrillingly suspenseful *Great Wave*, and the introspective geometry of Fernand Léger's *Still Life with a Beer Mug* (1921–22).

Artificial Ultramarine

The story of blue never ends. Our search for ever deeper shades is insatiable. While the prohibitive price that ultramarine commanded for centuries may explain an acute and urgent urge to find cheaper alternatives for such a lush shade - including the prize offered in 1824 by France's Société d'Encouragement pour l'Industrie Nationale for a suitable synthetic substitute - our perennial quest for blue is ultimately more existential than economic. Equated with the sea and sky and the breath between them, blue has become a metaphor for the very medium in which our souls are suspended in the universe. Looking for blue, we look for ourselves. In 1828, a French chemist working in Toulouse, Jean-Baptiste Guimet, was awarded the Société's prize of 6,000 francs (roughly 37,600 euros in today's money) for his canny concoction of sand and charcoal, soda and clay, which he cooked into a glossy green mirror that could be shattered into

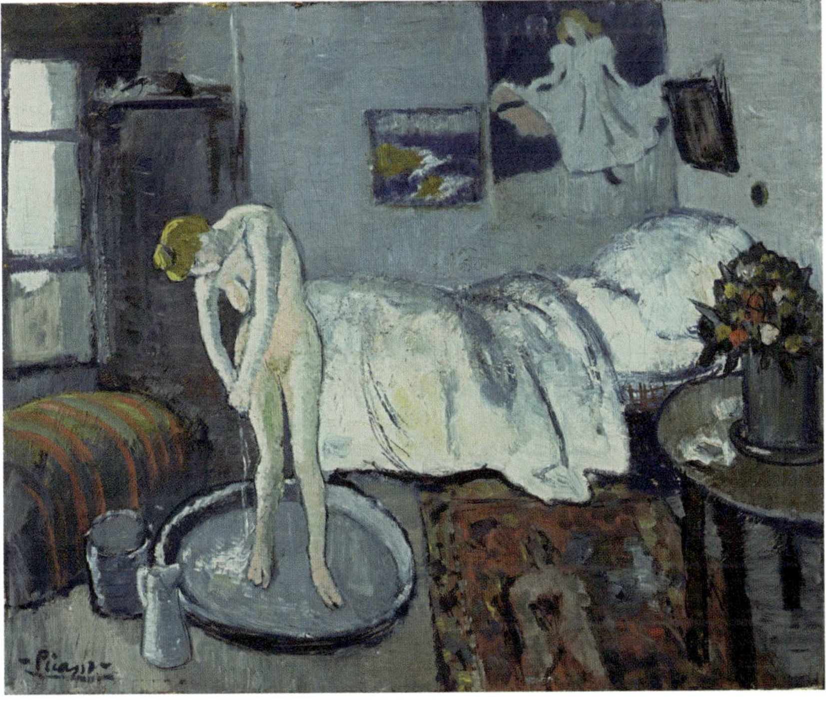

Pablo Picasso, *The Blue Room*, 1901

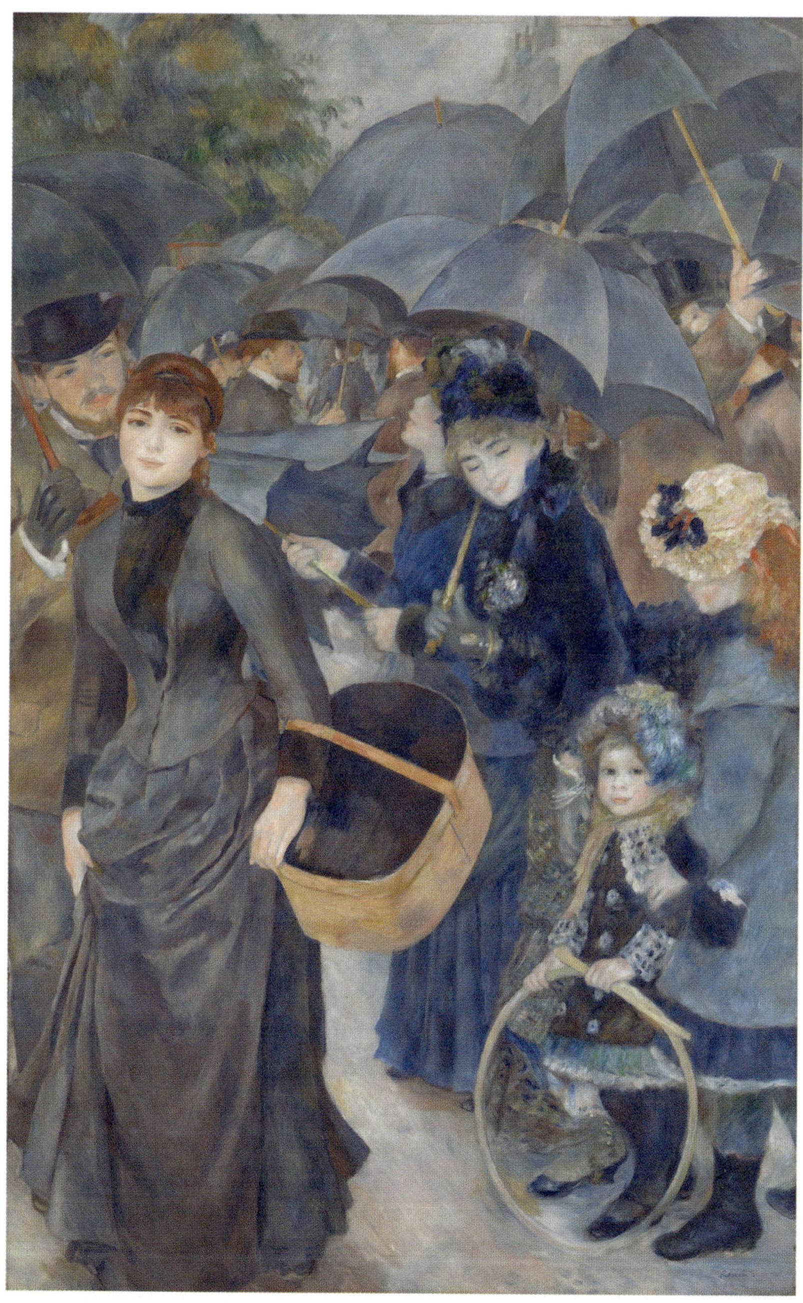

Pierre-Auguste Renoir, *The Umbrellas*, *c.* 1881–86

Artificial Ultramarine

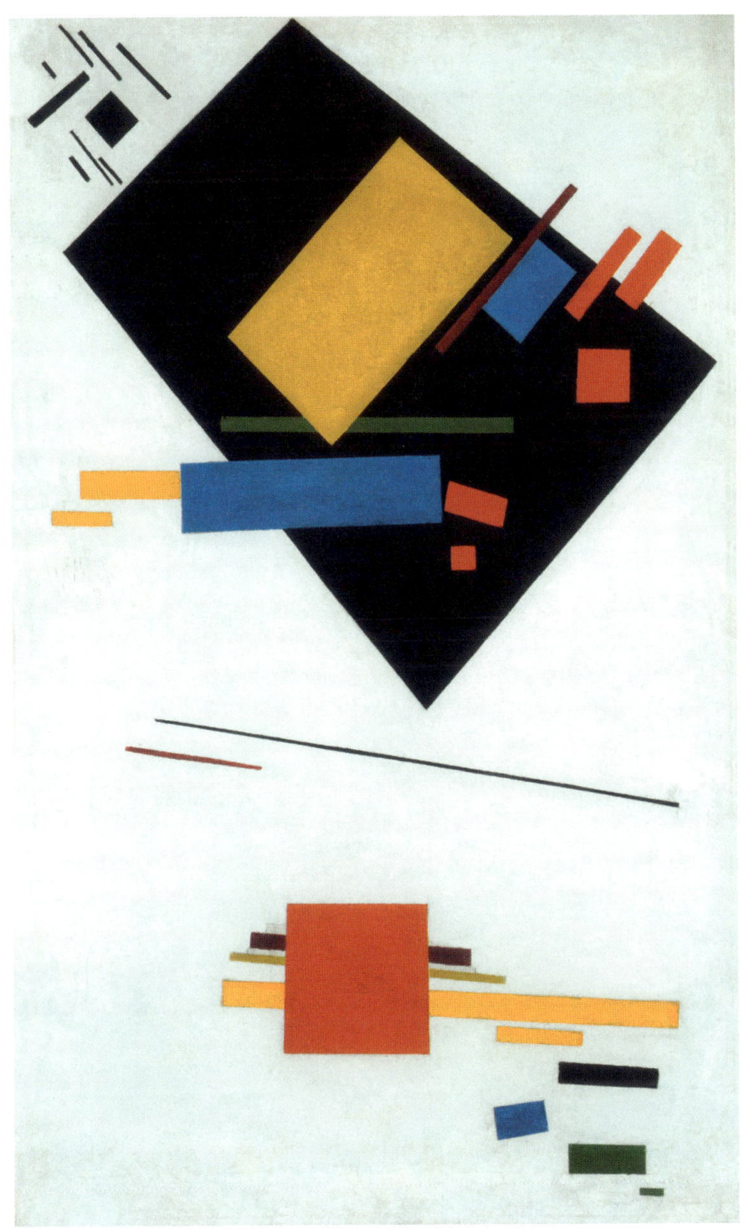

Kazimir Malevich, *Suprematist Painting (with Black Trapezium and Red Square)*, 1915

Yves Klein, *Untitled Blue Monochrome (IKB 181)*, 1956

bright blue powder. The new pigment would prove indispensable to such masterpieces as Pablo Picasso's *The Blue Room* (1901), Renoir's *The Umbrellas* (*c.* 1881–86) and Kazimir Malevich's *Suprematist Painting (with Black Trapezium and Red Square)* (1915). Placed side by side, the jostle of umbrellas in Renoir's canvas (which preserves both the cobalt blue the Impressionist favoured early in his career and the artificial ultramarine he preferred later) and the jumble of shapes in Malevich's create an invigorating dialogue of jousting geometries and bickering blues. Despite Guimet's breakthrough (an achievement matched simultaneously, if not slightly earlier, by a German chemist working in Tübingen), the persistent pursuit of an ever-bluer blue continued unabated.

International Klein Blue

In the 1950s, the French artist Yves Klein attached his name to a method for mixing ultramarine with a matte resin that helped the pigment retain its intensity. He called the proprietary process 'International Klein Blue', placed a premium on its license, and began unveiling works consisting solely of a field of pure, undifferentiated blue, unsullied by shape or shade – a savvy move that demonstrated beyond doubt that colour could transcend form or function; that the mere idea of colour could be elevated to the status of iconic, unforgettable art.

Philipp Otto Runge's Colour Sphere

(1810)

The year 1810 was a profound one for colour. Not only did it see the publication of Goethe's famous and influential *Theory of Colours*, it also witnessed the untimely death, at just thirty-three years of age, of Geothe's friend and fellow chromophile, the aspiring German Romantic painter Philipp Otto Runge. Runge had himself been tinkering with an ambitious model for mapping the complexities of colour. Conceived as a luminous globe that twists around an axis that runs between pure white at one pole and pure black at the other, Runge's *Farbenkugel* (Colour Sphere) spins off the flat surface of the page like an undiscovered celestial orb. Although Runge succumbed to tuberculosis in the same year in which his ideas were first published, and was therefore unable to help propel them into the realm of cultural discourse, their impact could still be detected a century later, whirring in the imagination of Bauhaus artists and thinkers.

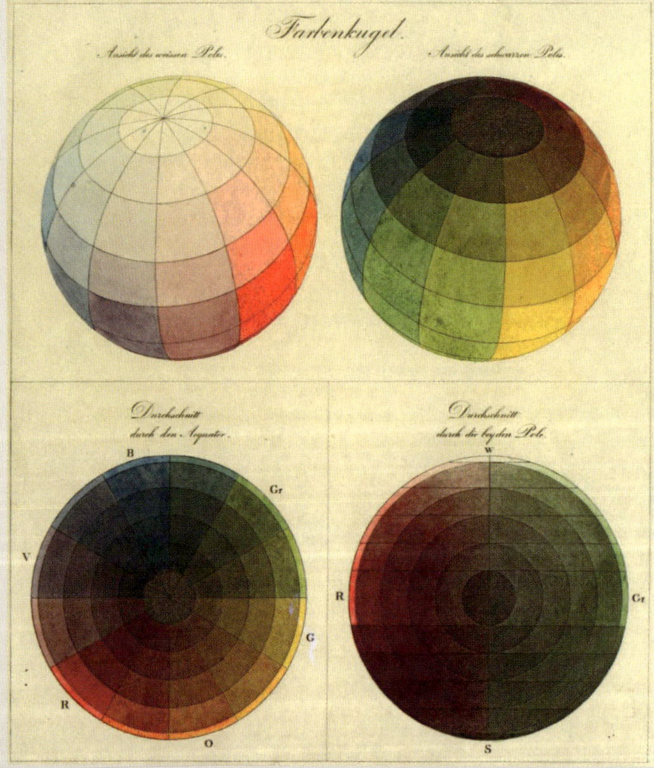

Resembling a globe, Runge's Colour Sphere is comprised of twelve longitudinal zones. The purest colours are found encircling the equator. Between each of the three primary colours (red, blue and yellow) are gradations of secondary colours (orange, green and purple). With white and black constituting the sphere's two poles, the remaining spaces of the globe, north and south of the equator, show lighter and darker hues of each colour.

With this diagram (right), appended to Runge's treatise, the theorist endeavoured to illustrate the 'harmonizing' and 'disharmonizing' effects of various colour combinations and how to modulate unwanted discordancies. Runge's invocation of musical terminology throughout his writings is striking, and recalls Isaac Newton's equation of individual colours with specific musical notes.

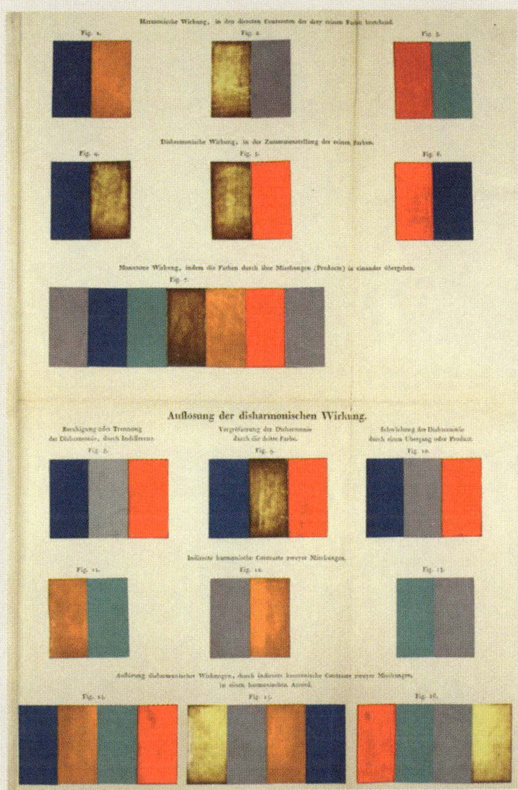

Contemporary Icelandic-Danish artist Olafur Eliasson's 2005 luminous sculpture *Flowerball* (below) recalls the kaleidoscopic spin of Runge's theoretical diagram. The work's halogen bulb casts prismatic shapes onto surrounding walls, echoing the splendour of Newton's first forays into colour theory.

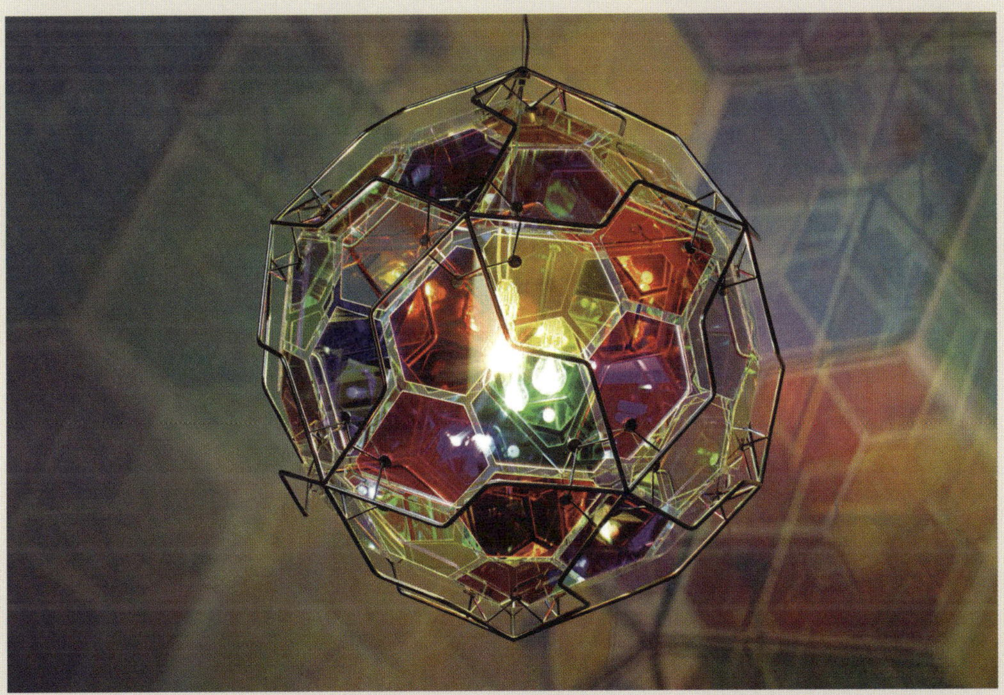

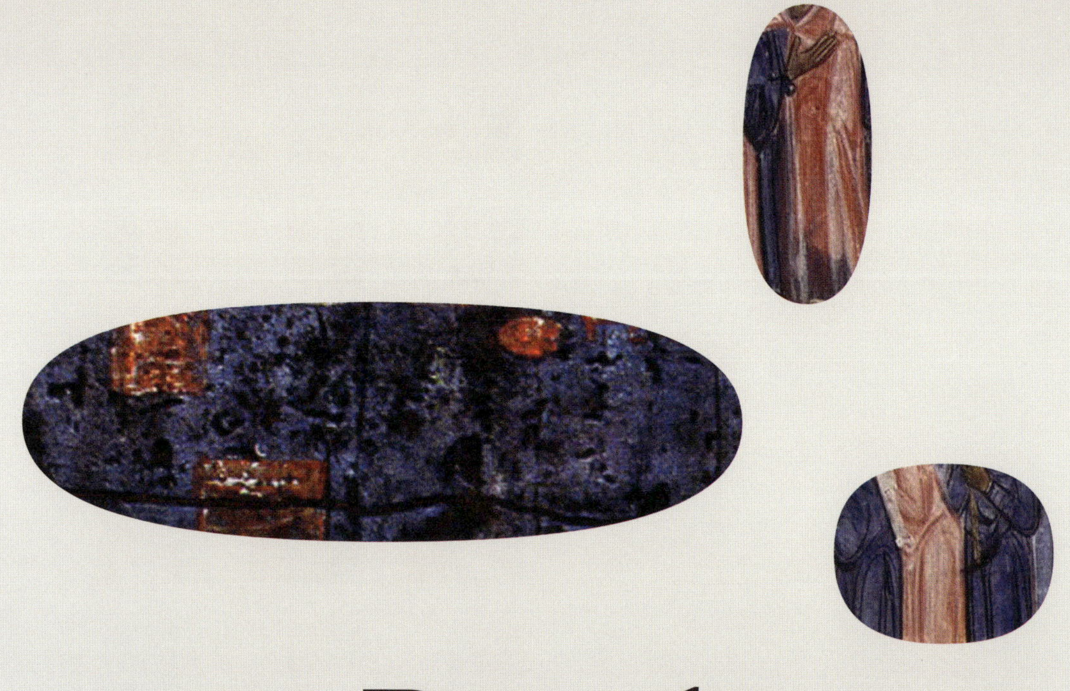

Purple

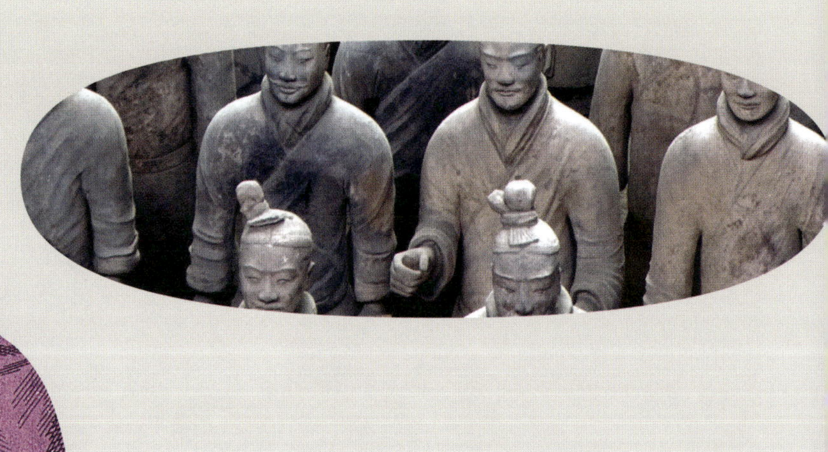

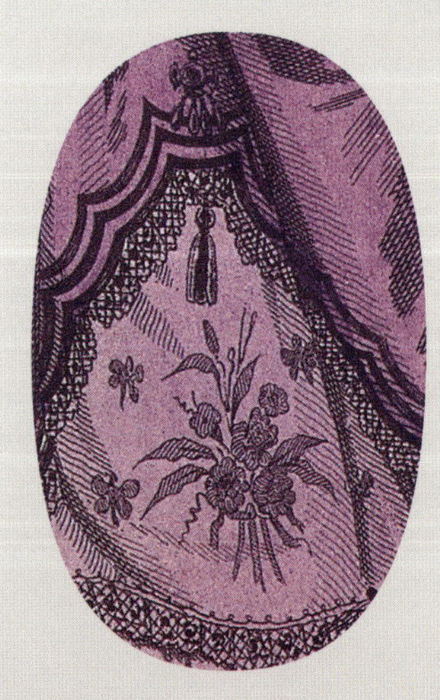

'A pigeon walking dainty in the street', observes Margaret Steele Anderson at the outset of her 1921 poem 'Purple' – an elegant six-line lyric with which the American writer endeavours to cleanse the colour of connotations that have encrusted it for centuries:

The morning mist where backyard fences meet;
An old Victoria and in it, proud,
An old, old woman, ready for her shroud:
These are the purple sights for me,
Not palaces nor pageantry.[1]

Anderson's effort to rescue purple from its elevated status – as a colour suited solely to 'palaces' and 'pageantry' – and to bring it down to earth is an uphill one. However evocatively the colour may describe the iridescent shimmer of a prosaic pigeon's pedestrian stride, the diaphanous brume that sweeps urban fences into a dazzling dawn-lit blur, or the lucent pallor of an 'old, old woman, ready for her shroud', our imaginations have long been conditioned to associate purple first and foremost with aristocratic privilege. We're prepared to accept the unpretentious rain as purple, but only if a prince tells us so.

While the blood of noblemen may be blue, the DNA of power is patently purple. A claim to have been 'born and bred in the purple', as Anna Komnene, the 12th-century Byzantine princess and author of the medieval chronicle *Alexiad*, insists she was, was more than merely a metaphorical assertion of one's royal legitimacy. It was a literal description of an extravagant nativity. 'The emperor returned to the capital with the laurels of victory', Komnene writes, setting the scene of her own origin story:

He found the empress in the throes of childbirth,
in the room set apart long ago for an empress's
confinement. Our ancestors called it the porphyra
hence the world famous name porphyrogenitus.

> *At dawn (it was a Saturday) a baby girl was born to them, who resembled her father, so they say, in all respects. I was that baby.*[2]

'The room set apart long ago for an empress's confinement', to which Komnene refers, was an extraordinary delivery chamber in the Great Palace of Constantinople reserved exclusively for expecting empresses. Perfectly square in its dimensions and crowned with a pyramidal ceiling, its walls were covered with a ravishing violet veneer derived from the igneous rock porphyry (meaning 'purple' in Greek). Since at least the 6th century, the concept of *porphyrogénnētos* (literally, 'begotten in the purple') had been invoked to distinguish (and to prioritize) potential heirs who were actually born during their father's reign from those who were born prior to his assumption of the throne. To be 'born in the purple' was to bear the indelible stain of one's divine right to rule.

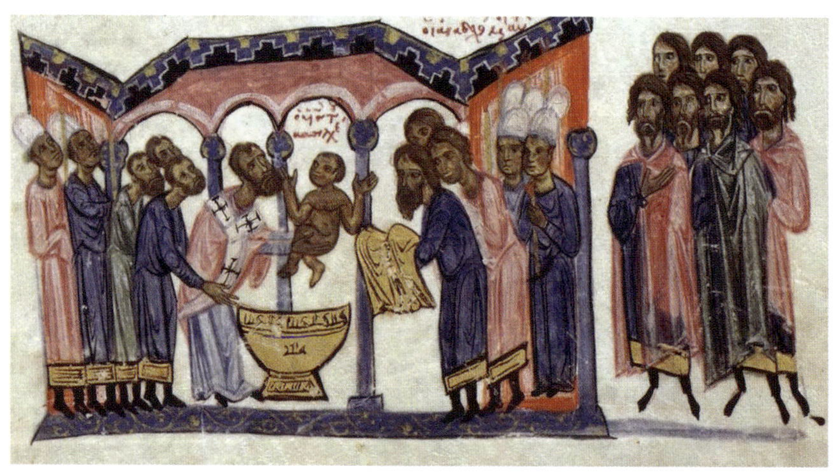

Illumination from the Byzantine Greek manuscript of John Skylitzes, 11th century CE

Tyrian Purple

Why purple? The connection between power and purple predates the periwinkle pampering of Anna Komnene by many millennia. Traces of a purple pigment composed of a barium copper silicate have been found on the walls of 1st-century BCE imperial tombs in China and on the 3rd-century terracotta soldiers discovered in Xian, China, in 1974. But its story starts much earlier still. It is suspected that in the 16th century BCE a process for procuring a prized and pricey purple dye had been perfected in ancient Phoenicia – whose complex place-name itself conflates the resonance of two Greek words: *phoinix* (meaning 'the colour purple') and *phoinos* (meaning 'blood red'). Produced in the Phoenician city of Tyre, among the world's oldest inhabited metropolises, the pigment known variously as 'Tyrian purple' or 'Phoenician red' was derived from putrid secretions of predatory murex sea snails.

As only the tiniest trickle of the malodorous dye could be coaxed from a given snail's hypobranchial gland – a defensive organ used by the creature when alive to paralyse its prey – the pigment was preposterously expensive. It is estimated that a quarter of a million snails were required to produce a single ancient *uncia* (or ounce) of the dazzling dye. Exceedingly scarce, the colour was reserved exclusively for the staining of royal apparel and paraphernalia. '[This] precious colour', notes Pliny the Elder, 'which gleams with the hue of a dark rose ...',

> *This is the purple for which the Roman fasces and axes clear a way. It is the badge of noble youth; it distinguishes the senator from the knight; it is called in to appease the gods. It brightens every garment and shares with gold the glory of the triumph. For these reasons we must pardon the mad desire for purple.*[3]

•

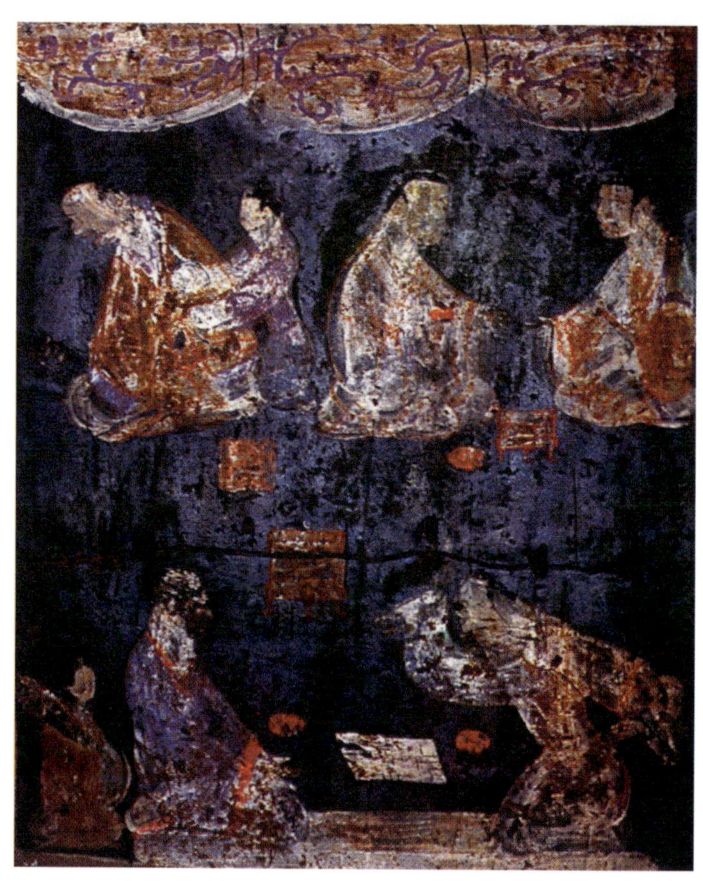

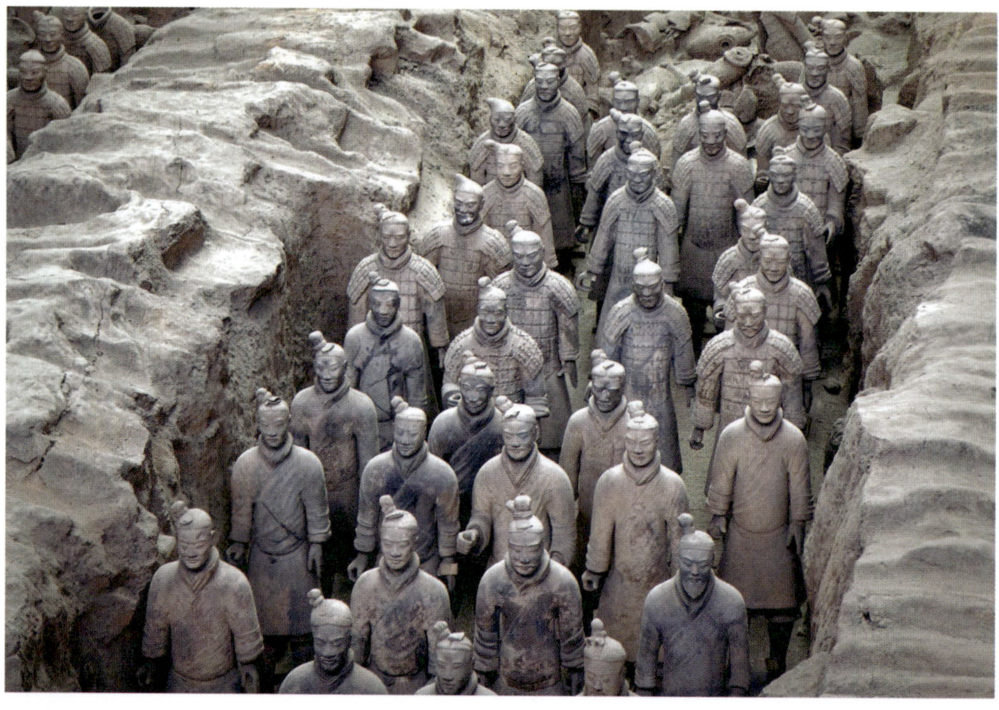

OPPOSITE TOP Mural from an Eastern Han tomb near Luoyang, China, 25–220 CE, showing a pair of Liubo players, containing both Han blue and Han purple pigments

OPPOSITE BOTTOM Terracotta Army (detail), tomb of Qin Shi Huang Di, near Xi'an, China, Qin dynasty, 221–207 BCE

That mollusc mucus should have yielded such a cherished hue, one synonymous with wealth and privilege, is among the more curious chromatic ironies in the history of image-making. The colour may have stood for a higher order, but it stank of a lower ordure. In his pioneering treatise on biology, *Historia Animalium*, Aristotle painstakingly describes the insalubrious process of pinching the paltry pigment from the disassembled diaphragm of the still-living creature. 'The murex', he says,

> *is caught in the spring-time when engaged in the construction of the honeycomb; but it is not caught at any time about the rising of the dog-star, for at that period it does not feed, but conceals itself and burrows. The bloom of the animal is situated between the mecon (or quasi-liver) and the neck, and the co-attachment of these is an intimate one. In colour it looks like a white membrane, and this is what people extract; and if it be removed and squeezed it stains your hand with the colour of the bloom. There is a kind of vein that runs through it, and this quasi-vein would appear to be in itself the bloom. And the qualities, by the way, of this organ are astringent. It is after the murex has constructed the honeycomb that the bloom is at its worst. Small specimens they break in pieces, shells and all, for it is no easy matter to extract the organ; but in dealing with the larger ones they first strip off the shell and then abstract the bloom. For this purpose*

> *the neck and mecon are separated, for the bloom lies in between them, above the so-called stomach; hence the necessity of separating them in abstracting the bloom. Fishermen are anxious always to break the animal in pieces while it is yet alive, for, if it die before the process is completed, it vomits out the bloom.*[4]

Once extracted, the secretions were put in a vat that was simmered and skimmed again and again. As the air thickened with a garlicky stench, the colour inside the vat deepened as the dye magically matured from a bilious yellow to a regurgitative green, to a wholly unexpected vibrant violet. Different species of snail yielded different shades. In time, it was determined that adding a proportion of secretions from the *Buccinidae* family, which tended to produce a reddish violet dye, to the matte purple generated by murex snails created the most intense and stable hue – a shade 'dark by reflected, and brilliant by transmitted light' that Pliny equated with 'the colour of clotted blood'.[5]

To make the repulsive operation of shucking miniscule droplets of mucus from the shattered bodies of living snails tolerable, the ancients wrapped the odious ordeal in heroic legend, crediting the Phoenician god Melqart (the chief deity of Tyre) with the pigment's discovery. The Greeks saw it slightly differently, attaching the dye's invention instead to the story of Hercules, their god of strength, who, so the myth went, noticed his dog's teeth and tongue were brilliantly besmirched after biting a snail while the two were walking along a beach. Hercules had been on his way to win the favour of the Thessalian princess Tyro, who, it is said, clapped eyes on the dog's stained lips and immediately fell in love with the dazzling colour. Demanding a gown dyed in the unprecedented hue, Tyro seductively squeezed Hercules into agreeing to produce the pigment.

In 1636, Peter Paul Rubens, the Baroque master whose obsession with a crimson derived from crushed kermes insects

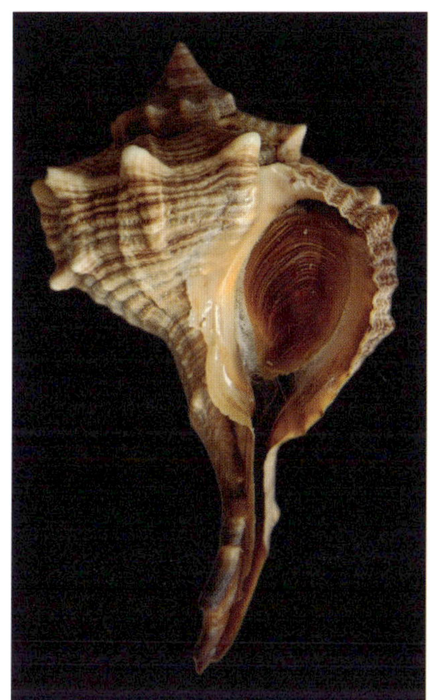
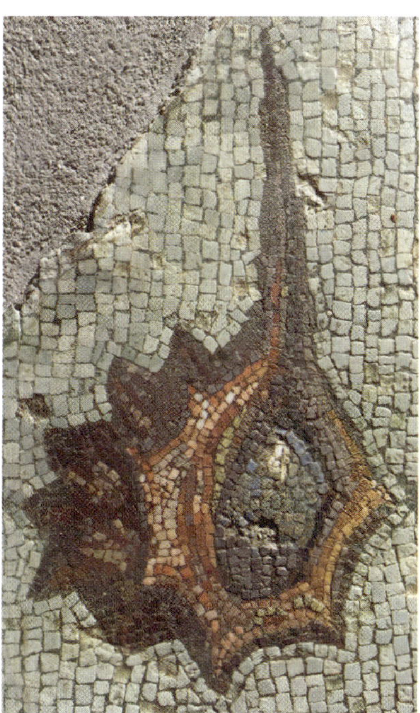

Bolinus brandaris, commonly known as the purple dye murex, and a Roman mosaic likely depicting a murex shell, late 2nd to early 1st centuries BCE

we looked at earlier, was taken by the colourful story, which he had come across in the *Onomasticon*, a reference book of names compiled by the 2nd-century Greek scholar Julius Pollux. Rubens selected it as one of the many classical scenes with which he would adorn the walls of the royal Spanish hunting lodge, Torre de la Parada, which he had been commissioned to decorate. Determined not to let conchological accuracy disfigure his picture, Rubens swaps the smaller murex shell for the alluring spiral of a much larger, canvas-ready nautilus as the victim of the dog's seaside snack. Although the myth of Tyrian purple's serendipitous discovery may have been permanently recorded

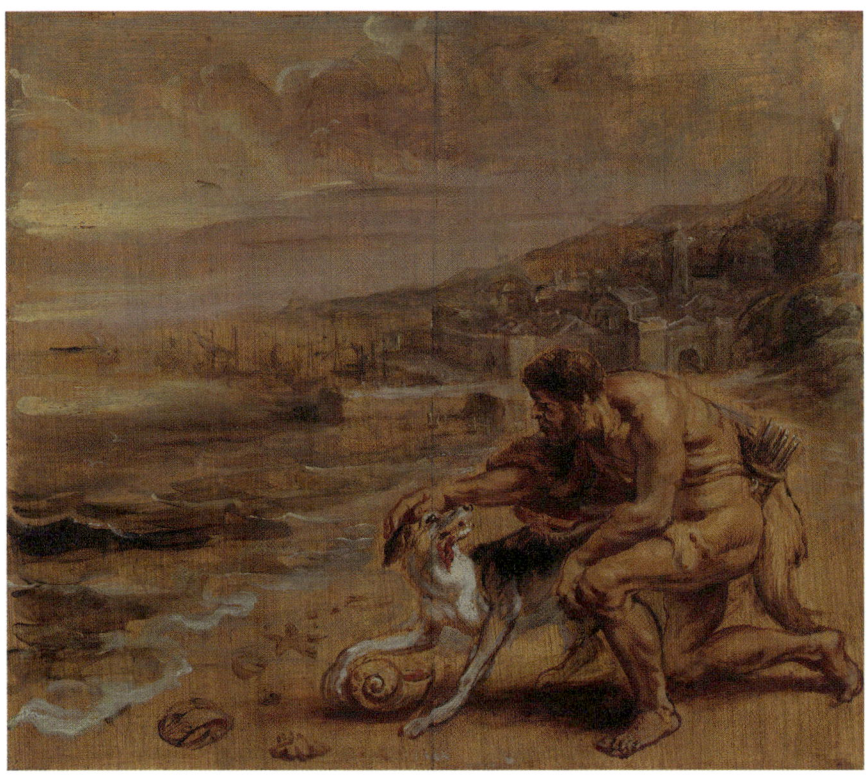

Peter Paul Rubens, *Hercules' Dog Discovers Purple Dye*, c. 1636

on Rubens's canvas (and on that of a contemporary, Theodoor van Thulden, who created an almost identical painting based on Rubens's original), the complex recipe itself had vanished from the pages of history with the fall of Constantinople two centuries earlier, in 1453, when the Turks captured the capital of the Byzantine empire. It would be another two centuries before the pioneering French malacologist Henri de Lacaze-Duthiers would sink his own teeth into the mystery of the missing purple in 1858, after stumbling across some molluscs in the Mediterranean, and dream the colour up again from scratch.[6]

Mauve

It was a red-letter year for violet. A few months earlier, a prodigious eighteen-year-old chemist by the name of William Perkin, working in a garden shed, had attempted to extract the anti-malarial elixir quinine from coal tar instead of the more costly South American cinchona tree and wound up creating a stunning purple emulsion by accident. Knowing his art history, Perkin quickly christened his chance concoction 'Tyrian purple', after the long-lost fabled pigment. Ultimately conceding that his contrived colour was in fact closer to the blossoms of the mallow plant (or *mauve* in French) than it was to the bloom of murex snails, Perkin revised the name accordingly.[7] Almost immediately, mauve caught fire with the public and seemed to seep into the fabric of every fashionable garment one could find. Not everyone liked it. *Punch* magazine labelled the frenzy

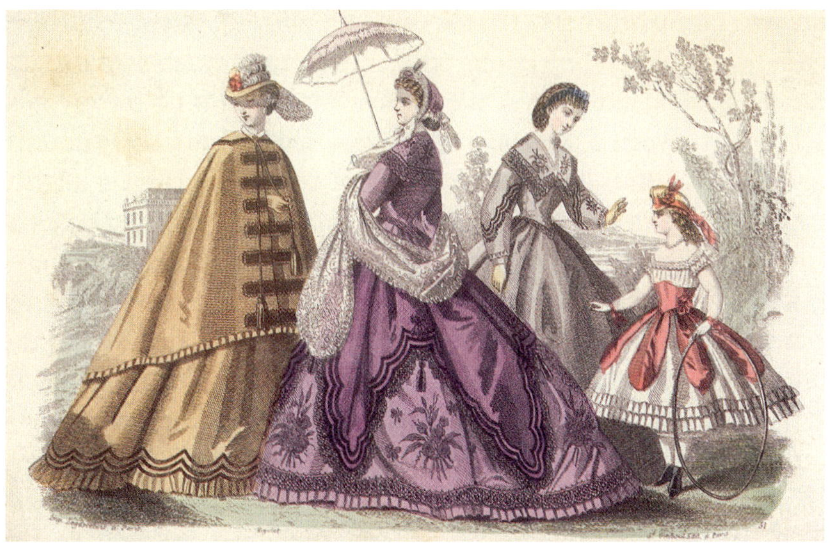

An illustration from *The Englishwoman's Domestic Magazine* showing the latest mauve fashions, 1864

'mauve measles' - a disease characterized by 'the eruption of a measly rash of ribbons above the head and neck'. Instantly rich, Perkin was tickled pink. 'Charles Dickens' periodical *All the Year Round*', notes the writer Philip Ball, 'sang Perkin's praises in September 1859':

> *As I look out my window, the apotheosis of Perkins's purple seems at hand - purple hands wave from carriages - purple hands shake each other at street doors - purple hands threaten each other from opposite sides of the street; purple-striped gowns cram barouches, jam up cabs, throng steamers, fill railway stations: all flying countryward, like so many migrating birds of Purple paradise.*[8]

Cobalt Violet

It wasn't only bonnets, shawls and bell-shaped skirts that were caught up in the contagious craze. The imaginations of artists were similarly stained. While it is estimated that no more than about 1 in every 2,000 paintings created before 1856 employ any semblance of purple, artists of the second half of the 19th century would soon be accused of falling victim to a virulent 'violettomania'. The same year that the lost code for Tyrian purple was reverse-engineered by Lacaze-Duthiers and mauve was mooted by Perkin, the French artist Eugène Delacroix was heralding the emergence, literally, of violet from the shadows. Writing in his journal in early September 1856, Delacroix meditates on the sight of 'a small urchin' who 'had climbed up one of the statues of [a] fountain in full sunlight'.[9] The painter noted that, properly observed, the shadows the boy cast were not, as commonly imagined and depicted, woven from shades of black, but from 'the most brilliant violets'.[10] Three years later, a French chemist, Jean Salvétat, succeeded in nudging the recipe for cobalt blue that Louis Jacques Thénard had devised in 1802 (see page 118) into the realm of violet, thereby creating the first purpose-built purple pigment in art history.[11]

Salvétat's innovation (which was superseded the following year by a more resilient manganese violet) was perfectly timed for the ensuing revolution in the way that artists perceived the world and where they stood to perceive it. The invention in 1841 by the American portraitist John Goffe Rand of a portable and collapsible paint tube, which replaced the cumbersome, easily rupturable pig's bladder purses that paint had previously been stored in, keeping easels indoors, was already pushing artists outside *en plein air*. Purple gave them purpose. Suddenly, natural shadows and the crepuscular light of the 'violet hour' (as T. S. Eliot would later describe it) could be scrutinized and transcribed first-hand. 'I have finally discovered the true colour of the atmosphere,' Édouard Manet would be overheard exclaiming to a group of friends in 1881. 'It's violet. Fresh air is violet. I found it! Three years from now everyone will do violet!'[12]

The reaction by some was scathing. The novelist and art critic Joris-Karl Huysmans insisted that the fascination with purple had gone too far: 'lands, skies, waters, flesh, everything', he said, 'was lilac and aubergine'.[13] The journalist Albert Wolff, writing in the influential French newspaper *Le Figaro*, was harsher still. In a devastating assessment of the lens through which the Impressionists saw life, Wolff compared the 'purplish spots' with which Renoir punctuated his bodies to 'heaps of decomposing flesh' and the 'complete putrefaction of a corpse'.[14]

The historian Alfred de Lostalot, however, reviewing an exhibition of Claude Monet's work in 1883, was rather more forgiving. He chalked up the obsession with purple to a congenital quirk that, he speculated, Monet and his circle may have shared. 'We know', he said,

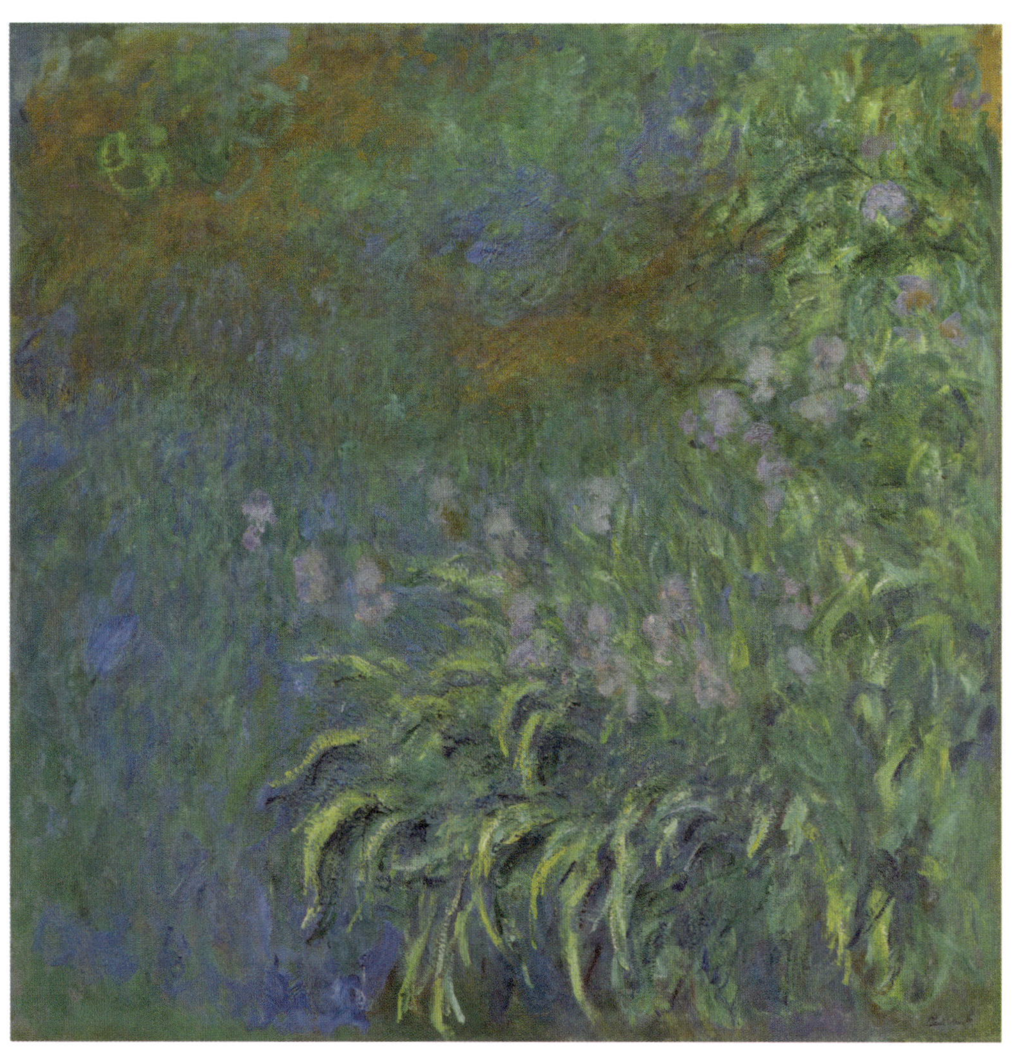

Claude Monet, *Irises*, 1914–17

> *that there is in the solar spectrum an area of rays that the lens intercepts in passing and which, therefore, do not impress the retina. This area, called ultra-violet because it extends beyond the violet radiations which everyone perceives, plays a considerable role in nature, but its effects are not of the optical order. However, recent experiments by M. de Chardonnet have absolutely demonstrated that this invisible part of the spectrum is keenly felt by a few people. M. Monet is certainly one of them; he and his friends see purple; the crowd sees differently, hence the disagreement.*[15]

Purple's multivalent past - the contradictory connotations it conjures of outmoded majesty, mollusc mucus, medicinal experimentation and modish whimsy - complicates the elegant light that glances off Monet's late, expressive portrait of irises (1914–17). Inspired by depictions of the flower he had seen in prints by Hokusai, Monet managed to import the Japanese flower into his own famous garden, recognizing that the colour was capable of collapsing seemingly irreconcilable cultural notes. Purple pulses through Monet's paintings like throbbing veins in polished marble. Whether, as Lostalot speculated, the artist's eye was unusually shaped, no one can say. That his soul was, however, is beyond doubt. His canvases are less the ledger of a colour he uniquely saw than proof of a world he uniquely felt. Monet's paintings do not merely evince violet. They breathe it.

Michel Eugène Chevreul's *The Principles of Harmony and Contrast of Colours* (1839)

While some theorists pull colours together, others pull them apart. Goethe and Philipp Otto Runge were very much of the former camp. Their wheels and globes, respectively, reweaved the colours of the rainbow that Newton's prism had prised apart by spinning them into ingeniously conceived shapes. In 1839, a formidable French chemist, whose research had revolutionized the manufacturing of candles and deepened our understanding of diabetes, proposed a new system for comprehending colour that blew chromatography to pieces, literally. Michel Eugène Chevreul had been summoned by a tapestry factory to investigate why its dyes were underperforming. Finding no problem with the dyestuffs themselves, Chevreul concluded that the problem lay with the weaving – that certain colours, when placed side by side, weaken each other's intensity, while others amplify their power. When he published his findings in the form of a treatise, *De la loi du contraste simultané des couleurs* (or *The Principles of Harmony and Contrast of Colours*, as it was known in English when translated in 1854), he included elaborate plates featuring a blizzard of coloured dots that show the effect of different colour combinations. The impact of Chevreul's ideas on the work of ensuing generations of artists, particularly the Neo-Impressionists, cannot be overstated.

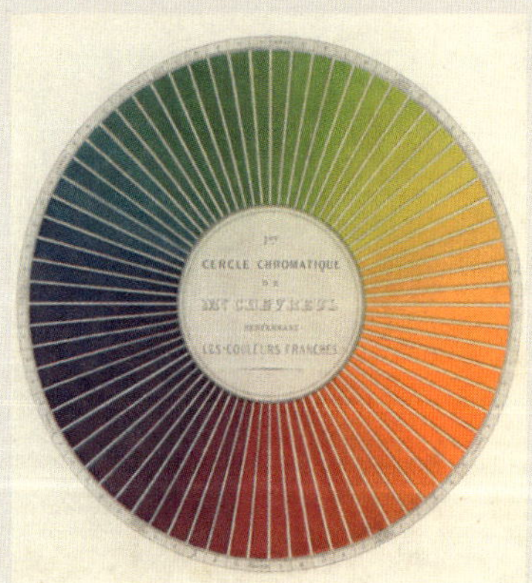

To help readers visualize his theory of colour contrast, Chevreul devised a series of colour wheels. Opposite each sliver of colour is the 'nuance' that most intensifies it.

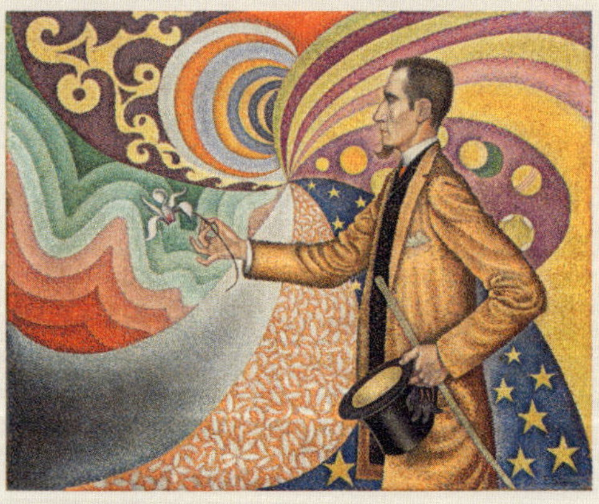

Translating Chevreul's ideas of contrast and harmony into artistic practice, French 'pointillist' artists Georges Seurat and Paul Signac developed a technique of applying small dots of paint side by side on their canvases.

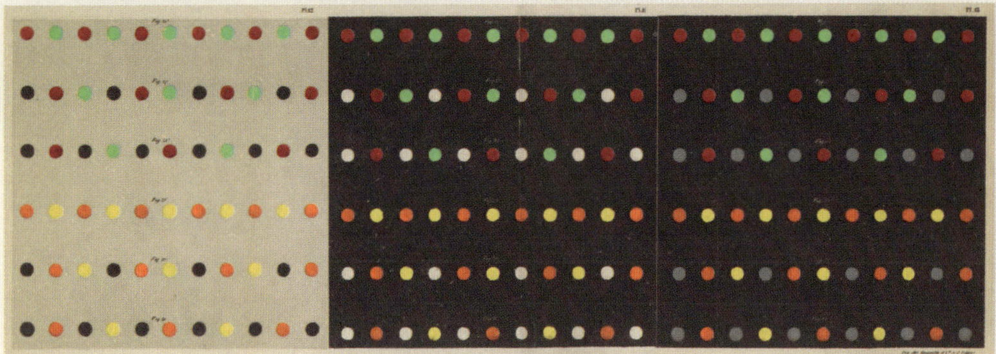

Chevreul's treatise illustrated how particular colour combinations, under varying conditions, created different effects – heightening or diminishing a given colour's power. The volume includes elaborate diagrams of painted dots against fields of neutral tones that anticipate abstract works by later, non-figurative artists. Above, plates 11, 12 and 13 from *The Principles of Harmony and Contrast of Colours* are captioned 'Assortments of two bright colours with white, black and grey'.

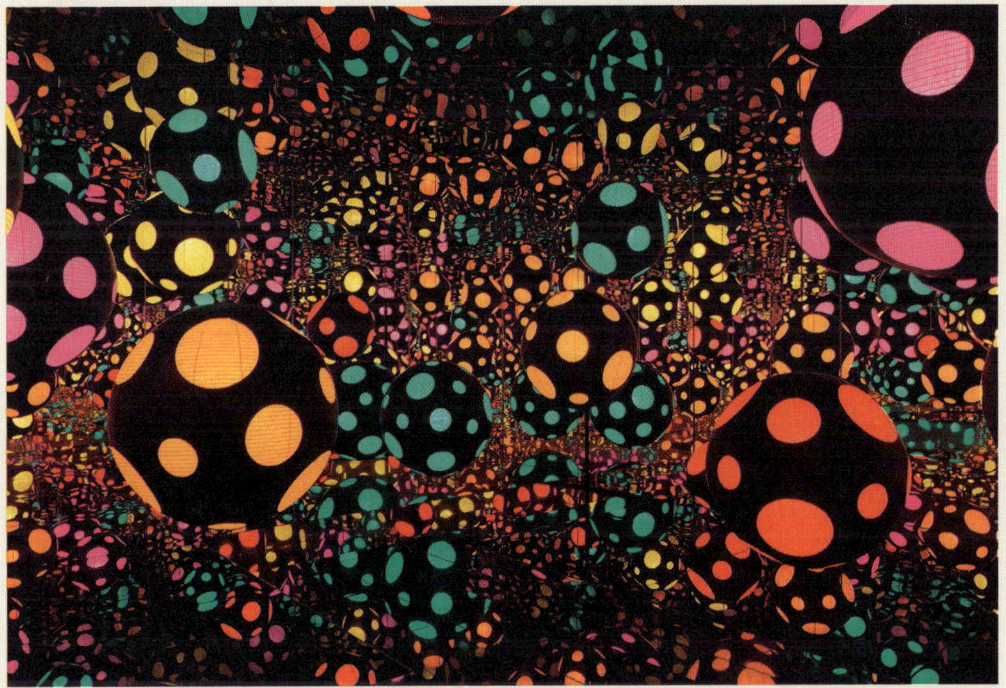

Contemporary Japanese artist Yayoi Kusama has spent a lifetime constructing an intensely personal visual language from the deceptively simple dot. When Kusama was around ten years old, she began having wild visions dominated by dots, flashes and fields of flowers that threatened to annihilate her. By covering her numerous prints, sculptures, installations and videos in an endless sea of polka dots, Kusama has sought to embrace, if not orchestrate, that obliteration. For the artist, dots symbolize the soul's simultaneously infinite and infinitesimal nature.

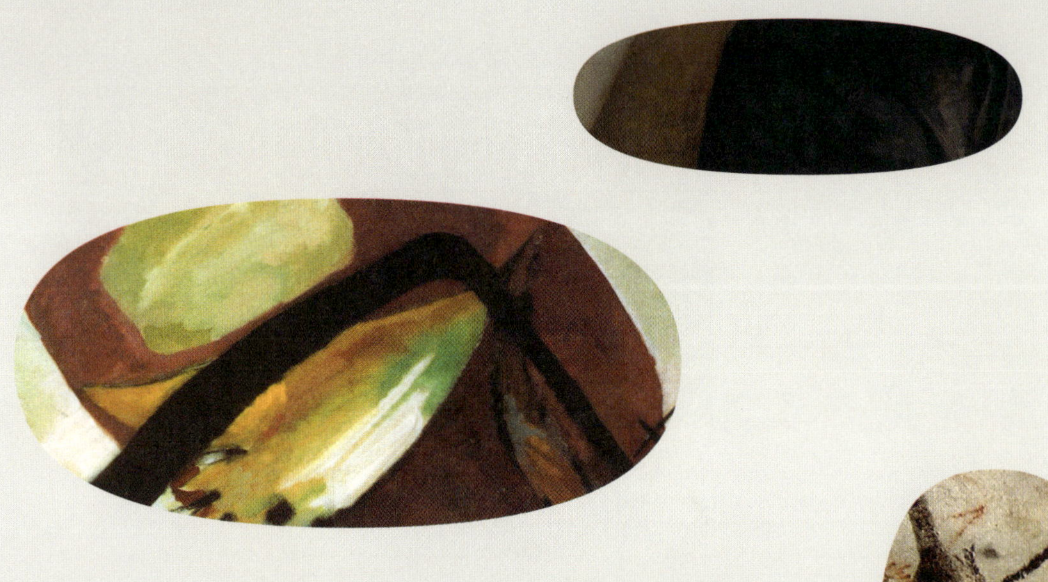

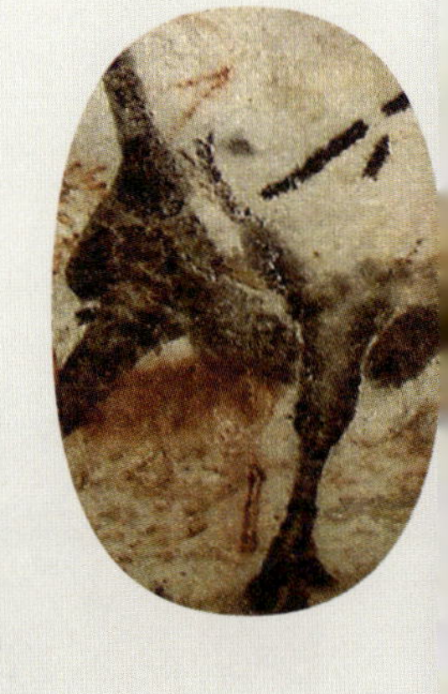

Black

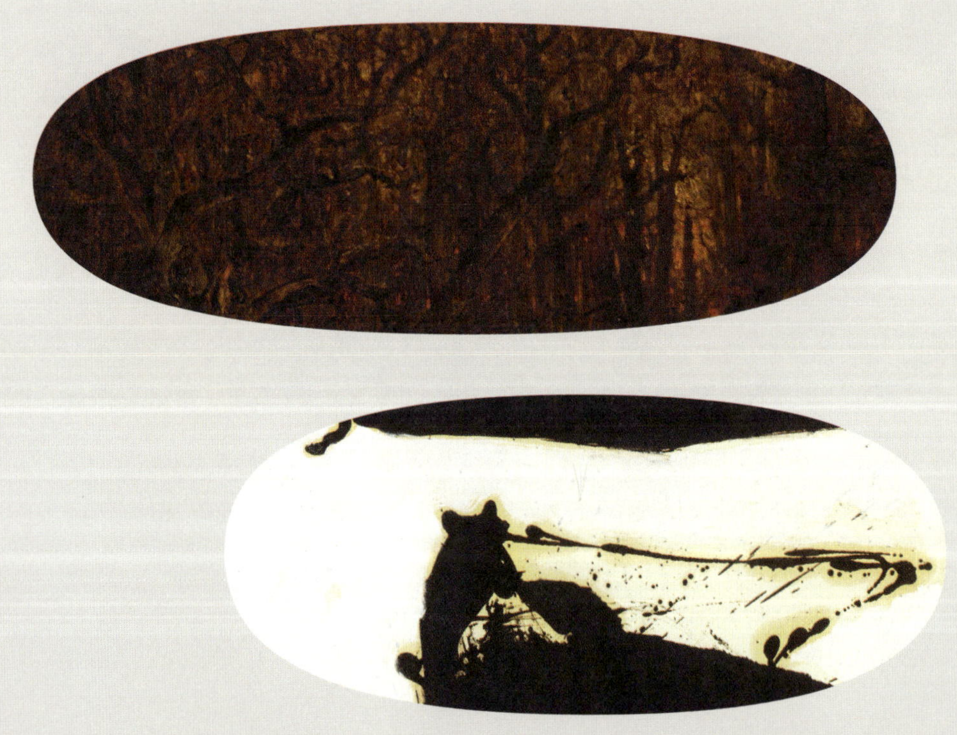

Black is where imagination begins – where art blazes into being. Contrary to culturally instilled prejudice that all too often equates the colour with negativities – emptiness and distrust, mourning and misfortune – black is the purest proof of illumination, not its opposite or enemy. Anyone who doubts black's fundamental vibrancy need merely consider the effulgent etymology of the word, lit as it is from inside by the still smouldering Proto-Indo-European root *bhel-*, meaning to 'shine' or 'gleam' or 'flash'. This largely forgotten fact is one that the Irish artist Guggi's 2009 sculpture, *Calix Meus Inebrians* – a colossal black cup whose polished bronze interior runneth over with the echoing light of falling stars in the Provençal gardens of Château La Coste – knows by heart.

Black's brilliance is a scintillating truth we used to cherish. The very earliest examples of creative expression ever discovered – charcoal drawings found in the Grotte Chauvet-Pont d'Arc in south-eastern France, thought to have been created around 37,000 BCE – were fashioned using the same charred pine branches that our pioneering Palaeolithic forebears also used to illumine the dim and dank hollows they inhabited, to keep themselves warm, and to cook their food. From its inception, in other words, art was an extension of vital rituals for survival, and black was the colour and form that that art took – the blood that pulsed incandescently through it.

The story of human culture is the tale of mankind's persistent efforts, however, to smother black's animating ember, to disconnect it from the brightness and heat with which it is indispensably entangled. From the black horse that Famine rides in the Book of Revelation to the grim gothic garb of Dracula (whom Bram Stoker introduces as 'clad in black from head to foot, without a single speck of colour about him anywhere'), black has been posited time and again as the irredeemable antithesis of life and joy. Mankind's forays into outer space have only served to amplify the enmity, demonizing darkness as a fearful void requiring our salvation - rather than celebrating it as the cradle of creativity from which everything, including life itself, emerges. A handwritten text by Carl Sagan, scribbled when the future astrophysicist and author was still an undergraduate student at the University of Chicago in the early 1950s, is indicative of the instinctive prejudice that has pitted black against light. 'There is a wide yawning black infinity,' Sagan wrote.

> *In every direction the extension is endless, the sensation of depth is overwhelming. And the darkness is immortal. Where light exists, it is pure, blazing, fierce; but light exists almost nowhere, and the blackness itself is also pure and blazing and fierce. But most of all, there is very nearly nothing in the dark; except for little bits here and there, often associated with the light, this infinite receptacle is empty. This picture is strangely frightening.*[1]

Not long after Sagan committed his anxious words to paper, the pioneering Abstract Expressionist Robert Motherwell gave visual voice to a similarly sombrous vision in his painting *The Black Sun* (1959), whose austere astral title is an allusion to a meditation on creative obsession by the French modernist poet Charles Baudelaire. In his intense prose poem 'The Desire to Paint', Baudelaire confesses to a hopeless yearning to capture the evaporated essence of 'a certain woman who has appeared to me so rarely, and so swiftly fled away, like some beautiful, regrettable thing the traveller must leave behind him in the night'. This 'overpowering' beauty that haunts Baudelaire's imagination is a malign magnificence that can only be evoked by one colour: 'The colour black preponderates in her,' he says, 'all that she inspires is nocturnal and profound.'

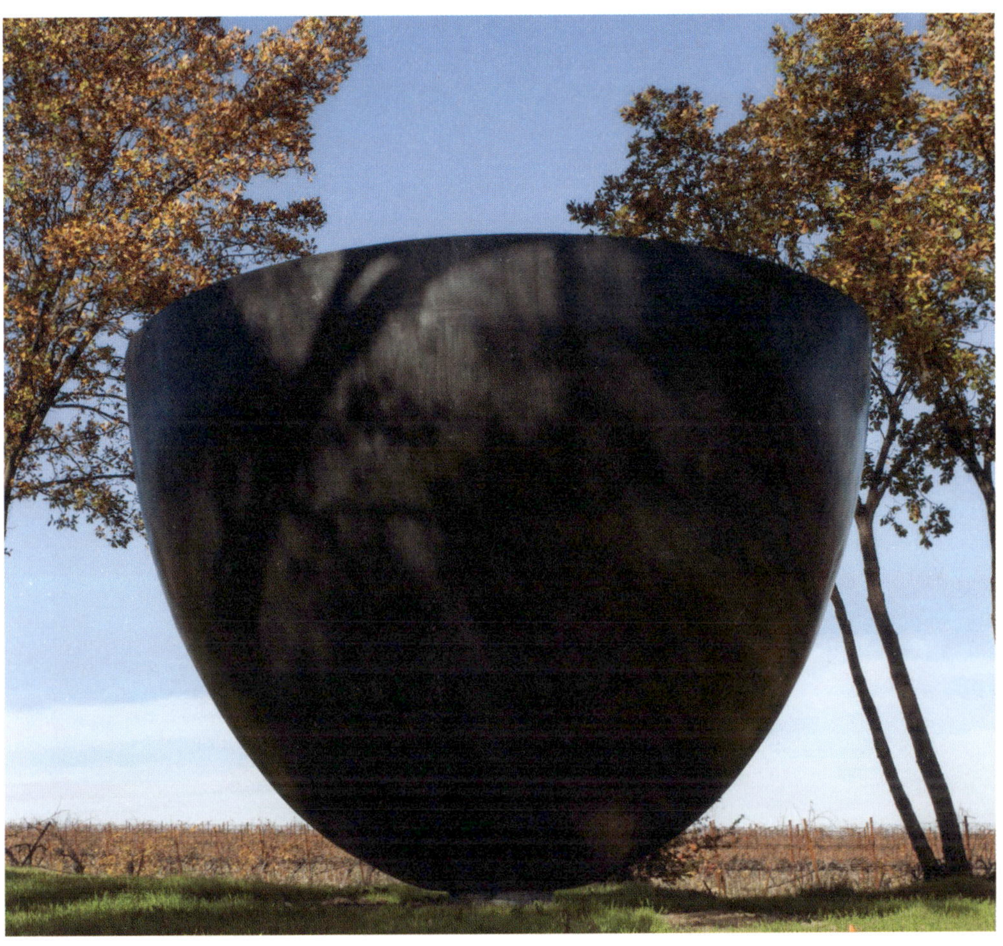

Guggi, *Calix Meus Inebrians*, 2009

Her eyes are two caverns where mystery vaguely stirs and gleams; her glance illuminates like a ray of light; it is an explosion in the darkness. I would compare her to a black sun if one could conceive of a dark star overthrowing light and happiness.[2]

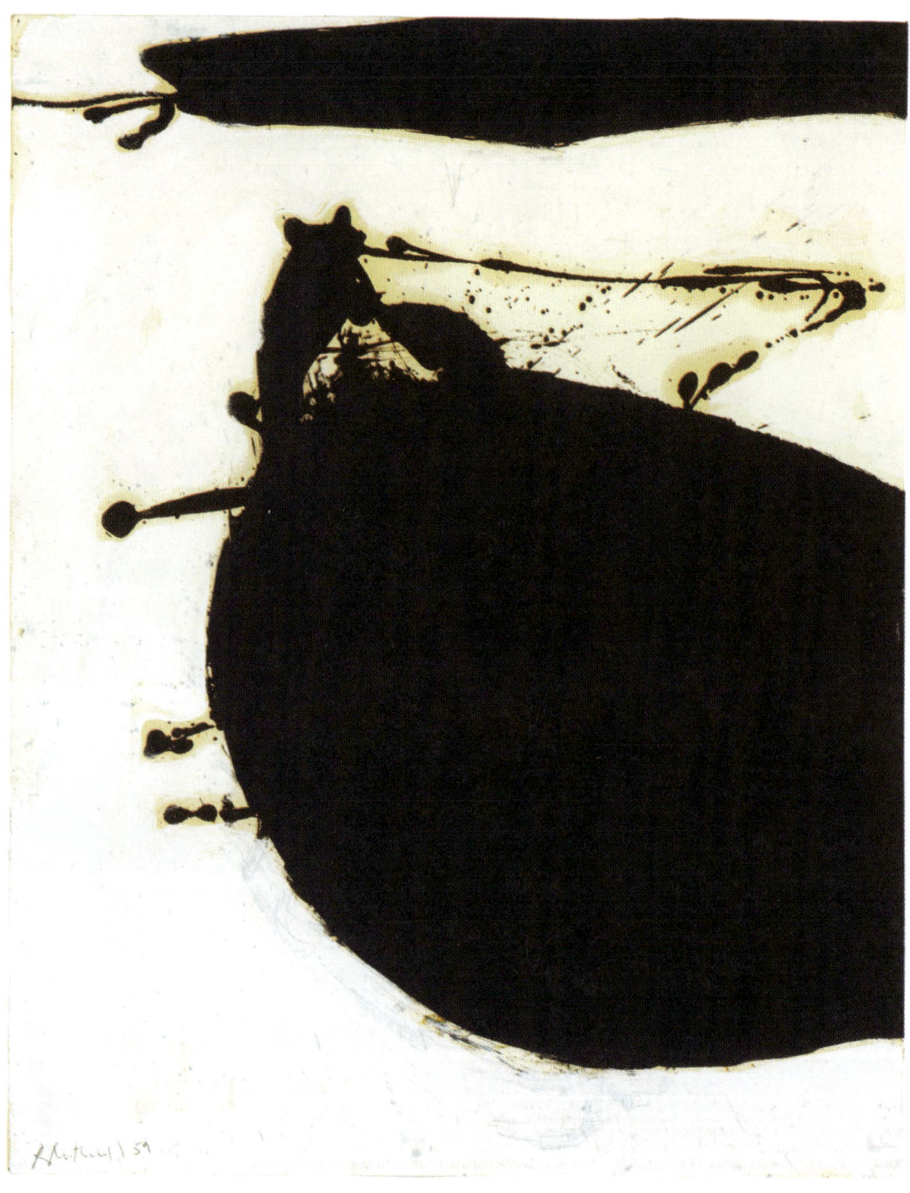

Robert Motherwell, *The Black Sun*, 1959

Charcoal

Like a gnostic secret, black's majesty has somehow survived the incessant efforts to tarnish it. A perennial counter-argument against the portrayal of the colour as blighted blankness can be found in the silent narrative of art history, as if in the muscle memory of creative expression, twitching since prehistory, an inextinguishable knowledge of the colour's true lustre ineluctably flexes. We know from scientific scrutiny of the earliest applications of a black pigment - charcoal - in the Chauvet cave paintings that careful consideration was given to which type of wood, when combusted, would yield the most alluring hue and could best be manipulated when scraped and smoothed on the contoured surface of the cave's walls and ceiling to produce a compelling simulation of texture and movement. In their study 'Illuminating the Cave, Drawing in Black: Wood Charcoal Analysis at Chauvet-Pont d'Arc', a team of archaeologists analysing the properties of this, art's earliest pigment, concluded that, in addition to the 'readily available supply of deadwood' pine used by the Palaeolithic artists, and the wood's advantageous 'combustion properties', 'its mechanical properties', carefully chosen, 'rendered it ideal for producing drawing charcoal and pigment for the smudging and blending techniques used in cave paintings.'[3]

Reliance on charcoal as a fundamental tool in image-making has persisted uninterrupted since its first use forty millennia ago. A direct line can be traced from the gleaming manes of stampeding horses thundering across the walls of the Grotte Chauvet to the arched eyebrows and onyx stares of the 2nd-century Romano-Egyptian Fayum portraits (the earliest known portraits of actual sitters), to the mute moan of Albrecht Dürer's unflinching portrait of a deceased Christ, whose anguished crown and gnarled countenance are softly spun from charcoal pencil, and to the lustrous railings that lead our eye from the hollow howl of Munch's *The Scream* to the electric sky beyond.

Art has a way of retaining and asserting black's restorative refulgence even when the wielders of sticks of charcoal themselves have succumbed to the falsities of the colour's undeserved alignment with desolation and decay. Wassily Kandinsky could hardly have been clearer about his opinion of what black denoted in his influential treatise *Concerning the Spiritual in Art*, despite the fact that works he created contemporaneously with that book's publication in 1911 vibrate vividly with a contrary consciousness. 'Black', Kandinsky insists,

> *is something burnt out, like the ashes of a funeral pyre, something motionless like a corpse. The silence of black is the silence of death. Outwardly black is the colour with least harmony of all, a kind of neutral background against which the minutest shades of other colours stand clearly forward. It differs from white in this also, for with white nearly every colour is in discord, or even mute altogether ... Not without reason is white taken as symbolizing joy and spotless purity, and black grief and death.*[4]

It is difficult, however, to square Kandinsky's insistence on black's allegedly nullifying nature with his own inspirative use of charcoal black in his thrumming *Picture with a Black Arch*, created at almost the same moment that his treatise first appeared in print. Far from casting a pall over the work, the eponymous black arch – a bold boomerang that rotates around the canvas's centre – marshals the vibrancy and verve of the painting's otherwise entropic energies. Black, in other words, doesn't temper or cancel the explosive splendour of the work's colours, it facilitates it. 'Of all the graphic elements running through the picture', notes the art historian Hajo Düchting,

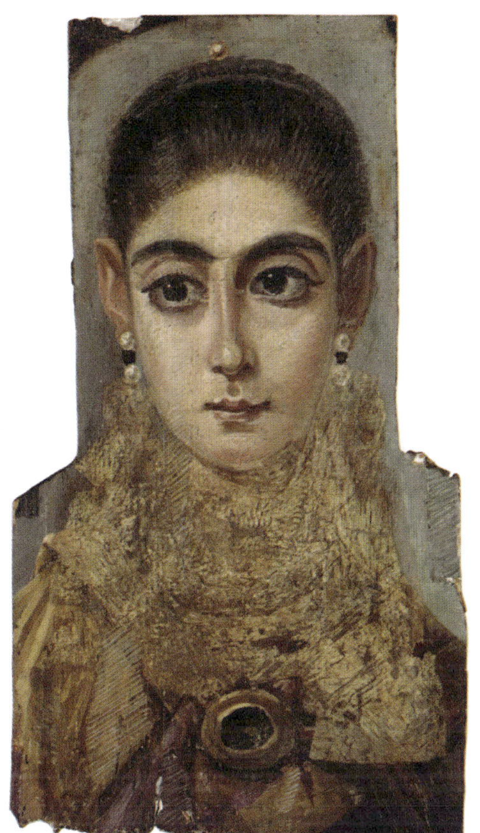

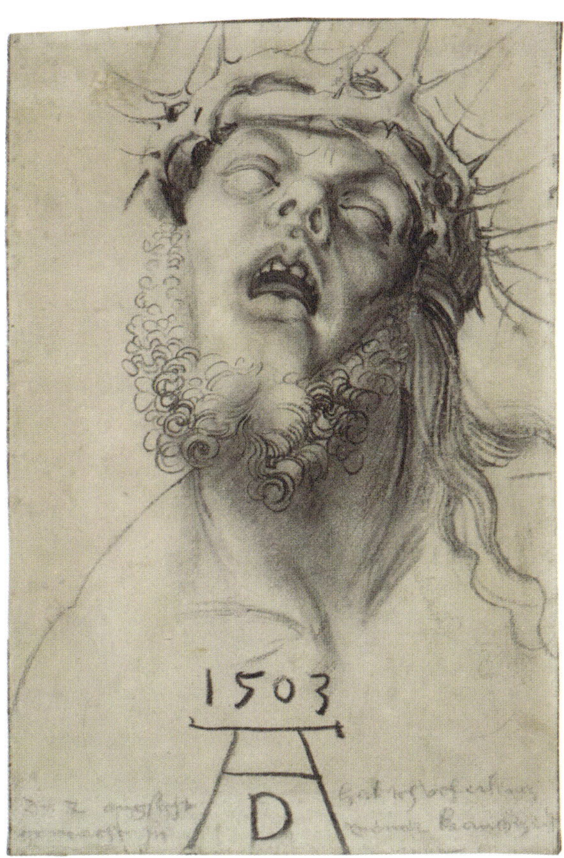

ABOVE LEFT Fayum mummy portrait of a woman ('L'Européenne'), Egypt, 100–150 CE

ABOVE RIGHT Albrecht Dürer, *Head of the dead Christ*, 1503

the arch that gives it its title carries particular weight. The arch, which actually looks more like a right angle, frames all three shapes and reinforces the stabilising function of the violet disc. But it can also be seen in terms of movement, starting in the red shape and, after bending slightly in the violet, moving down towards the blue. The black arch appears as an

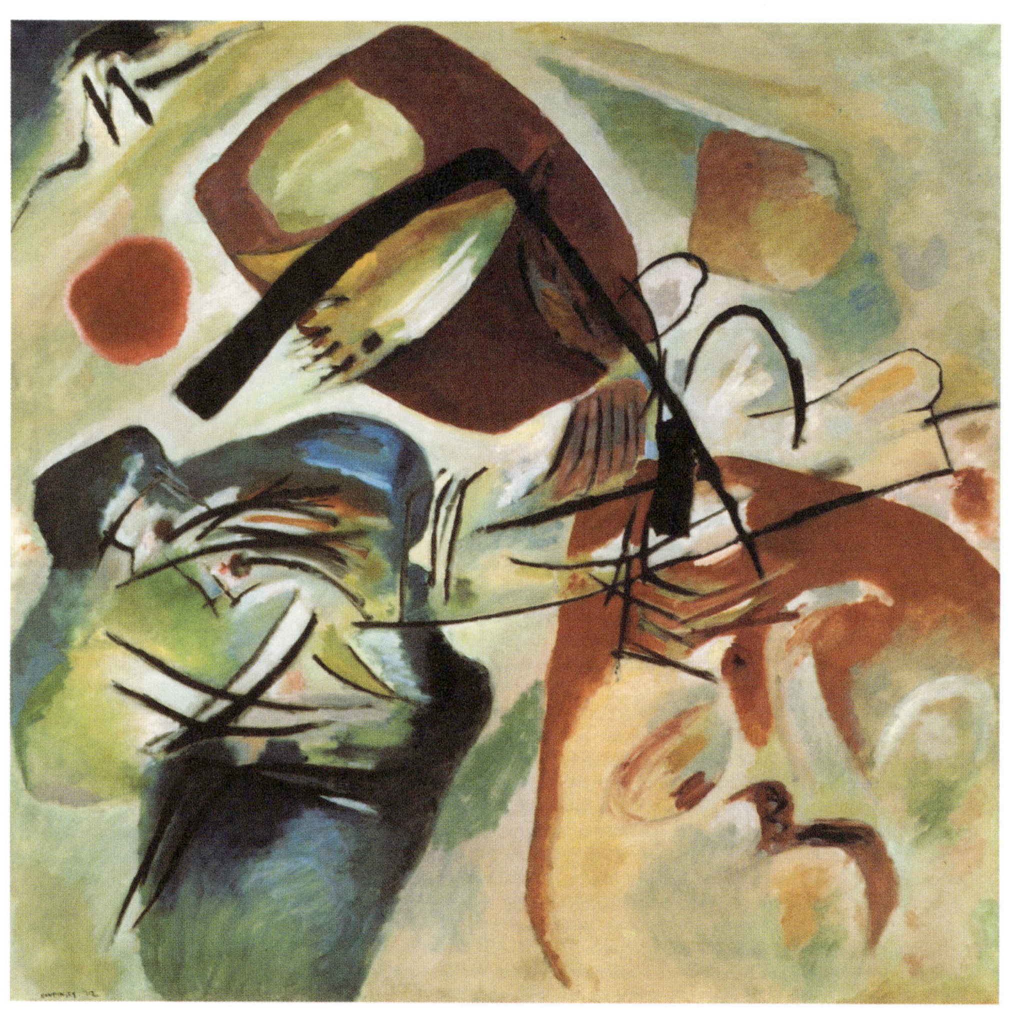

Wassily Kandinsky, *Picture with a Black Arch*, 1912

Charcoal

eruption of energy, as an image of violent struggle, in which the red forms represent one side and the retreating blue silhouette the other.[5]

If one were not already familiar with the contours and colours of Kandinsky's painting prior to reading Düchting's analysis, he or she could be forgiven for thinking that the critic was describing the refracting dynamism of a rainbow at the centre of the canvas rather than a black arch - with all the supposed disparaging connotations that that colour conjures for Kandinsky. That black absorbs colours and echoes them back rather than refuting or rejecting them is a truth that also underlies the power of works by British painter and writer Lynette Yiadom-Boakye and Nigerian-American contemporary visual artist Toyin Ojih Odutola. It is more than just the title of Yiadom-Boakye's charcoal and pen-and-ink drawing *Man Big Hands* (2006) that draws us to the tight weave of the figure's interlocking fingers. Although, like nearly all of the artist's subjects, the enigmatic sitter is a purely fictional presence, summoned from the shadows of the artist's imagination, he has nevertheless been sculpted into physical semblance by the squeeze of real fingers: the artist pinching a wand-like stick of charcoal, waving it over the blankness of white paper. Within the mystical consciousness of the work, the subject's hands are at once make-believe and the truest thing there is.

In Ojih Odutola's 2016 portrait *Confidence Building I*, the charcoal countenance at the centre of the work is the chromatic pivot around which the ephemeral mauves and perishable rusts fleetingly organize themselves. The black visage has a soft solidity to it that throws into doubt the reality of everything that orbits it - material elements which, upon further meditation, seem to evaporate into an insubstantial aura. The world may melt away but the ineradicable obsidian strength of spirit to which Ojih Odutola's portrait attests will pulsate forever.

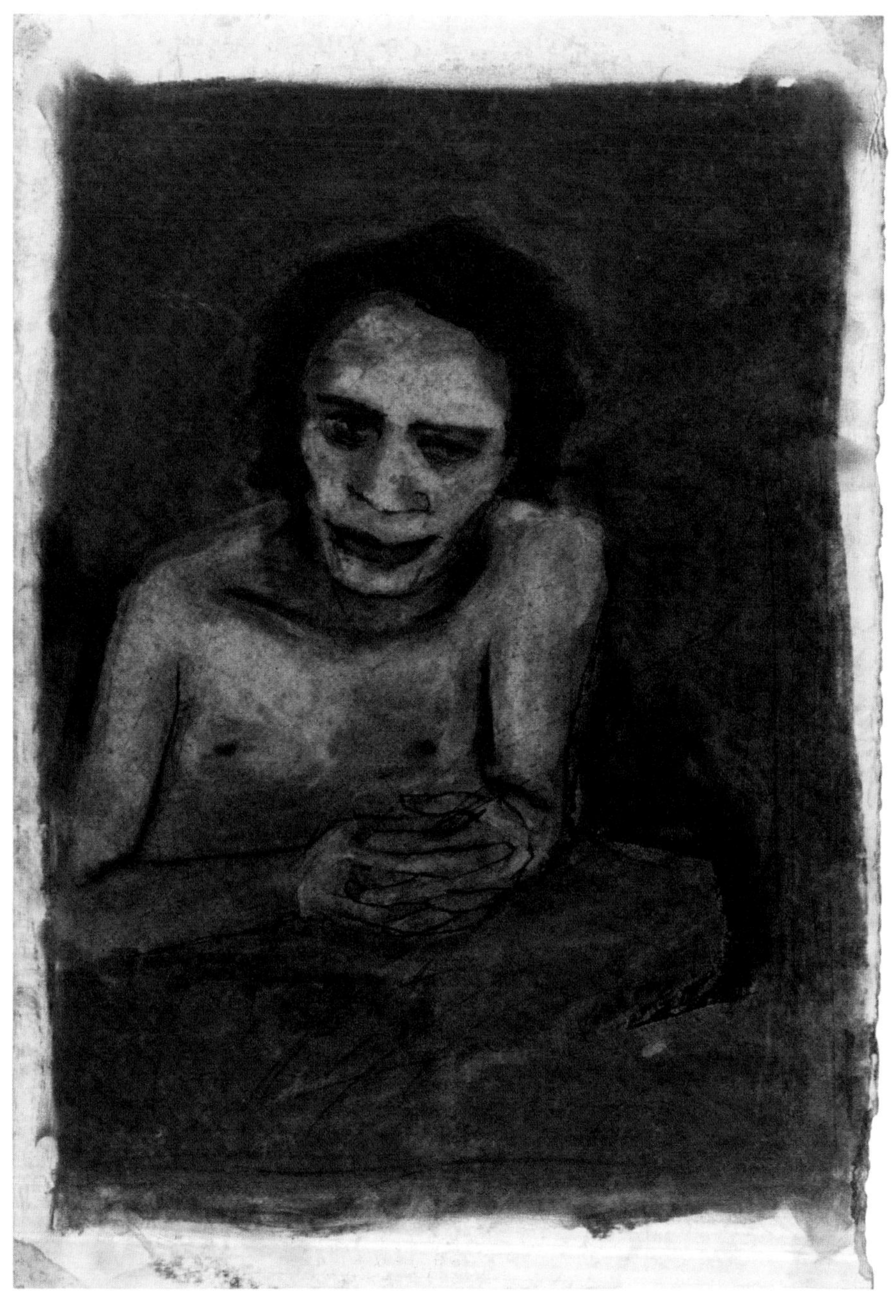

Lynette Yiadom-Boakye, *Man Big Hands*, 2006

Charcoal

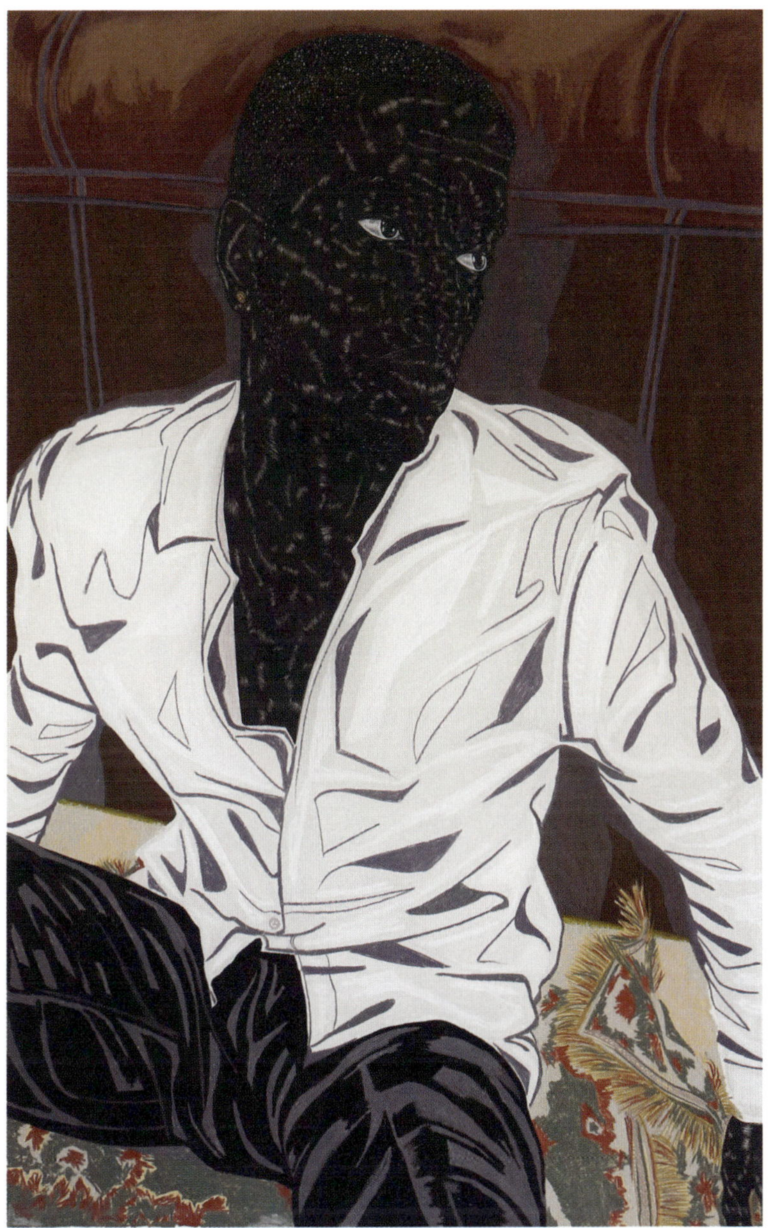

Toyin Ojih Odutola, *Confidence Building I*, 2016

Bone Black

Darkness gleaned from grinding incinerated branches and trunks was not the only way that black was handed down by our ancient antecedents. At some unremembered moment in prehistory, a trailblazing Late Stone Age draughtsman recognized too that combusting bones – roasting them with careful precision – produced a unique black that glistened distinctly from the absorbing matte finish that charcoal typically yielded. The static stampede of aurochs, ibex and bulls that rush across the walls of the Lascaux caves in France, estimated to be around 17,000 years old, is one of the earliest surviving examples of so-called bone black's breathtaking use.

Creating the striking colour requires considerable patience and attentiveness. It isn't enough merely to surround a disassembled skeleton with glowing embers. Animal bones have a

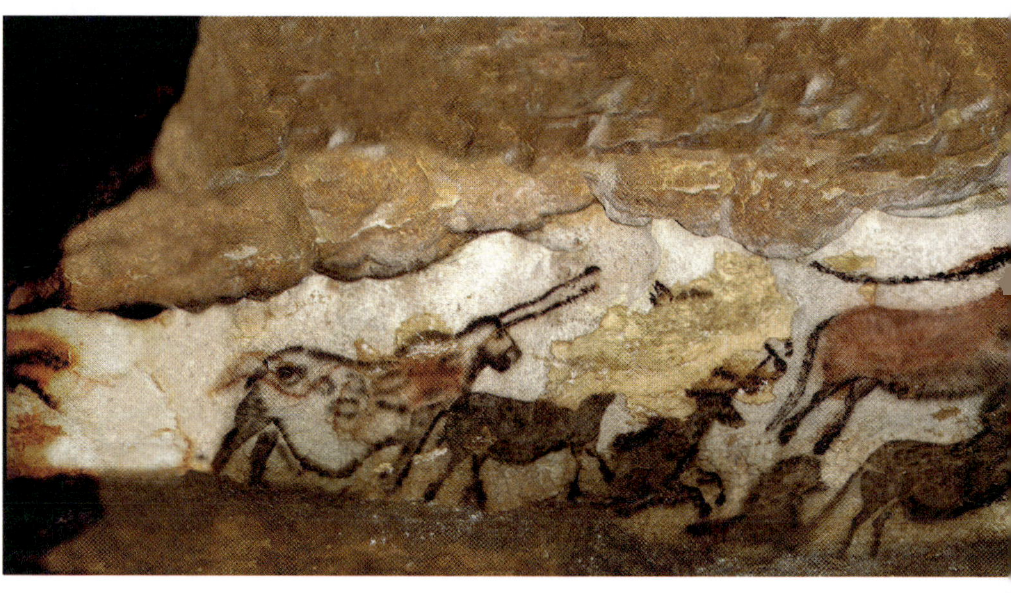

Hall of Bulls, Lascaux caves, Dordogne, France, *c.* 15,000 BCE

tendency to become friable when burned in open air and then crumble into ash. The key is to hot-box them in a sealed crucible, depriving the collagen and calcium phosphate that comprise their organic armature of oxygen. The result is carbonized fragments that can then be pestled into powder and employed as pigment. The more laboriously levigated and pulverized on a slab of stone the particalized bones are, the purer and more profound the black. An echoing underlayer of bone black used by Hieronymus Bosch in his ominous polyptych *Visions of the Hereafter* (after 1490) is indicative of the reverberating intensity of which the pigment was capable. That Bosch's choking darkness, which engulfs his smoggy glimpse of hell, should be created from a substance that, like the soul-sizzling soot it evokes, was forged in fire, only amplifies the quadtych's potency.

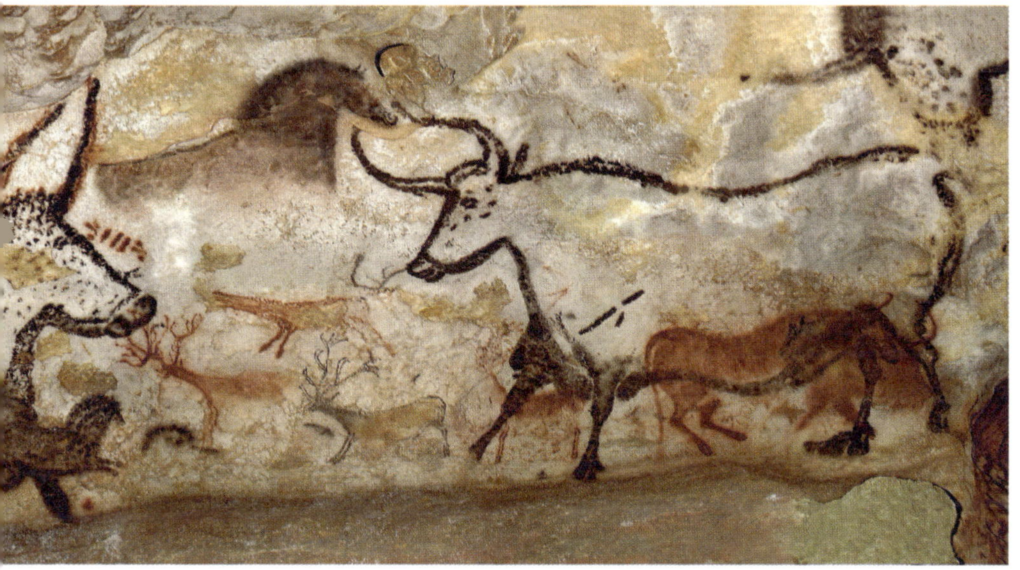

The precise provenance of the materials necessary to create bone black - animal or human - is the subject of some morbid speculation. Whether the pigment's use in works by Egyptian, Greek and Roman artists amounts to forensic evidence of ancient human sacrifice is difficult to prove. By the time that Rembrandt relied on bone black to construct the deep gloaming gloom from which his sitters mystically stare, any fabled use of human remains, had there ever been any, seems to have been abandoned. 'No one, thank God,' the art historian Simon Schama exclaims with relief in his magisterial study of the Dutch Golden Age master's achievement, *Rembrandt's Eyes*, 'robbed graves anymore for charring skeletons to make "bone black".'[6] Not everyone, however, is convinced that bone black was ever indeed manufactured in such an abominable manner. Discussing the origin of what she calls 'one of the more notorious ingredients in the seventeenth century ... which was said by some to be made from human corpses', Victoria Finlay, the cultural historian and expert on the history of pigments we met earlier, sounds a sensible note of scholarly caution:

> *I imagine the apprentices in artists' studios would have told wonderful ghost stories about bone black, although there is little reason to think these rumours were based on anything more than ghoulishness. In truth, bone black - a rich deep blue, black pigment - was usually derived from the thighs of cattle or the limbs of lambs: uncontroversial powdered and burned scraps from the slaughterhouse's remainder pit.*[7]

Finlay may well be right that human remains were never alchemized into blistering blackness. But substituting cattle thighs and 'limbs of lambs' for human bones does little to purge the pigment of menacing and murky mysticisms that time has baked into it. The symbolic significance of burning animal bones is itself ancient and still has suppressed resonance to this day. The word 'bonfire' is a thinly veiled contraction of 'bone-fire', and survives in our language as a relic of forgotten ceremonial traditions. 'The bone in the bonfire', according to one 19th-century historian writing in 1890,

> *was something more than a symbol. Its presence grew out of and illustrates the deepest and most remarkable phase of osteologic folk-lore. It represented the animal or man burned in the ancient sacrifice, because the notion is nigh universal in primitive mythology and modern superstition that the immaterial part of creatures, their indestructible element or soul, is connected with or resident in the bones. Such a belief has a ready foundation in the durability of the osseous skeleton, and its permanence when the soft parts have disappeared.*[8]

A work by the American expatriate artist John Singer Sargent, created a few years before these remarks appeared in the *Journal of American Folklore*, illustrates the mythic potency of a pigment fabricated from the fire of fired bones. Sargent's intriguingly titled *Madame X* (1883–84) is often described as a study in stark contrasts – a canvas that pits the chic black satin of the sleek evening dress worn by Virginie Amélie Avegno Gautreau (an American-born Parisian socialite and wife of a French banker) against the pale alabaster glimmer of her simultaneously silken and sepulchral complexion. Sargent has eerily tempered the sheen of Gautreau's skin (contrived from an audacious concoction of lead white, rose madder, vermilion and viridian) with a resplendent pinch of bone black.[9] By doing so, he complicates his seemingly seductive portrait and rescues it from a superficiality into which it risked slipping.

A subtle hint of bone black transforms the painting into a soulful meditation on the fleetingness of flesh – blurring the line between desire and decomposition. Gautreau's gorgeously gangrenous skin, suffused with the residue of ritualistically roasted bone, smoulders spookily – and hovers precariously, like us, between life-in-death and death-in-life. Little wonder that the work, which Sargent felt compelled to undertake without commission, was said to have caused 'a riot' when first shown at the Paris salon in 1884, or that the artist himself would look back on it later in life as 'the best thing I have ever done'.

Sargent's portrait of Gautreau is not the only masterpiece of the 19th century whose beguiling allure is underwritten by crushed, cremated remains. For more than twenty years, the French realist Théodore Rousseau tinkered with a painting in which he tried to record the contours of a sunset that he saw in December 1845, as light sieved itself through the tangled skeletons of leafless forest. The hulking trees in the work may be stripped by nature of their foliage, but, in their looming presence in Rousseau's ominous painting, they are anything but lifeless. Never before in art have trees hovered so imposingly or with such anthropomorphic energy. 'In it', Alfred Sensier, the artist's biographer, says of the intimidating work, 'Rousseau accumulated there multitudes of forest forms, generations of trees which embrace each other and arise in frenzied silhouettes, without obliterating each other; one might say they are like impatient people metamorphosed into trees, waiting only for the magic wand of some enchanter to utter the terrible cry of deliverance. If ever a forest had a voice about to burst into a mysterious choir, it's Rousseau's *Forest in Winter*.'[10] The semblance of ceaseless metamorphosis in the work – of shapes shape-shifting between

OPPOSITE John Singer Sargent, *Madame X*, 1883–84

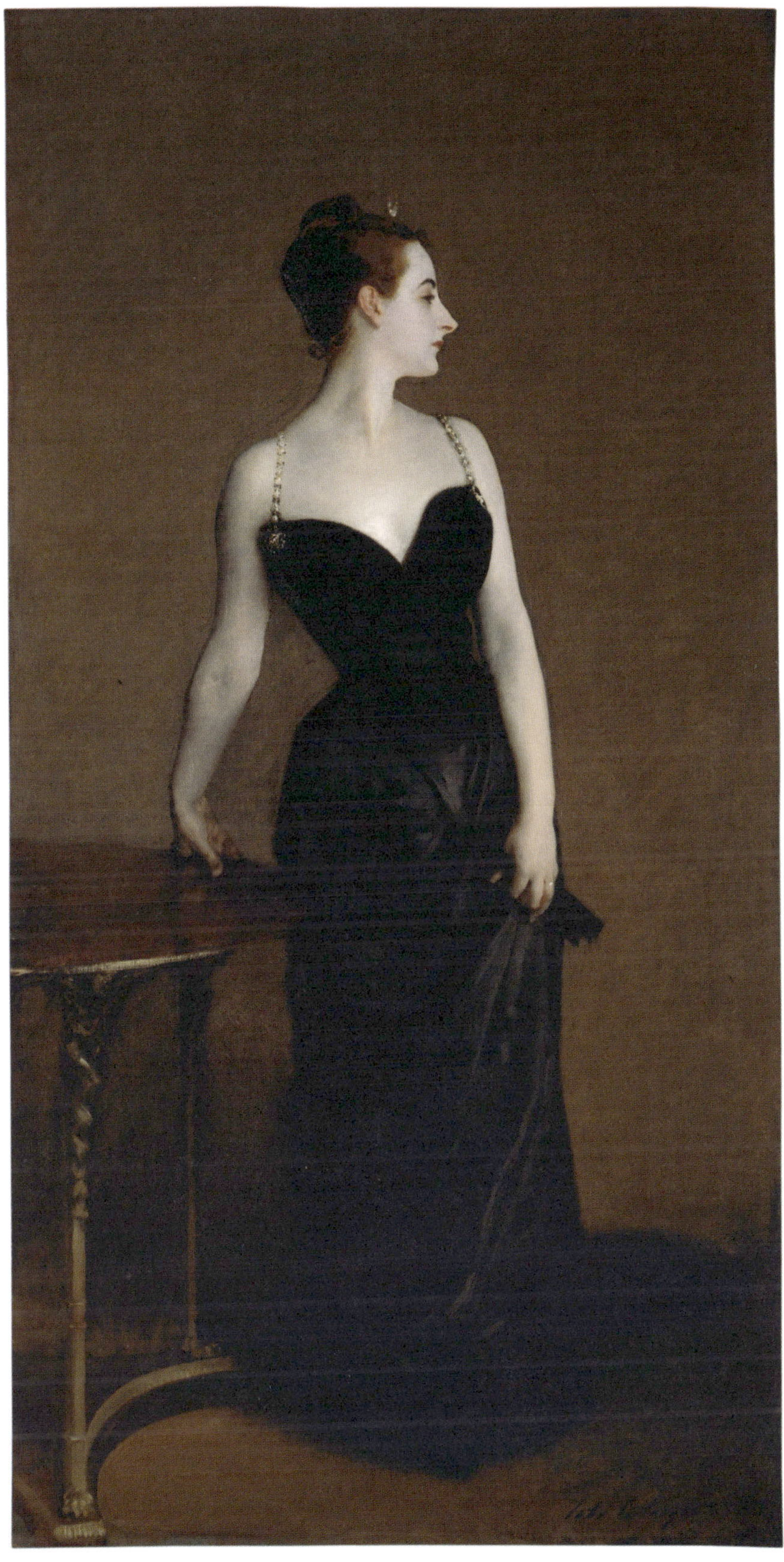

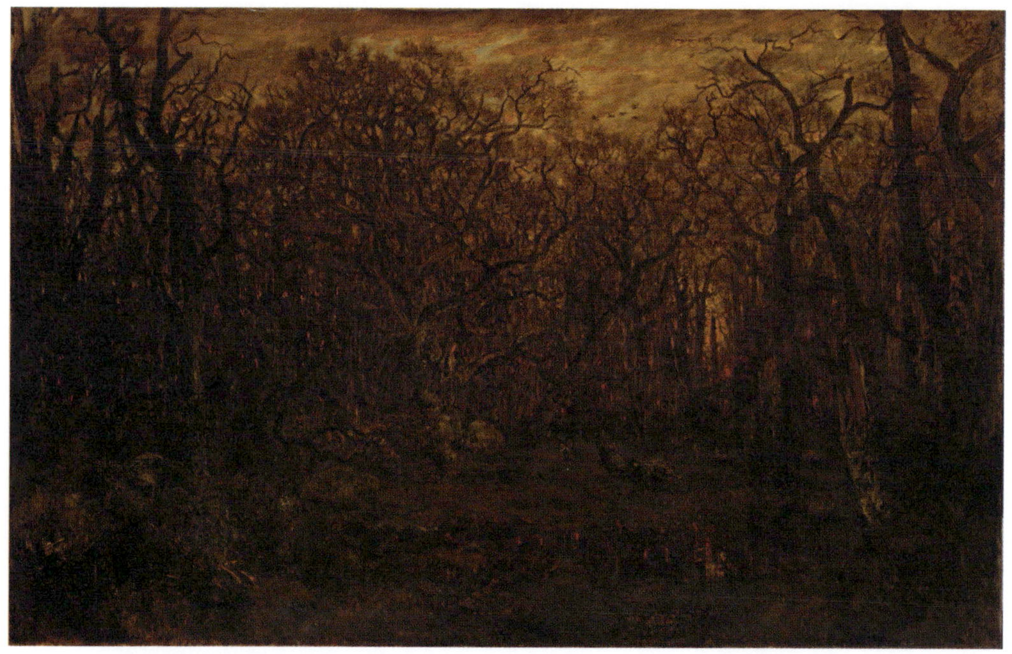

Théodore Rousseau, *The Forest in Winter at Sunset*, c. 1846–67

trees and people – is kindled from below the surface. An infrared photograph of the colossal canvas, whose tight trellis of trunks and web of wiry branches resembles the congested bronchi of a clotted chest X-ray, confirms the existence of carbon beneath the paint and reveals a reliance by Rousseau on bone black for his initial sketch of the work. The presence of fine fragments of fired femurs and fibulae, fossilized in oil beneath the varnish of a work that is all about the pulse of light and transmutation of inert and active forms, only intensifies its peculiar power. The hypnotizing gloam of buried bone breathes us in and coughs us out.

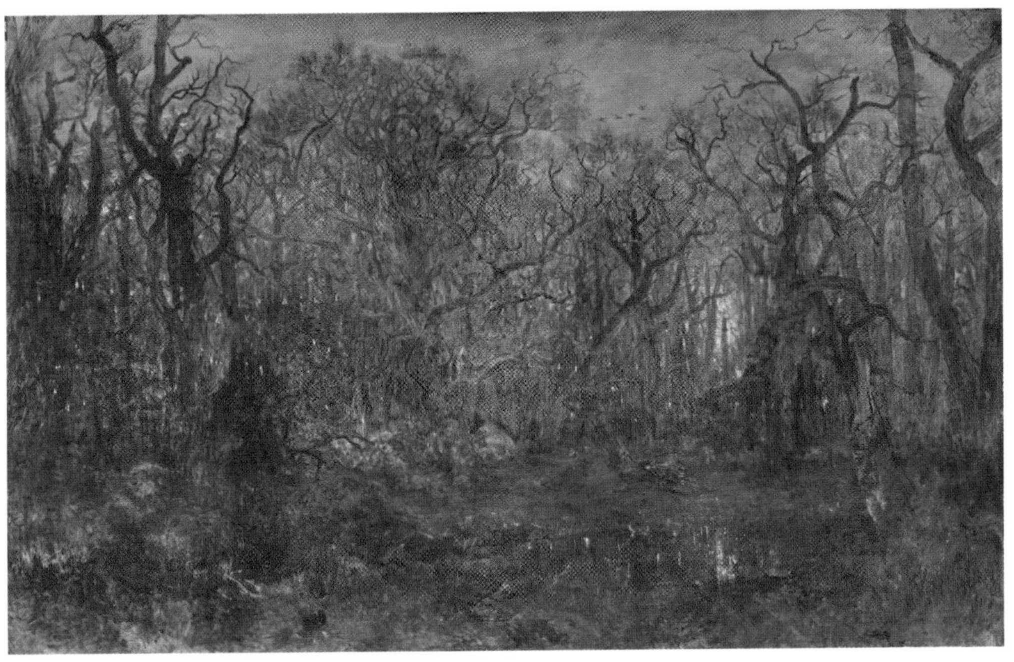

Infrared photograph of Rousseau's *The Forest in Winter at Sunset*

Emily Noyes Vanderpoel's *Color Problems*

(1902)

What if you could break an object down into nothing more than its constituent colours – sieve it through an immaterializing mesh of your mind's creation until all that is left is a grid of heft-less hues, a chromatic key? That is exactly what the American artist and writer Emily Noyes Vanderpoel did in a sequence of intriguing plates that she included in her treatise of 1902, *Color Problems: A Practical Manual for the Lay Student of Color*. Vanderpoel's eccentric charts extract the chromatic rhythm of a given object or creature – from an Egyptian mummy case to a teacup and saucer, a Chinese vase to Assyrian tiles, a butterfly to an antique rug – and construct from the analysis a 10 × 10 chessboard of proportional colour. Like quasi-QR codes of pure pixilated colour, these engrossing abstract grids look ahead to the spare music of Piet Mondrian and his minimalist descendants.

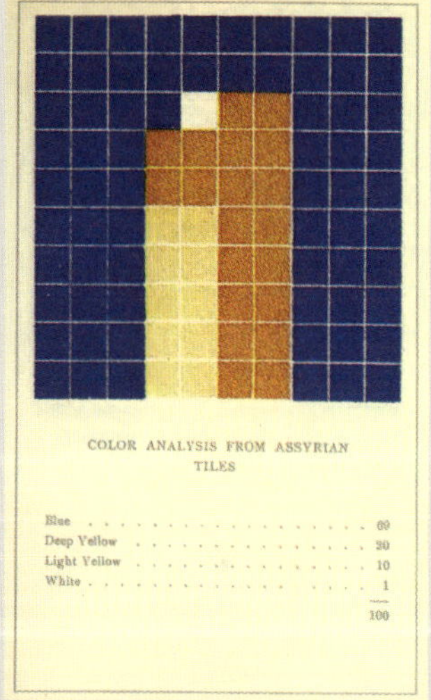

COLOR ANALYSIS FROM ASSYRIAN TILES

Blue	69
Deep Yellow	20
Light Yellow	10
White	1
	100

Plate LI, 'Color analysis from Assyrian tiles'

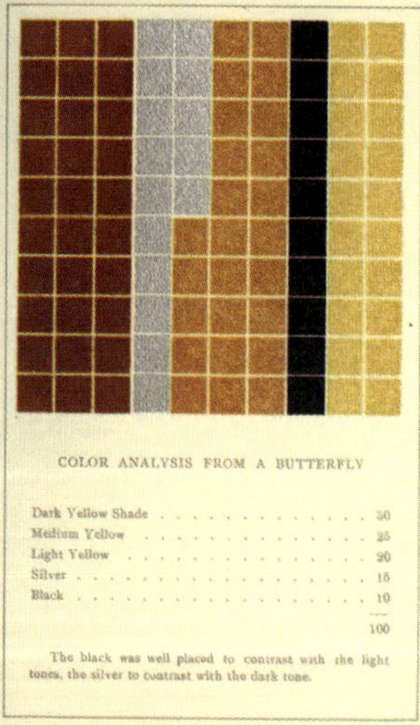

COLOR ANALYSIS FROM A BUTTERFLY

Dark Yellow Shade	30
Medium Yellow	25
Light Yellow	20
Silver	15
Black	10
	100

The black was well placed to contrast with the light tones, the silver to contrast with the dark tone.

Plate XCVIII, 'Color analysis from a butterfly'

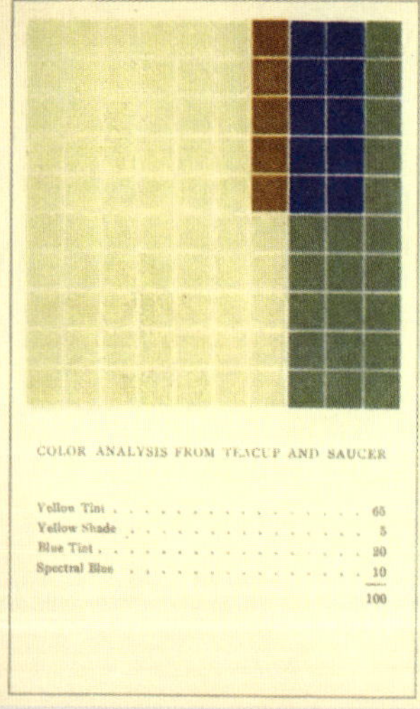

COLOR ANALYSIS FROM TEACUP AND SAUCER

Yellow Tint	65
Yellow Shade	5
Blue Tint	20
Spectral Blue	10
	100

Plate XXXII, 'Color analysis from a teacup and saucer'

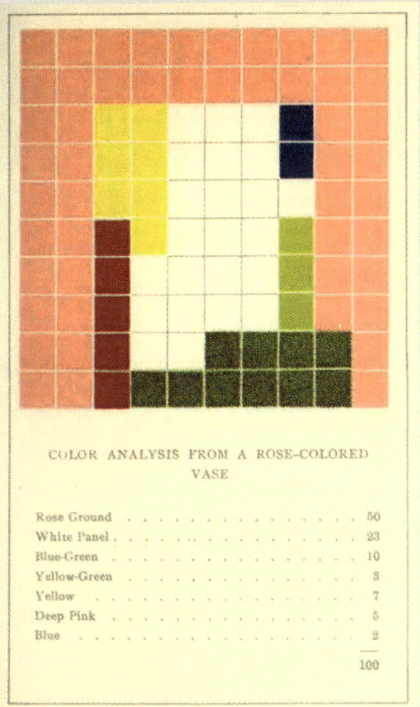

Plate xcv, 'Color analysis from a rose-colored vase'

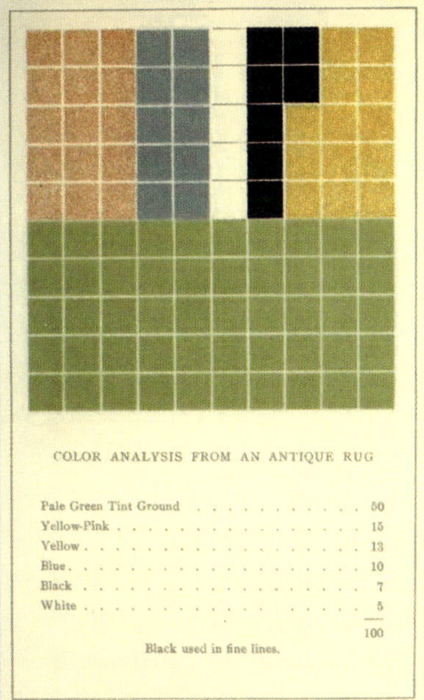

Plate LXXIX, 'Color analysis from an antique rug'

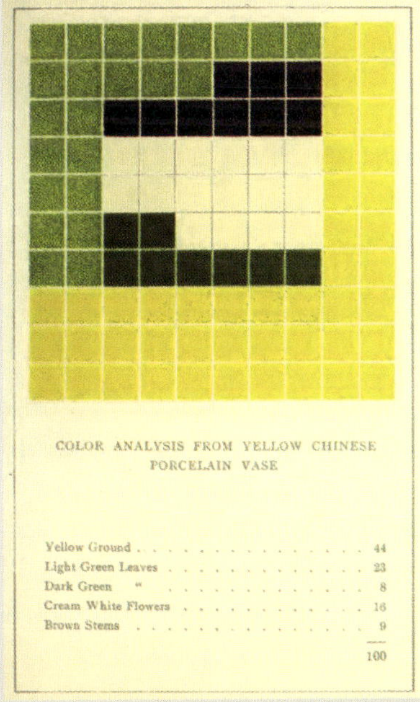

Plate xcvi, 'Color analysis from a yellow Chinese porcelain vase'

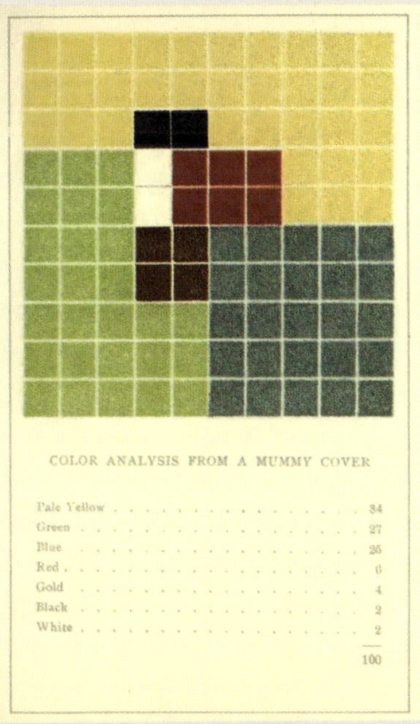

Plate LII, 'Color analysis from a Mummy cover'

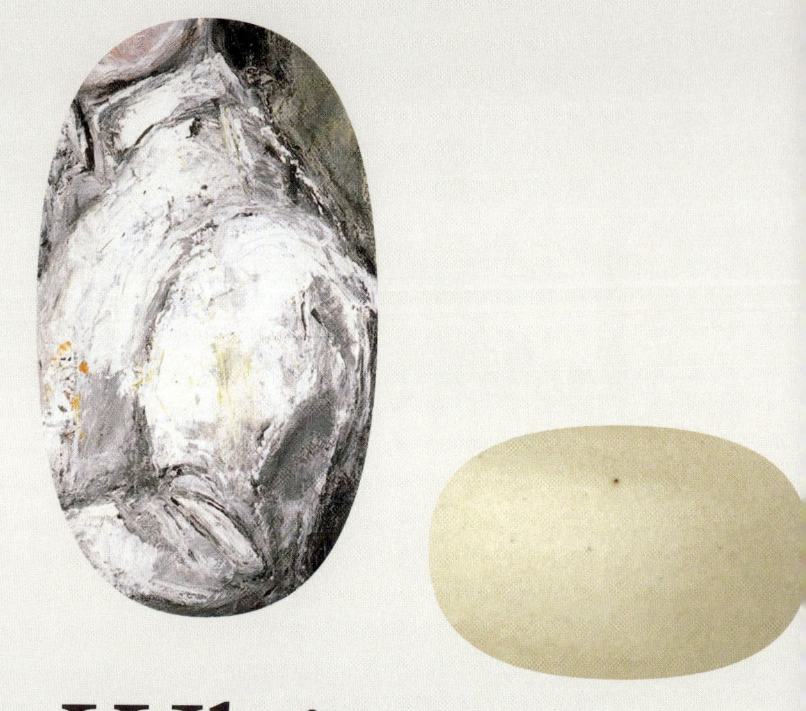

White

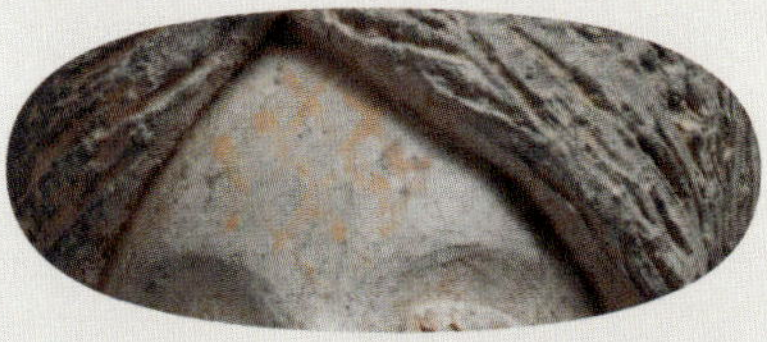

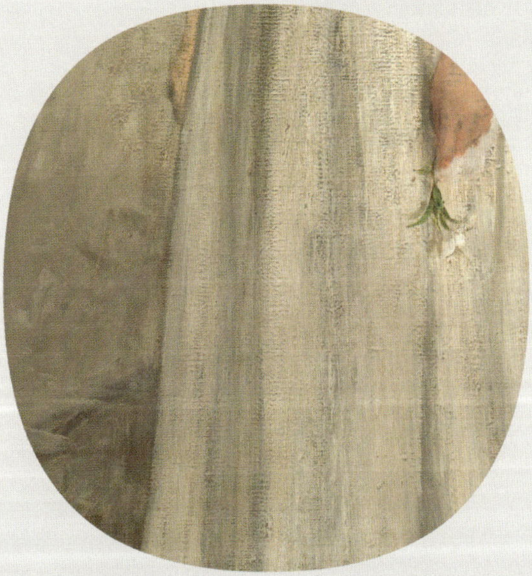

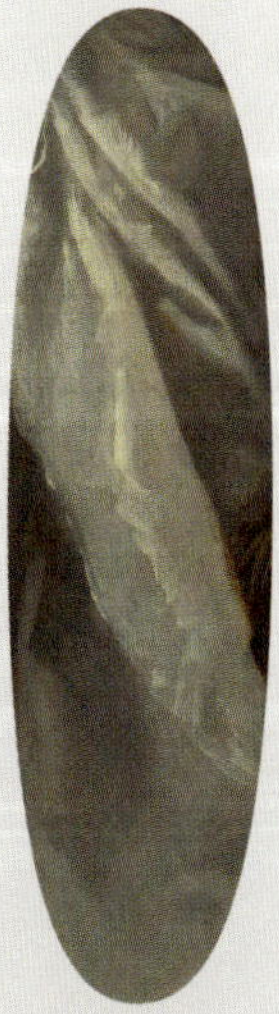

White has a dark side. For all its associations in Western culture with innocence and purity, white has a penchant for pivoting thought to the more sombre aspects of life. In her merrily macabre poem 'Cherry White', American writer Dorothy Parker illustrates white's propensity to propel even the most mirthful of meditations into bleakness:

I never see that prettiest thing –
A cherry bough gone white with Spring.
But what I think, 'How gay 'twould be
To hang me from a flowering tree.'[1]

That final twist in the braid of Parker's verse (a parody of an earlier, much-loved poem by A. E. Housman that measures life against the annual arrival of the 'cherry hung with snow'[2]) is genuinely shocking. So accustomed are we to equating the colour white with rebirth and renewal (the blooms in Housman's lyric are 'Wearing white for Eastertide'), we are caught off-guard – blindsided in the glare of white's blossoming brilliance – by the sudden snap of Parker's dark humour. This is the thing about white: it is never content with the contentment of its presumed immaculacy. White's whiteness is a white lie.

Take the arresting arrangement of white fabric flowers around sun-bleached bovine bone in the 1931 painting *Cow's Skull with Calico Roses* by Georgia O'Keeffe, Parker's contemporary. A stark study in the modalities of white, both real and artificial, the painting juxtaposes textures of calcified death in a skull that the artist found in a New Mexico desert with the satin petals of fake flowers used to adorn graves in the American Southwest. To amplify the endless regression of white's enigma, O'Keeffe has staged her still life on strips of pale parchment, giving the work a shallow, depth-less depth. The message is clear: whiteness is a choreographed cultural contrivance, a construct. Far from simple or pure, the true essence of white is a murky mystery.

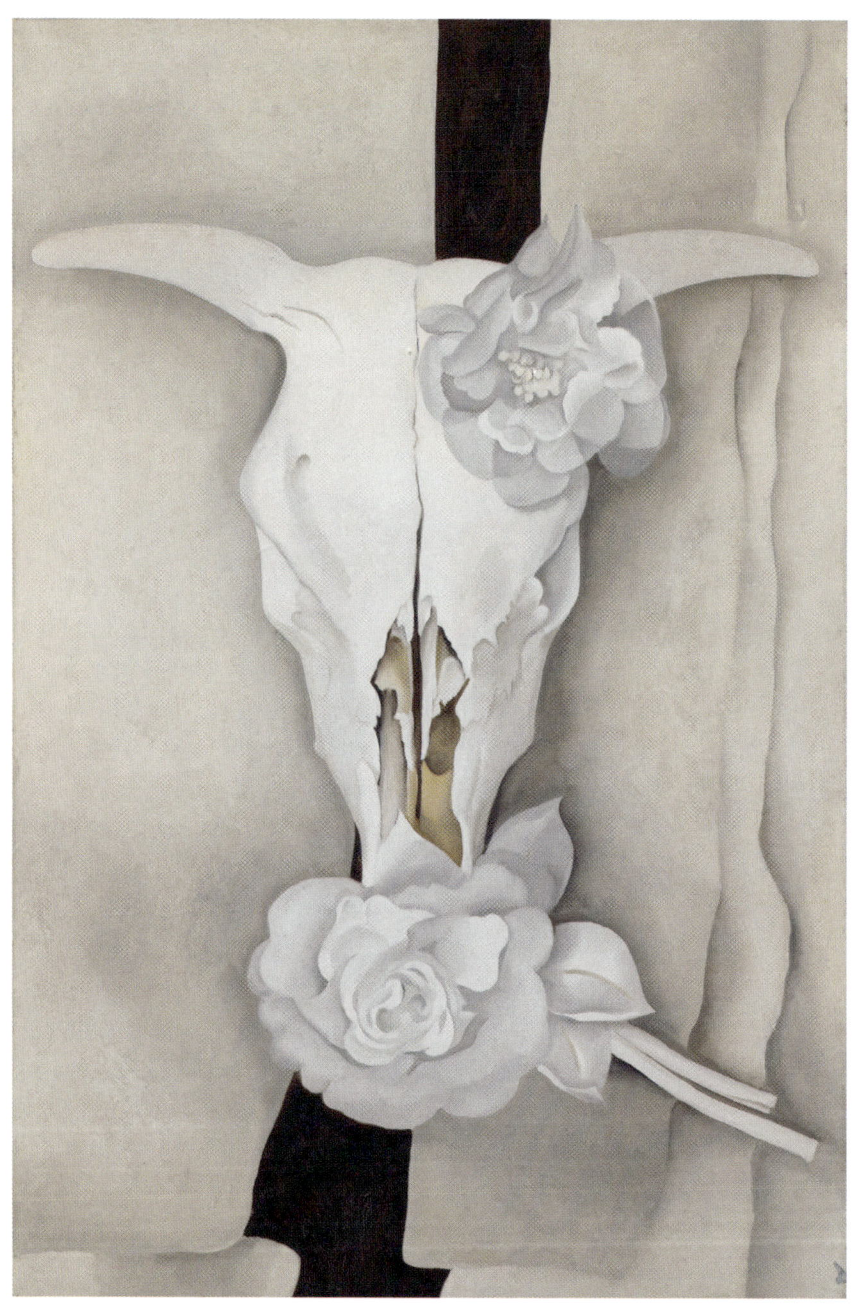

Georgia O'Keeffe, *Cow's Skull with Calico Roses*, 1931

Lead White

Lead white, the principal pigment used by Western artists from antiquity to the beginning of the 20th century to portray everything pristine and wholesome in the world - from drifts of unblemished snow to the unsullied sheen of flowing silk gowns - was itself the source of profound unpleasantness. Used to create everything from the flawless alabastrine skin of the doting Virgin Mary in Raphael's *Madonna of the Pinks* (c. 1506-07) to the excessive spotlessness of American artist James McNeill Whistler's *Symphony in White, No. 1: The White Girl* (1861-63, 1872), the seemingly benign pigment was the unlikely product of placing strips of lead beside a pool of vinegar for a month in an earthenware chamber, surrounded by piles of fermenting animal excrement.

The combination of an acetate formed by the proximity of lead and vinegar with the fumes of carbon dioxide emitted by festering faeces yielded a puffy white patina on the lead strips that was as alluring as it was lethal. The 'hateful brew', as 2nd-century Greek physician and poet Nicander of Colophon described it, triggered profound neurotoxic effects in those harvesting the lead carbonate, and resulted in both physical and psychological maladies. 'Over the victim's jaws and in the grooves of the gums', Nicander observed of those who prepare the pigment,

> *is plastered an astringent froth, and the furrow of the tongue turns rough on either side, and the depth of the throat grows somewhat dry, and from the pernicious venom follows a dry retching and hawking, for this affliction is severe; meanwhile his spirit sickens and he is worn out with mortal suffering. His body too grows chill, while sometimes his eyes behold strange illusions or else he drowses; nor can he bestir his limbs as heretofore, and he succumbs to the over mastering fatigue.*[3]

•

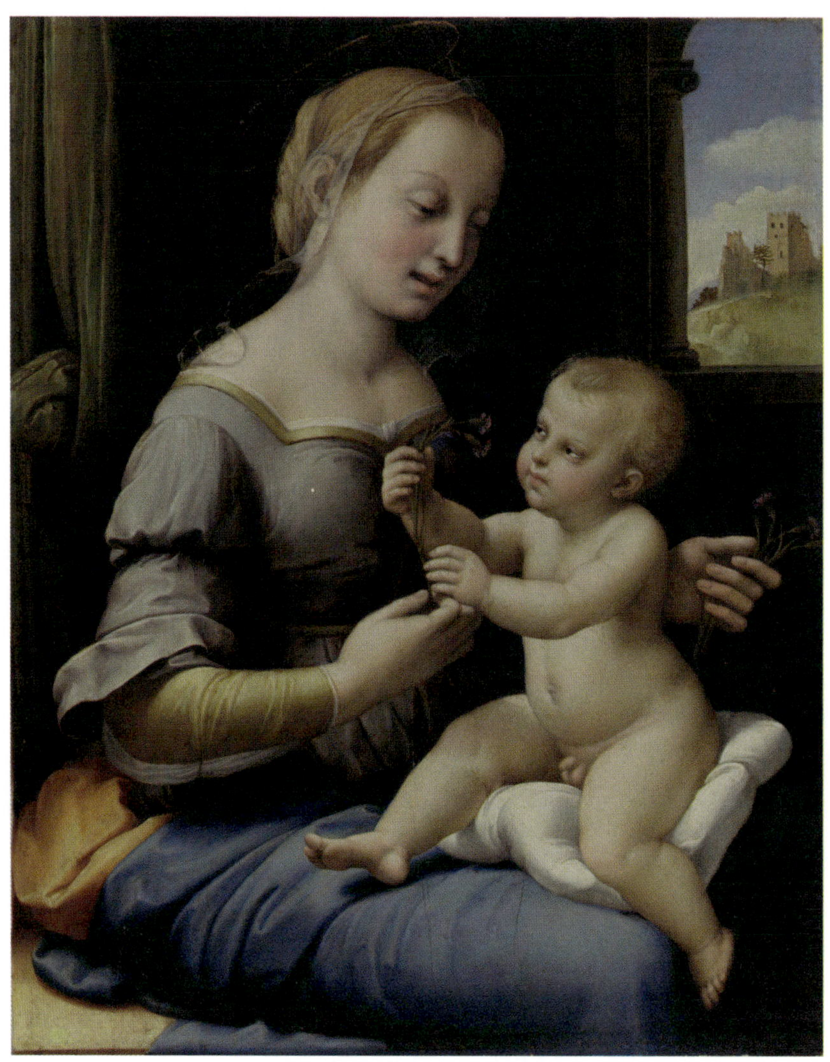

ABOVE Raphael, *The Madonna of the Pinks*, c. 1506–07

OPPOSITE James McNeill Whistler, *Symphony in White, No. 1: The White Girl*, 1861–63, 1872

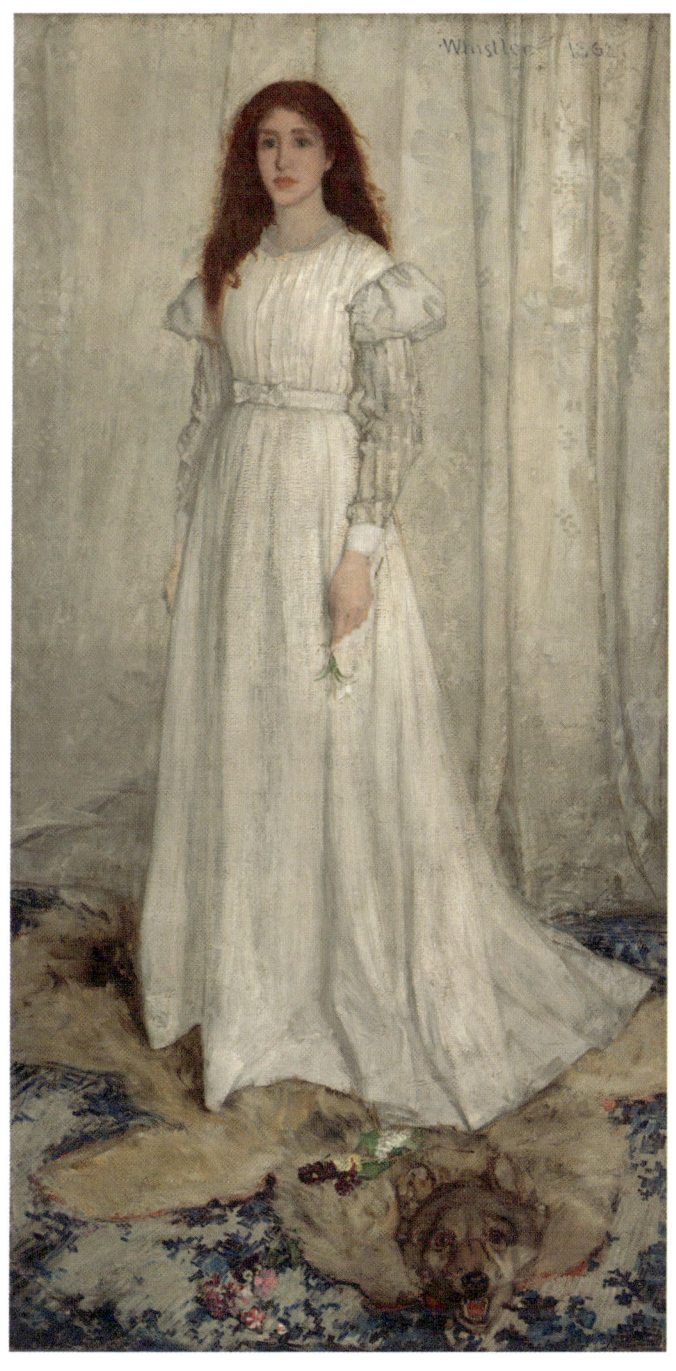

Lead White

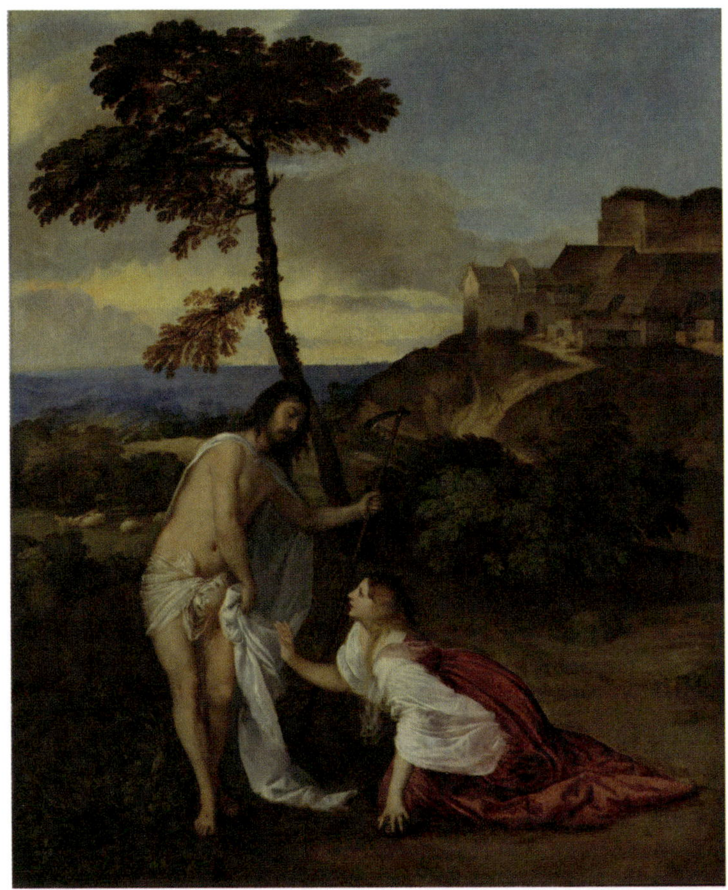

Titian, *Noli me Tangere*, c. 1514

It is difficult to square such suffering unfolding outside the fiction of the canvas with the delicate luminosity of the risen Christ's diaphanous cloak and loincloth in Titian's moving depiction of Christ's encounter with a grieving Mary Magdalene, *Noli me Tangere* (c. 1514). Meaning 'do not touch me', the Latin title of Titian's painting alludes to Christ's instruction to Mary Magdalene, who reaches out in awe to feel his resurrected flesh after she initially failed to recognize him. Christ's message, that the time has come for faith not tangible proof, is aesthetically amplified by the minor miracle of Titian himself weaving from a putrid and toxic chemical residue an exquisite translucency of fabric.

An intense self-portrait by the contemporary Welsh painter Shani Rhys James suggests just how indelibly the unsettling lore of lead white's noxiousness has stained cultural consciousness. Entitled simply *Lead White*, the work captures

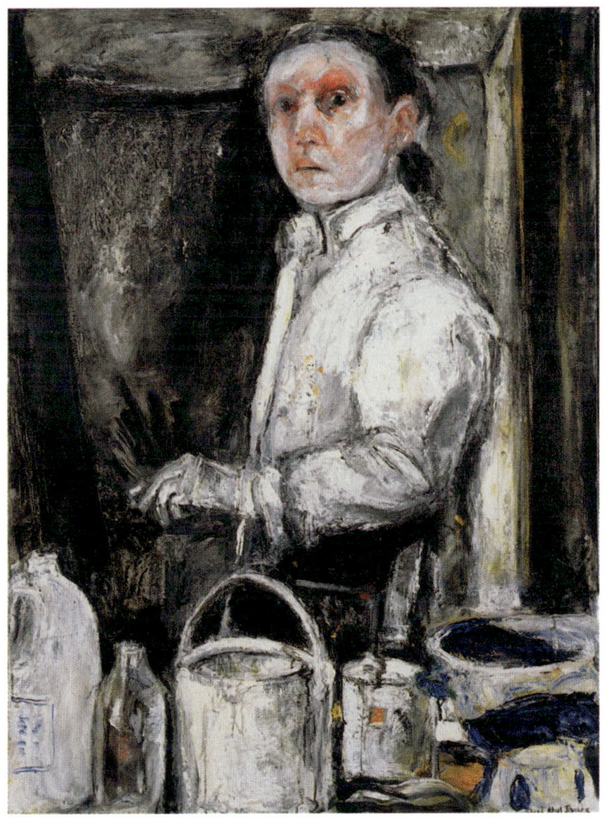

Shani Rhys James, *Lead White*, 1995

the artist in her laboratory-like studio. She appears startled by our gaze, caught as if in an illicit act of concocting colours. Her grubby gloves and lab coat are the same distressed white as her ashen face and the embattling barricade of receptacles she uses to brew her paint – as if the maker, the making and the made were all aspects of the same mephitic mixture. Her art is her life, her death, and her lingering ghost.

Calcite

White may have come, over the course of cultural history, to symbolize innocence, but that does not mean it is a colour unaware of danger or one that naively lets down its guard. While white may be pure, it is also among the most vigilantly protective colours found anywhere in nature – a calculating and calcifying defence against the insatiable rapacities of the universe. Take, for instance, if you can squint tightly enough to see it, the infinitesimal architecture of the brilliant and brilliantly white coccosphere – a microscopic, orb-shaped shell that serves as the armoured vessel in which a single-cell marine organism, the coccolithophore, navigates the treacherous seas.

Constructed from round calcium-carbonate shields, the teensy Death Star-shaped coccosphere (whose diameter is less than that of a grain of salt) does not merely protect its lone inhabitant against predation from such wandering hunters as microzooplankton. According to researchers at NASA, when the creatures come together in their incalculable trillions upon trillions, floating and frothing in sparkling 'blooms' on the ocean's surface, the resulting coccospherical white foam – acres of shimmering spume that are visible from space – can 'reflect nearly all the visible sunlight that hits [it]', a power that helps regulate the thermal climate of the ocean beneath, making it habitable for life.[4] Over time, emptied fragments of these calcite nannofossils

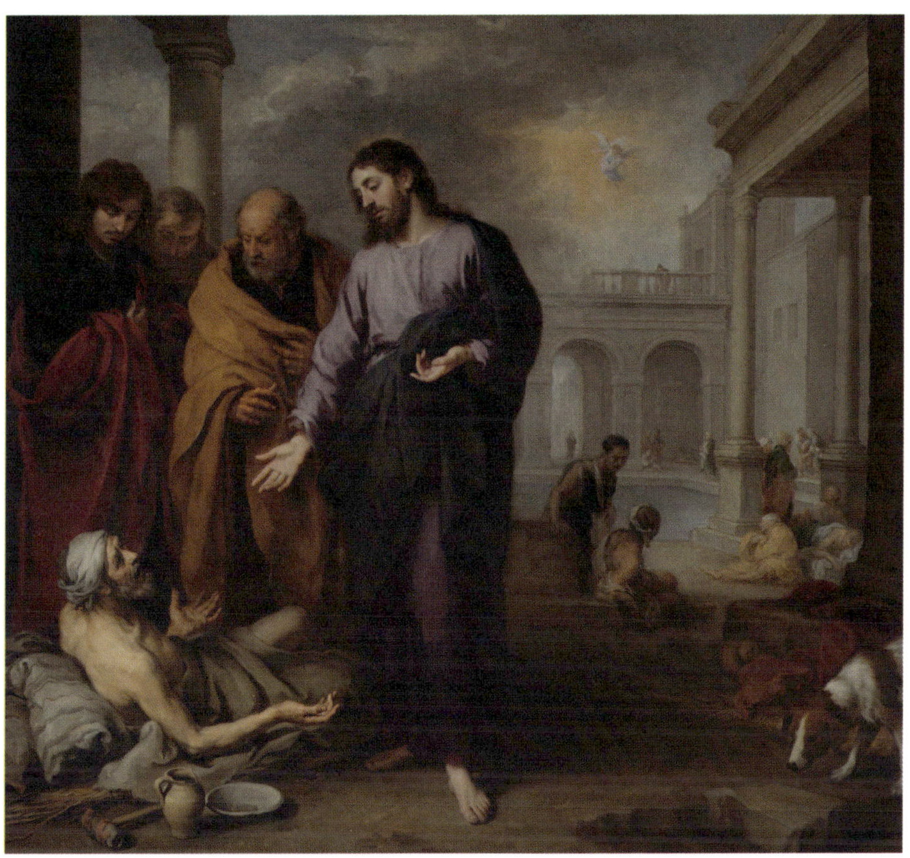

Bartolomé Esteban Murillo, *Christ healing the Paralytic at the Pool of Bethesda*, 1667–70

sink to the bottom of the sea and are slowly compressed into crumbly strata of pure white chalk – a material seized upon as an indispensable pigment since prehistory.

A miracle of microminiature engineering that is capable of protecting life from assaults both near and distant, chalk is an ideal medium, symbolically, for portraying preternatural power. In his poignant painting *Christ healing the Paralytic at*

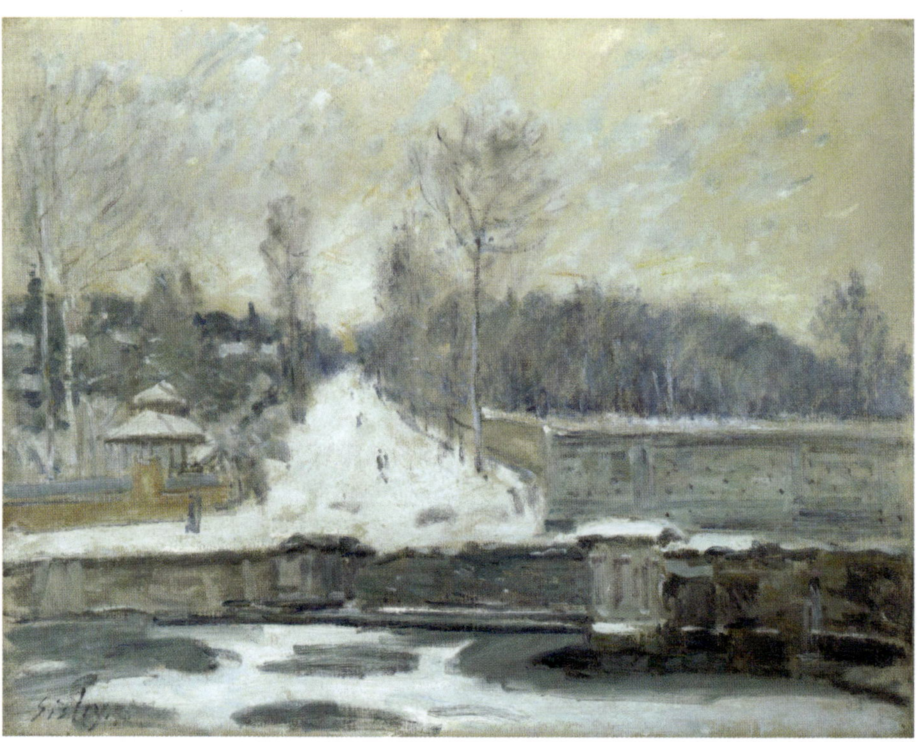

Alfred Sisley, *The Watering Place at Marly-le-Roi*, probably 1875

the Pool of Bethesda, the 17th-century Spanish Baroque master Bartolomé Esteban Murillo sculpts the open palm of Christ – the ineluctable focus of our eyes – from pure white chalk and intensifies the mineral's ethereal shimmer by setting Christ's hand against the orange and yellow-ochre folds of St Peter's robe, which droops behind it. Murillo's canvas depicts an affecting scene from the Book of Matthew in which Christ visits a healing pool in Jerusalem – a spot where an angel is said occasionally to appear. Whosoever steps in the pool first after the angel has blessed the water, according to local legend, is instantly healed. When Christ encounters a sick and disabled man who has never been able to reach the water first, Christ miraculously brings the restorative power to the infirmed figure. He offers his outstretched hand as if it were a healing husk that could envelop the suffering soul.

Chalk plays a crucial role too in the meditative intensity of French Impressionist Alfred Sisley's *The Watering Place at Marly-le-Roi* (probably 1875) – a contemplative depiction of the grand water gardens of a château built as a retreat from Versailles for Louis XIV, King of France, in the late 17th century. So still is the wintery scene, the snow and icy air appear to have slowed the world down to a near-glacial stasis. Only the gentle gush of pale blue water flowing from a spigot on the right side of the canvas, melting the otherwise frozen surface of the pond in the foreground into a kind of tar-pit-like inkiness, disrupts the frigid tranquillity. For the snow itself, which envelops the gardenscape like a dappled shroud, Sisley has relied on lead white. But it is the artist's use of chalk to articulate the suspended ebb and tussle of wispy winter clouds above the scene, encrusting the sky with the tactility of crushed microfossils salvaged from the sea, that transforms Sisley's vision into something more felt than seen. The crushed coccospheres with which the dingy opulence of the sky is crafted inflect the painting's atmosphere with a kind of timeless grandeur – preserving the fleeting moment like an ancient insect in the polished lens of rare white amber.

Kaolin

While many in the West are accustomed to equating black with mourning and the sombrous rituals of burial – the grim garb of grieving ('death-suited', as the poet Philip Larkin described those in funereal attire) – ancient cultures of Asia and Africa have long reached instead for white as the colour most appropriate for bereavement and the sending-off of souls to the hereafter. And not just any white, either. In both China and Africa, a chalky-white clay mineral called kaolin has played a particularly key function in the aesthetics of sepulchral works. Thickly encrusted in kaolin, a 19th-century Congolese statuette (which symbolically stood as a sentinel between this world and the next) illustrates the resilience of age-old associations between the colour white and the ancestral sphere to which souls emigrate. 'The realm of the living', according to Alisa LaGamma, an expert in the arts of Africa, Oceania and the Americas at the Metropolitan Museum of Art, New York,

> *is characterized as black, in contrast to that of the ancestors, Mpemba, which is blanched of color and identified with the chalk or white kaolin drawn from river beds. That material substance is a ritual symbol with long-standing and far-ranging significance across Central Africa and is identified with purity, contact with the ancestors, and virtue. Indeed, in missionary and ethnographer Karl Laman's Kikongo-French dictionary, the term for chalk or white clay is* phembe *or* phembi*, and its derivatives are* pemba*, 'to be' or 'to become white' and* pembisa*, 'to make white' or 'to whiten'.*[5]

The Western word 'kaolin' is derived from the name of a mountain in China, Gaoling (or 'High Hill'), where rich deposits of the white clay have been found in abundance for millennia. At some unremembered moment in ancient Chinese history, an enterprising potter experimented with adding a proportion of kaolin to petuntse (a generic term for the wide range of powdery rocks used to create stoneware vessels) and discovered that the combination, when heated to a preposterously high temperature, produced a glimmering white ceramic that was thinner,

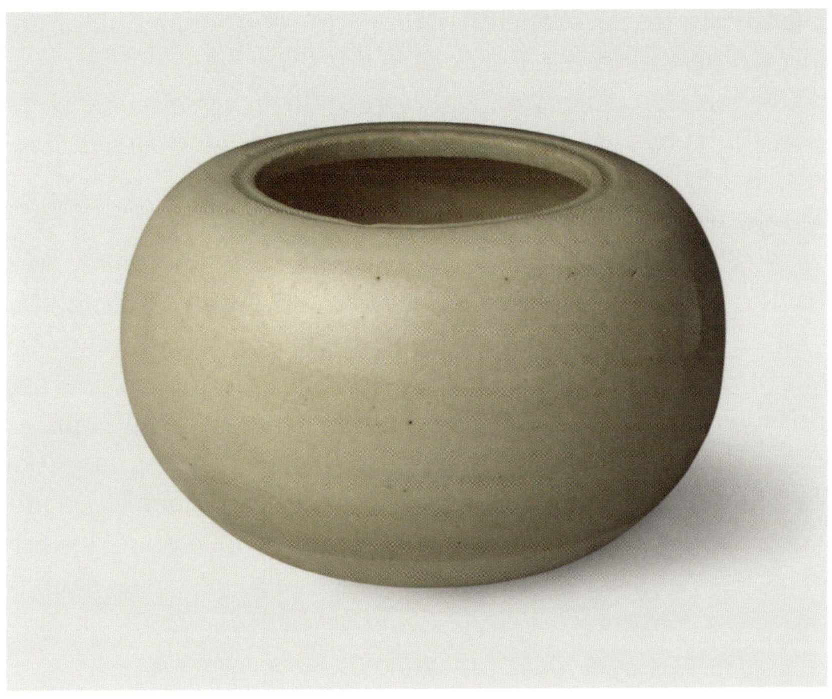

Bowl, China, Sui-Tang dynasty, 7th century CE

lighter, harder and more alluringly luminous than any ever known: porcelain.

Over the course of the ensuing centuries, more colourful and ornately decorated iterations of porcelain (especially cobalt blue-and-white 'china' from the 14th century onwards) would become among the most coveted commodities created by China. But that initial incarnation of ethereally austere translucent white vessels retained an association with honouring and communing with the dead. The contemporary British potter and writer Edmund de Waal, on a pilgrimage to the archives of the Ceramics Institute in Jingdezhen, in the very heart of China's rich kaolin deposits, recalls coming across an order placed on 'the twenty-fourth of the fifth month of 1909', on behalf of the last Chinese emperor, Pu Yi, then just three years old, for 'one white porcelain vase, four white porcelain ju vessels, one white porcelain bowl, and twelve large white porcelain dishes. The vessels will be placed in front of the portrait of the late Empress Xiao Qin Xian for ritual purposes.'[6]

The otherworldly, luminous lustre of porcelain proposes itself as a palpable pivot-stone between death and life, life and death. The chemical attributes of kaolin, as a catalyst for transforming the friable fleshiness of petuntse into something paradoxically both sturdier and more evaporatively light, is crucial to the transformation of the base materials into spiritual sublimity. 'Porcelain mass', according to Martin Schönfeld, a professor of philosophy and an expert on porcelain's cultural history,

> *is a mixture of fusible and infusible ingredients. Because of the materials' different melting points, one ingredient melts in the kiln while the other stays solid. Infusible china clay or kaolin is the 'bone' of the porcelain, as the Chinese called it. Fusible china stone or petuntse (a Western corruption of the Chinese 白墩子), a powdery blend of crystalline feldspar and quartz molded into small pellets, is the 'flesh' of the porcelain. When fired, the flesh attaches to the bone; the flux of petuntse fuses and binds to the heat-resistant kaolin.*[7]

Schönfeld's description of the forging of porcelain, the remarkable fusion of flesh and bone that the process entails, smacks of a curiously literal creation myth, as if kaolin were a secret ingredient for the moulding of life itself – the elusive elixir of being for which the alchemists strenuously searched for centuries. There is a very real sense in which kaolin can indeed be perceived, at least in the story of Western science, as the fabled Philosopher's Stone, ceaselessly sought after since at least the 3rd century BCE, when the ancient Greco-Egyptian alchemist Zosimos of Panopolis posited the existence of such a mysterious element in his legendary handbook *Cheirokmeta* (Handmade). Eventually dismissed as a red herring by scholars from the 18th century onwards, the elusive Philosopher's Stone came to be seen by many as a kind of mythical McGuffin – a material whose very unattainability was useful in motivating early scientific enquiry. A remarkable discovery made in 1708 by an obscure German mountebank, however, dares us to reassess that narrative and to reconsider whether the finest things in life are worth their weight in white, not gold.

It all started in 1700 when nineteen-year-old Johann Friedrich Böttger, an apprentice to an apothecary in Berlin, incautiously boasted that he had stumbled upon a substance that could indeed transform lead into gold. The son of a mint-keeper and nephew of a prosperous goldsmith, Böttger ought to have been more aware than most of the dangers of gold's irrepressible allure – the grave risks of claiming to have found the key to unlocking its mystery. Word of his feat reached the ear of the avaricious king of Prussia, Frederick I, who immediately dispatched a team to fetch the audacious alchemist. Tipped off, Böttger ran. But didn't look where he was going. He soon found himself running headlong into the territory and arms of the equally greedy monarch of Saxony, Augustus the Strong, who was all too happy to keep the teenager safe in a castle in Dresden – a hostage until he was able to produce a hefty pile of gold. Things looked hopeless for the hapless alchemist until the respected German physicist Ehrenfried Walther von Tschirnhaus was permitted to pay Böttger a visit – an encounter that would change the course of cultural history.[8]

Tschirnhaus recognized in Böttger a surprisingly genuine aptitude for scientific experimentation that, he believed, might be useful in a separate pursuit in which Tschirnhaus had himself

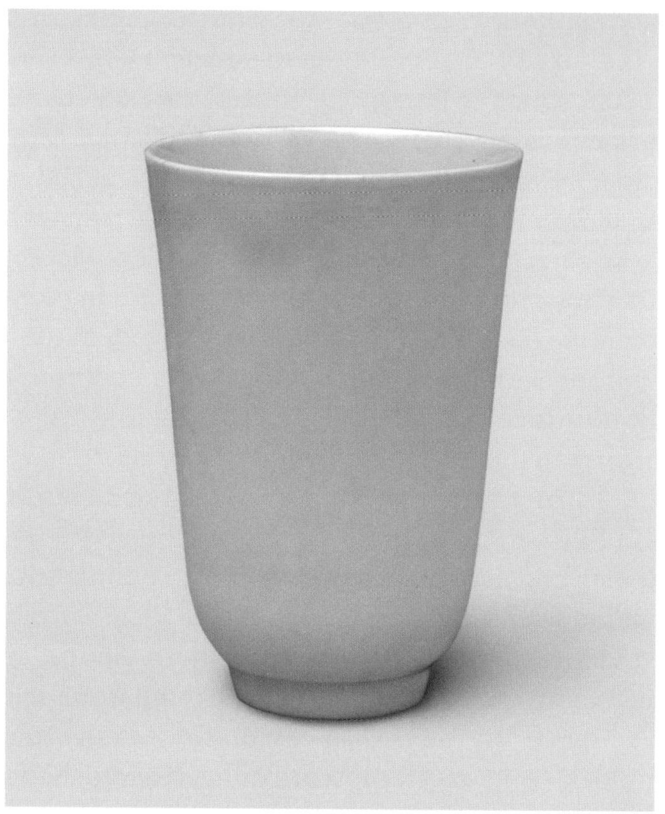

Johann Friedrich Böttger, beaker, 1709–10

been unsuccessfully engrossed: cracking the ancient chemical code for making Chinese porcelain. Known in Böttger's and Tschirnhaus's day as 'white gold', for the exorbitant prices that the merchant class in Europe was prepared to pay for the imported commodity, Chinese porcelain was, pound for pound, more valuable than the precious metal itself. Prepared to give Böttger one last chance to prove his worth, Augustus the Strong relocated the enterprising pair to Meissen and instructed them to produce white gold – or else.

Sure enough, the collaboration proved successful when Tschirnhaus and Böttger discovered (or rather rediscovered) that alabaster could indeed be transformed into the hard translucency of perfect porcelain when combined with kaolin – rich deposits of which had recently been discovered 100 km (62 miles) to the south-west of Meissen in Schneeberg. Production of a suitably pure-white porcelain substitute that came to be known as Böttgerware (a name that conceals the contribution of Tschirnhaus, who died soon after the pair's breakthrough) was quickly underway. In time, other ingredients (including quartz) would be added to the recipe to further strengthen the cleverly reverse-engineered ceramic. But the great breakthrough by Böttger and Tschirnhaus (there is still some debate over just whose insight it was that proved ultimately decisive[9]) was in recognizing the centrality of kaolin to forming the solid 'bone' around which the flesh of alabaster flux adhered under heat – in decrypting the secret of converting the lifeless dross of dull clay into a shimmering substance that pulsed with luminous life.

Albert Henry Munsell's *Atlas of the Munsell Color System* (1915)

Just as every place in the world occupies a specific geographic position (one to which latitudinal, longitudinal and altitudinal coordinates can be assigned), the American teacher and artist Albert Henry Munsell believed that every conceivable colour could likewise be placed along intersecting x, y and z axes. According to the deceptively simple 'Munsell Color Space', as the model was known, every colour that we perceive possesses a unique combination of quantifiable qualities (hue, value and chroma) and can be located accordingly in an elaborate colour 'atlas'. Like the theories of Philipp Otto Runge, whose colour sphere must have been spinning in the back of Munsell's mind, white and black occupy the poles in the latter's multidimensional scheme, forming a neutral axis around which the chromatic globe twists. Harmonious hues, or those in 'balance', will be found along similarly charted paths – as if mapping immaterial roads through a transcendent realm of pure colour.

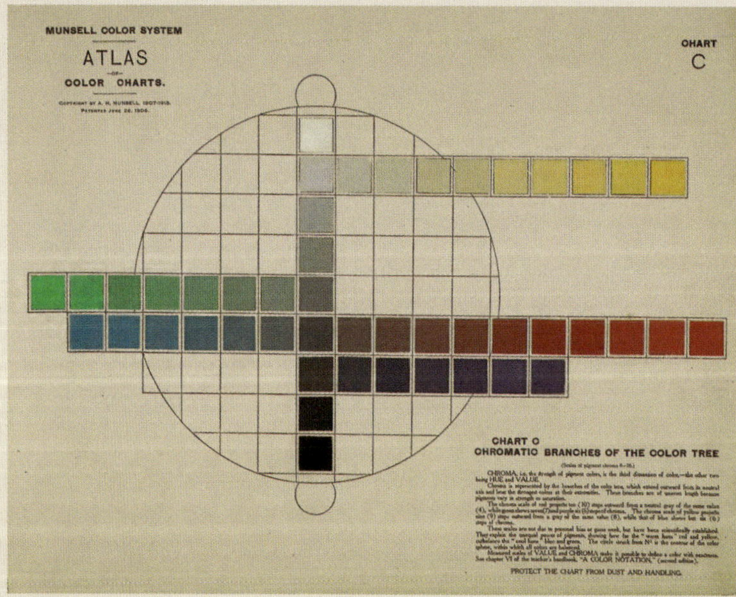

This chart is intended to illustrate Munsell's concept of 'chroma' – a colour's 'strength', or intensity, as opposed to its 'hue' or 'value' – and how it figures in pinpointing the position of a given colour. 'Chroma', Munsell explains in the key to the chart, 'is represented by the branches of the color tree, which extend outward from its neutral axis and bear the Strongest colors at their extremities. These branches are of uneven length because pigments vary in strength or saturation.'

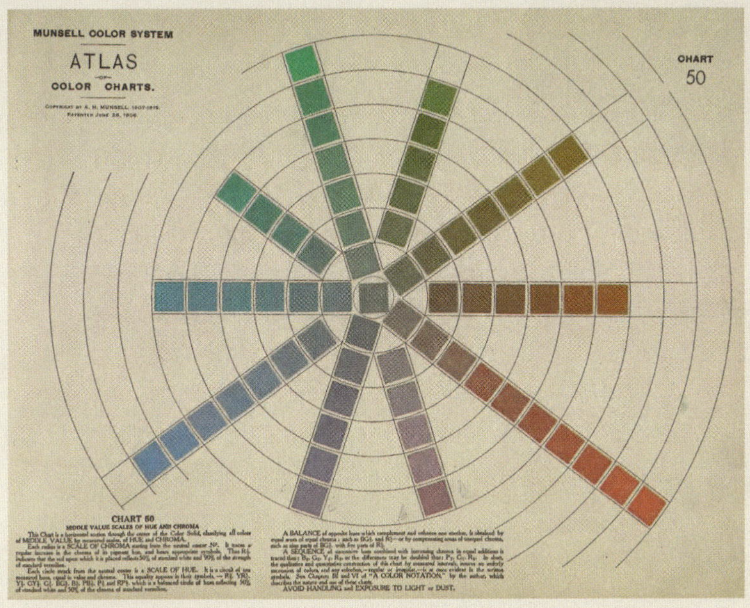

'Chart 50' from *Atlas of the Munsell Color System* is intended to illustrate 'a horizontal section through the center of the Color Solid', as if one were to slice the theorist's globe of colour in half along its equator and examine its core. Each resplendent spoke, or 'radius', in Munsell's model indicates a given colour's relative 'scale of chroma', or strength.

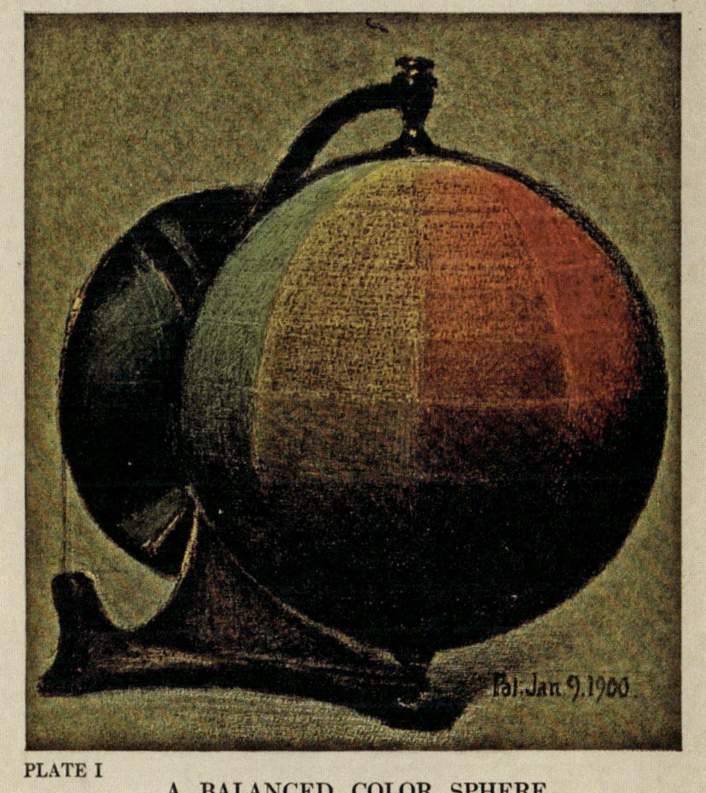

PLATE I

A BALANCED COLOR SPHERE

PASTEL SKETCH

Munsell's focus on multidimensional models capable of categorizing colours and unlocking how they interact with one another can be traced back to his early twenties. In 1879, when he was twenty-one, he constructed a spinning chromatic pyramid to observe the optical illusion of hues blurring together. In time, that proto device would evolve into a globe (seen here) and then into his better-known quasi-geographic colour atlas.

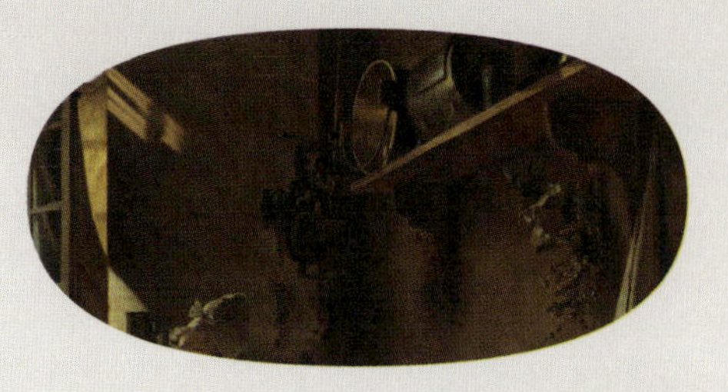

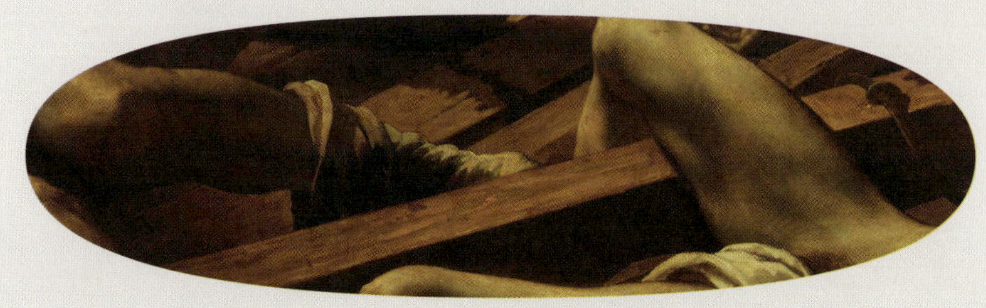

Brown

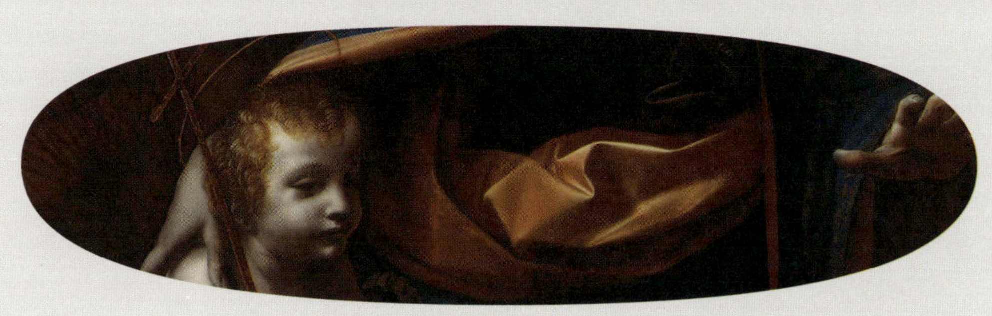

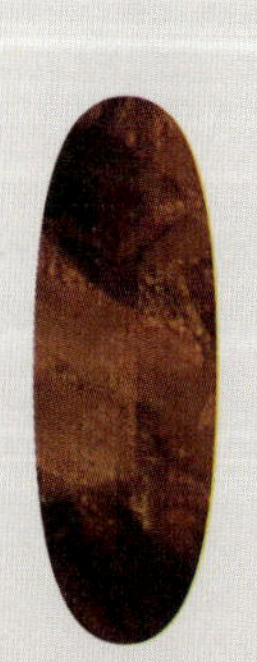

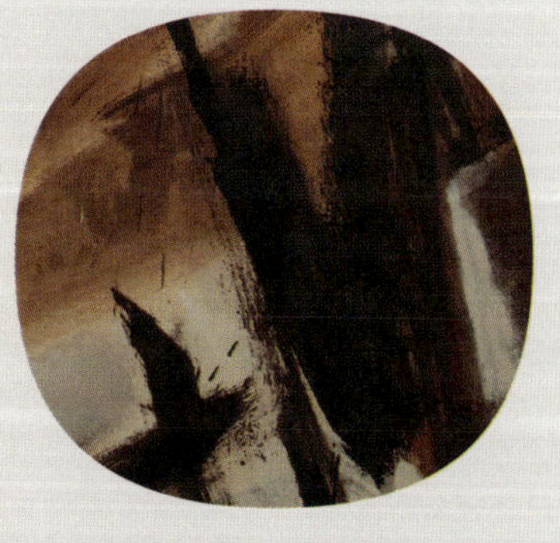

To get to the bottom of brown is to get to the bottom of being. Our souls may aspire to blue (its vaulted heavens and surging seas), crave gold, and rage red and green in fits of anger and jealousy, but brown is really the colour to which our bodies are closest in this world. Brown is the ground we stand upon and the abyss we are moving towards our entire lives. Brown draws us in. There's no resisting the beauty or gravity of its powerful pull. Brown undergirds our experience of lushness. It gives way to the ephemeral flush of flowers that blush for a season and are gone. Brown abides. Once we sync our minds to the music of brown, we begin to see its shades inflected in everything. In his poem 'The Fowlers', the 18th-century poet Moses Browne, who may have been congenitally attuned to russet rhythms, captures the smoulder of night smudging into morning more familiarly than one might have expected:

> *'Twas early dawn, when yet the glimm'ring light*
> *But dimly pierc'd the scatt'ring brown of night.*[1]

Umber

In 1959, Lee Krasner couldn't sleep. It had been three years since her husband, Jackson Pollock – with whom Krasner had been in a turbulent marriage for more than a decade – had died drunk behind the wheel. But reverberations of the untimely loss were still keeping the American abstract artist awake at night. Indulging her insomnia, Krasner hurled herself into a new nocturnal schedule. She swapped the natural light in which she was accustomed to working in her studio during the day for the artificial flicker of electric bulbs, and traded the vibrant hues for which her work was known for the muddy music of more sombrous shades. The result was a string of affecting canvases that

Krasner called the *Umber Paintings*, after the earthy brown that dominates their sober surfaces.

In works such as *Seeded* (1960), deep sorrel slashes wear away at the canvas as if it were the site of an excavation or hasty burial – as if Krasner were caught in a ceaseless cycle of putting to rest and resurrecting the fraught energy of her relationship with Pollock. 'My painting', Krasner once suggested, 'is so biographical, if anyone can take the trouble to read it.' In compiling the catalogue raisonné of Krasner's oeuvre after her death in 1984, the art historian Ellen Landau concluded that the artist's teasing confession 'is most easily proved by an examination' of the *Umber Paintings*. 'By using these pictures as vehicles to express the ongoing, and to all appearances death-defying, continuity of her tempestuous relationship with Pollock, Krasner exposed in a particularly poignant way the deeply personal roots of her artistic impulse. In the process, she produced a dramatic set of canvases whose mythic, explosive quality vividly projects her turmoil and inner rage.'[2]

That Krasner should reach for brown, and for umber in particular, as the shade best suited to reveal the grittier aspects of her soul is consistent with the murky pigment's muckiness. 'A course, greazy, and foule colour' is how the English artist and musician Edward Norgate – in a treatise on painting, 'Miniatura; or, the Art of Limning', that he left unpublished at the time of his death in 1650 – described the pigment, which is derived principally from raw deposits unearthed in Turkey. Despite its insalubrious texture and tone, the pigment was, Norgate concedes, 'very useful for shadowes, hair, perspective and almost any thing'. 'It is extreamly dry and, as you find it in the shopps, troublesome to worke,' he points out, 'but burnt in a Crusible, works neatly and well.' The nearness of umber to the shade of shadows probably explains its name – a version of Latin *ombra* (meaning 'shadow').[3] Umber was a paradox, aligned equally to the materiality of tangible earth and the immateriality of

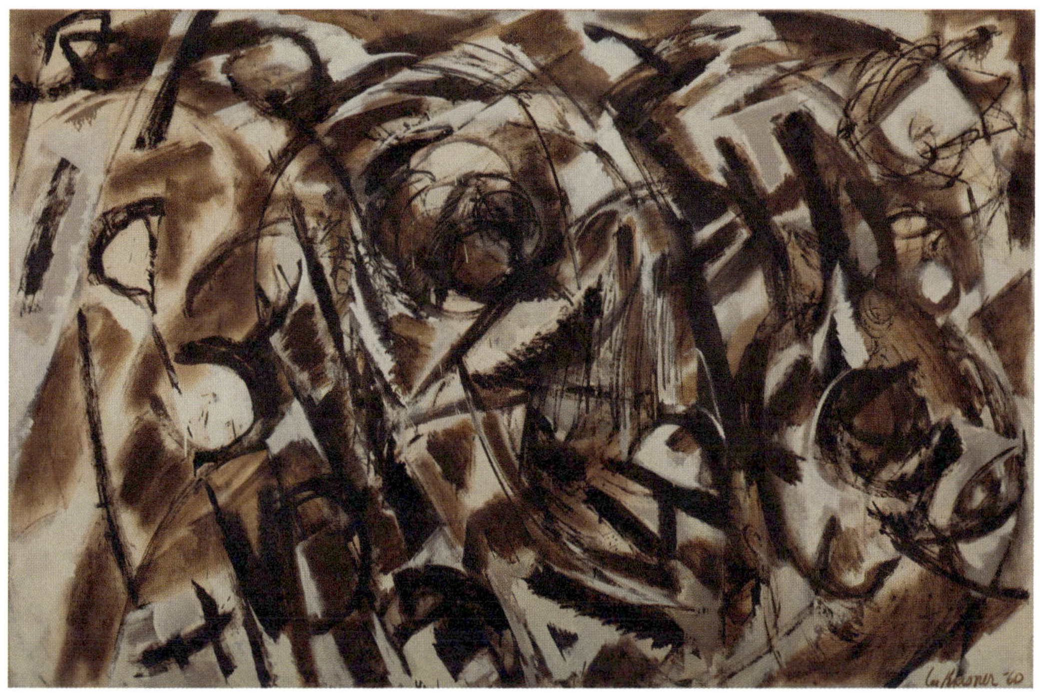

Lee Krasner, *Seeded*, 1960

impalpable gloom. The gashes of umber with which Krasner conducts her dramatic self-interrogation ensure her work tills the same serious soil that furrows Rembrandt's brow in his 1659 self-portrait – a broody depiction that is, itself, sculpted from psychological shadows and untempered rage.

Van Dyke Brown

When it came to casting shadows, the Old Masters were spoiled for choice. In addition to umber, there was an effective derivative of peat found in the iron oxide-rich soils around Kassel and

Cologne, Germany. Eventually known by the end of the 18th century as 'Van Dyke brown' - in honour of the 17th-century Flemish master and protégé of Rubens, Anthony van Dyke, whose paintings widely employ a distinctive glaze made from the pigment - so-called Cassel earth (or Cologne earth) was fashioned from naturally compressed turf, or lignite - a sedimentary rock also known as 'brown coal'. As such, Van Dyke brown is a close sibling of the mineraloid gemstone jet, whose depth of darkness gives birth to the phrase 'jet black'. Millennia before European colourmen had begun pestling lignite into pigment, our prehistoric forebears were forging pendants from the same stuff and polishing them into Venus figurines.

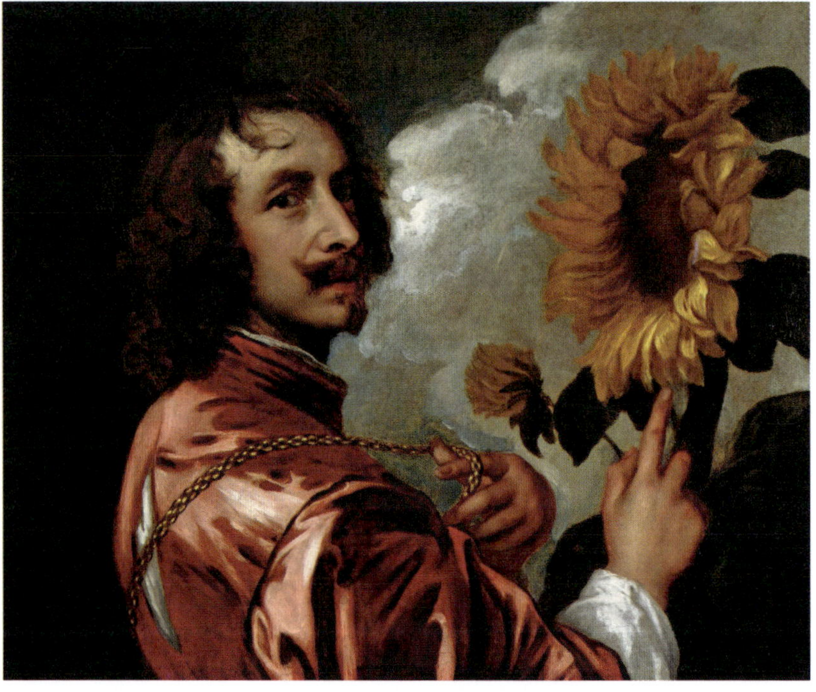

Anthony van Dyke, *Self-Portrait with a Sunflower*, 1632-33

By the 1st century CE, the use of lignite as a fuel was a practice capable of radiating more than merely heat. According to Pliny the Elder, long before the Renaissance succeeded in extracting the pigment Van Dyke brown, the crude rock vibrated with almost supernatural power. 'The kindling' of the sedimentary substance, Pliny insists,

> *drives off snakes and relieves suffocation of the uterus. Its fumes detect attempts to stimulate a disabling illness or a state of virginity. Moreover, when thoroughly boiled with wine it cures toothache, and if combined with wax, scrofulous tumours. The Magi are said to make use of it in what they call 'divination by axes', and they assert it will not burn away completely if a wish is destined to come true.*[4]

In time, lignite, when not burned for fuel but dried and pounded, was found to produce an absorbing brown hue – one that Norgate described as 'very good to close upp the last and deepest touches of the Shaddowe places of pictures by the life, and likewise very useful in Landscape'. In *The Virgin of the Rocks*, Leonardo found Cassel earth useful in sculpting the cave-like rocky recess in which, according to the narrative of a non-biblical story, the infant John the Baptist, escorted by the archangel Uriel, adores the Christ child as he, and the Virgin Mary, journey from Bethlehem to Egypt to foil King Herod's plot to kill him. Analysis of the artist's materials by curators at London's National Gallery has revealed that the rich russet rocks that surround the travelling party owe their simmering radiance to a calibrated inflection of lignite; 'where the rocks are warmer in tone', the curators note, 'the paint mixture is dominated by Cassel earth.'[5]

When placed in proximity to Leonardo's work, Pliny's allusion to the use of lignite as an amulet of protection and divine guidance sheds curious light on the masterpiece. Crafted

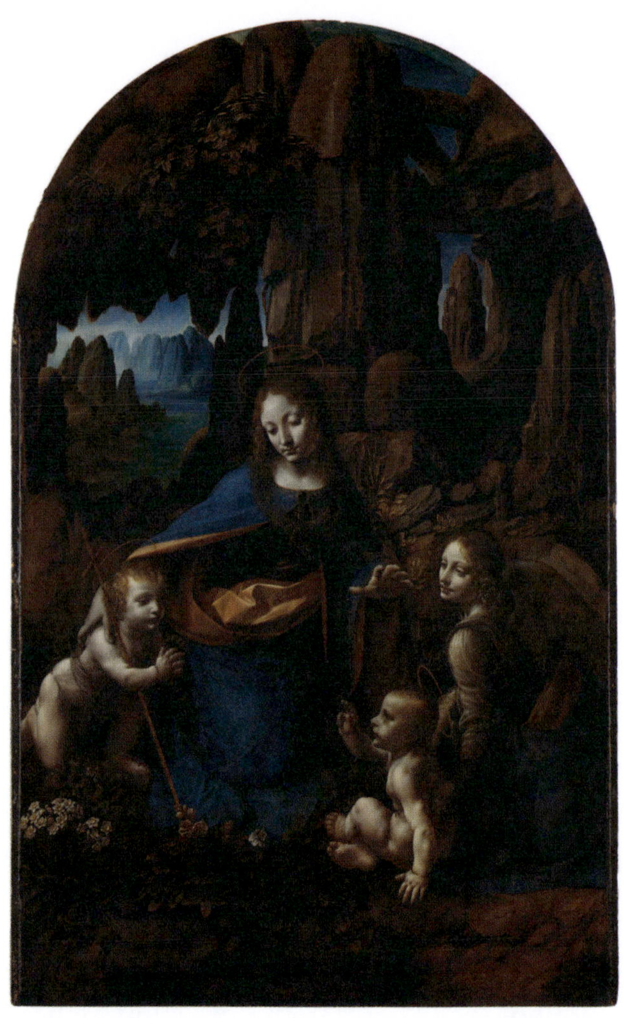

Leonardo da Vinci, *The Virgin of the Rocks*, c. 1491/92–99 and 1506–08

from the same substance that was once employed by ancient axinomancers (who heated lignite axe heads until they glowed and interpreted the shifting shapes they saw in the smouldering blades), the rocks that Leonardo sharpens and ignites in his painting glimmer ambiguously and demarcate a strange spiritual sanctuary that collapses the distance between superstition and faith. Three centuries later, Théodore Géricault will rely on Cassel earth to define a very different kind of intense space when staging a reconstruction of the tragedy that befell the passengers and crew of the French naval frigate *Méduse*, which struck a sandbank off the West African coast on 2 July 1816. To choreograph convincingly the faces and physiques of those left clinging for two weeks to a makeshift float, Géricault scoured the morgues and hospitals in and around Paris to acquaint himself with physiognomies of suffering. But it isn't just his keen observation of emaciated muscle that makes *The Raft of the Medusa* so compelling. Like Leonardo, Géricault has sculpted from lignite the ambiance of a plane that sits outside time and space. The scene may portray a maritime disaster, but there is an eerie earthiness to the air that is piled on top of the dead and dying. In this, the most subterranean sea painting in art history, the cadaverous sheen of lignite allows the painter to sync with his subject like few works before ever have. Géricault makes us feel the paradoxical claustrophobia

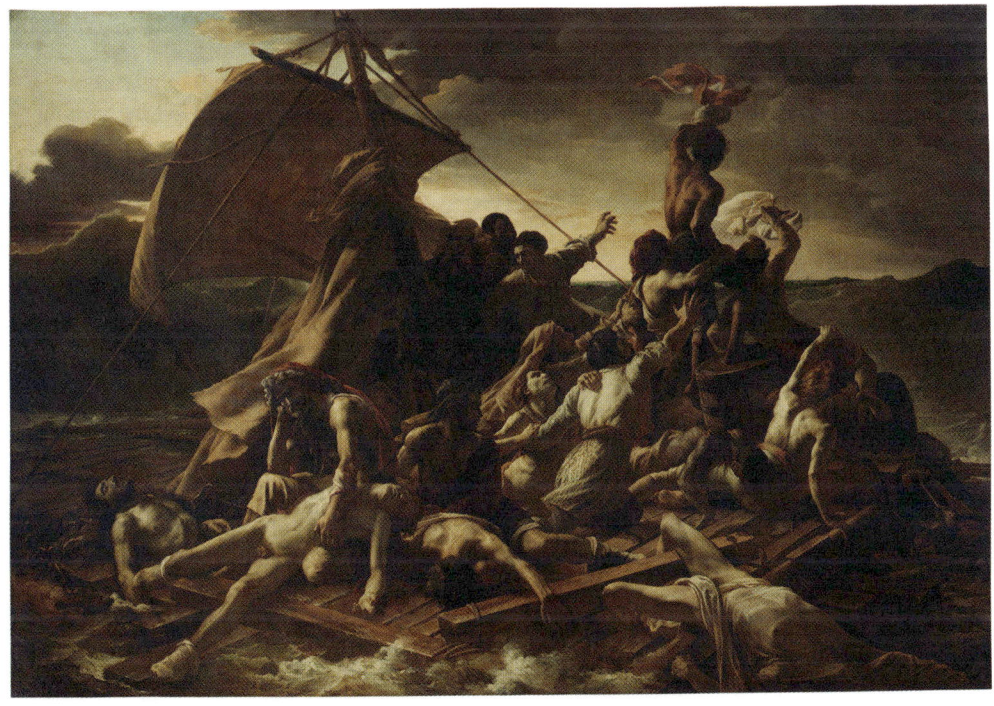

Théodore Géricault, *The Raft of the Medusa*, 1818–19

of the catastrophe – fatally cramped on a wide sea – by interring us alive with it.

Mumia

The disquieting conceit of art as entombment would be taken to a deeper and more alarmingly literal level by contemporaries of Géricault (if not indeed by the Rouen-born Romantic himself, who died before his time in 1824, aged just thirty-two) with the reliance on one of the most extraordinary pigments in the history of art: mumia, or 'mummy brown'. Due to a linguistic slip sometime around the 14th century, *mumiya*, the Persian word for 'bitumen' (a substance derived from crude oil that, since antiquity, had been celebrated as a magical cure-all for assorted ailments), found itself synonymous with ancient Egyptian corpses that had merely been embalmed with the sticky stuff – a lazy lexical slide that still trips off our tongues today. Before long (and despite local laws prohibiting the practice), Europeans desperate for the fabled elixir unwittingly facilitated a gruesome trade in smuggled bodies from Egypt, which were powderized into a dark, bitumen-brown medicine that could be acquired at almost any pharmacy. Unflinching testimony preserved by a 16th-century British merchant, John Sanderson, who participated in the morbid market first-hand, fleshes out the appalling enterprise of procuring desiccated relics. 'We were lett doun by ropes as into a well,' Sanderson recalls of a subterranean expedition into the necropolis of Saqqara in ancient Memphis,

> *with waxe candles burninge in our hands, and so waulked upon the bodies of all sorts and sised* [sic], *great and smaul, and some imbalmed in little earthen potts, which never had forme, these are sett at the feete of great bodies. They gave no*

> *noysome smell at all, but are like pitch beinge broken. For I broke off all the parts of the bodies to see how the fleshe was turned to drugge, and brought home divers heads, hands, armes and feet, for a shewe. We brought allso 600 lbs for the Turkie Companie in peces; and brought into Ingland in the Hercules, together with a whole bodie. They are lapped in 100 double of cloth, which rotting and pilling off, you may see the skin, flesh, fingers and nayles firme, altered blacke. One little hand I brought into Ingland, to shew; and presented it to my brother, who gave the same to a doctor in Oxford.*[6]

In time, misguided enthusiasm for the miracle extract, ingestion of which remedied nothing, gave way to a realization by some colourmen that pulverized people did, however, yield an unexpectedly effective hue. In a letter published in the influential learned journal *Annals of Philosophy* in 1823, the Anglo-Saxon scholar John Josias Conybeare reflects on the journey that mumia had taken from panacea to pigment. 'My dear sir,' Conybeare writes, 'it is well known that the substance found in the interior of Egyptian mummies, and thence termed mumia, once obtained not only a place, but a high reputation, in the Materia Medica ... Mumia, though long since discarded from the Pharmacopaeia, has, I believe, retained some value as a pigment, especially with those artists who are somewhat of dilettanti in the choice of their materials. I am not sufficiently acquainted with the practical part of oil-painting to say with what justice. It may possibly afford a somewhat richer brown than the common asphaltum.'[7]

The use of 'common asphaltum' proved itself a kind of curse. Géricault, who employed it extensively in *The Raft of the Medusa* to inflect the fetid sea air with a tawdry tawny gloam, was doubtless unaware that, over time, the pigment would cause colours to curdle and the canvas itself to rumple. However

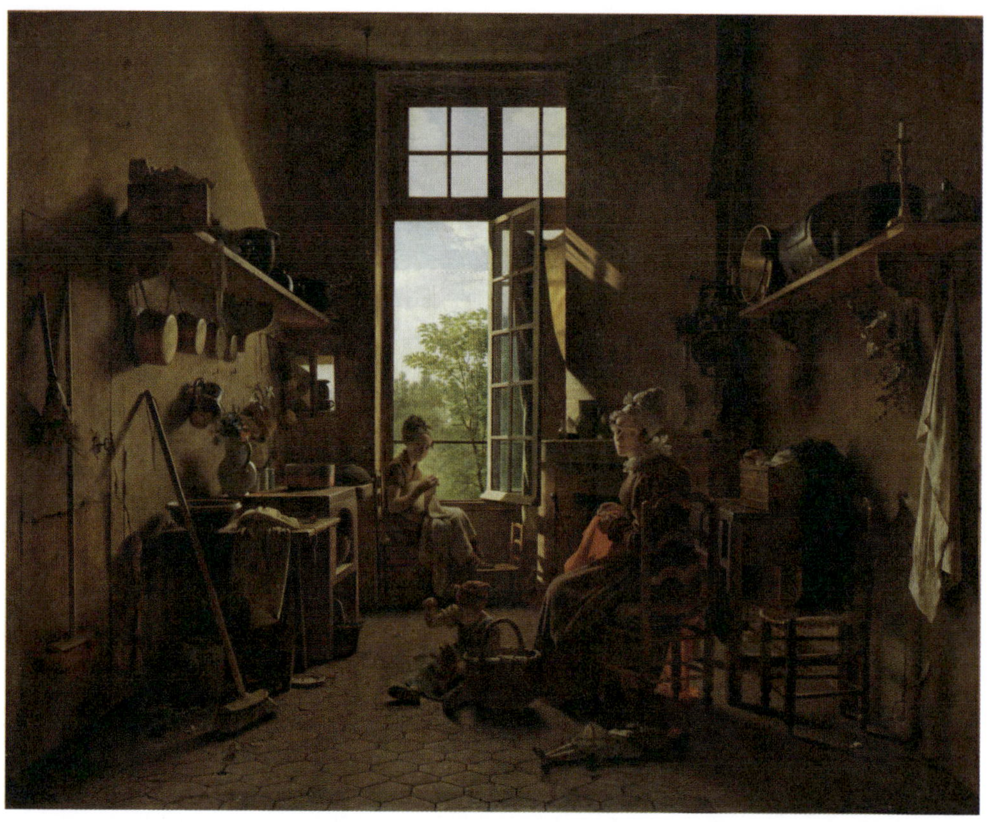

Martin Drölling, *L'intérieur d'une cuisine*, 1815

macabre its essence and abhorrent its procurement, mumia produced a brown that was ironically less fugitive in application than asphaltum – more comfortable in its own skin. Precisely how widespread its use was and in which works, specifically, it can be found have proved tricky for art historians to pin down, given the tools at hand. Nor is it easy to know for certain whether a given batch of 'mummy brown' was derived from far-flung ancient Egyptian bodies or corpses closer to home. It has long been rumoured that a simulation of mumia, concocted from the shrivelled remains of French kings riffled from their rest in the abbey of Saint-Denis, is responsible for setting the temperature and tone of French artist Martin Drölling's late masterpiece *L'intérieur d'une cuisine* (1815), created two years before the painter died. Knowing that dollops of death disbalanced Drölling's palette is helpful in comprehending more consciously the troubling tombiness of the scene, which looks less like a cosy kitchen than a timeless crypt – hived off forever from the world of shifting sunlight we glimpse through the window in the distance. When perceived as shellacked in pulverized flesh and linen, the eerie otherworldliness we detect in the placid countenances of the eternal seamstresses, whose ungainly gawk our gaze awkwardly meets, suddenly makes sense.

The early 19th century witnessed an accelerating fascination in Europe with all things Egyptian – a craze serially stoked by the gradual release after 1809 of the multi-volume encyclopedic *Description de l'Ėgypte*, compiled in the wake of Napoleon's campaign in Egypt in 1798 and intended to comprise everything that could be known about the place. To paint with mumia was to have one's finger not just on ground-up fingers, but on the very pulse of cultural resuscitation. In England, we know that Turner turned to it,[8] and that, later, the Pre-Raphaelites were obsessed with the murky mystery with which the ghoulish pigment seemed uniquely capable of imbuing a scene. Not everyone was a fan. George Field concedes that the pigment 'brought from the catacombs of Egypt' has, 'as a rule, a more solid and lasting texture than simple asphaltum' and is 'less liable to crack or move on the canvass'. But he is also quick to caution that 'mummy varies exceedingly both in its composition and qualities; and as from its very nature and origin nothing certain can be said of it, but little reliance should be placed on this brown', before recycling a quip that 'nothing is to be gained by smearing one's canvass with a part, perhaps, of the wife of Potiphar [the captain of the Pharaoh's guard from the Book of Hebrews, who is said to have purchased Joseph as a slave]'. 'It is not particularly prudent', Field concludes, 'to employ without necessity these crumbled remains of dead bodies, which must contain ammonia and particles of fat in a concrete state and so be more or less apt to injure the colours with which they may be united.'[9]

That many artists were not fully cognizant of what, exactly, they were trafficking in or squeezing on to their palettes when they got hold of a tube of 'mummy brown' seems likely from the reaction of the British artist Edward Burne-Jones when he finally realized what exactly a product so-marketed truly entailed. Burne-Jones's wife vividly remembered the moment when a guest over Sunday lunch recounted a recent visit he'd paid to a colourman's laboratory, where he had witnessed first-hand the grisly process of pestling a person into pigment. 'Edward', Georgiana Burne-Jones recalled, 'scouted the idea of the pigment having anything to do with a mummy' and 'said the name must be only borrowed to describe a particular shade of brown'.

> *But when assured that it was actually compounded of real mummy, he left us at once, hastened to the studio, and returning with the only tube he had, insisted on our giving it decent burial there and then. So a hole was bored in the green grass at our feet, and we all watched it put safely in, and the spot was marked by one of the girls planting a daisy root above it.*[10]

The bizarre ritual left an indelible impression too on the artist's young nephew, the writer Rudyard Kipling, who had come round for lunch that Sunday as well. 'He descended in broad daylight with a tube of "Mummy Brown" in his hand,' Kipling recalled with 'delightful shivers' decades later, 'saying that he had discovered it was made of dead Pharaohs and we must bury it accordingly. So we all went out and helped – according to the rites of Mizraim and Memphis, I hope - and to this day I could drive a spade within a foot of where that tube lies.'[11]

For those artists who were aware of mummy brown's grim ingredients, the use of mortal remains as a medium of aesthetic expression was doubtless indicative of an urge to merge not just emotionally with a work but materially - to collapse the distance between a mere meditation on being human and human beings themselves. That Eugène Delacroix is believed to have reached for mummy brown to create his now lost decorations for the Salon de la Paix at the Hôtel de Ville in Paris, including a portrayal of Neptune calming the waves, implies a poignant transformation of the mythic scene (which Bernini famously chiselled from marble) from remote indifference of stolid stasis to something grittily integral to death and life. After all, however mighty gods may seem, they're nothing more than a murky mosaic of our own festering grime.

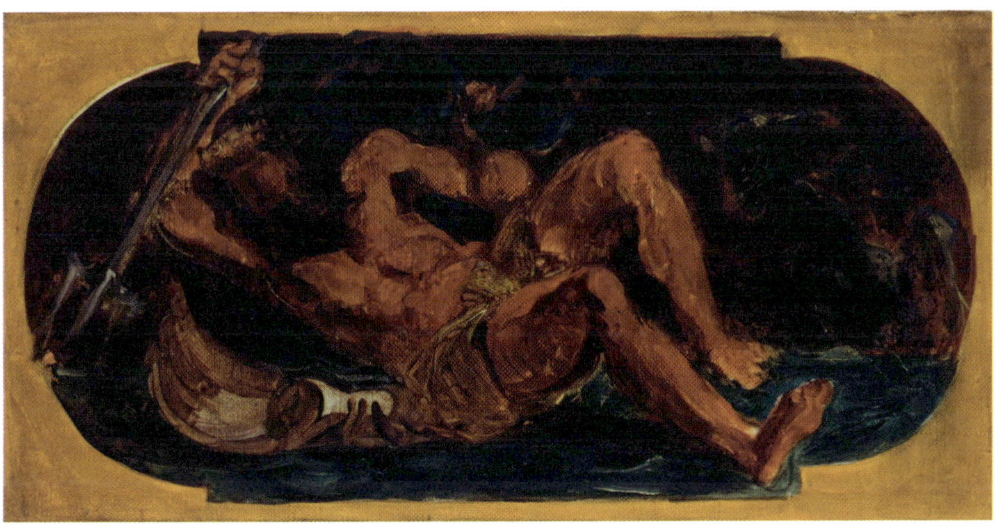

Eugène Delacroix, 'Neptune Calms the Waves', design for the Salon de la Paix at the Hôtel de Ville in Paris, 1849–52

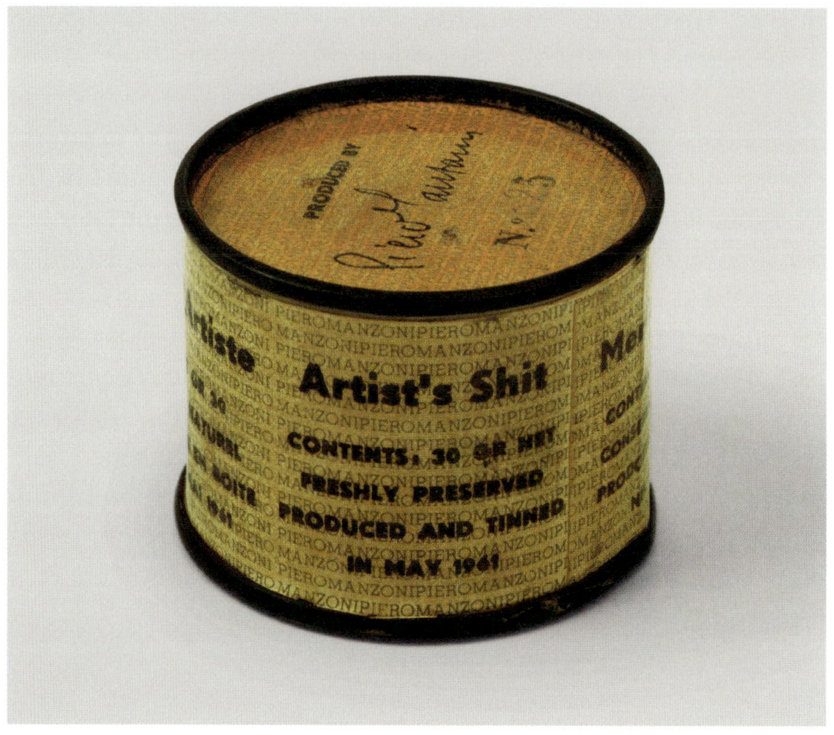

Piero Manzoni, *Artist's Shit*, 1961

Excrement

One needn't, of course, wait for death, or for an elapse of centuries to ferment buried flesh into the raw stuff of pigment, in order to squeeze the human body into potent colour. As Picasso realized in a moment of epiphany while observing his infant daughter, Maya, fill her nappy, we, all of us, are living tubes of paint. 'According to him,' the artist's granddaughter Diana Widmaier Picasso recently revealed, 'excrement from an infant breast-fed by its mother had a unique texture and ocher color.'[12] To what extent Picasso's preoccupation with poo – which the art critic Jonathan Jones astutely traces back to his portrayal of one of the five prostitutes is his epoch-making *Les Demoiselles d'Avignon* (1907) 'squat[ting] on the ground, her arse towards the onlooker, about to do a shit' - may be memorialized in surviving works is difficult to know.[13] He never itemized the medium as such on any given painting or collage.

It wasn't until 1961, when the impish Italian avant-garde artist Piero Manzoni unveiled ninety pantry-ready and professionally labelled cans filled with his own faeces, *Merda d'artista* (or *Artist's Shit*), that a work comprised of excrement was prepared to say so on the tin. A wry comment on rampant commercialization, Manzoni's irreverently cheeky work (which predates Andy Warhol's tamer, albeit more famous, simulacra of commodities) bears down on the question of how much of themselves artists put into their work - what, exactly, we are buying and admiring when we acquire them. The fact that Manzoni's cans, made as they are of steel, cannot easily be scanned to confirm what it is that really gives them their plausible heft, leaves a level of indeterminacy about the veracity of the artist's insistence that they are indeed filled with his faeces. Manzoni's serves as a pungent metaphor for what we've always suspected about works of art. They're all Schrödinger cats: simultaneously shit and not shit until we have the courage to open them up and look inside.

Johannes Itten's *Utopia*

(1921)

Among the more ingenious models ever devised for understanding the shades and harmonies of colour is one conceived by the Swiss-German painter Johannes Itten in 1921. Alternately a flat, two-dimensional twelve-pointed star when opened and a vibrant 3D globe when closed, Itten's curiously kinetic device flexed like the moon-shy petals of a morning glory or African daisy. The intriguing chromatic tool was inspired by Philipp Otto Runge's colour sphere and was first included in Itten's first book published as a Bauhaus tutor, *Utopia: Documents of Reality*. In accordance with his unique teaching methods at the Bauhaus (where he began classes with meditative exercises), the star/sphere embodied Itten's conviction that 'colours are primordial ideas' - that they precede forms, not serve them. In his still-used guidebook published in 1961, *The Art of Color,* Itten presented a series of chessboard-like colour grids devoted to the feelings evoked by the four seasons. At once calibrated yet expressive, these matrices of melodious hues echo the contours and chromatic genius of the grids created by his friend and fellow artist Paul Klee.

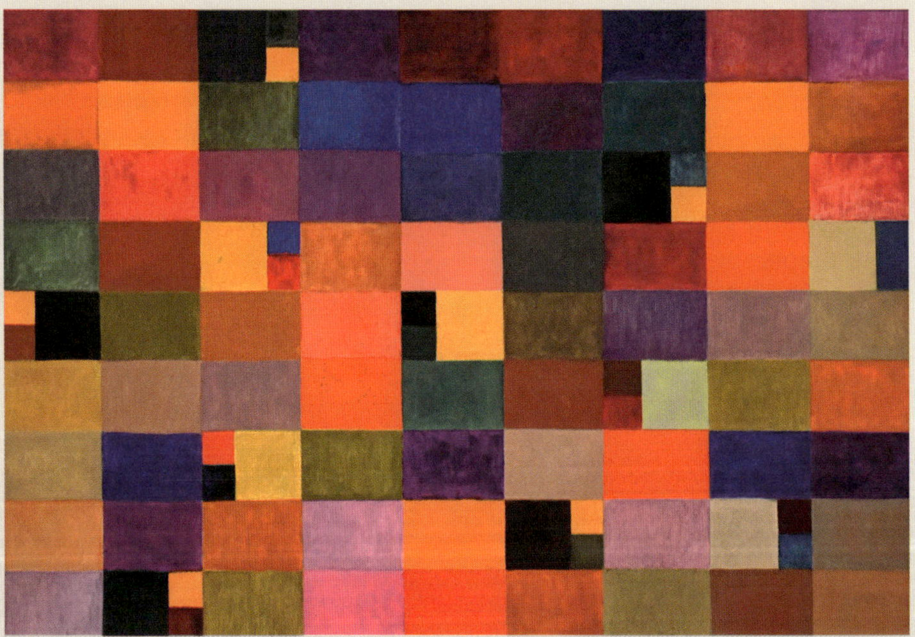

Recalling the colour analyses of objects created by Emily Noyes Vanderpoel, Itten endeavoured to tabularize in evocative chromatic grids one's emotional response to each of the four seasons - an exercise he often asked his students to undertake as well. Above is Itten's luminous ledger accounting for how autumn feels.

Itten's model was a sophisticated elaboration on Runge's innovative colour sphere from a century earlier. Not only did it shuttle conceptually between two and three dimensions as the twelve petals of its outstretched star clenched into a globe, it was also tuned to the twelve pitches of the musical scale - advancing a purported correlation between colour and music that stretches back centuries.

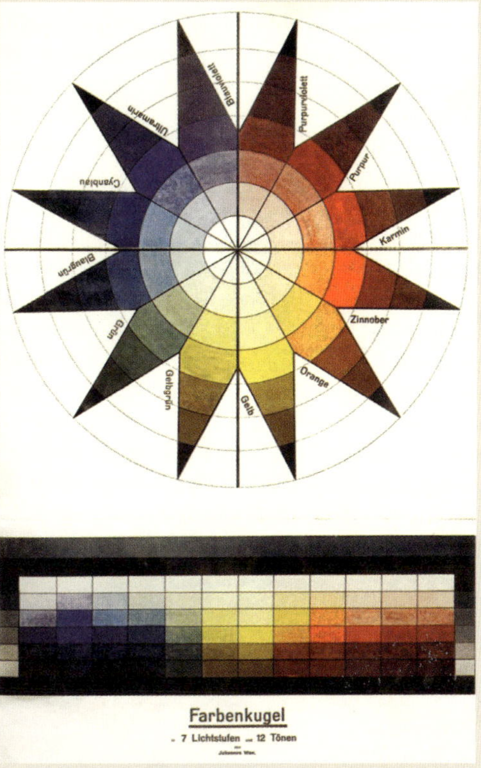

Like Itten, Swiss-born German artist Paul Klee taught at the renowned design school the Bauhaus, where he too emphasized the importance of colour contrast and harmony. Klee's celebrated colour grids echo Itten's efforts to organize the intensity of experience into a chromatic order that is at once lyrical and precise.

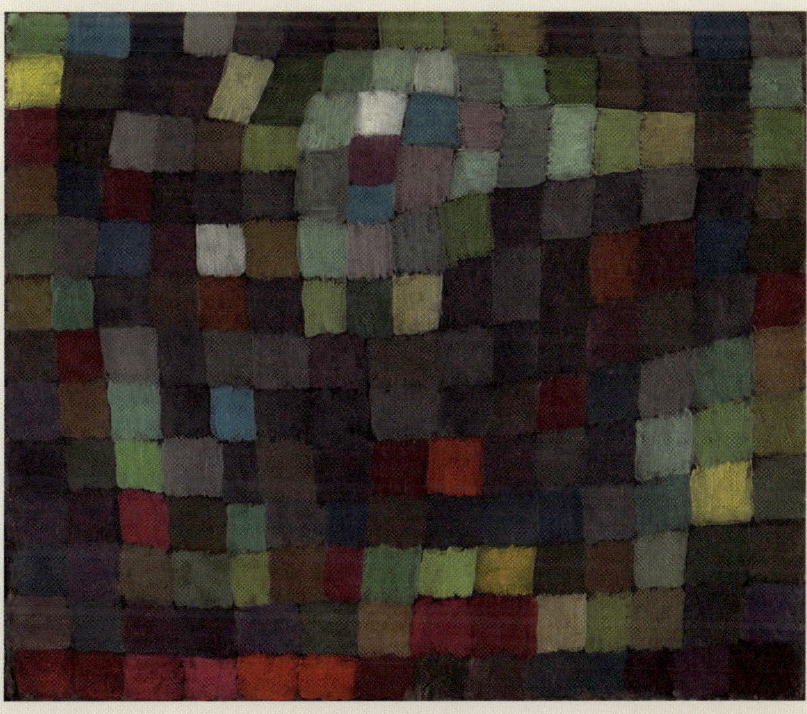

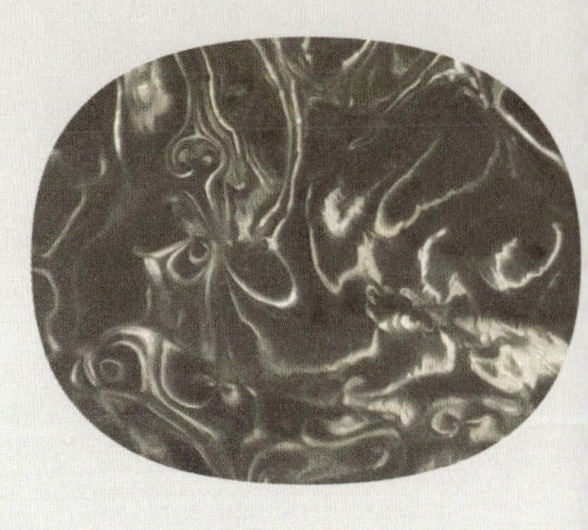

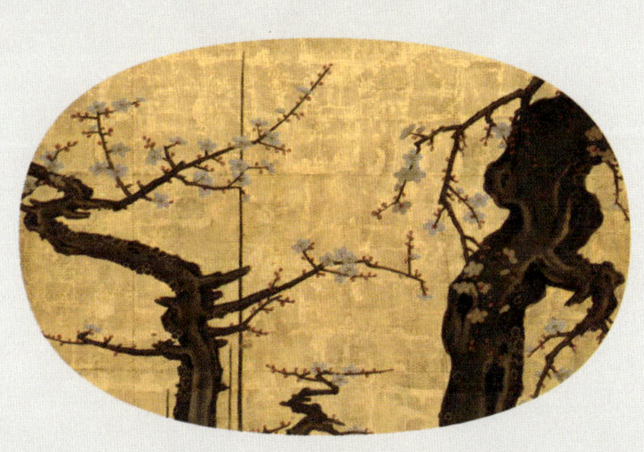

Precious Metals

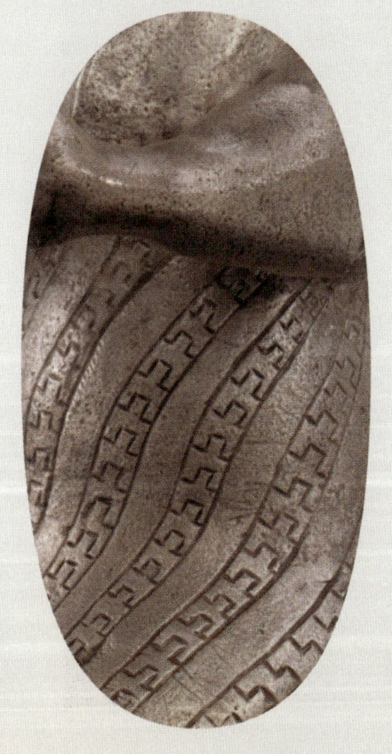

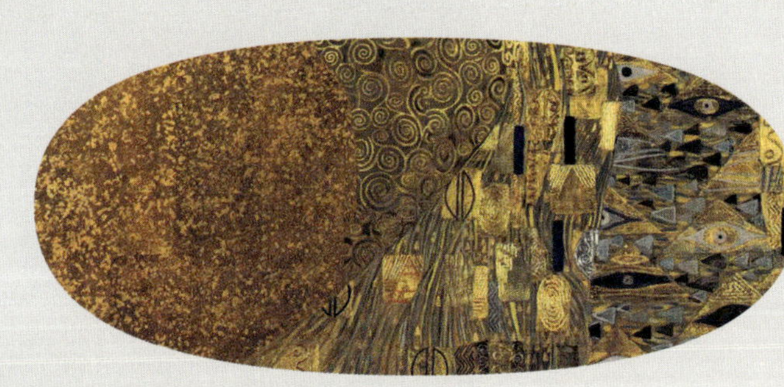

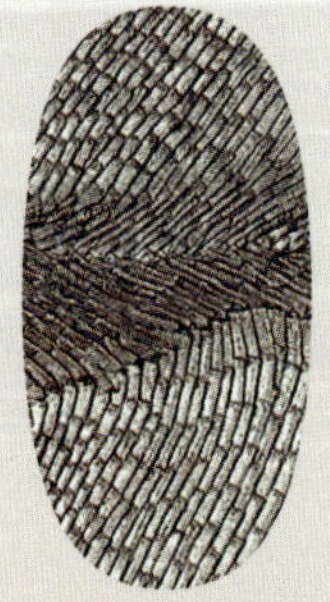

When prospectors pan the gravel of glittery streams or palpate the earth's veins for a hidden pulse, for what are they really searching? Gold? Silver? Something priceless in themselves? 'As in digging for precious metals in the mines,' the 19th-century American writer Herman Melville wrote of the process of separating what's dross from what's dear in his psychological novel *Pierre,* published the year after *Moby-Dick* in 1852, 'much earthly rubbish has first to be troublesomely handled and thrown out; so in digging one's soul for the fine gold of genius, much dullness and common-place is first brought to light.'[1]

It may not be too poetic to propose that behind every work that flaunts the trophies of literal prospecting is an invisible pickaxe swung by an artist desperate to tap into something eternal and true. Such is the subject of Argentinian artist Mariana Telleria's intriguing 2014 collage *Depredador*, which surreally depicts a stiffened lamé-suited torso collapsed in the desert, like a golden cobra that's shed its skin. The incongruously lavish form, alien among rocks, casts a shadow on the rich terrain in the shape of a prospector's mattock, as if the fled figure's spirit is still fumbling forever for the mythic mother lode.

Since prehistory, art has dared us to determine just how precious precious metals truly are. From a finely wrought Bronze Age penis sheath excavated from a grave in Bulgaria in 1972 (one of the earliest examples of metalwork ever discovered[2]) to the gaudy potty that the contemporary Italian artist Maurizio Cattelan fashioned from 18-karat gold in 2016, the use of precious metals has defined, defiled and deified who we are.

Gold

On 17 March 1852 in Naples, a previously unknown, potato-shaped asteroid swam into the ken of Annibale de Gasparis, an Italian astronomer with a knack for spotting overlooked

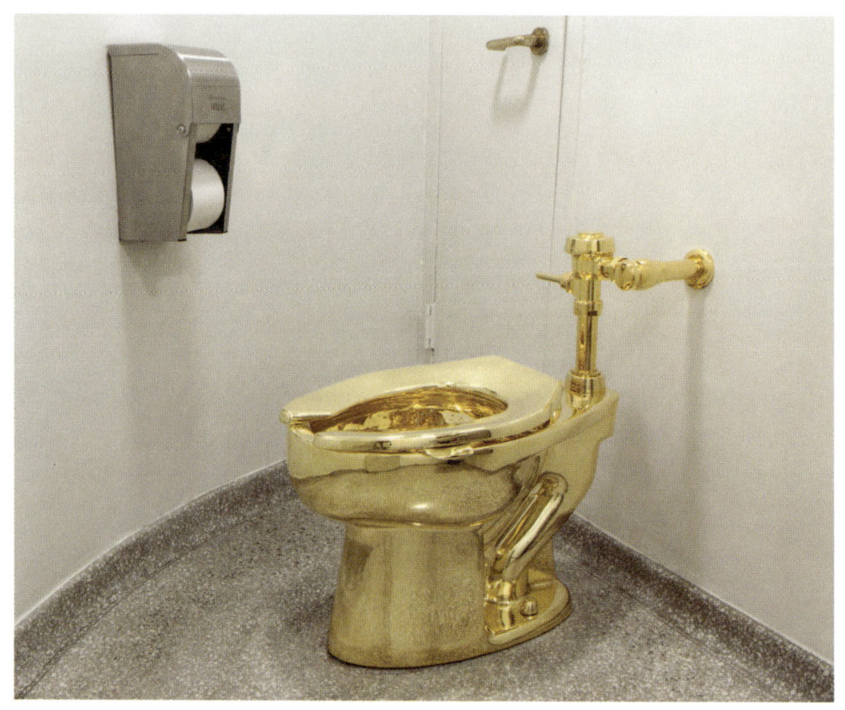

Maurizio Cattelan, *America*, 2016

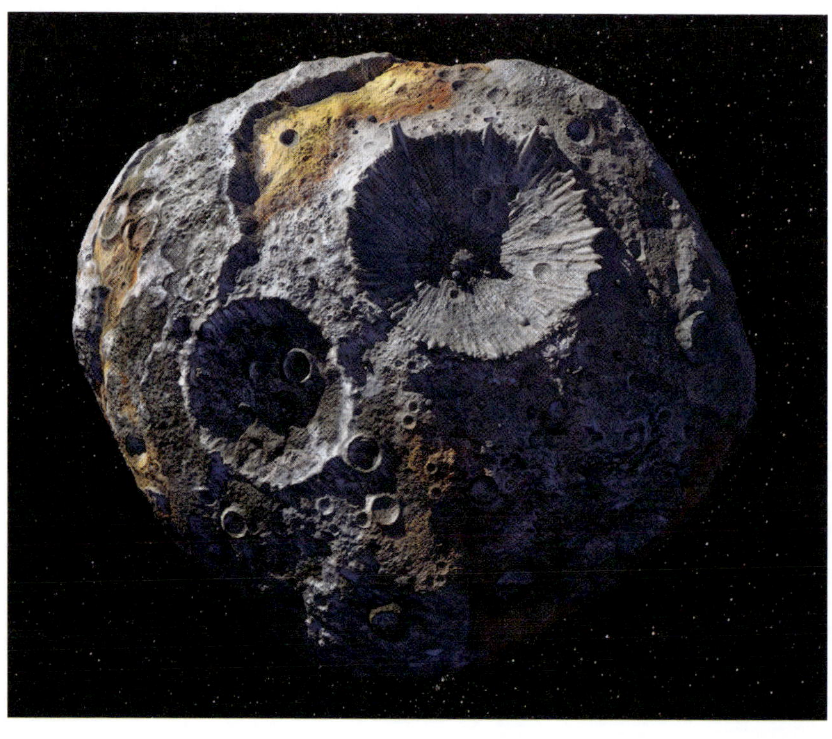

Peter Rubin, *Asteroid Psyche*, 2021

interplanetary bodies. Over the course of his career, Gasparis would be credited with locating nine such minor planets (as they are also known) lurking among the broad band of cosmic rubble that orbits the sun between Mars and Jupiter. Unbeknown to Gasparis, the very next day in Marseilles, a French astronomer by the name of Jean Chacornac would independently spy the same object through his telescope and, stealing Gasparis's thunder, allow the director of his observatory, Benjamin Valz, to give the lumpen mass its name: 'Psyche', after the Greek goddess of the soul.[3]

Fast-forward to the present day, and the astrophysical descendants of Gasparis and Chacornac working for NASA are still squinting with fascination at their near-simultaneous discovery. So fixated on Psyche is NASA, the agency has begun preparing an exploratory mission to the surface of the planetoid with the aim of testing a breathtaking hypothesis: that the rugged clump that Benjamin Valz poetically equated with the transcendent soul may in fact be packed with precious metals, and may even contain enough extraterrestrial gold to make each and every person on earth a billionaire twenty-three times over.[4]

That intense tension, between gold's seductive opulence on the one hand and its evaporative evocation of soulful sublimity on the other, has stimulated artists for millennia. The same unique constellation of properties that make the element a compelling symbol for the beckoning gleam of a realm beyond our material world is what makes gold the most coveted of substances in it. While gold may not be the rarest metal on our planet (rhodium and tantalum are both scarcer) nor the most durable (tungsten and titanium are stronger), it is its possession of these qualities to an exceptionally high degree, combined with its almost unrivalled malleability and incorruptibility (almost nothing tarnishes it), that distinguishes the substance. And it's beautiful. Believed by scientists to have been created in the smallest fraction of a second during the fallout of a collision between a pair of nearby neutron stars, the gold that bombarded earth billions of years ago, and which now shimmers in its deep veins, is indeed the proof of both unfathomable power and a spectacular elsewhere.[5]

Among the final elements to be forged in the exploding furnace of smashing stars and hurled our way across the interstellar medium before those stars collapsed into a massive black hole, gold is the glittering last gasp of oblivion. Given its extraordinary origin, its recurring use by Byzantine and medieval artists as a kind of cosmic backdrop to sacred portraits and scenes is all the more dazzling and literal. In the elaborate illumination that portrays the evangelist Matthew in the Jaharis Byzantine Lectionary, created for the great church of Hagia Sophia in Constantinople (modern-day Istanbul), the 12th-century artist has used so-called shell gold (a suspension of gold applied with a brush[6]) to create the luminous eternal realm in which the wizened gospel-writer patiently sits, waiting for divine inspiration to shower upon him. In the top right-hand corner of the gold field, which time has worn away to reveal a carmine preparatory ground beneath, the pointing hand of God juts like a burst of elemental energy, or the thrust of precious metals across the solar system.

An awareness of gold's celestial origin intensifies the reading not only of Christian manuscripts and paintings. A set of four Japanese sliding-door panels created in the middle of the 17th century by the Edo-period master Kano Sansetsu is similarly unsettled. Created for the abbot's residence in a Zen Buddhist temple in Kyoto, the panels are dominated by the contorting trunk and branches of an outsized plum tree, just beginning to blossom against the lustre of a gold-leaf background. In accord with convention, we ought to interpret the blooming plum, particularly in the context of the flowering azalea to the left, as a reassuring symbol of seasonal rebirth and the unending cycle of life.[7] But the surging ocean of egregious gold that threatens to engulf the old plum – hammered levitatingly thin into weightless

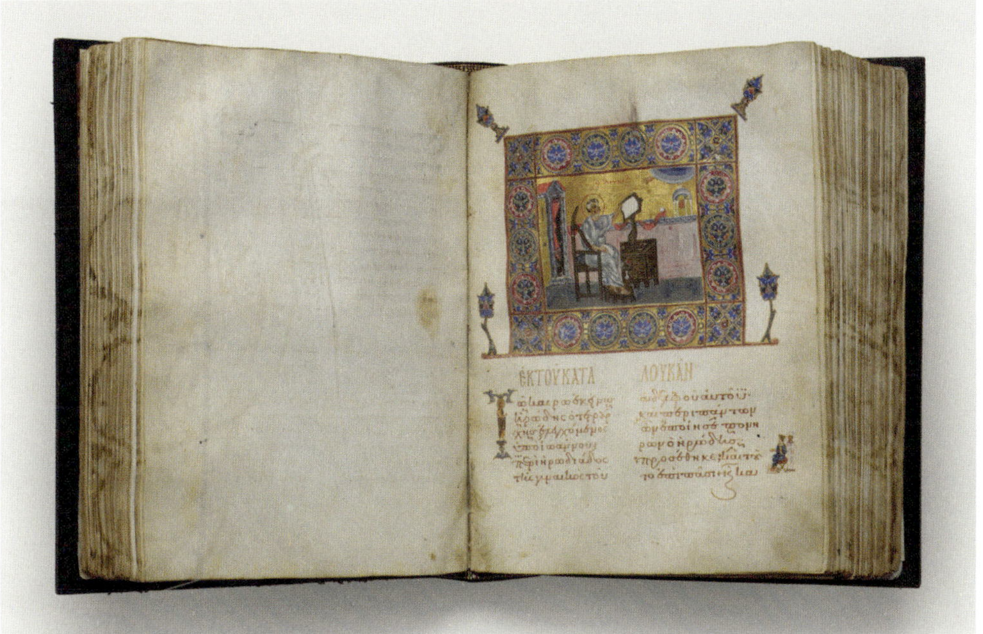

Jaharis Byzantine Lectionary, Byzantine Empire, *c.* 1100

gold leaf by Sansetsu – complicates the work's message. An echo of stellar annihilation, gold is anything but an unambiguous emblem of eternal renewal. In the ever-unfolding narrative of the universe's ceaseless expansions and implosions, what cosmic cataclysm awaits our own solar system behind the sliding doors of temporal existence can never be taken for granted.

A comparable tension between terrestrial forces and celestial energies inflects the shine of Gustav Klimt's scintillating *Portrait of Adele Bloch-Bauer I* (1907). Commissioned by Adele's husband, Ferdinand Bloch-Bauer (a wealthy Austrian banker and sugar magnate), the portrait and the fervently reverential manner in which it is executed are often suspected to be evidence of a passionate affair between Klimt and the sitter,

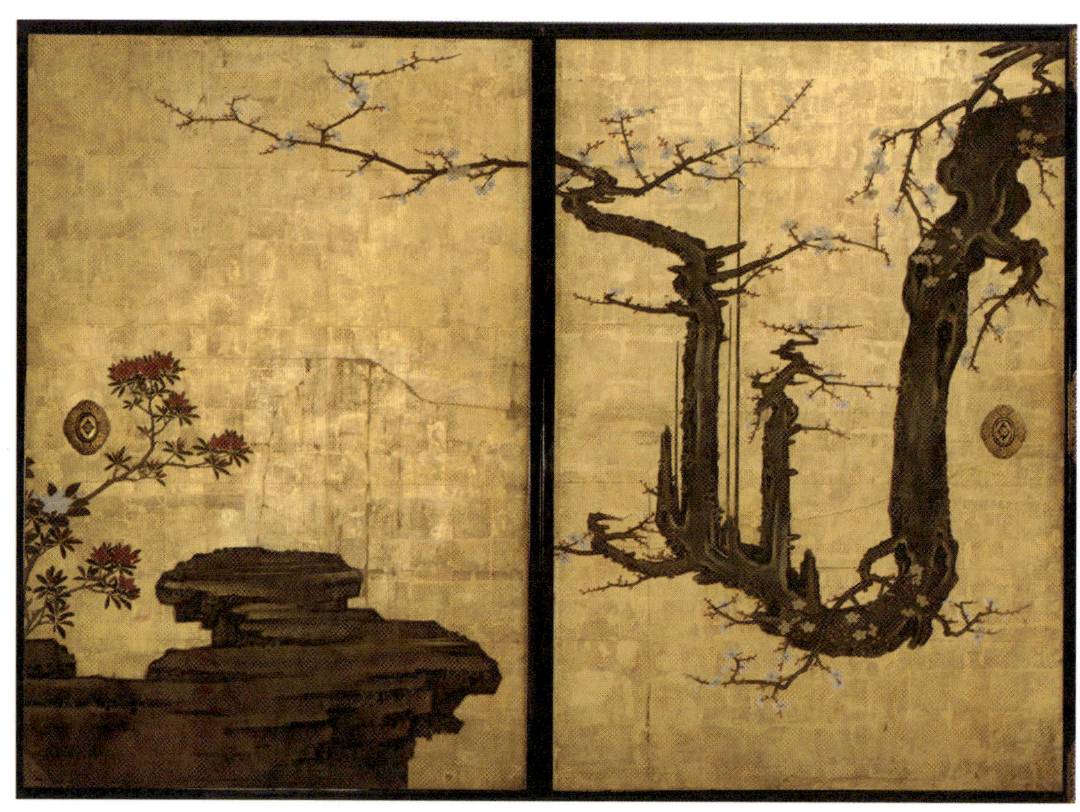

Kano Sansetsu, *Old Plum*, 1646

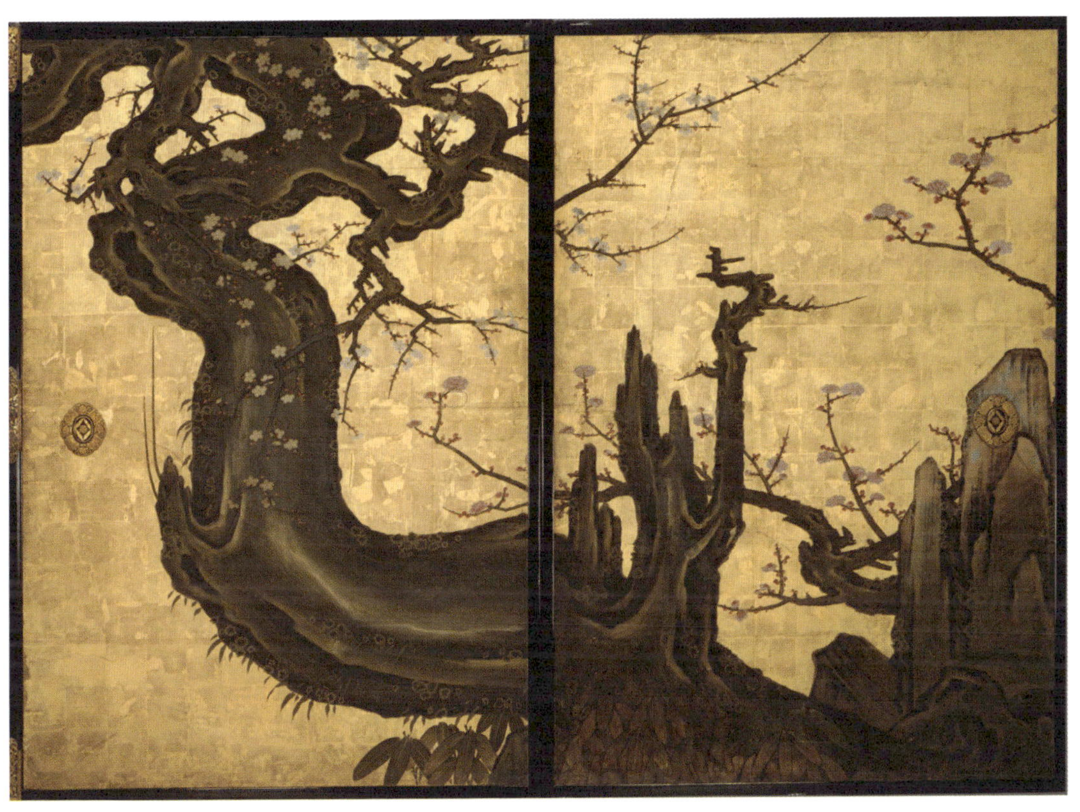

a glamorous Viennese socialite. Years after Adele's death from meningitis in 1923 (aged just forty-three), the painting was seized by the Nazis after Ferdinand fled Austria, leaving the work behind, and was temporarily renamed *The Lady in Gold* to conceal the Jewish identity of its subject.[8] Bloch-Bauer's longing eyes, poised head and sculpted alabaster arms pierce through a lavish vortex of enveloping gold leaf – now twisting in tight, triskelion swirls, now cascading like a cosmic shower laced with atoms freshly fashioned in a stellar collision.

The polished opulence is at once sensationally sophisticated and irreducibly raw – elementally unrefined like an undiscovered vein still pulsing beneath the earth's crust. 'Klimt's ornamentation', posits Ludwig Hevesi, a Hungarian art critic and contemporary advocate of Klimt's work, 'is the figurative expression of primal matter, which is always, without end, in a state of flux, turning and twisting in spirals, entangling itself, a whirlpool that takes on every shape.'[9] What makes Klimt's portrait so limitlessly alluring isn't the costly extravagance of its materials but the ostentatious awareness they seem to possess of their otherworldly provenance – the work's equation of fleshly passion with the reverberation of galactic convulsions. That same cosmic consciousness compounds the surface of a strange solar tondo that British artist Mark Alexander created in 2016. Resembling an undiscovered Homeric shield with a self-portrait of the artist as a child fitted to its centre, *The Golden Wonder* flares with vainglorious verve. Gold may be ancient and alien, but from it Alexander forges something fresh and intimate – a new art history.

Gold's scarcity on our planet means that the value of every fleck of the precious metal fluctuates in proportion to the

OPPOSITE TOP Gustav Klimt, *Portrait of Adele Bloch-Bauer I*, 1907

OPPOSITE BOTTOM Mark Alexander, *The Golden Wonder*, 2016

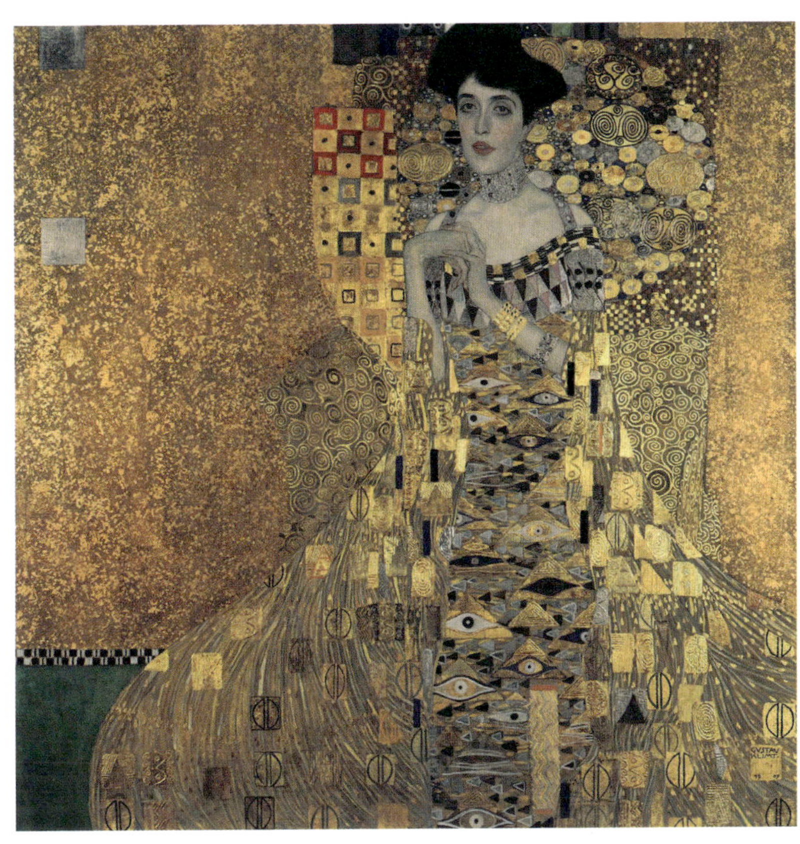

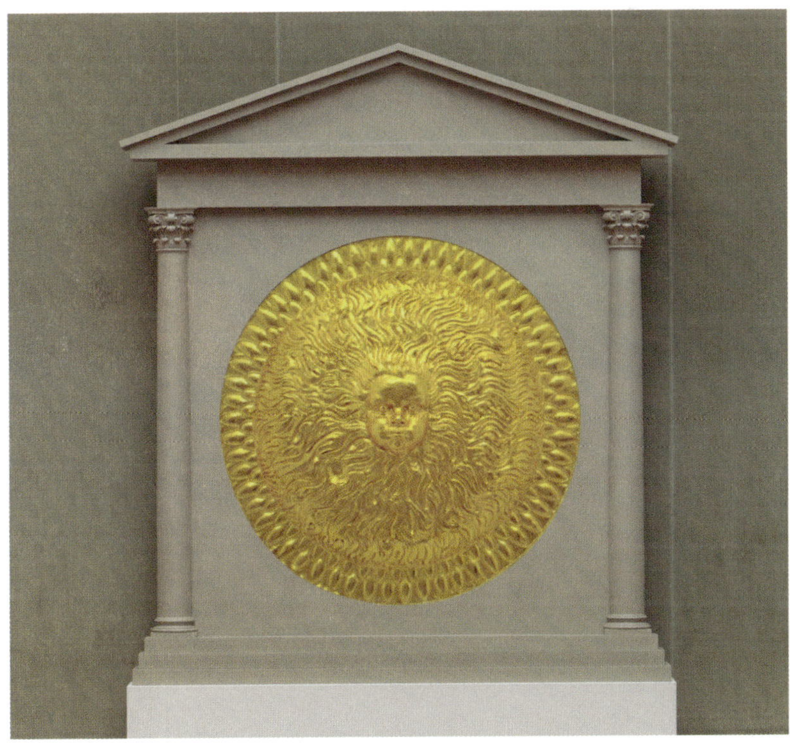

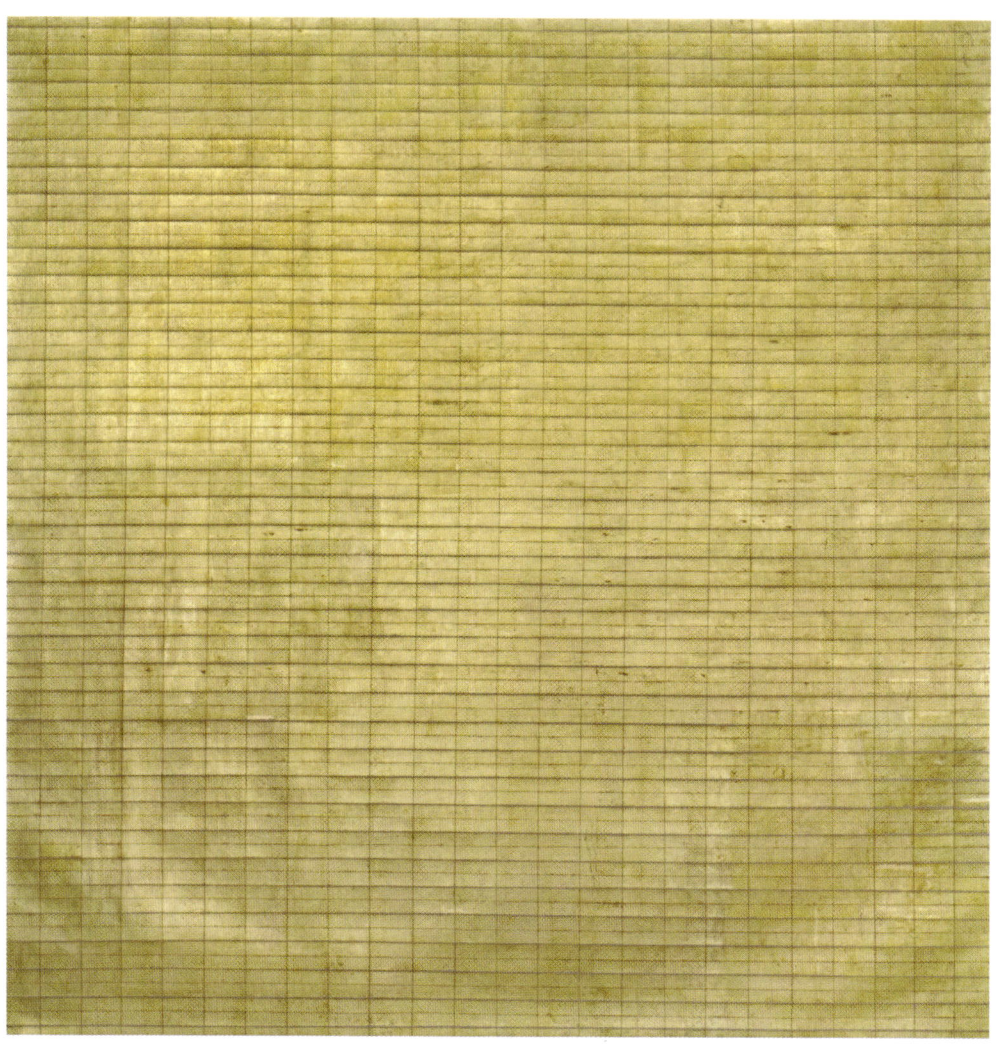

Agnes Martin, *Friendship*, 1963

volume of all the element ever extracted (a fact that means, of course, that if a colossal mass of it were ever lassoed back to our planet from a passing asteroid, such as Psyche, its worth would collapse). More than almost any other element, therefore, gold comprises an indissoluble community of atoms. Every gold work speaks to every other – a poetic assertion given scientific weight by the element's excellence as a conductor and ability to transmit efficiently across expanses. It is impossible, in other words, to appraise the meaning of American abstract artist Agnes Martin's geometric meditation *Friendship* (1963) – a 190.5 × 190.5-cm (75 × 75-in.) canvas covered edge-to-edge, corner-to-corner with gold leaf – in isolation from gold's use by Klimt before Martin, or every medieval icon-maker before that. On to the gilded surface of her work, Martin has incised a tight grid of 1,776 rectangular cells (a matrix that measures 24 across by 74 down) – each etched cell distinctive in its making, yet repetitive. The glittering circuitry posits itself as a sort of massive motherboard of eternal connectivity, facilitating an ever-evolving fellowship between artworks and ages. *Friendship* marks a pivot point towards a deceptively simple geometry of imperfect perfection in the imagination of the reclusive Martin, who spiritually sought through her work not just to tap into a rich lode of joy in our existence, but also to follow that deep vein back to its cosmic origins. 'Happiness', she once asserted, 'is being on the beam with life – to feel the pull of life.'[10]

Silver

However meditative Martin's *Friendship* may be, the gold that encrusts its surface cannot ultimately compete with the reflective power of silver – the only element capable of bouncing back 95 per cent of the light that hits it. The remarkable reverberance of silver, however, whose lustre has been prized by artists since at least the 4th millennium BCE, is undermined by the ease with which it tarnishes, or darkens, when exposed to even the slightest amount of sulphur in the air. A quick glance at a work that employs both gold and silver, such as Paolo Uccello's *The Counterattack of Michelotto da Cotignola at the Battle of San Romano* (1450–75), where the gold bridles of the horsemen still glister undiminished to this day while the silver leaf of the soldiers' armour has dimmed to black, vividly illustrates the contrast between metals.[11] That paradoxical capacity for intense brilliance on the one hand and irrepressible corruption on the other renders silver among the most poignant materials with which artists have ever worked. Its inherent hybridity of dazzling and disappointing qualities mirrors our own and has made it an ideal substance, both materially and metaphorically, to coat not only the mirrors we stare into but also objects of art upon which we reflect.

The relationship between tangible silver we can squeeze into shape in this world and the just-out-of-reach silvery sheen of that other great reflector, the moon, has troubled the imaginations of artists and writers since time immemorial. The British poet Walter de la Mare's enchanting children's lyric 'Silver' begins by evoking the circuitry between earth and heaven that silver quietly conducts:

> *Slowly, silently, now the moon*
> *Walks the night in her silver shoon;*
> *This way, and that, she peers, and sees*
> *Silver fruit upon silver trees*

Second only to gold in malleability, silver has spun itself mysteriously into myriad folkloric legends, or 'lies … "breathed through silver"', as C. S. Lewis once described the nature of myth.[12] The precise function of an exquisite Proto-Elamite *objet* of a kneeling bull holding a spouted vessel from the 4th millennium BCE, one of the earliest surviving artefacts to make use of

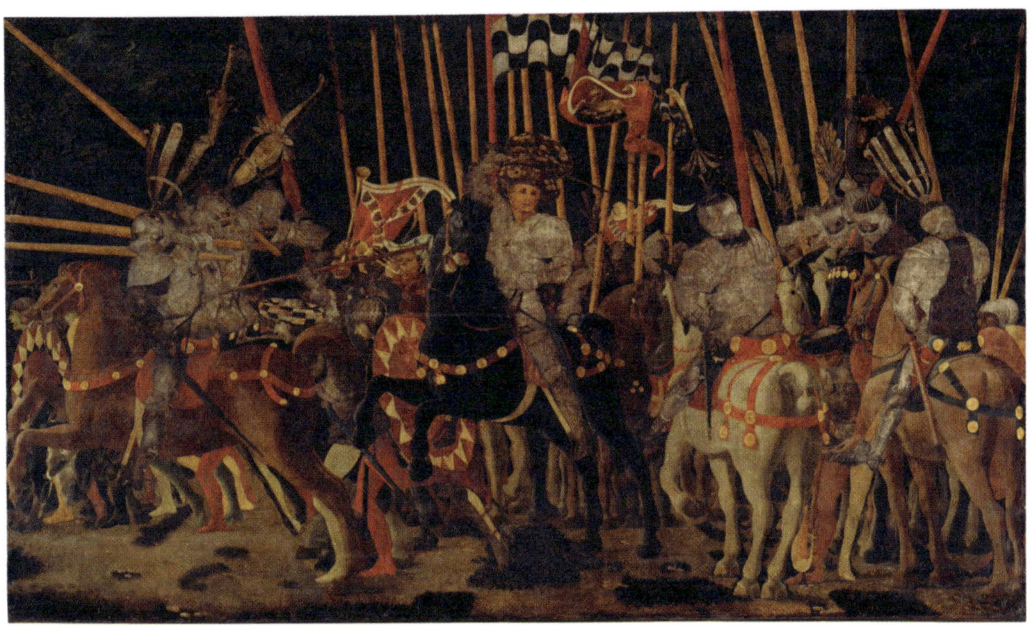

Paolo Uccello, *The Counterattack of Michelotto da Cotignola at the Battle of San Romano*, 1450–75

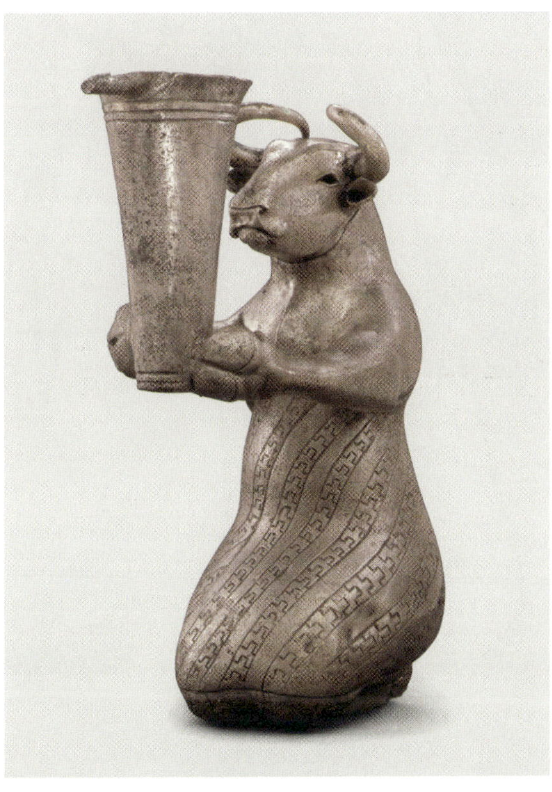

Kneeling bull holding a spouted vessel, Iran, *c*. 3100–2900 BCE

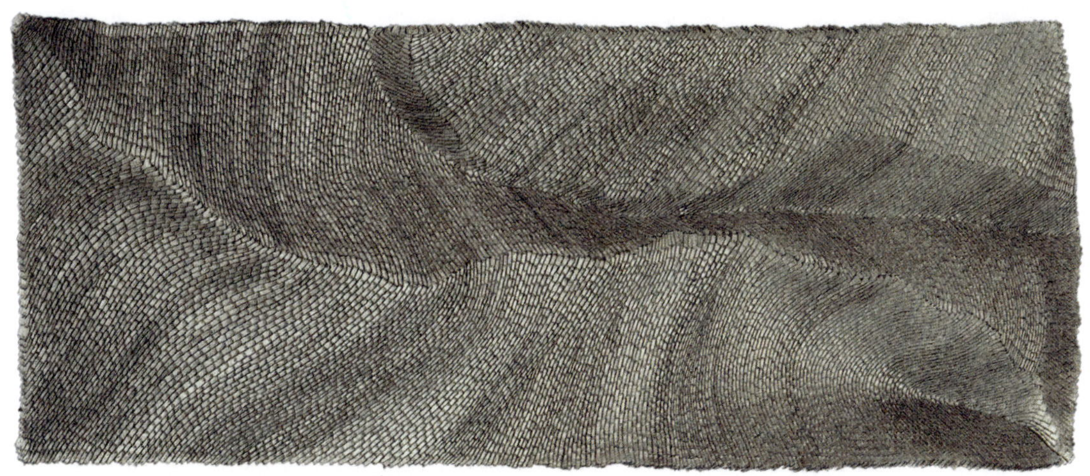

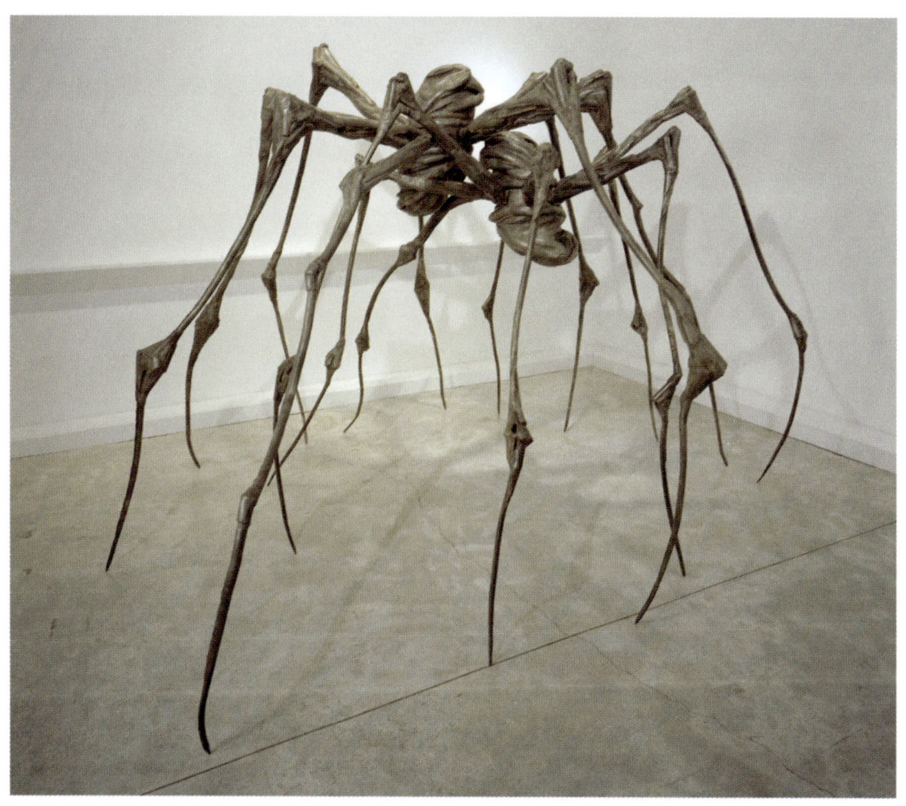

Silver

silver, has yet fully to be worked out by archaeo-anthropologists. Its part-bovine, part-human physique and sweetly supplicating posture (with reverential hoofs raising a receptacle to the sky) invite speculation about what mystical communion it might be commanding with silvery showers of light from above. Flash-forward five millennia to the glittering tapestries, or so-called woven walls, of the contemporary Colombian artist Olga de Amaral, and that ancient impulse to pay tribute to the mysterious magic of silvery light shimmers undiminished. An intense textile whose linen surface is painstakingly textured with silver leaf, *Umbra 30* (2003) echoes the undulations of the artist's native land – its silver-laced mountains and valleys – where deposits of the metal have been found for centuries. In Amaral's work, strips of indigenous silver weave physical and cultural reflections into a scintillating tissue – a flickering fabric our eyes feel as much as see.

A material link between silver and sight was scientifically established in the early 1880s when a German physician, Carl Siegmund Franz Credé, published the results of experiments in which newborn babies' eyes were washed with a 2 per cent solution of silver nitrate as a balm against neonatal conjunctivitis. Widely practised for a century (until the treatment was replaced in the 1980s by antibiotic drops), the silver in so-called Credé's procedure is credited with preserving the vision of an incalculable number of infants worldwide. As salve against blindness, silver nitrate provides a poignant layer of meaning to one of French-American artist Louise Bourgeois's many sculptural studies of the spider – a recurring symbol in her work that she has described as, collectively, 'an ode to my

OPPOSITE TOP Olga de Amaral, *Umbra 30*, 2003

OPPOSITE BOTTOM Louise Bourgeois, *Spider Couple*, 2003

mother' (a gifted weaver who died when the artist was still a student). *Spider Couple* (2003), which depicts an unexpectedly tender snuggle between two oversized bronze arachnids, is leant the lustre of a more affectingly reflective patina by the application of silver nitrate, a coating that, in addition to protecting infant eyes, syncs a work with the pulsing veins of our deepest memories. The use of such 'silver nitrate patina[s]' by contemporary artists, according to the art historian Bruce Nixon, 'can project an intense dream-like silence, paradoxically ethereal and subtly archaized, especially in low light'. The result, Nixon says, are figures that 'might be fugitives from the silt beds of the subconscious'.[13]

Bourgeois's work, wrought large in sculptural terms, illustrates silver's ability to conduct very private feelings. The element, of course, has also served as a public sounding board for our collective consciousness. Since the earliest days of photography, silver solutions have been used to capture images and, more recently, as in the case of Gerhard Richter's affectingly encrusted *Abstraktes Foto* (1989), bewitchingly occlude them. A metallic coating used in cinemas to intensify projection in the early 20th century gave rise to the still-used cinematic sobriquet 'silver screen'. In the 1960s, American Pop artist Andy Warhol delved deeper into that vein with his disquieting *Silver Car Crash (Double Disaster)*. On one of the unsettling serigraph's two panels, a mosaic of fifteen corroded images captures the still-trapped body of a fatal automobile accident. Opposite those corroded images, a blank silver panel resists meaningful reflection.

The construction of *Silver Car Crash* echoes the carpentry of a religious diptych while offering no spiritual comfort. Here, silver is a dispiriting shroud that serves only to insulate anguish and loss. Warhol's work, which enshrines anonymous tragedy, is conscious of the cultural irony of using incorrigibly corruptible silver as a common currency of celebration and tribute. A similar instinct invigorates a poetically powerful sculpture by the

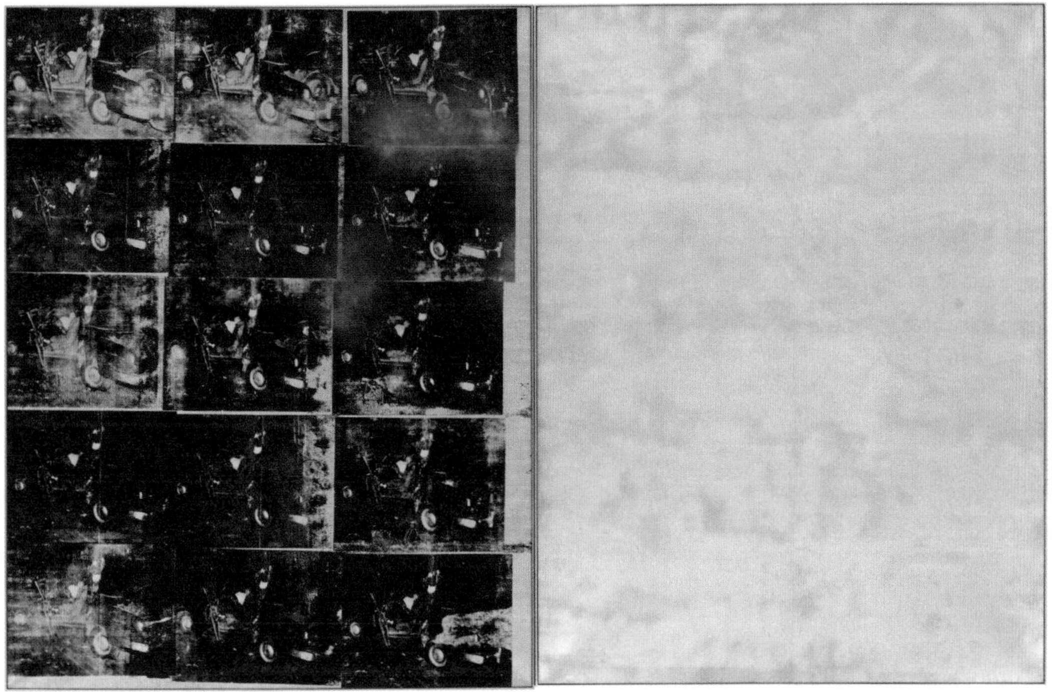

Andy Warhol, *Silver Car Crash (Double Disaster)*, 1963

contemporary British artist Cornelia Parker, who is also obsessed with crushing silver into meaning. To create her intriguing installation *Thirty Pieces of Silver* (1988–89), Parker orchestrated the steamrolling of more than a thousand silver objects, from trophies to trombones, candlesticks to cutlery. The flattened flatware was then arranged by Parker into thirty separate orbiting clusters (or 'discs', as she calls them), which she then suspends with long wires from the ceiling of a given gallery, such that the discs appear to levitate a few centimetres above the floor. The trampled detritus of forgotten achievements each object symbolizes – milestones in life, from a child's christening, perhaps, to first place in a flute competition – appears poignantly to defy

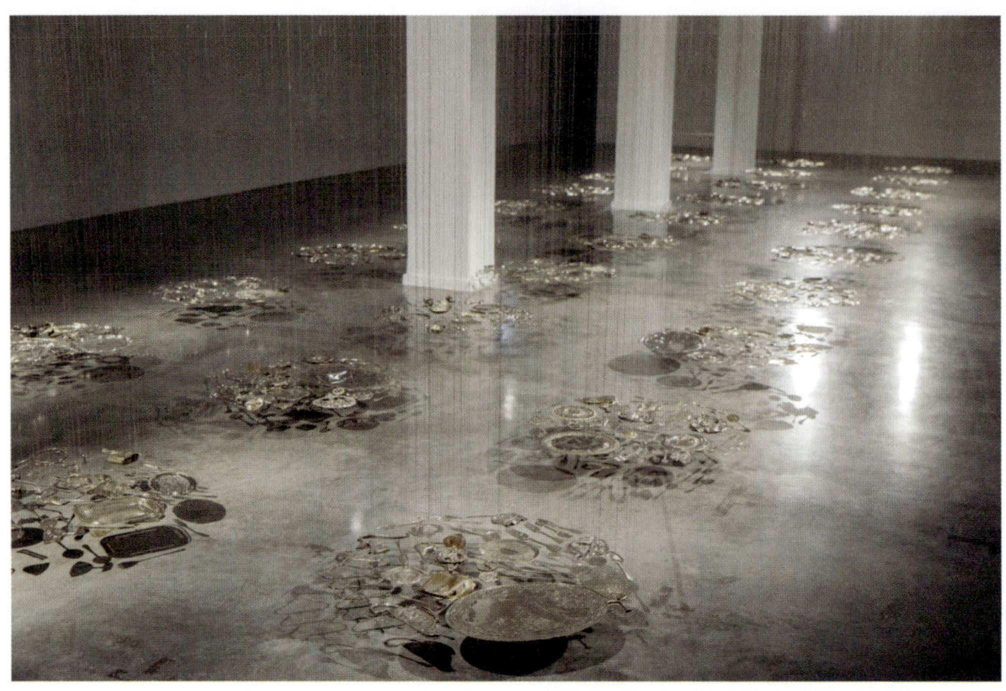

Cornelia Parker, *Thirty Pieces of Silver*, 1988–89

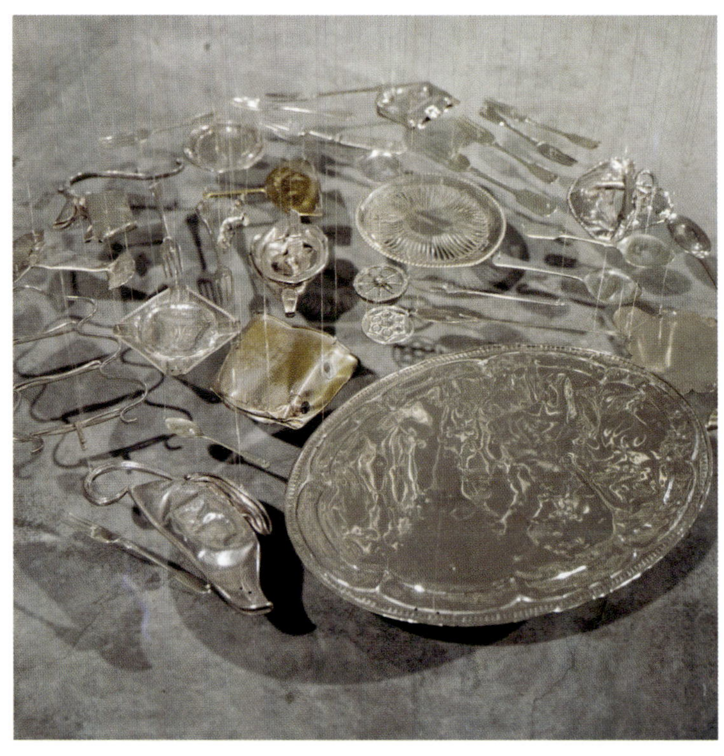

Cornelia Parker, *Thirty Pieces of Silver*, 1988–89

the gravities of physical being and float into memory. 'Silver is commemorative,' Parker has said of the work's message,

> *the objects are landmarks in people's lives. I wanted to change their meaning, their visibility, their worth, that is why I flattened them, consigning them all to the same fate. As a child I used to crush coins on a railway track – you couldn't spend the money afterwards but you kept the metal slivers for their own sake, as an imaginative currency and as physical proof of the destructive powers of the world. I find the pieces of silver have much more potential when their meaning as everyday objects has been eroded.*[14]

Parker's *Thirty Pieces of Silver*, like all works that employ precious metals, seeks in a sense a reverse alchemy – a transformation of the materialities of this world to something eternal that lies beyond.

Notes

Introduction

1 Maurice Merleau-Ponty, *Basic Writings*, ed. Thomas Baldwin. London and New York: Routledge, 2003, p. 312.
2 John Ruskin, *The Two Paths: Being Lectures on Art, and Its Application to Decoration and Manufacture, Delivered in 1858–9*. New York: John Wiley & Sons, 1889. p. 216.
3 Dillian Gordon, 'Duccio di Buoninsegna, "The Virgin and Child with Saint Dominic and Saint Aurea, and Patriarchs and Prophets"', in *National Gallery Catalogues: The Italian Paintings before 1400*. London: National Gallery, 2011, pp. 188–201.
4 *From the Past and for the Future: Safeguarding the Cultural Heritage of Afghanistan – Jam and Herat*. Paris: UNESCO, 2015, p. 16.
5 Quoted in Donald Hall and Pat Corrington Wykes, eds, *Anecdotes of Modern Art: From Rousseau to Warhol*. Oxford: Oxford University Press, 1990, p. 37.
6 Richard Owen, 'Florence skull yields portrait of Giotto'. *The Times*, 20 September 2000.
7 Kelly Grovier, '"Giotto"'. *Quadrant*, 45/11 (2001), p. 86.
8 Marcia B. Hall, *The Power of Color: Five Centuries of European Painting*. New Haven, CT: Yale University Press, 2019, p. 6.
9 David Scott Kastan, with Stephen Farthing, *On Color*. New Haven, CT: Yale University Press, 2018, p. 15.

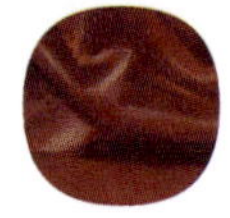

Red

1 Gregory Curtis, *The Cave Painters: Probing the Mysteries of the World's First Artists*. New York: Knopf, 2006, pp. 49–52.
2 H. Valladas *et al.*, 'Radiocarbon AMS Dates for Paleolithic Cave Paintings'. *Radiocarbon*, 43/2B (2001), pp. 977–86.
3 Neil Harrison, *The Origins of Europeans and Their Pre-historic Innovations from 6 Million to 10,000 BCE*. New York: Algora Publishing, 2019, p. 216.
4 *Nanotechnology: Concepts, Methodologies, Tools, and Applications*. Hershey, PA: IGI Global, 2014, p. 1010.
5 *The Natural History of Pliny*, trans. John Bostock and H. T. Riley, vol. 6. London: Henry G. Bohn, 1857, p. 362.
6 Quoted in Don Emerson, 'Haematite: The Bloodstone'. *Preview*, 2017/191 (2017), p. 46.
7 Andrew Graham-Dixon, *Caravaggio: A Life Sacred and Profane*. London: Penguin Books, 2011, p. xcvi.
8 Quoted in John Elliot, 'Anish Kapoor on show in India'. *Financial Times*, 7 December 2010.
9 Shelley Fletcher, Lisha Glinsman and Doris Oltrogge, 'The Pigments on Hand-Colored Fifteenth-Century Relief Prints from the Collections of the National Gallery of Art and the Germanisches Nationalmuseum'. *Studies in the History of Art*, 75 (2009), p. 286.
10 Godfrey Smith, *The Laboratory, or School of Arts ... Compiled for the use, benefit, and entertainment of the curious: illustrated with a variety of curious copper-plates. Volume II*. London: C. Hitch and L. Hawes, R. Baldwin, S. Crowder and H. Woodgate, 1756, p. xxv.
11 Mary Virginia Orna, *The Chemical History of Color*. Heidelberg: Springer, 2013, p. 86.
12 In Charles Hutton, George Shaw and Richard Pearson, *The Philosophical Transactions of the Royal Society of London from Their Commencement, in 1665, to the Year 1800 ....* London: C. and R. Baldwin, 1809, vol. 8, p. 79.
13 In John Lowthorp *et al.*, *The Philosophical Transactions and Collections, to the End of the Year 1700. Abridg'd and Dispos'd Under General Heads ... By John Lowthorp ... The Third Edition (From*

... *MDCC ... to ... MDCCXX ... by Benj. Motte ... From ... 1719, to ... 1733 ... By Mr. John Eames ... and John Martyn ... From ... 1732, to ... 1744 ... By John Martyn ... From ... 1743, to ... 1750 ... By John Martyn*). London: J. Knapton, R. Knaplock, R. Wilkin, J. and B. Sprint, D. Midwinter, W. Taylor, W. and J. Innys, R. Robbinson [*sic*], and J. Osborn, 1747, p. 103.
14 John Belchier, 'An Account of the Bones of Animals being changed to a Red Colour by Aliment only'. *Philosophical Transactions of the Royal Society*, 39/442 (1736), pp. 287–88.
15 Hubertus von Sonnenburg and Frank Preusser, 'El Grecos "Entkleidung Christi" (Espolio) in der Alten Pinakothek'. *Maltechnik-Restauro*, 82/3 (July 1976), pp. 142–56.
16 Hermann Kühn, 'A Study of the Pigments and the Grounds Used by Jan Vermeer'. *Reports and Studies in the History of Art*, 2 (1968), pp. 154–75.
17 Wassily Kandinsky, *The Art of Spiritual Harmony*, trans. M. T. H. Sadler. London: Constable and Company Limited, 1914, p. 79.
18 *Ibid.*, p. 49. In English, the book is best known by the title of a later translation, *Concerning the Spiritual in Art*. The original German title is *Über das Geistige in der Kunst*.
19 Victoria Finlay, *Colour: Travels Through the Paintbox*. London: Hodder & Stoughton, 2002, p. 180.
20 Quoted in Daniel Varney Thompson, *The Materials of Medieval Painting*. New Haven, CT: Yale University Press, 1936, p. 103.
21 Cennino Cennini, *Il libro dell'arte*, trans. Daniel Varney Thompson. New Haven, CT: Yale University Press, 1933, p. 24.
22 Theophilus, *On Divers Arts*. Garden City, NY: Dover Publications, 1979, p. 40.
23 François Delamare and Bernard Guineau, *Colour: Making and Using Dyes and Pigments*. London: Thames & Hudson, 2000, p. 140.
24 Joseph Priestley, *Experiments and Observations on Different Kinds of Air*. London: J. Johnson, 1775, vol. 2, p. 37.
25 David Bomford *et al.*, *Art in the Making: Degas*. London: National Gallery, 2004, pp. 142–49.

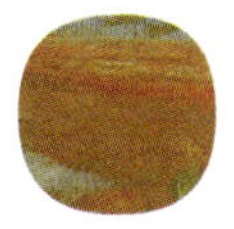

Orange

1 *The Natural History of Pliny*, trans. John Bostock and H. T. Riley, vol. 6. London: Henry G. Bohn, 1857, pp. 104–05.
2 Georg Eberhard Rumpf, *The Ambonese Curiosity Cabinet*. New Haven, CT: Yale University Press, 1999, p. 251.
3 Cennino Cennini, *Il libro dell'arte*, trans. Daniel Varney Thompson. New Haven, CT: Yale University Press, 1933, p. 29.
4 Anonymous, 'Saffron'. *Canadian Pharmaceutical Journal*, 9/10 (May 1876), p. 363.
5 www.businessinsider.com/why-real-saffron-is-so-expensive-2020-6?r=US&IR=T (accessed 28 October 2022).
6 Friedrich August Flückiger and Daniel Hanbury, *Pharmacographia: A History of the Principal Drugs of Vegetable Origin, Met with in Great Britain and British India*. London: Macmillan, 1874, p. 604.
7 Anonymous, 'Saffron'. *Canadian Pharmaceutical Journal*, 9/10 (May 1876), p. 363.
8 Pat Willard, *Secrets of Saffron: The Vagabond Life of the World's Most Seductive Spice*. Boston, MA: Beacon Press, 2001, p. 2.
9 John Watkins and Hugh Latimer, *The Sermons of the Right Reverend Father in God, and Constant Martyr of Jesus Christ, Hugh Latimer, Sometime Bishop of Worcester: Now First Arranged According to the Order of Time in which They Were Preached, Collated by the Early Impressions, and Occasionally Illustrated with Notes Explanatory of Obsolete Phrases, Particular Customs, and Historical Allusions. To which is Prefixed A Memoir of the Bishop, by John Watkins*. London: James Duncan, 1824, p. 56.
10 Pat Willard, *Secrets of Saffron: The Vagabond Life of the World's Most Seductive Spice*. Boston, MA: Beacon Press, 2001, p. 2.
11 Theophilus, *An Essay Upon Various Arts*, trans. and with notes by Robert Hendrie. London: John Murray, 1847, p. 41.
12 Quoted in *Journal of Natural Philosophy, Chemistry, and the Arts: Illustrated with Engravings. By William Nicholson*, vol. 2. London: G. G. and J. Robinson, 1799, p. 145.
13 Cynthia P. Avakian, Jacques Guertin and James A. Jacobs, eds, *Chromium(VI) Handbook*. London: CRC Press, 2004, p. 9.
14 Michel Eugène Chevreul, *The Principles of Harmony and Contrast of Colours, and Their*

Applications to the Arts ..., trans. Charles Martel. London: Longman, Brown, Green, and Longmans, 1854.
15 Ashok Roy, 'The Palettes of Three Impressionist Paintings'. *National Gallery Technical Bulletin*, 9 (1985), pp. 12–20.
16 Keren Rosa Hammerschlag, *Frederic Leighton: Death, Mortality, Resurrection*. Abingdon: Routledge, 2016, p. 105.

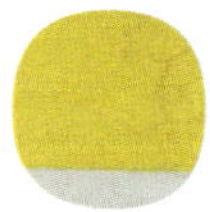

Yellow

1 Jorge Luis Borges and María Kodama, *Atlas*. New York: Dutton, 1985, p. 28.
2 Tom Stoppard, *Rosencrantz & Guildenstern Are Dead*. New York: Grove Press, 1967.
3 *The Archaeology of Phrygian Gordion, Royal City of Midas*, Gordion Special Studies 7. Philadelphia, PA: University of Pennsylvania Press, 2013, p. 166.
4 Ashok Roy, ed., *Artists' Pigments: A Handbook of Their History and Characteristics*, vol. 2. Washington DC: National Gallery of Art, 1993, p. 85.
5 Richard Jacobi, 'Über den in der Malerei verwendeten gelben Farbstoff der Alten Meister'. *Zeitschrift für Angewandte Chemie*, 54 (1941), pp. 28–29.
6 Ashok Roy, ed., *Artists' Pigments: A Handbook of Their History and Characteristics*, vol. 2. Washington DC: National Gallery of Art, 1993, p. 85.
7 Quoted in Charles Joseph Biederman, *The New Cézanne: From Monet to Mondriaan*. Red Wing, MN: Art History, 1958, p. 20.
8 In Michael Doran, ed., *Conversations with Cézanne*. Berkeley, CA: University of California Press, 2001, p. 62. Cf. John Gage, *Color and Culture: Practice and Meaning from Antiquity to Abstraction*. Berkeley, CA: University of California Press, 1999, p. 224.
9 Quoted in David Levy and Marcos Zayat, eds, *The Sol-Gel Handbook: Synthesis, Characterization, and Applications*, 3 vols. Weinheim: Wiley, 2015, p. 1153.
10 Pierre Louis Bouvier and Laughton Osborn, *Handbook of Young Artists and Amateurs in Oilpainting* .... New York: Wiley & Halsted, 1856, p. 10.
11 T. N. Mukharji, 'Piuri or "Indian Yellow"'. *Journal of the Society of Arts*, 32/1618 (November 1883), pp. 16–17.
12 Victoria Finlay, *Colour: Travels Through the Paintbox*. London: Hodder & Stoughton, 2002, p. 240.
13 R. Ploeger *et al.*, 'Late 19th Century Accounts of Indian Yellow: The Analysis of Samples from the Royal Botanic Gardens, Kew'. *Dyes and Pigments*, 160 (2019), pp. 418–31.
14 Robert L. Feller, ed., *Artists' Pigments: A Handbook of Their History and Characteristics*, vol. 1. Washington DC: National Gallery of Art, 1986, p. 69.
15 Quoted in Ross King, *Mad Enchantment: Claude Monet and the Painting of the Water Lilies*. London: Bloomsbury, 2016.

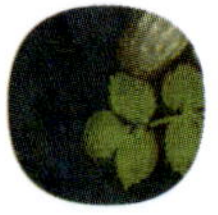

Green

1 Author's translation.
2 Quoted in Robert Havard, *From Romanticism to Surrealism: Seven Spanish Poets*. Totowa, NJ: Barnes & Noble, 1988, p. 195.
3 Richard L. Lewis and Susan Ingalls Lewis, *The Power of Art*, rev. 3rd edn. Australia: Cengage, 2018, p. 159.
4 *Theophrastus's History of Stones. With an English Version, and Critical and Philosophical Notes ... by John Hill*. London: C. Davis, 1746, p. 135.
5 Quoted in David A. Scott, *Copper and Bronze in Art: Corrosion, Colorants, Conservation*. Los Angeles: Getty Conservation Institute, 2002, p. 287.
6 Cennino Cennini, *Il libro dell'arte*, trans. Daniel Varney Thompson. New Haven, CT: Yale University Press, 1933, p. 33.
7 Philip Ball, *Bright Earth: The Invention of Colour*. London: Vintage, 2008, p. 299.
8 Stan Hendrickx *et al.*, eds, *Egypt at Its Origins: Studies in Memory of Barbara Adams – Proceedings of the International Conference 'Origin of the State, Predynastic and Early Dynastic Egypt', Krakow,*

28th August – 1st September 2002. Leuven: Peeters, 2004, p. 784.
9 Cennino Cennini, *Il libro dell'arte*, trans. Daniel Varney Thompson. New Haven, CT: Yale University Press, 1933, p. 31.
10 Quoted in Francis Young, ed., *A Medieval Book of Magical Stones: The Peterborough Lapidary*. Cambridge: Texts in Early Modern Magic, 2016, p. 82.
11 Giorgio Vasari, *The Lives of the Most Excellent Painters, Sculptors, and Architects*, trans. Gaston du C. Vere, ed. Philip Jacks. New York: Modern Library, 2006.
12 Quoted in Richard Ellmann, *Oscar Wilde*. London: Penguin, 1988, p. 546.
13 Ruth Siddall *et al.*, *Pigment Compendium*. London: Routledge, 2008, p. 155.
14 George Field, *Field's Chromatography; or, Treatise on Colours and Pigments as Used by Artists*, revised by Thomas W. Salter. London: Winsor & Newton, 1869, p. 272.
15 Philip Ball, *Bright Earth: The Invention of Colour*. London: Vintage, 2008, p. 177.
16 George Field, *Field's Chromatography; or, Treatise on Colours and Pigments as Used by Artists*, revised by Thomas W. Salter. London: Winsor & Newton, 1869, p. 269.
4 Cennino Cennini, *Il libro dell'arte*, trans. Daniel Varney Thompson. New Haven, CT: Yale University Press, 1933, p. 37.
5 Hugh Aldersey-Williams, *Periodic Tales*. London: Penguin, 2012, p. 309.
6 Kristie Macrakis, *Prisoners, Lovers, and Spies: The Story of Invisible Ink from Herodotus to Al-Qaeda*. New Haven, CT, and London: Yale University Press, 2014, p. 71.
7 In Kelly Grovier, *On the Line: Conversations with Sean Scully*. London: Thames & Hudson, 2021, p. 13.
8 Henry Hilton Brown and James Campbell Brown, *A History of Chemistry from the Earliest Times*. London: J. & A. Churchill, 1920, p. 209. Cf. Andrea Feeser, Maureen Daly Goggin and Beth Fowkes Tobin, eds, *The Materiality of Color: The Production, Circulation, and Application of Dyes and Pigments, 1400–1800*. Farnham: Ashgate, 2012, pp. 368 ff.
9 Philip Ball, *Bright Earth: The Invention of Colour*. London: Vintage, 2008, p. 274.
10 Quoted in Jo Kirby, 'Fading and Colour Change of Prussian Blue: Occurrences and Early Reports'. *National Gallery Technical Bulletin*, 14 (1993), p. 66. Cf. Philip Ball, *Bright Earth: The Invention of Colour*. London: Vintage, 2008, p. 274.

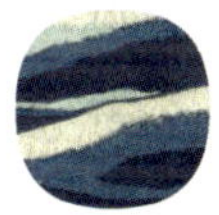

Blue

1 Yves Klein, 'Speech to the Gelsenkirchen Theatre Commission' (1959), in *Overcoming the Problematics of Art: The Writings of Yves Klein*, trans. Klaus Ottmann. Putnam, CT: Spring, 2007, p. 40.
2 Robert Burton, *The Anatomy of Melancholy, What It Is, with All the Kinds, Causes, Symptomes, Prognostics, and Several Cures of It …*, 2 vols. London: Longman, Rees, Orme, and Company [and 16 others], 1827, vol. 2, p. 110.
3 John Wood, *A Personal Narrative of a Journey to the Source of the River Oxus: By the Route of the Indus, Kabul, and Badakhshan, Performed Under the Sanction of the Supreme Government of India, in the Years 1836, 1837, and 1838*. London: John Murray, 1841, p. 265.

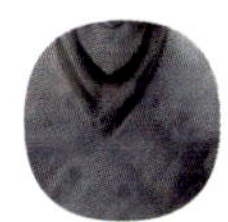

Purple

1 Margaret Steele Anderson, 'Purple'. *Poetry: A Magazine of Verse*, 17/6 (1921), p. 315.
2 In Thalia Gouma-Peterson, ed., *Anna Komnene and Her Times*. Abingdon and New York: Routledge, 2014, p. 117.
3 Quoted in John Gage, *Color and Culture: Practice and Meaning from Antiquity to Abstraction*. Berkeley, CA: University of California Press, 1999, p. 25.
4 *The Complete Works of Aristotle: The Revised Oxford Translation*, ed. Jonathan Barnes. Princeton, NJ: Princeton University Press, 1995, vol. 1, p. 863.
5 John Gage, *Color and Meaning: Art, Science, and Symbolism*. Berkeley, CA: University of California Press, 1999, p. 72.

6 Henri de Lacaze-Duthiers, ‘Mémoire sur la pourpre’. *Annales des Sciences Naturelles*, 12 (1859), pp. 5–84.
7 Victoria Finlay, *Colour: Travels Through the Paintbox*. London: Hodder & Stoughton, 2002, p. 476.
8 Quoted in Philip Ball, *Bright Earth: The Invention of Colour*. London: Vintage, 2008, p. 241.
9 *The Journal of Eugène Delacroix*, ed. Hubert Wellington, trans. Lucy Norton. London: Phaidon, 1951, p. 319.
10 *Ibid.*
11 Jean Salvétat, ‘Matières minérales colorantes vertes et violettes’. *Comptes Rendus des Séances de l'Académie des Sciences*, 48 (1859), pp. 295–97.
12 Quoted in Oscar Reutersvärd, ‘The “Violettomania” of the Impressionists’. *Journal of Aesthetics and Art Criticism*, 9/2, 1950, p. 110.
13 *Ibid.*, p. 107.
14 Albert Wolff, *Le Figaro*, 3 April 1876, p. 1.
15 Alfred de Lostalot, ‘Exposition des oeuvres de M. Claude Monet’. *Gazette des Beaux-Arts*, 1 April 1883, p. 344.

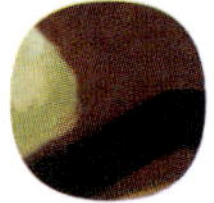

Black

1 Quoted in Joel Achenbach, ‘Why Carl Sagan is Truly Irreplaceable’. *Smithsonian Magazine*, March 2014, available online at www.smithsonianmag.com/science-nature/why-carl-sagan-truly-irreplaceable-180949818 (accessed 30 September 2022).
2 *The Poems of Charles Baudelaire*, trans. F. P. Sturm. London: W. Scott, 1905, p. 120.
3 Isabelle Théry-Parisot *et al.*, ‘Illuminating the Cave, Drawing in Black: Wood Charcoal Analysis at Chauvet-Pont d'Arc’. *Antiquity*, 92/362 (2018), pp. 320–33.
4 Wassily Kandinsky, *Concerning the Spiritual in Art*, trans. M. T. H. Sadler. New York: Dover Publications, 1977, p. 39.
5 Hajo Düchting, *Wassily Kandinsky, 1866–1944: A Revolution in Painting*. Cologne: Taschen, 2000, p. 40.
6 Simon Schama, *Rembrandt's Eyes*. London: Penguin, 2015, p. 216.
7 Victoria Finlay, *Colour: Travels Through the Paintbox*. London: Hodder & Stoughton, 2002, p. 112.
8 Daniel G. Brinton, ‘Folk-Lore of the Bones’. *Journal of American Folklore*, 3/8 (January–March 1890), p. 18.
9 Deborah Davis *et al.*, *Sargent's Women*, exhib. cat. New York: Adelson Galleries, 2003, p. 14.
10 Alfred Sensier, *Souvenirs sur Th. Rousseau*. Paris: Léon Techener, 1872, p. 155.

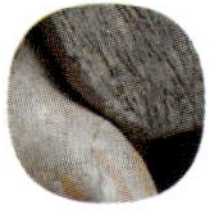

White

1 Dorothy Parker, *Collected Poems: Not So Deep as a Well*. New York: Viking, 1936, p. 161.
2 A. E. Housman, *A Shropshire Lad*. New York: Dover Publications, 1990, p. 2.
3 A. S. F. Gow and A. F. Scholfield, *Nicander: The Poems and Poetical Fragments*. Cambridge: Cambridge University Press, 2014, p. 99.
4 See https://earthobservatory.nasa.gov/features/Coccolithophores/coccolith_3.php (accessed 2 November 2022).
5 Alisa LaGamma, *Kongo: Power and Majesty*. New York: Metropolitan Museum of Art, 2015, p. 30.
6 Edmund de Waal, *The White Road: A Journey Into Obsession*. London: Vintage, 2016, p. 90.
7 Martin Schönfeld, ‘Was There a Western Inventor of Porcelain?’ *Technology and Culture*, 39/4 (1998), p. 717.
8 Suzanne L. Marchand, *Porcelain: A History from the Heart of Europe*. Princeton, NJ: Princeton University Press, 2022, pp. 31–32.
9 Sarah Richards, *Eighteenth-Century Ceramics: Products for a Civilised Society*. Manchester: Manchester University Press, 1999, p. 33.

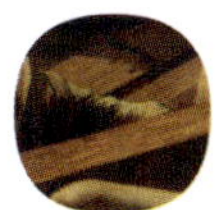

Brown

1 Moses Browne, *Angling Sports: In Nine Piscatory Eclogues. A New Attempt to Introduce a More Pleasing Variety and Mixture of Subjects and Characters Into Pastoral. On the Plan of Its Primitive Rules and Manners. Suited to the Entertainment of Retirement, and the Lovers of Nature in Rural Scenes. With an Essay in Defence of this Undertaking*. London: Edward and Charles Dilly, 1773, p. 111.
2 Ellen G. Landau, *Lee Krasner: A Catalogue Raisonné*. New York: Abrams, 1995, p. 182.
3 Cf Philip Ball, *Bright Earth: The Invention of Colour*. London: Vintage, 2008, p. 152.
4 *The Natural History of Pliny*, trans. John Bostock and H. T. Riley, vol. 6. London: Henry G. Bohn, 1857, p. 142.
5 Larry Keith *et al.*, 'Leonardo Da Vinci's "Virgin of the Rocks": Treatment, Technique and Display'. *National Gallery Technical Bulletin*, 32 (2011), p. 45.
6 In Sir William Foster, ed., *The Travels of John Sanderson in the Levant, 1584–1602: With His Autobiography and Selections from His Correspondence*. London: Hakluyt Society, 2017.
7 J. J. Conybeare, 'Examination of Mumia, etc.'. *Annals of Philosophy*, 21 (January–June 1823), pp. 124, 126.
8 Simon Schama, *Wordy: Sounding Off on High Art, Low Appetite and the Power of Memory*. London: Simon & Schuster, 2019.
9 George Field, *Field's Chromatography; or, Treatise on Colours and Pigments as Used by Artists*, revised by Thomas W. Salter. London: Winsor & Newton, 1869, p. 347.
10 Georgiana Burne-Jones, *Memorials of Edward Burne-Jones*. London: Macmillan, 1906. p. 114.
11 Rudyard Kipling, *Something of Myself and Other Autobiographical Writings*, ed. Thomas Pinney. Cambridge: Cambridge University Press, 1991, p. 10.
12 Quoted in Magnus Resch and Thomas Girst, *100 Secrets of the Art World: Everything You Always Wanted to Know about the Arts but Were Afraid to Ask*. London: Koenig Books, 2016, p. 81.
13 Jonathan Jones, 'Picasso's brown period: was he the first to make art from excrement?' *The Guardian*, 2 November 2016.

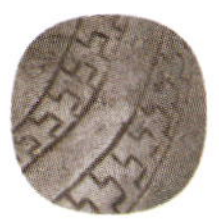

Precious Metals

1 Herman Melville, *Pierre; or, The Ambiguities*, Norton Critical Editions, ed. Robert S. Levine and Cindy Weinstein. New York: W. W. Norton, 2017.
2 Brian M. Fagan, ed., *The Oxford Companion to Archaeology*. New York: Oxford University Press, 1996, p. 740.
3 Paul Murdin, *Rock Legends: The Asteroids and Their Discoverers*. Cham: Springer International Publishing, 2016, p. 90.
4 For more on NASA's Psyche mission, see www.nasa.gov/psyche.
5 Stephan Rosswog, 'Out of Neutron Star Rubble Comes Gold'. *Physics*, 10 (2017), p. 131.
6 John Lowden, *The Jaharis Gospel Lectionary: The Story of a Byzantine Book*. New York: Metropolitan Museum of Art, 2009, p. 53.
7 Kathryn Calley Galitz, *The Metropolitan Museum of Art: Masterpiece Paintings*. New York: Skira Rizzoli in association with The Metropolitan Museum of Art, 2016, p. 289.
8 Anne-Marie O'Connor, *The Lady in Gold: The Extraordinary Tale of Gustav Klimt's Masterpiece, Bloch-Bauer*. New York: Knopf, 2012, p. 179.
9 Quoted in Gilles Néret, *Gustav Klimt: 1862–1918*, trans. Charity Scott Stokes. Cologne: Taschen, 2000, p. 60.
10 Quoted in Anna Chave *et al.*, *Agnes Martin*, exhib. cat. New York: Whitney Museum of American Art, 1992, p. 12.
11 Dillian Gordon, *National Gallery Catalogues: The Fifteenth Century Italian Paintings, Volume 1*. London: National Gallery, 2003, pp. 378–97.
12 Paul Brazier, *C. S. Lewis: The Work of Christ Revealed*. Eugene, OR: Pickwick Publications, 2012, p. 227.
13 Bruce Nixon, *Manuel Neri: The Figure in Relief*. Hamilton, NJ: Grounds for Sculpture, 2006, p. 6.
14 Quoted in *The British Art Show 1990*, exhib. cat. London: South Bank Centre, 1990, p. 88.

Bibliography

- Achenbach, Joel, 'Why Carl Sagan is Truly Irreplaceable'. *Smithsonian Magazine*, March 2014.
- Adelson, Warren, *et al.*, *Sargent's Women*, exhib. cat. New York: Adelson Galleries, 2003.
- Albers, Joseph, *Interaction of Colour*, 50th Anniversary Edition. New Haven, CT: Yale University Press, 1963.
- Alberti, Leon Battista, *On Painting: A New Translation and Critical Edition*, ed. and trans. Rocco Sinisgalli. Cambridge: Cambridge University Press, 2011.
- Aldersey-Williams, Hugh, *Periodic Tales*. London: Penguin, 2012.
- Anderson, Margaret Steele, 'Purple'. *Poetry: A Magazine of Verse*, 17/6 (1921).
- *The Archaeology of Phrygian Gordion, Royal City of Midas*, Gordion Special Studies 7. Philadelphia, PA: University of Pennsylvania Press, 2013.
- Aristotle, *Complete Works*. New York: Delphi Classics, 2013.
- Avakian, Cynthia P., Jacques Guertin and James A. Jacobs, eds, *Chromium(VI) Handbook*. London: CRC Press, 2004.
- Balfour-Paul, Jenny, *Indigo: Egyptian Mummies to Blue Jeans*. London: British Museum Press, 2011.
- Ball, Philip, *Bright Earth: The Invention of Colour*. London: Vintage, 2008.
- Batchelor, David, *Chromophobia*. London: Reaktion Books, 2000.
- Baty, Patrick, *The Anatomy of Colour: The Story of Heritage Paints and Pigments*. London: Thames & Hudson, 2017.
- Baudelaire, Charles, *The Poems of Charles Baudelaire*, trans. F. P. Sturm. London: W. Scott, 1905.
- Belchier, John, 'An Account of the Bones of Animals being changed to a Red Colour by Aliment only'. *Philosophical Transactions of the Royal Society*, 39/442 (1736).
- Bemiss, Elijah, *The Dyers Companion*. New York: Dover Publications, 1973.
- Bomford, David, *et al.*, *Art in the Making: Degas*. London: National Gallery, 2004.
- Borges, Jorge Luis, and María Kodama, *Atlas*. New York: Dutton, 1985.
- Bouvier, Pierre Louis, and Laughton Osborn, *Handbook of Young Artists and Amateurs in Oilpainting. Being Chiefly a Condensed Compilation from the Celebrated Manual of Bouvier ... Appended: A New Explanatory and Critical Vocabulary*. New York: Wiley & Halsted, 1856.
- Brazier, Paul, *C. S. Lewis: The Work of Christ Revealed*. Eugene, OR: Pickwick Publications, 2012.
- Brinton, Daniel G., 'Folk-Lore of the Bones'. *Journal of American Folklore*, 3/8 (January-March 1890).
- *The British Art Show 1990*, exhib. cat. London: South Bank Centre, 1990.
- Broecke, Lara, *Cennino Cennini's 'Il Libro dell'Arte': A New English Translation and Commentary with Italian Transcription*. London: Archetype, 2015.
- Brown, Henry Hilton, and James Campbell Brown, *A History of Chemistry from the Earliest Times*. London: J. & A. Churchill, 1920.
- Browne, Moses, *Angling Sports: In Nine Piscatory Eclogues. A New Attempt to Introduce a More Pleasing Variety and Mixture of Subjects and Characters Into Pastoral. On the Plan of Its Primitive Rules and Manners. Suited to the Entertainment of Retirement, and the Lovers of Nature in Rural Scenes. With an Essay in Defence of this Undertaking*. London: Edward and Charles Dilly, 1773.
- Brusatin, Manlio, *A History of Colours*. Boulder, CO: Shambhala, 1991.
- Bucklow, Spike, *The Alchemy of Paint: Art, Science, and Secrets from the Middle Ages*. London: Marion Boyars, 2009.
- Burton, Robert, *The Anatomy of Melancholy, What It Is, with All the Kinds, Causes, Symptomes, Prognostics, and Several Cures of It. In Three Partitions. With Their Several Sections, Members, and Subsections, Philosophically, Medicinally, Historically Opened and Cut Up*, 2 vols. London: Longman, Rees, Orme, and Company [and 16 others], 1827.
- Cennini, Cennino, *Il libro dell'arte*, trans. Daniel Varney Thompson. New Haven, CT: Yale University Press, 1933.
- Chave, Anna, *et al.*, *Agnes Martin*, exhib. cat. New York: Whitney Museum of American Art, 1992.
- Chevreul, Michel Eugène, *The Principles of Harmony and Contrast of Colours, and Their Applications to the Arts: Including Painting, Interior Decoration, Tapestries, Carpets, Mosaics, Coloured Glazing, Paper-Staining, Calico-Printing, Letterpress-Printing, Map-Colouring, Dress, Landscape and Flower Gardening, etc.*, trans. Charles Martel. London: Longman, Brown, Green, and Longmans, 1854.

- Chirimuuta, Mazviita, *Outside Color: Perceptual Science and the Puzzle of Color in Philosophy*. Cambridge, MA: MIT Press, 2015.
- Clarke, Mark, 'Anglo-Saxon Manuscript Pigments'. *Studies in Conservation*, 49/4 (2004), pp. 231–44.
- Coles, David, *Chromatopia: An Illustrated History of Colour*. New York: Thames & Hudson, 2021.
- Collings, Michael R., *GemLore: An Introduction to Precious and Semi-Precious Stones*, 2nd edn. Rockville, MD: Borgo Press, 2009.
- Conybeare, J. J., 'Examination of Mumia, etc.'. *Annals of Philosophy*, 21 (January–June 1823).
- Curtis, Gregory, *The Cave Painters: Probing the Mysteries of the World's First Artists*. New York: Knopf, 2006.
- Daniels, Vincent, Rebecca Stacey and Andrew Middleton, 'The Blackening of Paint Containing Egyptian Blue'. *Studies in Conservation*, 49/4 (2004), pp. 217–30.
- Delacroix, Eugène, *The Journal of Eugène Delacroix*, ed. Hubert Wellington, trans. Lucy Norton. London: Phaidon, 1951.
- Delamare, François, and Bernard Guineau, *Colour: Making and Using Dyes and Pigments*. London: Thames & Hudson, 2000.
- Delistraty, Cody C., 'Seeing Red: How the Color of Passion, Romance, and Anger can Influence Behavior'. *The Atlantic*, 5 December 2014.
- Derksen, Goverdina C. H., and Teris A. Van Beek, '*Rubia tinctorum* L.'. *Studies in Natural Products Chemistry*, 26 (2002), pp. 629–84.
- Doran, Michael, ed., *Conversations with Cézanne*. Berkeley, CA: University of California Press, 2001.
- Doran, Sabine, *The Culture of Yellow; or, The Visual Politics of Late Modernity*. New York: Bloomsbury, 2013.
- Düchting, Hajo, *Wassily Kandinsky, 1866–1944: A Revolution in Painting*. Cologne: Taschen, 2000.
- Dusenbury, Mary M., ed., *Color in Ancient and Medieval East Asia*. New Haven, CT: Yale University Press, 2015.
- Eastaugh, Nicholas, *et al.*, *Pigment Compendium: A Dictionary and Optical Microscopy of Historical Pigments*. Oxford: Butterworth-Heinemann, 2008.
- Eckstut, Joann, and Arielle Eckstut, *The Secret Language of Color*. New York: Black Dog & Leventhal, 2013.
- Eiseman, Leatrice, and E. P. Cutler, *Pantone on Fashion: A Century of Color in Design*. San Francisco, CA: Chronicle Books, 2014.
- Eiseman, Leatrice, and Keith Recker, *Pantone: The 20th Century in Color*. San Francisco, CA: Chronicle Books, 2011.
- Elliot, Andrew J., and Markus A. Maier, 'Color and Psychological Functioning'. *Current Directions in Psychological Science*, 16/5 (2007), pp. 250–54.
- Ellmann, Richard, *Oscar Wilde*. London: Penguin, 1988.
- Emerson, Don, 'Haematite: The Bloodstone'. *Preview*, December 2017.
- Fagan, Brian M., ed., *The Oxford Companion to Archaeology*. New York: Oxford University Press, 1996.
- Feeser, Andrea, Maureen Daly Goggin and Beth Fowkes Tobin, eds, *The Materiality of Color: The Production, Circulation, and Application of Dyes and Pigments, 1400–1800*. Farnham: Ashgate, 2012.
- Feller, Robert L., ed., *Artists' Pigments: A Handbook of Their History and Characteristics*, vol. 1. Washington DC: National Gallery of Art, 1986.
- Field, George, *Chromatography; or, A Treatise on Colours and Pigments, and of Their Powers in Painting, &c*. London: Charles Tilt, 1835.
- Field, George, *Field's Chromatography; or, Treatise on Colours and Pigments as Used by Artists*, revised by Thomas W. Salter. London: Winsor & Newton, 1869.
- Finlay, Victoria, *Colour: Travels Through the Paintbox*. London: Hodder & Stoughton, 2002.
- Finlay, Victoria, *The Brilliant History of Color in Art*. Los Angeles, CA: Getty, 2014.
- Fletcher, Shelley, Lisha Glinsman and Doris Oltrogge, 'The Pigments on Hand-Colored Fifteenth-Century Relief Prints from the Collections of the National Gallery of Art and the Germanisches Nationalmuseum'. *Studies in the History of Art*, 75 (2009).
- Flückiger, Friedrich August, and Daniel Hanbury, *Pharmacographia: A History of the Principal Drugs of Vegetable Origin, Met with in Great Britain and British India*. London: Macmillan, 1874.
- Foster, Sir William, ed., *The Travels of John Sanderson in the Levant, 1584–1602: With His Autobiography and Selections from His Correspondence*. London: Hakluyt Society, 2017.
- Friedman, Joseph, *Paint and Colour in Decoration*. London: Cassell Illustrated, 2003.
- Gaetani, Maria Carolina, Ulderico Santamaria and Claudio Seccaroni, 'The Use of Egyptian Blue and Lapis Lazuli in the Middle Ages: The

Wall Paintings of the San Saba Church in Rome'. *Studies in Conservation*, 49/1 (2004), pp. 13–22.

- Gage, John, *Color and Culture: Practice and Meaning from Antiquity to Abstraction*. Berkeley, CA: University of California Press, 1999.
- Gage, John, *Color and Meaning: Art, Science, and Symbolism*. Berkeley, CA: University of California Press, 1999.
- Gage, John, *Colour in Art*. London: Thames & Hudson, 2006.
- Galitz, Kathryn Calley, *The Metropolitan Museum of Art: Masterpiece Paintings*. New York: Skira Rizzoli in association with The Metropolitan Museum of Art, 2016.
- Garfield, Simon, *Mauve: How One Man Invented a Colour that Changed the World*. London: Faber, 2000.
- Gartside, Mary, *An Essay on Light and Shade, on Colours, and on Composition in General*. London: T. Davison, 1805.
- Gartside, Mary, *An Essay on a New Theory of Colours, and on Composition in General; Illustrated by Coloured Blots Shewing the Application of the Theory to Composition of Flowers, Landscapes, Figures, &c*. London: J. Barfield, 1808.
- Gettens, Rutherford J., Robert L. Feller and W. T. Chase, 'Vermilion and Cinnabar'. *Studies in Conservation*, 17/2 (May 1972), pp. 45–69.
- Gettens, Rutherford J., Elisabeth West Fitzhugh and Robert L. Feller, 'Calcium Carbonate Whites'. *Studies in Conservation*, 19/3 (August 1974), pp. 157–84.
- Goethe, Johann Wolfgang von, *Theory of Colours*, trans. Charles Lock Eastlake. London: John Murray, 1840.
- Gordon, Dillian, 'Duccio di Buoninsegna, "The Virgin and Child with Saint Dominic and Saint Aurea, and Patriarchs and Prophets"', in *National Gallery Catalogues: The Italian Paintings before 1400*. London: National Gallery, 2011, pp. 188–201.
- Gorton, Thomas, 'Vantablack Might Not Be the World's Blackest Material'. *Dazed*, 27 October 2014.
- Goswamy, B. N., 'The Color Yellow'. *Tribune India*, 7 September 2014.
- Graham-Dixon, Andrew, *Caravaggio: A Life Sacred and Profane*. London: Penguin Books, 2011.
- Grovier, Kelly, 'Giotto'. *Quadrant*, 45/11 (2001), p. 86.
- Grovier, Kelly, *On the Line: Conversations with Sean Scully*. London: Thames & Hudson, 2021.
- Hall, Donald, and Pat Corrington Wykes, eds, *Anecdotes of Modern Art: From Rousseau to Warhol*. Oxford: Oxford University Press, 1990.
- Hall, Emily, *et al.*, *Color Chart: Reinventing Color, 1950 to Today*, exhib. cat. New York: Museum of Modern Art, 2008.
- Hall, Marcia B., *Color and Meaning: Practice and Theory in Renaissance Painting*. Cambridge: Cambridge University Press, 1992.
- Hammerschlag, Keren Rosa, *Frederic Leighton: Death, Mortality, Resurrection*. Abingdon: Routledge, 2016.
- Harley, R. D., *Artists' Pigments c. 1600–1835: A Study in English Documentary Sources*. London: Butterworths, 1970.
- Harrison, Neil, *The Origins of Europeans and Their Pre-historic Innovations from 6 Million to 10,000 BCE*. New York: Algora Publishing, 2019.
- Harvey, John, *The Story of Black*. London: Reaktion Books, 2013.
- Havard, Robert, *From Romanticism to Surrealism: Seven Spanish Poets*. Totowa, NJ: Barnes & Noble, 1988.
- Heather, P. J., 'Color Symbolism: Part I'. *Folklore*, 59/4 (December 1948), pp. 165–83.
- Hendrickx, Stan, *et al.*, eds, *Egypt at Its Origins: Studies in Memory of Barbara Adams – Proceedings of the International Conference 'Origin of the State, Predynastic and Early Dynastic Egypt', Krakow, 28th August – 1st September 2002*. Leuven: Peeters, 2004.
- Herbert, William, *A History of the Species of Crocus*. London: William Clowes & Sons, 1847.
- Hicks, Carola, *Girl in a Green Gown: The History and Mystery of the Arnolfini Portrait*. London: Vintage, 2012.
- Hoeppe, Gotz, *Why the Sky Is Blue: Discovering the Color of Life*, trans. J. Stewart. Princeton, NJ: Princeton University Press, 2007.
- Hutton, Charles, George Shaw and Richard Pearson, *The Philosophical Transactions of the Royal Society of London from Their Commencement, in 1665, to the Year 1800 ....* London: C. and R. Baldwin, 1809.
- Jackson, Holbrook, 'Colour Determination in the Fashion Trades'. *Journal of the Royal Society of Arts*, 78/4034 (March 1930), pp. 492–513.
- Jacobi, Richard, 'Über den in der Malerei verwendeten gelben Farbstoff der Alten Meister'. *Zeitschrift für Angewandte Chemie*, 54 (1941), pp. 28–29.
- Kandinsky, Wassily, *The Art of Spiritual Harmony*, trans. M. T. H. Sadler. London: Constable and Company Limited, 1914.
- Kandinsky, Wassily, *Concerning the Spiritual in Art*, trans. M. T. H. Sadler. New York: Dover Publications, 1977.

- Keith, Larry, *et al.*, 'Leonardo Da Vinci's "Virgin of the Rocks": Treatment, Technique and Display'. *National Gallery Technical Bulletin*, 32 (2011).
- King, Ross, *Mad Enchantment: Claude Monet and the Painting of the Water Lilies*. London: Bloomsbury, 2016.
- Klein, Yves, 'Speech to the Gelsenkirchen Theatre Commission' (1959), in *Overcoming the Problematics of Art: The Writings of Yves Klein*, trans. Klaus Ottmann. Putnam, CN: Spring Publications, 2007.
- Klinkhammer, Barbara, 'After Purism: Le Corbusier and Color'. *Preservation Education & Research*, 4 (2011), pp. 19–38.
- Kraft, Alexander, 'On Two Letters from Caspar Neumann to John Woodward Revealing the Secret Method for Preparation of Prussian Blue'. *Bulletin of the History of Chemistry*, 34/2 (2009), pp. 134–40.
- Kühn, Hermann, 'Lead-Tin Yellow'. *Studies in Conservation*, 13/1 (February 1968), pp. 7–33.
- Kühn, Hermann, 'A Study of the Pigments and the Grounds Used by Jan Vermeer'. *Reports and Studies in the History of Art*, 2 (1968), pp. 154–75.
- LaGamma, Alisa, *Kongo: Power and Majesty*. New York: Metropolitan Museum of Art, 2015.
- Landau, Ellen G., *Lee Krasner: A Catalogue Raisonné*. New York: Abrams, 1995.
- Lee, Raymond L., 'Cochineal Production and Trade in New Spain to 1600'. *The Americas*, 4/4 (April 1948), pp. 449–73.
- Levy, David, and Marcos Zayat, eds, *The Sol-Gel Handbook: Synthesis, Characterization, and Applications*. Weinheim: Wiley, 2015.
- Lewis, Richard L., and Susan Ingalls Lewis, *The Power of Art*, rev. 3rd edn. Australia: Cengage, 2018.
- Loske, Alexandra, *Colour: A Visual History*. London: Ilex, 2019.
- Lowden, John, *The Jaharis Gospel Lectionary: The Story of a Byzantine Book*. New York: Metropolitan Museum of Art, 2009.
- Lowthorp, John, *et al.*, *The Philosophical Transactions and Collections, to the End of the Year 1700. Abridg'd and Dispos'd Under General Heads ... By John Lowthorp ... The Third Edition (From ... MDCC ... to ... MDCCXX ... by Benj. Motte ... From ... 1719, to ... 1733 ... By Mr. John Eames ... and John Martyn ... From ... 1732, to ... 1744 ... By John Martyn ... From ... 1743, to ... 1750 ... By John Martyn)*. London: J. Knapton, R. Knaplock, R. Wilkin, J. and B. Sprint, D. Midwinter, W. Taylor, W. and J. Innys, R. Robbinson [*sic*], and J. Osborn, 1747.
- McCouat, Philip, 'The Life and Death of Mummy Brown'. *Journal of Art in Society* (2013).
- McKeich, Cherie, 'Botanical Fortunes: T. N. Mukharji, International Exhibitions, and Trade Between India and Australia'. *Journal of the National Museum of Australia*, 3/1 (March 2008), pp. 1–12.
- Macrakis, Kristie, *Prisoners, Lovers, and Spies: The Story of Invisible Ink from Herodotus to Al-Qaeda*. New Haven, CT, and London: Yale University Press, 2014.
- Maerz, Aloys John, and Morris Rea Paul, *A Dictionary of Color*. New York: McGraw-Hill, 1930.
- Marchand, Suzanne L., *Porcelain: A History from the Heart of Europe*. Princeton, NJ: Princeton University Press, 2022.
- Melville, Herman, *Pierre; or, The Ambiguities*, Norton Critical Editions, ed. Robert S. Levine and Cindy Weinstein. New York: W. W. Norton, 2017.
- Morris, Errol, 'Bamboozling Ourselves'. *New York Times*, 7 parts, 27 May – 4 June 2009.
- Mukharji, T. N., 'Piuri or "Indian Yellow"'. *Journal of the Society of Arts*, 32/1618 (November 1883), pp. 16–17.
- Murdin, Paul, *Rock Legends: The Asteroids and Their Discoverers*. Cham: Springer International Publishing, 2016.
- *The Natural History of Pliny*, trans. John Bostock and H. T. Riley, vol. 2. London: Henry G. Bohn, 1855.
- *The Natural History of Pliny*, trans. John Bostock and H. T. Riley, vol. 6. London: Henry G. Bohn, 1857.
- Nixon, Bruce, *Manuel Neri: The Figure in Relief*. Hamilton, NJ: Grounds For Sculpture, 2006.
- O'Connor, Anne-Marie, *The Lady in Gold: The Extraordinary Tale of Gustav Klimt's Masterpiece, Bloch-Bauer*. New York: Knopf, 2012.
- Owen, Richard, 'Florence skull yields portrait of Giotto'. *The Times*, 20 September 2000.
- Pastoureau, Michel, *Blue: The History of a Color*, trans. M. I. Cruse. Princeton, NJ: Princeton University Press, 2000.
- Pastoureau, Michel, *Black: The History of a Color*, trans. Jody Gladding. Princeton, NJ: Princeton University Press, 2009.
- Pastoureau, Michel, *Green: The History of a Color*, trans. Jody Gladding. Princeton, NJ: Princeton University Press, 2014.
- Paterson, Ian, *A Dictionary of Colour: A Lexicon of the Language of Colour*. London: Thorogood, 2004.
- Paul, Stella, *Chromaphilia: The Story of Colour in Art*. London: Phaidon, 2017.

- Pavey, Don, *Colour and Humanism: Colour Expression and Patterns of Thought about Colour, the Lost Tradition of the Great Venetians, the Dynamics of the Classical Palette of Earths, and the Power of Colour as a Cultural Instrument Today*, 2nd rev. edn. London: Micro Academy, 2009.
- Peplow, Mark, 'The Reinvention of Black'. *Nautilus*, 11 August 2015.
- Perkin, W. H., 'The History of Alizarin and Allied Colouring Matters, and Their Production from Coal Tar'. *Journal of the Society of Arts*, 27/1384 (May 1879), pp. 572–602.
- Phipps, Elena, 'Cochineal Red: The Art History of a Color'. *The Metropolitan Museum of Art Bulletin*, 67/ 3 (Winter 2010), pp. 4–48.
- Photos-Jones, E., *et al.*, 'Kean Miltos: The Well-Known Iron Oxides of Antiquity'. *Annual of the British School of Athens*, 92 (1997), pp. 359–71.
- Pleij, Herman, *Colors Demonic and Divine: Shades of Meaning in the Middle Ages and After*. New York: Columbia University Press, 2004.
- Ploeger, R., *et al.*, 'Late 19th Century Accounts of Indian Yellow: The Analysis of Samples from the Royal Botanic Gardens, Kew'. *Dyes and Pigments*, 160 (2019), pp. 418–31.
- Priestley, Joseph, *Experiments and Observations on Different Kinds of Air*, vol. 2. London: J. Johnson, 1775.
- Reutersvärd, Oscar, 'The "Violettomania" of the Impressionists'. *Journal of Aesthetics and Art Criticism*, 9/2 (December 1950), pp. 106–10.
- Richter, Ernst Ludwig, and Heide Härlin, 'A Nineteenth-Century Collection of Pigments and Painting Materials'. *Studies in Conservation*, 19/2 (May 1974), pp. 76–82.
- Riley, Charles A., II, *Color Codes: Modern Theories of Color in Philosophy, Painting and Architecture, Literature, Music, and Psychology*. Lebanon, NH: University Press of New England, 1995.
- Rood, Ogden N., *Modern Chromatics, With Applications to Art and Industry*. New York: D. Appleton, 1879.
- Rose, Mark, '"Look, Daddy, Oxen!": The Cave Art of Altamira'. *Archaeology*, 53/3 (May/June 2000), pp. 68–69.
- Rosswog, Stephan, 'Out of Neutron Star Rubble Comes Gold'. *Physics*, 10/131 (December 2017).
- Roy, Ashok, 'The Palettes of Three Impressionist Paintings'. *National Gallery Technical Bulletin*, 9 (1985), pp. 12–20.
- Roy, Ashok, ed., *Artists' Pigments: A Handbook of Their History and Characteristics*, vol. 2. Washington DC: National Gallery of Art, 1993.
- Royal Botanic Gardens, Kew, 'Indian Yellow'. *Bulletin of Miscellaneous Information*, 1890/39 (March 1890), pp. 45–50.
- Rumpf, Georg Eberhard, *The Ambonese Curiosity Cabinet*. New Haven, CT: Yale University Press, 1999.
- St Clair, Kassia, *The Secret Lives of Colour*. London: John Murray, 2016.
- Salvetat, J., 'Matières minérales colorantes vertes et violettes'. *Comptes Rendus des Seances de l'Academie des Sciences*, 48 (1859).
- Schafer, Edward H., 'Orpiment and Realgar in Chinese Technology and Tradition'. *Journal of the American Oriental Society*, 75/2 (April–June 1955), pp. 73–89.
- Schafer, Edward H., 'The Early History of Lead Pigments and Cosmetics in China'. *T'oung Pao*, 44/4 (1956), pp. 413–38.
- Schama, Simon, *Rembrandt's Eyes*. London: Penguin, 2015.
- Schama, Simon, *Wordy: Sounding Off on High Art, Low Appetite and the Power of Memory*. London: Simon & Schuster, 2019.
- Schauss, A. G., 'Tranquilizing Effect of Color Reduces Aggressive Behavior and Potential Violence'. *Journal of Orthomolecular Psychiatry*, 8/4 (1979), pp. 218–21.
- Schönfeld, Martin, 'Was There a Western Inventor of Porcelain?' *Technology and Culture*, 39/4 (1998), pp. 716–27.
- Scott, David A., *Copper and Bronze in Art: Corrosion, Colorants, Conservation*. Los Angeles: Getty Conservation Institute, 2002.
- Siddall, Ruth, *et al.*, *Pigment Compendium*. London: Routledge, 2008.
- Smith, Godfrey, *The Laboratory, or School of Arts ... The Second Edition. Illustrated with Copper-Plates. To which is added An Appendix ... Translated from the High Dutch*. London: J. Hodges, J. James and T. Cooper, 1740.
- Stanlaw, James M., 'Japanese Color Terms, from 400 CE to the Present: Literature, Orthography, and Language Contact in Light of Current Cognitive Theory', in Robert E. MacLaury, Galina V. Paramei and Don Dedrick, eds, *Anthropology of Color: Interdisciplinary Multilevel Modeling*. Amsterdam: John Benjamins, 2007, pp. 295–318.
- Stoppard, Tom. *Rosencrantz & Guildenstern Are Dead*. New York: Grove Press, 1967.
- 'Techniques: The Passing of Mummy Brown'. *Time*, 2 October, 1964.

- Theophilus, *An Essay Upon Various Arts*, trans. and with notes by Robert Hendrie. London: John Murray, 1847.
- Theophilus, *On Divers Arts*. Garden City, NY: Dover Publications, 2012.
- *Theophrastus's History of Stones. With an English Version, and Critical and Philosophical Notes ... by John Hill*. London: C. Davis, 1746.
- Théry-Parisot, Isabelle, *et al.*, 'Illuminating the Cave, Drawing in Black: Wood Charcoal Analysis at Chauvet-Pont d'Arc'. *Antiquity*, 92/362 (2018), pp. 320–33.
- Thompson, Daniel V., *The Materials and Techniques of Medieval Painting*, reissue of 1st edn, published in 1936 as *The Materials of Medieval Painting*. New York: Dover Publications, 1956.
- Townsend, Joyce H., 'The Materials of J. M. W. Turner: Pigments'. *Studies in Conservation*, 38/4 (November 1993), pp. 231–54.
- Trinder, Kingston, *An Atlas of Rare and Familiar Colour: The Harvard Art Museums' Forbes Pigment Collection*, Los Angeles: Atelier Éditions, 2018.
- Valladas, H., *et al.*, 'Radiocarbon AMS Dates for Paleolithic Cave Paintings'. *Radiocarbon*, 43/2B (2001), pp. 977–86.
- Vanderpoel, Emily Noyes, *Color Problems: A Practical Manual for the Lay Student of Color*. London: Longmans, Green, and Co., 1902.
- Vasari, Giorgio, *Lives of the Painters, Sculptors and Architects*, trans. Gaston du C. Vere, 2 vols. London: D. Campbell, 1996.
- von Sonnenburg, Hubertus, and Frank Preusser, 'El Grecos "Entkleidung Christi" (Espolio) in der Alten Pinakothek'. *Maltechnik-Restauro*, 82/3 (July 1976), pp. 142–56.
- Watkins, John, and Hugh Latimer, *The Sermons of the Right Reverend Father in God, and Constant Martyr of Jesus Christ, Hugh Latimer, Sometime Bishop of Worcester: Now First Arranged According to the Order of Time in which They Were Preached, Collated by the Early Impressions, and Occasionally Illustrated with Notes Explanatory of Obsolete Phrases, Particular Customs, and Historical Allusions. To which is Prefixed A Memoir of the Bishop, by John Watkins*. London: James Duncan, 1824.
- White, Raymond, 'Brown and Black Organic Glazes, Pigments and Paints'. *National Gallery Technical Bulletin*, 10 (1986), pp. 58–71.
- Willard, Pat, *Secrets of Saffron: The Vagabond Life of the World's Most Seductive Spice*. Boston, MA: Beacon Press, 2001.
- Wolff, A., *Le Figaro*, 3 April 1876, p. 1.
- Wood, John, *A Personal Narrative of a Journey to the Source of the River Oxus: By the Route of the Indus, Kabul, and Badakhshan, Performed Under the Sanction of the Supreme Government of India, in the Years 1836, 1837, and 1838*. London: John Murray, 1841.
- Woodcock, Sally, 'Body Colour: The Misuse of Mummy'. *The Conservator*, 20/1 (1996), pp. 87–94.
- Wouters, Jan, Luc Maes and Renate Germer, 'The Identification of Haematite as a Red Colorant on an Egyptian Textile from the Second Millennium BC'. *Studies in Conservation*, 35/2 (May 1990), pp. 89–92.
- Wreschner, Ernst E., 'Red Ochre and Human Evolution: A Case for Discussion'. *Current Anthropology*, 21/5 (October 1980), pp. 631–44.
- Young, Francis, ed., *A Medieval Book of Magical Stones: The Peterborough Lapidary*. Cambridge: Texts in Early Modern Magic, 2016.
- Young, Jean I., 'Riddle 15 of the Exeter Book'. *Review of English Studies*, 20/80 (October 1944), pp. 304–06.

List of Illustrations

Unless noted otherwise, the details used on the jacket, in the table of contents, on the chapter openers and in the notes are all taken from images reproduced elsewhere in the book. Dimensions are given in centimetres followed by inches; height precedes width precedes depth.

century. Photo: The Granger Collection/ Alamy Stock Photo

45 (TOP LEFT AND RIGHT) Title page and page from Isaac Newton, *Opticks: or, A treatise of the reflexions, refractions, inflexions and colours of light. Also two treatises of the species and magnitude of curvilinear figures*, London, 1704. Library of Congress, Washington DC

45 (BOTTOM) Gabriel Dawe, *Plexus No. 29*, 2014. Thread, painted wood and hooks. Site-specific installation at the BYU Museum of Art, Provo. Photo: Jana Iverson Last. © Gabriel Dawe

50 Circle of Lucas Cranach the Elder, *Portrait of a Man*, 1537. Oil on alder, 55.9 × 42.5 (22 × 16 ¾). The Metropolitan Museum of Art, New York. The Friedsam Collection, Bequest of Michael Friedsam, 1931

53 The 'Saffron Gatherers' fresco (detail) from the upper storey of Xeste 3 in Akrotiri, Thera (Santorini), Greece, 16th century BCE

54 Christo and Jeanne-Claude, *The Gates, Central Park, New York City, 1979–2005*. Photo: Wolfgang Volz. Christo and Jeanne-Claude © ADAGP, Paris and DACS, London 2023

57 Pierre-Auguste Renoir, *The Skiff (La Yole)*, 1875. Oil on canvas, 71 × 92 (28 × 36 ¼). The National Gallery, London

59 Frederic Leighton, *Flaming June*, 1895. Oil on canvas, 119.1 × 119.1 (46 ⅞ × 46 ⅞). Museo de Arte de Ponce. The Luis A. Ferré Foundation, Inc.

62 Jules Olitski, *Cadmium Orange of Dr. Frankenstein*, 1962. Acrylic on canvas, 229.5 × 203.2 (90 ⅜ × 80). Smithsonian American Art Museum, Washington DC. © Estate of Jules Olitski/VAGA at ARS, NY and DACS, London 2023

64 (LEFT) Georg Christoph Lichtenberg's representation of Tobias Mayer's colour triangle, plate from Tobiae Mayeri, *Opera Inedita Vol. I*, edited by Georg Christoph Lichtenberg, Göttingen, 1775

64 (RIGHT) RGB colour cube, 3D illustration. Photo: Simone Brandt/Alamy Stock Photo

65 (TOP) Johann Heinrich Lambert's three-dimensional adaptation of Tobias Mayer's colour triangle, from J. H. Lambert, *Beschreibung einer mit dem Calauschen Wachse ausgemalten Farbenpyramide*, Berlin, 1772

65 (BOTTOM) 'Harmonious Arrangement of Twenty-Five of the Most Useful Pigments', plate from George Barnard, *The Theory and Practice of Landscape Painting in Water-Colours*, London, 1855

69 Raphael, *The Mond Crucifixion*, c. 1502–03. Oil on poplar, 283.3 × 167.3 (111 ⅝ × 65 ⅞). The National Gallery, London

71 Johannes Vermeer, *Woman Holding a Balance*, c. 1664. Oil on canvas, 39.7 × 35.5 (15 ⅝ × 14). National Gallery of Art, Washington DC. Widener Collection

72 Rembrandt, *Belshazzar's Feast*, c. 1636–38. Oil on canvas, 167.6 × 209.2 (66 × 82 ⅜). The National Gallery, London

75 Orazio Gentileschi, *The Lute Player*, c. 1612–20. Oil on canvas, 143.5 × 129 (56 ½ × 50 ¾). National Gallery of Art, Washington DC

76 David Hockney, *A Bigger Splash*, 1967. Acrylic on canvas, 243.8 × 243.8 (96 × 96). Tate, London. © David Hockney

80 Vincent van Gogh, *Wheat Field with Cypresses*, 1889. Oil on canvas, 73.2 × 93.4 (28 ⅞ × 36 ¾). The Metropolitan Museum of Art, New York. Purchase, The Annenberg Foundation Gift, 1993

83 (TOP) Claude Monet, *Water Lilies*, 1919. Oil on canvas, 101 × 200 (39 ¾ × 78 ¾). The Metropolitan Museum of Art, New York. The Walter H. and Leonore Annenberg Collection, Gift of Walter H. and Leonore Annenberg, 1998, Bequest of Walter H. Annenberg, 2002

83 (BOTTOM) Piet Mondrian, *Broadway Boogie Woogie*, 1942–43. Oil on canvas, 127 × 127 (50 × 50). The Museum of Modern Art, New York

84 Fred Becker, *Hansa Yellow, Hooks and Eyes* series, 1947. Engraving and etching, 7.8 × 6.4 (3 ⅛ × 2 ⅝). The British Museum, London. Courtesy of Dolan/Maxwell and the Estate of Fred Becker. Photo: The Trustees of the British Museum

86 Title page of Mary Gartside, *An Essay on Light and Shade, on Colours, and on Composition in General*, London, 1805

87 'Orange', 'Violet' and 'Scarlet', plates from Mary Gartside, *An Essay on Light and Shade, on Colours, and on Composition in General*, London, 1805

90 Auguste Rodin, *The Thinker*, 1903. Bronze, 189 × 98 × 140 (74 ½ × 38 ⅝ × 55 ⅛). Musée Rodin, Paris. Photo: Joël Saget/AFP via Getty Images

93 Rogier van der Weyden, *The Magdalen Reading*, before 1438. Oil on mahogany,

Index

Page numbers in italic refer to illustrations. Highlighted page numbers refer to 'Colourful Minds' references, including text and illustrations.

I

J

K

L

M

Acknowledgments

My sincerest thanks go to Roger Thorp, Thames & Hudson's editorial director for its art list, who believed in this project from the start. I am grateful, too, to his extraordinary team of editors and designers for elevating my words into such a beautiful book. The journey of my thoughts about colour as a secret language can be traced in the many features, articles, reviews and poems I have written over the past twenty years. I am very grateful to the editors who have allowed me to audition my ideas in their pages - from the late Australian poet and literary editor of *Quadrant* magazine, Les Murray, who published my first musings on the materiality of colour, to BBC Culture's Rebecca Laurence and Fiona Macdonald, who so warmly embraced my pitch for a series of articles on colour in art in 2018. Profound thanks are owed as well to Anna Vaux at the *Times Literary Supplement*, to Mark Robinson at *Wired* magazine, and to Sam Phillips at the *RA Magazine*, for inviting me to share my reflections with their readers. *The Art of Colour* is dedicated to my wife, Sinéad, and to our son, Caspar, weaver of rainbows. Without their love, encouragement and support, there would be no colours to decode.

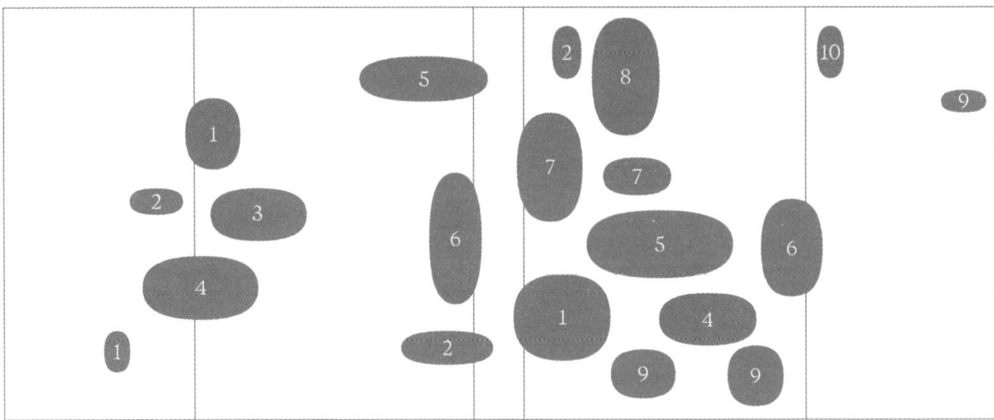

On the jacket

El Greco, *The Disrobing of Christ* (detail), 1577–79 (SEE PAGE 34)

Pierre-Auguste Renoir, *The Skiff (La Yole)* (detail), 1875 (SEE PAGE 57)

Michelangelo Merisi da Caravaggio, *Martha and Mary Magdalene* (detail), *c.* 1598 (SEE PAGE 27, TOP)

Edgar Degas, *Combing the Hair ('La Coiffure')* (detail), *c.* 1896 (SEE PAGE 42)

Frederic Leighton, *Flaming June* (detail), 1895 (SEE PAGE 59)

Kazimir Malevich, *Suprematist Painting (with Black Trapezium and Red Square)* (detail), 1915 (SEE PAGE 131)

Margareta Haverman, *A Vase of Flowers* (detail), 1716

Vincent van Gogh, *The Starry Night* (detail), 1889 (SEE PAGE 9)

Peter Paul Rubens, *Samson and Delilah* (detail), *c.* 1609–10 (SEE PAGE 30)

Hilma af Klint, *Group X, No. 1, Altarpiece* (detail), 1915 (SEE PAGE 2)

First published in the U.S. and Canada in 2023
by Yale University Press, P.O. Box 209040,
302 Temple Street, New Haven, CT 06520-9040
yalebooks.com

Published by arrangement with
Thames & Hudson Ltd, London

Library of Congress Control Number:
2022947346

ISBN 978-0-300-26778-5

Printed and bound in China through
Asia Pacific Offset Ltd